The Dynamics of International Migration and Settlement in Europe

IMISCOE **(International Migration, Integration and Social Cohesion)**

IMISCOE is a European Commission-funded Network of Excellence of more than 350 scientists from various research institutes that specialise in migration and integration issues in Europe. These researchers, who come from all branches of the economic and social sciences, the humanities and law, implement an integrated, multidisciplinary and internationally comparative research program that focuses on Europe's migration and integration challenges.

Within the program, existing research is integrated and new research lines are developed that involve issues crucial to European-level policy making and provide a theory-based design to implement new research.

The publication program of IMISCOE is based on five distinct publication profiles, designed to make its research and results available to scientists, policymakers and the public at large. High-quality manuscripts written by IMISCOE members, or in cooperation with IMISCOE members, are published in these five series. An Editorial Committee coordinates the review process of the manuscripts. The five series are:
1. Joint Studies
2. Research
3. Dissertations
4. Reports
5. Textbooks

More information on the network can be found at: www.imiscoe.org

IMISCOE **Joint Studies** include publications resulting from joint initiatives of IMISCOE members. These publications target a broad audience, including policymakers.

The Dynamics of International Migration and Settlement in Europe

A State of the Art

Rinus Penninx
Maria Berger
Karen Kraal
(eds.)

IMISCOE Joint Studies

AMSTERDAM UNIVERSITY PRESS

Cover design: Studio Jan de Boer BNO, Amsterdam
Layout: Fito Prepublishing, Almere

ISBN-13   978 90 5356 866 8
ISBN-10   90 5356 866 2
NUR   741 / 763

Contents

1. Introduction

Rinus Penninx

1. Times are changing

In recent decades, international migration has become a major phenomenon. While the number of persons living outside their country of birth worldwide was estimated at 'more than 105 million' in 1985 (United Nations, 1998: 1) this number had nearly doubled to approximately 200 million 20 years later (GCIM 2005). Figures for the European continent show an even steeper increase of residents in European countries that have been born outside their present country of residence: in a shorter period of 15 years their number grew from an estimated 23 million in 1985 (United Nations, 1998: 1) to more than 56 million, or 7.7 per cent of the total European population in 2000 (IOM 2003: 29).

Such absolute numbers already demonstrate that Europe has factually become an immigration continent. The relevance of this thesis is reinforced if we look at the relative importance of migration in the demography of Europe. Recent analyses of Eurostat show that since 1988 net migration has become a more substantial contributor to the growth of the population of the 15 original member states of the EU than natural growth (i.e. births minus deaths). For the year 2005 this holds also for the EU-25: in that year a total net migration of 1.69 million (on a total population of 462 million) contributed significantly more to population growth than 0.327 million natural growth. For the near future prognoses of Eurostat expect a negative natural growth from 2010 on. Net migration is expected to prevent an absolute decrease of the EU population until the year 2025 (Eurostat 2005, 2006).[1]

How impressive such general figures for Europe may be, they do not mirror the differential impact of immigration. Migration and settlement patterns of immigrants are basically uneven, both in time and in space. Some West European countries, such as Switzerland, Belgium and France, have a history of immigration before World War II and immigration resumed soon after 1945. Other countries in the western part of Europe only started to acquire their immigration experience in the decades following the Second World War; these include the United Kingdom, Sweden, Germany, Austria and the Netherlands. For a number of European countries such as Italy, Spain, Portugal, Greece and Ireland, which used to be emigration countries until the 1980s, the current immigration experience spans a period of about two decades. Still other countries, among them most of the ten recently accessed EU member states, are experiencing emigration, transit migration and immigration at the same time. Obviously, such historical differences are reflected in the size and composition of their immigrant populations.

The unevenness of the immigration experience in scale and in time is as much noticeable *within* the countries in question. More than in the past, new immigrants in recent decades have tended to concentrate in urban areas. This pattern of migration, in terms of destination, is not specifically European. Large cities and conurbations have seen their composition changed rapidly. They have become the visible face of globalisation. In the Netherlands, for example, more than 60 per cent of all immigrants and their direct descendants live in the Western conurbation. In Amsterdam, immigrants and their offspring constitute about half of the total population, and more than half of the pupils in primary schools are of non-Dutch origin. Similar observations can be made about other large European cities (Penninx et al. 2004). Within these metropolises, moreover, there is almost always a skewed distribution of these newcomers over districts and wards, contributing to their visibility.

The picture is further complicated by what is called the new geography of migration. The pattern of origin of migrants in Europe up to the 1980s could conveniently be grouped under three headings: a) migration with a colonial background that connected certain European countries to their former colonies; b) labour migration that connected a number of 'recruiting countries' to a limited number of 'sending countries', and c) refugee migration that was strongly dominated by refugee migration from Eastern Europe to the West. In terms of the origins of immigrants this led to a number of geographical patterns of migration that embraced Europe and the Mediterranean countries, plus a limited number of (former) colonies. That picture is now completely blurred. Nowadays, immigrants, moved by varying motives and coming under different guises, come to Europe from all over the world in significant numbers: expatriates working for multinational companies and international organisations, skilled workers from all over the world, nurses and doctors from the Philippines, refugees and asylum seekers from African, Near Eastern and Asian countries, from the Balkan and former Soviet Union countries, students from China, undocumented workers from African countries, just to single out some of the major immigrant categories. The result in some places is so heterogeneous that Vertovec (2006) recently coined the new term 'super-diversity', illustrating the case of the UK in general and the London metropolis in particular.

All these facts on the changing size, origin, destination and composition of international migration do seem to relate to a broader context of change: that of increasing globalisation. This has expressed itself in several domains: the financial world has been one of the first doing away with national barriers; agricultural and industrial production and part of the world of service supply have increasingly developed new divisions of labour across borders; trade across borders has been eased and has increased; culture and knowledge have developed new and rapid ways of dissemination that are not hindered by national borders.

These changes have had far-reaching consequences for the mobility of people across borders. The first is that in such a globalising world the type of mobility of people in general has also changed significantly, particularly when it comes to short-term stays like those for business travel, study and tourism, but also for longer stays of those who are directly related to or needed for the aforementioned forms of globalisation, such as employees of international organisations and multinational enterprises and highly skilled people in general. One could bring these together under the category of the wanted travellers and migrants. The expected benefits for global actors and national governments in given spatial territories coincide and thus their mobility is facilitated, if not promoted. But this is not necessarily the case for others, who as a consequence of the same process of globalisation – more and rapid information on possibilities elsewhere, denser and relatively cheaper communication and transport, etc. – decide themselves to look for an economically better and/or politically safer new destination. Paradoxically, for them national boundaries and borders and the sovereign right of states to decide on admission of non-nationals have gained importance. For the non-solicited and non-invited migrants new and increasing barriers have been erected. The new notions in scientific analysis have thus become 'supply versus demand driven mobility and migration' and in policy terms 'the wanted versus unsolicited'. This ambivalent reaction to international mobility and migration in a globalising context has taken a special form within the European Union. On the one hand, the EU (and its predecessors) created essentially a fundamental right to move and settle within the EU area for citizens and residents of its member states. On the other hand, EU member states have developed restrictive and defensive immigration policies to keep out unasked-for migrants. This amounts to the paradoxical trend towards 'free mobility' for those within, and increasing closure for those outside the EU.

A second consequence of globalisation and the specific selection of migration and the movements it stimulates, concerns changes to the forms of settlement. While migration tended to be viewed in the past predominantly as a once off movement leading to permanent resettlement (a conception that prevailed in the literature on classic immigration countries), recent migration – helped by strongly increased transport and communication facilities – has shifted to more fluid practices of international mobility in which more migrants have consecutive stays in different countries, alternate their residence between countries, etc. This may lead to new practices of residence, integration and community formation. Researchers are exploring these new phenomena under the notion of transnationalism. Policymakers are asking the uneasy question what such practices mean for integration.

2. Reactions of societies: changing policies

Behind the facts of change listed above, the dynamics of both migration and integration have changed. And the policies for these, in themselves quite different, processes have become more and more intertwined. Let us look briefly at each of the two fields and illustrate how they tend to become interwoven.

As for migration one first observation to be made is that European countries have consistently defined themselves as non-immigration countries, in contrast to countries such as Canada, Australia and the United States. While the rhetoric about being a 'nation of immigrants' is strong in the latter countries, it is singularly absent in Europe. Such a framing of the migration question has been a constant factor in Europe, irrespective of the fact that quite a few countries have had higher immigration rates than classic immigration countries, measured simply by the percentages of foreign-born in their total populations: Switzerland and Germany, for instance, have higher percentages than the United States of America.

This framing has had pervasive consequences. In Northwest European countries the 'temporary' labour migration policies developed since the mid-1950s were abandoned after the first oil crisis of 1973. In general, ad hoc and lenient migration policies were replaced by restrictive policies that were justified by a simultaneous decrease or absence of demand, particularly for lower-skilled migrants, and an increase of supply-driven migration presenting itself under the policy categories of family reunion and formation, and refuge and asylum. In a spiral pattern of reactionary new measures of restriction and control and 'innovative' new forms of immigration, new actors and new dynamics developed. Immigration was increasingly criminalised: tougher regulations by definition led to more illegality and irregularity, creating opportunities for new actors like smugglers and traffickers. International political terrorism has furthermore put migrants into focus from a security perspective. Migration thus became first and foremost associated with problems and threats and as such it rose to the top of the political agenda in many countries in recent times. (Problems and perceived threats as a consequence of integration problems concur to reinforce this tendency, as we shall see later).

The idea of not being an immigration country has also had direct consequences for settlement and policies of integration. Northwest European countries had 'solved' the contradiction of not being an immigration country and importing significant labour in the 1950s and 1960s by defining these migrants as 'temporary guests'. That meant limited facilities for accommodation in anticipation of their eventual return. But here, too, the 'fact' that a significant portion stayed for good and formed communities that gradually grew by using their rights to bring families and spouses, contradicted perceptions and expectations. Some national governments identified these tensions relatively early and initiated some form of policy of inclusion or integration, like Sweden in the mid-1970s and the Netherlands in the early 1980s. Most countries, however, acknowledged the need to formulate 'integration policies' much later in the 1990s, often hesitantly and partially (Penninx 2005).

The idea that integration of long-term residents was a necessity for sound and cohesive societies was initially, particularly in the early policies of states like Sweden and the Netherlands, inspired by a philosophy of equality and equity in a welfare state context. It was not seen as contradicting the philosophy of not being an immigration country. On the contrary, restrictive immigration policies were seen as a necessary condition for a successful integration policy (too much and continuous immigration would make integration an impossible task). These early integration policies were strongly rights-based, embracing not only the socio-economic but also the political and cultural domains of life. For most other European national governments, however, such ideas went too far and they were content to maintain ad hoc adaptive measures, leaving in most cases the integration responsibility to parties in civil society, such as trade unions, churches and welfare organisations.

Whatever the intensity and content of integration policies, and irrespective of the question whether such policies have been primarily initiated by national or local authorities, integration has become a central theme in politics in Europe since the 1990s. And in becoming so, it showed that integration policies inevitably go far beyond the simple idea of providing facilities for newcomers to adapt and function in the new society. The premise of any integration policy ultimately leads to questions of how the society in which newcomers 'integrate' essentially defines itself and whether it is able and willing to change. This made integration policies as sensitive politically as immigration itself. Northwest European countries seem to have moved in recent years from earlier conceptions of integration policies that focused on the position of newcomers in society to one that is primarily focusing on the cohesion of societies as a whole and on commonalities that are supposed to be crucial for such social cohesion. This has led, using the newcomers as a trigger or a threat, to much more fundamental questions and discussions on the identity of our societies: who are we? The outcomes of such discussions have consequences for newcomers and for what their integration should mean. Some observers have called the recent policies in countries like Denmark and the Netherlands 'neo-assimilationist'.

It is at this point that the nexus between the two policy fields of migration and integration becomes stronger and inextricable. To the old policy assumption that restrictive immigration is a necessary condition for the success of an integration policy, a new one is added: integration policy measures are used to select those immigrants that are able and willing to integrate and deter those who are not. Making first admission dependent on tests in the country of origin, extension of residence permits on success in integration courses, and naturalisation on ever more elaborate requirements of integration are examples of measures that fit this inversion.

The picture outlined here is strongly based on the Northwest European experience. South European countries have a much more recent experience in immigration and integration, but at the same time a stronger growth of immigration than Northwest Europe. Their institutional framework for regulation is new and their practices are much less determined by a long history of migration regulation and the path dependency that it may entail. In certain respects this leads to quite different measures of regulation, such as the frequent regularisations. For most of the ten new members of the EU the topic of migration and integration is relatively new and takes multiple forms: emigration, immigration and transit migration co-exist in most of these countries. The European Union has become an important forum for policy development through its initiatives to create a framework for common migration policies (since the late nineties) and integration policies (since 2003).

3. Research on migration, settlement and social cohesion: IMISCOE

In the wake of the developments outlined above, research in Europe has developed and expanded in the course of time and followed roughly the timing of the migration phenomenon itself. Initially in the

1960s and 1970s, individual researchers engaged in such research, often focusing on one particular flow of migrants or immigrant group. The 1980s saw the first research institutes with more comprehensive programmes in the United Kingdom, Sweden, France and the Netherlands; a pattern that expanded to other West European countries and to the Southern countries in the late 1990s.

This migration and integration research was traditionally strongly embedded in national contexts, both in terms of its framing of the questions and its funding. As a consequence it reflected strong national concerns and perspectives. Topics and priorities were accordingly those that related primarily to destination countries. Most of that research was furthermore mono-disciplinary.

It was the 6th Framework Programme for research of the European Union that offered a possibility to try and overcome the fragmented nature of research, and in doing so provide a coherent and more comprehensive analytic and empirical basis for policies and the public discourse on international migration and integration. In 2004, nineteen research institutes from ten European countries established the Network of Excellence IMISCOE: International Migration, Integration and Social Cohesion in Europe, funded by the Directorate General for Research of the European Commission. The task of IMISCOE is to build an infrastructure for research in the domain of international migration, integration and social cohesion by developing a coherent, multidisciplinary, cross-national comparative research programme. Furthermore, it should develop an infrastructure for training of future researchers and a system of dissemination of results of research to a wide audience. Such activities should contribute to a sound and solid basis for public discourse and policy making in this area.

This volume is the first comprehensive result of that cooperation that has by the time of this publication expanded to 22 research institutes and more than 400 researchers in Europe. In order to take stock of research, IMISCOE has formed nine clusters of researchers that cover the most important sub-domains. Two clusters have worked on the process of international migration itself: one from the perspective of the destination countries, specifically focusing on regulation efforts, and one from the perspective of sending countries, looking at causes and consequences of migration for these countries. Four clusters of researchers have worked on different dimensions of the process of settlement and integration: on political aspects, on economic integration, on social aspects and on the cultural and religious dimension of integration respectively. Three more clusters of researchers have worked on cross-cutting themes of a) interethnic relations, identity, representation and discrimination, b) gender, age, generations and family structures, and c) the multilevel governance of migration and integration, particularly focusing on the process of policy making. Each of these clusters was tasked with writing a state of the art of ongoing research with the additional purpose of creating a common analytical framework and identifying directions for future joint research.[2] The elaborate versions of most of these overviews have been published on the IMISCOE website.[3] The nine chapters that follow are based on these overviews. Consequently they are the result of work done by groups of researchers that is larger than the ones who actually wrote the chapters.

The focus in this book is in principle on Europe and European research, but certainly not exclusively so. In fact much of the early traditions of research on migration and integration research were developed in North-America and thus will be referred to frequently. There is furthermore some variation in the chapters as to the form. All chapters introduce their specific perspective that leads to a (strategic) choice of topics and questions to be covered, but the extent to which varies. Some bring the discussion between disciplines (or the obvious lack of it) to the forefront as in chapters 5 and 6 on economic and social integration respectively. We have tried to enhance the programmatic function of these overviews by concluding each of the chapters with directions and priorities of future research to be developed within the IMISCOE network. The final concluding chapter builds on these overviews, trying to draw lines for future research together across the subdomains surveyed in the separate chapters.

4. The organisation of this book

Chapter 2 focuses specifically on the *processes of international migration to Europe, its causes and the efforts of states to regulate migration*. It sets the scene by an analytical description of major changes in Europe since the 1970s and their consequences for the changed demand for workers, possibly migrants. It goes on to describe the efforts of national states to 'regulate' migration processes, which in practice in many cases equals to restrict or prevent them. This mismatch of defensive and reactive policies, a mismatch with the internal demand on the one hand and with the external pressure for migration on the other, leads to a growing irregularity of migration movements and migrants. The staunch restrictiveness fuels in a spiral of new 'innovative' intermediaries of all kinds to help migrants reach their desired destinations and new governmental efforts to combat them, bringing migration and migrants more and more in the criminal sphere.

While chapter 2 looks at processes of international migration from the perspective of European destination countries, chapter 3 focuses attention on the causes and consequences in and for the countries of origin. *Causes and selectivity of migration and their consequences for development of the countries or regions of origin* are the central themes here. The topics of remittances of migrants and the possible accumulation of human resources through migration as two possible 'gains' from migration are weighted against possible 'losses'. Crucial questions to be answered by empirical research are under what conditions gains can be increased and losses reduced and for whom, and what policies could possibly help here.

Chapters 4 to 7 focus on different aspects of integration processes of immigrants: political, economic, social and cultural integration. In chapter 4, the *political aspects of integration processes* are the central topic. *Migrants' citizenship; legal status, rights and political participation* are described with the help of three analytical concepts: the political opportunity structure, political integration and political transnationalism.

The second aspect of integration processes, *economic integration*, is the central focus of chapter 5. *Migrants' work, entrepreneurship and economic integration* is discussed here. The authors of this chapter have chosen for an approach in which general concepts of the discipline of economics are taken as a starting point to survey research on economic integration of immigrants in various disciplines. The two ways in which individual immigrants may be inserted into the economic system, as a wage worker or as an independent entrepreneur, are systematically surveyed.

Social integration is the third aspect, treated in chapter 6: *Social integration of immigrants with special reference to the local and spatial dimension*. The authors of this chapter have chosen to develop an analytical approach that focuses primarily on local processes of integration, choosing a unit of analysis in which the spatial implications can be built in as a strong analytical component. In such an approach much of what has been developed by geographers, for example in studies on segregation, is integrated with other approaches to integration and assimilation studies in the social sciences in general.

Chapter 7 focuses on the fourth aspect of integration: that of culture in the anthropological sense. The chapter describes the *cultural, religious and linguistic diversity in Europe*. Central in this chapter is what the authors call the governance of culture, religion and language of immigrants: how do governments deal with the policy challenges these issues evoke, what normative connotations underpin these policies, and what arguments, pro and con, are to be distinguished?

In the following three chapters a number of special topics are treated, often cutting across the basic distinction between processes of migration on the one hand, and processes of settlement on the other. The first of these topics in chapter 8 is *Identity, representation, interethnic relations and discrimination*. This chapter focuses on the relations between immigrants and the society of settlement, and the mechanisms that underpin such relations. The authors provide an overview of theoretical and methodological tools to grasp the concepts that are of utmost relevance to this field.

Chapter 9 covers the broad topics of *age, generations and gender in migration and integration processes*. The authors of this chapter have chosen to single out the time dimension of these processes as a central organising perspective. They discuss theoretical concepts regarding the time factor in research, and focus on methodological approaches such as the life-course approach and longitudinal studies. Additionally they survey research on gender, the family and generations, again highlighting the factor of time.

Chapter 10 has defined its special domain as *the multilevel governance of migration and integration*. The authors adopt an analytical perspective that focuses on the various levels of governmental policy making and their increasing interconnectedness on the one hand, and at the involvement of non-governmental actors in formal and informal decision making processes on the other.

Finally, in chapter 11, general conclusions are drawn on the state of the art of research in Europe and some overarching themes that cut across the sub-domains surveyed in the nine thematic chapters of this book will be discussed. In doing so, this concluding chapter points to research directions for the future, arguing both from a scientific and a policy point of view. These can be read as challenging tasks of the IMISCOE Network of Excellence in the years to come.

Notes

1   The increased significance of international migration for Europe as a whole becomes even more clear when the comparison in time is extended: one of the first comprehensive analyses of the 1950-1975 period (United Nations 1979: 64) showed that Europe as a whole had a negative migration balance in the 1950s, an approximately zero balance in the 1960s and a slightly positive one in the first half of the 1970s. While the Eastern, Northern and Southern parts of Europe showed consistently a negative migration result over the whole period, Western Europe's migration balance was positive and growing in that same period.

2   Apart from this effort to create a joint programme of research starting from the current research of the participating institutes and researchers, three 'feasibility studies' were commissioned by IMISCOE to start new strategic research lines: one on the systematic study of Europe as a migration system (EUROLINKS), one on the systematic comparative study of integration processes and policies (INTPOL) and one on social cohesion (SOCO). These studies will be published independently. We will refer incidentally to these programming initiatives in the concluding chapter of the book.

3   www.imiscoe.org.

Literature

Eurostat (2005), *EU-25 population rises until 2025, then falls.* News release. Luxemburg: Eurostat.

Eurostat (2006), First demographic estimates. *Statistics in Focus 1/2006.* Luxemburg: Eurostat.

GICM (2005), *Migration in an interconnected world: New directions for action.* Global Commission on International Migration October 2005. http://www.gcim.org/en/finalreport.html

IOM (2003), *World Migration 2003: Managing Migration: Challenges and Responses for People on the Move,* IOM World Migration Report Series, No. 2. Geneva: International Organization for Migration.

Penninx, R. (2005), 'Integration of migrants: economic, social, cultural and political dimensions', 137-152, in: M. Macura, A.L. MacDonald and W. Haug (eds.), *The new demographic regime. Population challenges and policy responses.* New York/Geneva: United Nations.

Penninx, R., K. Kraal, M. Martiniello & S. Vertovec (eds.) (2004), *Citizenship in European cities. Immigrants, local politics and integration policies.* Aldershot/Burlington: Ashgate.

United Nations (1979), *Labour Supply and Migration in Europe. Demographic dimensions 1950-1975 and prospects.* New York: United Nations.

United Nations (1998), *Population Distribution and Migration. Proceedings of the United Nations Expert Group Meeting on Population Distribution and Migration, Santa Cruz, Bolivia, 18-22 January 1993.* New York: United Nations.

Vertovec, S. (2006), *Super-diversity and its implications.* http://www.compas.ox.ac.uk/publications/wp-06-25.shtml.

2. International Migration and Its Regulation[1]

Maria I. Baganha, Jeroen Doomernik, Heinz Fassmann,
Sonia Gsir, Martin Hofmann, Michael Jandl, Albert Kraler,
Matthias Neske and Ursula Reeger

1. Introduction

At the centre of this chapter are the process of migration, its structural trends, geographical patterns, conceptual delineation and statistical measurement. In describing and analysing these, we do not follow traditional theoretical concepts that interpret migration as a 'natural' function and only as a consequence of economic or political disparities. This perception of migration as an automatic flow in an uneven world does not do justice to the complexity of this phenomenon. Migration is regulated and defined by various forces, two of which will be in the centre of attention in this chapter: the economy and the society. The economy and its specific demand for qualified and unqualified labour are of critical importance because they have the societal power to define the size and the structure of the labour markets to which the migrants have to adapt. The institutional approach, by contrast, is central to explaining why and which migration takes place. It underlines the significance of policy and administrative procedures for canalising migration flows. Of course, these two forces interact. The enterprises and their political representatives formulate their needs and economic interests and influence the institutional rules. The institutional rules, in turn, delimit the scope and options of entrepreneurial action.

The economy and the societal institutions open and close gates for migrants; they also define and differentiate between spatial mobility and migration. Usually, only some forms of spatial mobility are perceived as migration – a fact not reflected in the general and rather technical definition of migration given by the United Nations recommendation dating back to 1998: 'a long-term migrant should be defined as a person who moves to a country other than that of his or her usual residence for a period of at least a year (12 months), so that the country of destination effectively becomes his or her new country of usual residence.' According to these guidelines, EU citizens moving within the EU are migrants while in reality they may not be perceived as such. On the other hand, in some countries labour migrants are categorised as guest workers and not as migrants. And it is also a matter of public perception whether asylum seekers, who are obviously mobile, are migrants.

The two sections of this chapter serve to prove and to illustrate the above statements. The first section provides a comprehensive overview of migration to Europe over the last decades with a particular focus on the links between the needs of the economy and the structural selection of labour migrants. This overview will show that migration is not a natural process and is not driven primarily by economic disparities but is controlled and regulated by society.

The second section very briefly describes when and how migration becomes a policy concern, how policies try to select migrants and 'to protect' Europe from unwanted migration and how this impacts on migration flows. As will become apparent, migration policies do not always reach the intended target but often have unintended side effects. The concluding remarks will supply a brief outlook on possible directions for further research in this area.

2. Economic restructuring and flows of migration in Europe

The annual inflow into the 15 EU member states from both other member states and third countries amounted to 1.87 million people for the period from 1995 to 1999. In the same period, 1.26 million people emigrated either to another EU country or to a third country. So the positive net migration per year was around 610,000 which is more than the net migration from and to the USA.

The flow data clearly show that migration is more important for population development than the natural increase (births minus deaths). The annual gain due to the surplus of the migratory inflow is much higher than the natural increase. Furthermore, the flow data prove that economic restructuring and international migration are inextricably intertwined. The in- and outflows fluctuate parallel to economic cycles. These temporal fluctuations allow us to divide the history of international migration in Europe since World War II into three periods: the post-war period until the oil crisis, the economic recession of the 1970s and 1980s and the economic take-off in the 1990s.

Economic development and migration

From the end of World War II up to the oil crisis in the early 1970s, Western European countries actively tried to tap into new pools of labour. For this purpose, they strategically signed bilateral agreements for the recruitment of foreign labour and eased legal proceedings for the issuing of resident permits to economic migrants entering their borders.

They fostered this massive import of labour on the assumption that the millions of foreign workers would only stay temporarily. The idea was that after accomplishing their own projects a significant part of the immigrants would return to their home countries, while another sizeable part would depart when the economy would cease to need foreign labour. Those remaining would thus be a kind of small residual that would not pose serious social or cultural problems.

The economic recession that followed the oil crisis of the 1970s falsified this assumption. In fact, not only did relatively few immigrants return to their countries of origin, but numerically significant and highly concentrated immigrant communities had been established for good within the borders of the majority of the Northwestern European countries, in a substantial number of cases evidencing signs of social and cultural exclusion.

With the failure of the so-called 'rotation system', Western Europe discovered that, independently of its own political representations, it had become a region of immigration. Furthermore, the recognition of this new situation came in a period of high unemployment among the domestic and the foreign resident population, of growing xenophobic attitudes towards immigrants and ethnic minorities, and of increasing social and economic problems with the so-called 'second-generation'.

This new reality led governments to subscribe to policies aimed at fostering the integration of those already established in the country. As for immigration, they curtailed the entrance of new economic migrants, while facilitating family reunification. Furthermore, the continuously high unemployment rates across Western Europe helped to reinforce the conviction at both governmental and societal levels that Europe did not need more economic migrants with few or no skills.

The economic explanation for this prevailing belief may be summarised as follows: after World War II Europe saw a phase of mass production on massive industrial plants that required a large supply of poorly qualified manpower. This phase was followed by automatisation and the expansion of the service sector that needs numerically less but more qualified personnel. This restructuring of the European economy, which has been underway since the 1970s, went hand in hand with a displacement of a great number of labour-intensive industries which greatly decreased the need for low-skilled labour in Europe. Simultaneously, the changes opened up new opportunities, namely in activities connected with information and knowledge, essentially dependent on highly qualified manpower. In this process, rising unemployment came to be seen as the result of 'the mismatch between the supply of and the demand for, different skill types' (Bean et al. 1990: 20). It is widely accepted that this mismatch will increase, if more economic immigrants with poor or no skills are allowed to enter (Vogler-Ludwig 1994).

European governments acted accordingly, closing their borders to economic migrants and only reluctantly and exceptionally regularising illegal or irregular immigrants. However, the incoming migrants seem to hold quite a different view of the opportunities the restructuring of the European economy opens up to them. Regardless of the general closing of the borders, they keep entering not only on family grounds and as asylum seekers, but also as temporary migrants, as tourists overstaying their visas, or simply as undocumented migrants. In sum, Europe as a whole has unintentionally become a continent of immigration after decades of global emigration.

Geographical pattern

In order to demonstrate the effect of policy in defining and producing migration, it is useful to consider recent changes from a geographical perspective. The following will therefore concentrate on East-West and South-North migration.

East-West migratory flows in Europe

Until 1950, the dominant migration flows in Europe were East-West due to ethnic cleansing in countries with significant ethnic minorities. After 1950, the Cold War reduced this pattern to a flow from East to West Germany and to a small flow of political refugees escaping from communism. Since the mid-1950s, migration from the South to Northwestern Europe became more important. This only changed after the fall of the Iron Curtain when European East-West migration gained importance and Poland, the former Soviet Union/CIS, the former GDR, former Yugoslavia and other countries, mainly Bulgaria and Romania, once again became main sending areas.

Within this European East-West migration, Germany was and remains the main country of destination. Between 1950 and today some two thirds of all East-West migrants moved to Germany. Most immigrants were either ethnic Germans, labour migrants or family dependents. The German government was actively involved in attracting migrants coming 'back' to the country of their ancestors. So the idea that Germany was or is overrun by migrants and had no possibility to influence this process was and is not in conformity with the real situation.

During the last decade, a shift of East-West migration is taking place. The traditional countries of origin in Eastern Europe such as Poland, Hungary or Slovakia more and more became countries of destination.

With the shift of the EU border after the accession of the new member countries and the implementation of the transitional rule, East-West migration of post-war Europe came to an end. The changes in the economic differences, which are of crucial importance in traditional theoretical approaches, are less significant than the shift in the political perspective. From the political point of view, migrants from Eastern Europe are no longer victims of communism and the German resettlers can not be used any more as a proof for the superiority of the market system.

Immigration to Southern Europe
Southern European countries that have been major providers of labour migrants in the decades after WW II, have become a powerful magnet to a growing number of immigrants coming from neighbouring Eastern countries and from Africa in the last decade. While in the EC countries the stock of the foreign population was growing at an average rate of approximately 2 per cent per year between 1981 and 1991, in Southern European countries this same process was occurring at the much higher rate of 10 per cent per year[2], with Italy, Spain, Greece and Portugal roughly tripling the size of the legal foreign population within their borders.

This was an entirely new situation for this region, since for more than a hundred years, with the remarkable exception of France, all Southern European countries were engaged in mass migration movements, but as sending areas. The traditional role of the Southern European countries as labour suppliers was, thus, decisively inverted during the 1980s.

At the end of the 1980s, Italy, Greece, Spain and Portugal hosted close to 1.4 million regular migrants and an estimated 1.3 to 1.5 million irregular migrants (1988/89). This raised unprecedented legal, social and economic problems that caught these countries unprepared at all levels.

Political turmoil, progressive instability, acute ethnic conflicts and lower standards of living in Eastern Europe, growing demographic pressure, oppressive poverty, the search for economic betterment, religious strife and war in Africa are external factors that have greatly enhanced the attraction of Southern European countries both for economic migrants and for refugees. But it is not only the growth of geoeconomic inequalities that is changing the world. The intensification of the globalisation process has promoted a deep restructuring of the industry, a relocation of labour supplies, a redirection of capital flows, and new patterns of international competition. Southern European countries themselves to a certain degree accept the new migration as a proof for their economic progress and as a clear sign of superiority of the economic and political system produced by the EU, which guarantees peace, welfare and economic progress. Moreover, cheap and flexible labour migrants are welcome to produce extra profit in agriculture, tourism and small craft industry. Also here it is wrong to draw a picture of the South of Europe as an innocent victim of mass migration from the South not linked to certain societal and political processes.

The new dualism of migrants and segmented labour markets

Structural aspects of migration are thus closely linked to economic processes in the countries of destination. Contrary to common belief, the process of economic globalisation does not only create a growing number of opportunities for highly qualified labour in activities such as banking, finance, insurance and communication services, but it also generates numerous opportunities for poorly qualified persons in agriculture, construction, cleaning, catering, security, and a 'panoply' of other activities connected with leisure.

This last set of activities is undoubtedly traditional. Nevertheless, it would be a mistake to consider them simply as remnants of the past: they increasingly appear directly connected to the growth of modern service sectors and share the same urban space. This phenomenon has been documented not only in the 'global' cities of New York and London, and in lower rank world cities like Paris and Amsterdam, but in all the major cities of Southern Europe. In these cities, immigrants carry out these kinds of jobs that requires no special training or qualification and are not attractive for the domestic population. Due to present immigration restrictions, this demand for labour leads to an increasing number of undocumented migrants. These new unwelcome but useful migrants often suffer victimisation, economic exploitation and social exclusion.

So there are currently two kinds of migratory movements. At the one end, there is a growing number of highly skilled migrants that the receiving countries are eager to attract in order to complement or expand their high-skilled labour force. This serves both multinational corporations that have to protect their foreign investment, but also the receiving countries that aim to foster a knowledge-based society in order to become or to remain a central node in the globalised world. At the other extreme, we have a flow of migrants that regardless of their qualifications can only find jobs in the least qualified occupations, in sectors such as agriculture, construction, hotels, contract cleaning, domestic service and catering.

This migration of low or unskilled persons to the central economies of the globalised world can be conceptualised as an answer to the intrinsic need for migrant labour in the advanced economies, as postulated several decades ago by segmented labour market theory. Advanced industrial societies are marked by four characteristics that create an intrinsic need for migrant labour, namely structural inflation, hierarchical constraints on motivation, economic dualism and the demography of labour supply.

In modern industrial societies wages are not only income, they are associated with hierarchies of prestige and status. This essentially means that 'wages must be increased proportionately throughout the job hierarchy in order to keep them in line with social expectations, a problem known as structural inflation' (Massey et al. 1998: 29). Thus, employers have an interest in keeping wages low at the bottom of the occupational structure.

Hierarchical constraints on motivation result from the fact that at the bottom of the job hierarchy there is no status to be maintained and there are few chances for upward mobility, which makes these jobs undesirable for the vast majority of the native working population. In other words, there is no motivation for natives to enter the lowest class of jobs. This does not always hold true for immigrants, who, at least in the beginning, essentially look for income and do not immediately connect employment with the accumulation or maintenance of social status in the receiving society.

The third relevant characteristic of modern industrial societies is economic dualism that generates bifurcated labour markets. These are a capital-intensive primary labour market where jobs are essentially stable and skilled and a labour-intensive secondary labour market where jobs are essentially unstable and unskilled. Natives have little motivation to accept the low wages, unstable labour conditions and few prospects for mobility that characterise the secondary labour market. Thus employers must turn to immigrants in order to satisfy demand in this segment of the labour market.

As Douglas Massey and his colleagues concluded: 'The problems of motivation and structural inflation inherent to modern occupational hierarchies, together with the dualism intrinsic to market economies create a permanent demand for workers who are willing to labour under unpleasant conditions, at low wages, with great instability, and facing little chance for advancement' (Massey et al. 1998: 32). This demand is basically satisfied by migrant labour since women, teenagers and rural to urban migrants, the historical suppliers of this segment of the labour market, are no longer available in sufficient numbers.

Segmented labour market theory was developed during the 1970s (Piore 1979) based on the migratory experience of the advanced industrial economies in the 1960s and early 1970s. It remains, however, a powerful explanatory device for present-day international migration because the economic restructuring of the 1980s and 1990s did not significantly change the above-described characteristics that generate an intrinsic need for migrant labour. Actually, economic restructuring opened up a whole new set of the lowest occupations, namely in the service sector, for which the native population shows no interest, thus increasing the need for immigrant labour.

However, not all propositions of segmented labour market theory are equally valuable in explaining present-day international migration. In fact, the idea that 'international labour migration is [...] usually initiated through recruitment by employers in developed societies, or by governments acting on their behalf' (Massey et al. 1998: 33) is clearly outdated since today recruitment practices are no longer the main mechanism generating or sustaining international migration. Family reunification and the migration industry are indeed the main mechanisms that foster and perpetuate the present migratory flows.

3. Migration as a policy concern

This brief historical overview has clearly shown that the governments of the industrialised nations try both to adapt to the societal attitudes towards migration and to cater for the specific needs and demands of the economic sphere. Hence they are in principal critical as to whom they allow to settle within their borders. This is especially true for European countries where generally speaking policies are aimed at reducing unsolicited migrants to a minimum. It is these migrants and policies related to them that interest us most at this juncture; for, in comparison, solicited or wanted migrants are clearly a minor policy concern.

The control of migration has preoccupied the minds of policymakers ever since the relatively liberal[3] migration regime that prevailed during the classical period of post-war labour immigration came under increasing pressure in the early 1970s, and much more forcefully, in the late 1980s and early 1990s. As a result migration policy in general came to be seen as being essentially about controlling and preventing unwanted flows. While the shift to the term 'migration management' introduced some new nuances to policy discourse, the policies of European governments continued to follow this basic philosophy, though sometimes combining control with the encouragement of some forms of migration (Brochmann 1999).

National policy responses

During the 1990s European states, first and foremost those in the northwestern part of the continent, took measures aimed at curbing the 'floods of asylum seekers'. The tone and pace were set by the German government. Chancellor Kohl spoke of a '*Staatsnotstand*' (emergency situation) when the number of aliens hoping to benefit from the relatively generous German asylum provisions approached half a million annually in 1992.

The German government believed that the 'problem' demanded an amendment to the Constitution.[4] After considerable political bargaining, the opposition agreed with the drafting of catalogues of countries that a) as a rule do not cause their citizens to flee and seek international protection (safe countries of origin) or b) are foreign countries where a refugee ordinarily would receive protection if requested (safe third countries). An asylum seeker stemming from a safe country of origin can since be rejected in a fast-track procedure. In cases where an asylum seeker arrives over land (all Germany's neighbours are safe third countries), the application is deemed to be inadmissible since the asylum seeker was already safe from persecution before s/he arrived in Germany. The numbers of asylum requests in Germany indeed dropped markedly in the following years (1992: 438,000; 1994: 128,000). To a considerable extent, however, this was the result of a general reduction in the number of people seeking refugee protection in Europe.

At the same time, the changes in German law increased the number of asylum claims in the countries bordering Germany. These, however, were not so much the countries these asylum seekers would presumably have come through on their way to Germany (the Central European ones, for instance), but countries to the West, such as the Netherlands and the United Kingdom. Not surprisingly, these countries planned and implemented their own interventions. In fact, they did not want to become 'Europe's shower drain', as a Dutch politician phrased it at the time.

During the early to mid-1990s, most European states introduced a range of similar measures that can be summarised as follows:

- If an airline, haulage or shipping company imports an alien who has no authorisation to enter or is not properly documented, the responsible company is liable to (high) fines (carrier sanctions). In this way, states transferred and privatised law enforcement on which they used to have a monopoly.
- Nationals of countries known to 'produce' significant quantities of asylum seekers, refugees and undocumented migrants require a visa that has to be checked by the carrier.
- Procedures for the adjudication of asylum requests were streamlined. This implies that the relevant bodies check all technical grounds for rejection (safe country of origin, safe third country, noncredible travel account) before they look into a case as such.

- More law enforcement capacity was freed up to guard borders. This not only pertains to the external borders of the Schengen area but also to the internal ones that formally are open, in the latter case under the guise of behind the border spot-checks.
- Depending on their administrative capacities, states imposed internal controls. Welfare states with comprehensive population and aliens registers are best equipped for this and effectively exclude non-eligible aliens from most or all welfare state provisions. Other countries, like the United Kingdom have much fewer possibilities to do so effectively.
- Assisting unsolicited migrants in their attempts to cross a country's borders was criminalised, especially if the aim is to make profit. All European countries have by now introduced high penalties for human smuggling.

Most recently, governments have tended to concentrate on integration policies. This would not immediately appear to have a bearing on immigration control but its impact can be significant. Here it suffices to point out that several countries, first of all Denmark and the Netherlands, require all newcomers from third countries to attend integration courses unless they pass a language test or are otherwise excused. The general feeling appears to be that many newcomers – and especially those who have been admitted after they arrived unsolicited – keep too much to themselves and account for an unduly high percentage of those depending on welfare. In as far as such courses equip newcomers to become self-reliant, few observers would argue against them. Nevertheless, it is obvious that control mechanisms and integration measures follow a different logic. While foreigners who arrive uninvited are, as a rule, not to remain in the country, are excluded from any form of participation in society (e.g. during the asylum procedure or when they are undocumented) and sooner or later are expelled, the exceptions to this rule, e.g. refugees or spouses of legal residents, are to integrate and make an unequivocal decision for their new country and society.

International policy responses

The management of migration flows has long been a prerogative of the nation-state. Each state has the sovereign right to control its borders as well as to decide on admission and stay of aliens on its territory. Although new approaches to the management of migration flows have evolved during the last decade, such responsibilities ultimately remain with the state. In practice, most of the migration policies are reactive, in particular those trying to tackle irregular immigration and trafficking or smuggling.

In the process of European integration the EU member states have tried to find common responses to migration flows,[5] negotiating common measures on the level of the European Union. One of the first joint measures aimed to stop asylum seekers from filing multiple claims across Europe (so-called asylum shopping). This resulted in the Dublin Convention regulating member state responsibility for asylum claims. In essence, this Convention stipulates that the first country entered by an asylum seeker is the one to decide on the claim. It thus formalises the safe third country principle among a number of EU countries. The Convention has recently been incorporated into the EU's body of law and now goes by the name of Dublin Agreement.

The Schengen Information System (SIS) and EURODAC aim to make available to member states two databases containing the fingerprints and other personal data of aliens who are of concern to the authorities of the member states. Since EURODAC has become operational (January 2003), all asylum seekers have to be registered. Thus multiple applications should be easily detectable.

The common regulations introduced by the European Union appear to be more elaborate than most of the other international attempts of joint migration management. According to some authors including Aristide Zolberg, James Hollifield, Mark Miller, Eytan Meyers and Wayne Cornelius, 'supranational organisations and international regimes usually have had little impact on immigration policies of individual countries, with the partial exception of the EU and the refugee regime' (Meyers 2000: 1266). However, more recently Sandra Lavenex and Emek Uçarer have highlighted 'the policy-pushing role of the international organisation which becomes an additional actor' (2002: 216). Several UN agencies and programmes, specific intergovernmental bodies and NGOs attempt to shape migration policies. In 1994, Jonas Widgren counted 'about 25 intergovernmental organisations and fora, and a myriad of subgroups, [...] involved in different activities relating to international migration' (Widgren 1994: 4). Ten years later, their number has undoubtedly increased (see IOM 2003).

Different UN bodies and programmes play an important part in migration management.[6] Some intergovernmental organisations provide reports and policy-oriented studies on international migration.[7] International organisations such as the IOM or the ILO have become more important for policy making.[8] The Council of Europe, a regional intergovernmental body, has mandated the CDMG (European Committee on Migration) to enhance European cooperation on migration.

The 1990s also saw the development of regional consultative processes on migration on all continents.[9] Aiming to manage migration on a regional basis, these are important for at least two reasons. First of all, they consider the migration process as a whole, including destination countries as well as countries of origin and transit countries. And second, although the participants are not obliged to implement decisions, it has been observed that some participating governments have changed their national migration policy in line with previous process recommendations (Klekowski von Koppenfels 2001: 75).

Several NGOs, such as Amnesty International, the Churches Commission for Migrants in Europe (CCME) and Caritas, have voiced their concern about international migration processes (Geddes 2000: 132). These statements mainly focus on migrants' rights and in particular on immigration policy. Nevertheless, they may also have an impact on migration management. Indeed, managing migration flows and dealing with immigrants might be two discrete policy areas but they involve overlapping realities of one complex process.

Since the beginning of this century, governments and agencies have come up with several new initiatives regarding the management of international migration. For example, in 2001 the Swiss government initiated a consultative process to assess inter-state cooperation (the Berne Initiative). In 2003, the heads of six international organisations have established the Geneva Migration Group, an intergovernmental body that counts more than 100 member states and aims to facilitate policy discussion relating to international migration management. In January 2004, the Global Commission on International Migration, initiated by UN-secretary Kofi Annan, began to work on proposals for a comprehensive response to migration issues. It is certainly too early to assess the impact of these initiatives, but it has to be highlighted that they involve receiving, sending and transit countries whereas thus far most attempts to regulate migration are initiated by destination countries.

In most of these multilateral fora tackling illegal migration and trafficking of human beings have become priorities over the last twenty years. The Europeanisation of immigration policy has entailed the rapid development of instruments aiming to fight illegal migration (Guiraudon & Joppke 2001). This same issue has also been at the centre of most of the regional consultative processes on migration.

The emergent international policy responses seem to encourage the participation of different levels of government (national, regional and supra-national), the input of non-governmental and private agencies, multilateral rather than bilateral fora and partnership between the countries involved in the migration pattern (sending, receiving and transit countries). The fact that numerous agencies have come to influence the process of policy-shaping or even policy making requires a less state-centric analysis of migration policies and also the study of the evolving modes of cooperation. The concept of multilevel govern-ance seems to be useful for the development of such new approaches.

4. Policy aims, migratory processes and unintended outcomes

Most measures discussed above aimed at curbing unsolicited migration to Europe – first and foremost when targeted at asylum seekers and re-fugees. However, they have unintended, secondary, or even perverse ef-fects that question the legitimacy, the efficiency and efficacy of current migration management, both on the national and on the EU level.

Categorisation of migrants in policy

One intended outcome of migration policy in the developed world is the categorisation of migrants that serves to differentiate between de-sired and unsolicited ones. More and more categories have been devel-oped so that governments can tailor their control mechanisms to speci-fic target groups. This should guarantee efficiency and seems to be cost-effective. Yet at the same time it makes the regulation regime more and more complex and difficult to handle, let alone that it is still understandable for a broader audience.

The categorisation of migrants is not only within the mandate of the nation-state. Some migrants can claim the right to move and resettle on the basis of interests beyond the scope of national policy making, notably the UN's Refugee Convention or the European Convention on Human Rights. Adhering to those international obligations, which have their inherent virtues, is instrumental to the self-perception of all European states. Liberal democratic states lose legitimacy if they *only* pursue realist goals, as much as they put it at risk by solely pursuing idealistic, universalistic goals. As a result, controlling migration is me-taphorically akin to walking a tightrope, as the governments have to try and keep these two political positions in balance.

The outcome of this balancing act has been that European govern-ments are willing to accept a limited number of asylum seekers, of whom they will recognise an even smaller number as refugees. As be-came manifest in the 1990s, when the numbers of asylum seekers reached record heights, procedures and the adjudication processes were restructured: governments tried both to fast-track procedures and to keep potential asylum seekers away from European territories in or-der to avoid having to process their requests in the first place. Further-more, the countries started to outbid each other in the enforcement of these rules. The fluctuation of the number of asylum seekers coming to Europe since the 1990s may partly be attributed to such increasingly restrictive policies and their stricter implementation. However, it is just as likely that decreases in asylum requests are the consequences of either a) fewer conflicts generating refugees, b) fewer people making themselves known to the authorities, or c) increased applications elsewhere.

States also allow immigration for the purpose of family formation and reunification but usually impose restrictions on their numbers and the ensuing rights (e.g. by barring him/her from the labour market) or require the (prospective) immigrant to fulfil certain criteria. The purpose of these policy instruments is to deter unsolicited migrants who cannot meet these criteria. However, the extent to which restrictive admission rules actually keep migrants from coming is difficult if not impossible to gauge. We merely know for a fact that many feel not bound by the rules set by the governments of countries to which they would like to move (assuming they know the relevant rules in the first place). This is testified by illegal arrivals, overstaying of visas and use of alternative gates of entry (e.g. marriage where work is the prime motive or vice versa).

At the other end of the spectrum are the desired and welcome migrants, e.g. EU citizens who have the right to settle unrestrictedly in the territory of the EU. Their rights are similar to those of the citizens of their new country of residence. Only some voting rights and the right to hold sensitive public occupations are withheld from them. As a consequence, a new form of stratification has developed which divides the migrant population into different categories, often reinforced by both public opinion towards and daily treatment of migrants. This also impacts on politics. Politicians focus on particular entry gates (e.g. asylum) while ignoring other entry gates or groups of persons not covered by them or out of reach of policymakers for constitutional reasons (e.g. family reunion of EU/EEA citizens). Yet these entry gates or groups that are absent from political discourse are nonetheless important in quantitative terms.[10]

Immigrant communities as intermediary structures

As a response to the policy restrictions, migrants increasingly draw on the resources offered by transnational communities. Migration within a transnational community can, as a rule, be arranged without the involvement of third parties. The members of the community know each other or of each other. The motive for migration is often linked to existing relations, with the most prominent example being marriage. The existence of a community, however, also allows mobility for other motives. Legal residents (or naturalised members of the community) can stand guarantee for tourist visa, they can arrange marriages for money (or other rewards), supply work contracts to prove stable income if that is required to have a spouse come over, provide information, lend money to a prospective migrant, and the like. In short, if the need for migration arises and is recognised, it can usually be arranged within the transnational community. In terms commonly used in migration theory, immigrant communities can be described as intermediary structures that facilitate migration from country A (origin) to B (destination). In turn, they also allow to predict volume and direction of migration processes.

Intermediary structures can be understood as a 'section' of economic, political, social and cultural spheres in which migrants were involved before migration and that remain intact following migration. Migrants can be conceptualised as acting in a transnational social field (Basch et al. 1994) or a transnational social space (Faist 2000) that connects the country or region of origin with the country of destination. Within such a field or space migrants interact with other migrants and non-migrants in both places.[11] Transnational mobility has been growing significantly in recent decades due to a) encouragement from countries of origin, who are keen to retain influence on the financial resources of emigrants, b) increasing tolerance of dual nationality by host governments and c) advances in communication and transport technologies which enable transnational ties to be maintained much more economically than in the past (Vertovec 2004). It has also been pointed out that while transnationalism may not be new it at least represents a new way of studying migration (Al-Ali & Koser 2002).

Irregular migration and human smuggling

During the 1990s, the phenomenon of organised human smuggling, i.e. the facilitation of illegal entry to states for profit, has gained increasing notoriety. Numerous police reports and even parliamentary inquiries have thrown glimpses of light on the harsh realities of a business which is assumed to be generating billions of dollars of profit on a worldwide scale. Increasingly, this illicit business has been linked to organised crime, threats to the sovereignty and the internal security of states and the exploitation of human beings in desperate situations (Aronowitz 2001; Doomernik 2004; Doomernik & Kyle 2004; Ghosh 1998; Salt & Stein 1997; Salt 2000; Salt & Hogarth 2000). At the same time researchers find little substantiation for claims that organised crime is generally involved. Staring (2001, 2004), Van Liempt (2004), Van Liempt and Doomernik (forthcoming), Bilger, Hofmann and Jandl (forthcoming) and Neske (forthcoming) for instance suggest that many smuggling operations take place within the respective ethnic community, are based on trust and are thus relatively benign in nature.

These, however, are usually not cases likely to make headlines in the European newspapers. Thus today, far from regarding human smuggling as a benign 'crime without victims' (Nadig 2002: 7), human rights organisations have taken to counting the deaths of illegal and smuggled migrants.[12] At the same time, European states as well as the Council and the Commission of the European Union have accorded the fight against illegal migration and human smuggling one of the highest priorities in the area of Justice and Home Affairs.[13]

We have many indications that virtually all asylum seekers arriving today have at some stage used the services of smugglers. Efionayi-Mäder, Chimienti, Dahinden and Piguet (2001), for instance, found that all persons requesting asylum in Switzerland had been smuggled. For the Netherlands, Hesseling and Taselaar (2001) found this to be the case for certain nationalities and less so for others, largely depending on the presence in the country of established transnational networks. Others concur that access to more network diminishes reliance and dependency on professional migration help (Jordan & Düvell 2002; Koser 1997; Koser & Pinkerton 2002; Staring 2001).[14] This implies a perverse pre-selection of those who come into the asylum system: those who have the means to buy their way across borders, do not necessarily have the most urgent cause to flee and seek protection (Morrison 1998; Doomernik 2004).

That (growing) investments are needed to buy a trip to Europe makes it also very likely that processes of cumulative causation are set in motion (see e.g. Massey et al. 2003). Consider the case in which it is part of a household's survival strategy to send one member abroad in order to contribute remittances to the household's budget and perhaps to become a bridgehead for chain migration. The household thus decides to invest scarce resources into the migration project of one of its members. This investment may require selling off a piece of land or another potential means of production or taking up a loan from a third party. In any case, the investment has considerable and potentially even detrimental consequences for the economic situation of the household members staying behind. Their future depends on the success of the migration project. No matter whether this project fails or succeeds, it is obvious that under these conditions return migration (voluntarily or forcefully) is hardly ever an option. Either the household becomes dependant on the remittances generated by the member abroad, or the member cannot return without enormous social and economic consequences. These pressures to some extent explain why governmental attempts to deport growing numbers of aliens have usually failed.

If smugglers determine the final destination of the migration process, they do not necessarily serve the interests of their clients but may target what they consider to be the softest port of entry to the EU (physical and administrative entry, which may well be found in different countries). Consider, for example, a migrant from Nigeria who would prefer to seek a future in the United Kingdom (the country's former coloniser). The smuggler he contracts takes him via Moscow to Prague and from there across the green border to Germany. This is as far as the smuggler knows to bring his client. The odds are considerable that this migrant ends up applying for asylum in Germany (or perhaps in a country closer to the UK like Belgium or the Netherlands).

Once this principle collides with arrangements made on the European level, migration outcomes become even more unpredictable and are – arguably – less satisfactory for all parties involved. This is perhaps best illustrated with a few concrete examples.

The fictitious Nigerian applying for asylum in Germany gets 'stuck' in that country because an application for asylum should (and increasingly can) only be filed once. The fact that the Nigerian migrant speaks no German, has no relatives or acquaintances in Germany, has an education based upon the English school system etc. is not taken into consideration. He will therefore either try to move on to the UK in an irregular fashion (to live there undocumented or again apply for asylum hoping the UK has not yet joined the SIS) or bide his time in Germany. After seven years he can naturalise and become a German citizen (provided he was granted Convention status and not subsidiary protection, which is likely if he cannot prove to have arrived without passing through a safe third country), which implies freedom of movement in the Union. Whether this person then still has the energy to move on, is an open question.

5. Outlook for further research

As we have stated in the beginning of this chapter our research group focuses primarily on the process of international migration itself, its conceptual delineation, its statistical recognition, its regulation and its concrete forms and directions. This turns out to be a complicated task, the more so since the concrete manifestations of it often defy existing theoretical conceptions, statistical categorisations, policy notions and expectations of the migrants' behaviour. We have indicated some of these in the preceding text.

This has led us to define our research priorities for the future accordingly into five thematic areas:
- International migration: concepts and measurements
- Changing paradigms in migration theory
- Structural aspects of international migration
- Modes of regulation

– Migration industry: means and routes of migration.

Within this still broad delineation we have furthermore given priority to those areas where the lack of empirical data and adequate approaches is most urgent by defining three short-term tasks:

The first one is to develop a better insight in irregular migration by establishing an empirically based typology of such irregular migration processes. Such a typology should be based on various data sources including court files, observations and interviews with smuggled migrants and with smugglers. Three different dimensions may be included: the smuggling methods (green border, hidden, fake visa, false documents, legal travelling), the 'geography' of irregular migration processes (countries of origin, transit countries, transit hubs, countries of destination, routes) and the smugglers' organisation (pyramid-like hierarchy, service, outsourcing, ethnic/family/other networks).

The second task is to develop a typology of modes of regulation. Since irregular migration is – to some extent – 'produced' by migration policies, it will be clear that this task is linked to the first one. The assumption here is not that policies force people directly to migrate irregularly, but that the official definition of regular migration automatically determines all other forms to be irregular.

The task here is to look at the different modes of regulation of types of migrants, such as asylum seekers, ethnically privileged migrants, family related migration and labour and see whether and how these fit into a common typology. The practice of policies related to the treatment of such migrants, the processes of border control and eviction for them will allow for an analysis of similarities and dissimilarities between countries.

The third task will identify structural aspects of interrelations between different categories of migrants and the dynamics of flows. Irregular flows and legal flows can either oppose or complement each other. They can cover the same geographical areas or different ones. Their demographic and socio-economic structures can converge or diverge.

In working on such concrete tasks we will eventually also accumulate material for the other thematic areas. One of these is that this empirical work will run into the lack of adequate and comparable statistical data on international migration and the selective nature of existing data. Development of viable alternative information sources is crucial and can best be based on empirical research.

The three concrete tasks should also help to eventually develop adequate medium range theories and concepts that help to explain present changing migration patterns. The traditional theoretical approaches are of a too general nature, whether they explain international movements of economically active individuals by economic equilibrium models, by neo-classical theory (Todaro 1976; Harris & Todaro 1970; Sjaastad 1962), by push-and-pull models (Lee 1966), by the economics of family migration that considers the effects of earnings differentials across space (Stark 1991), by dual labour market models (Piore 1979) or a differentiated approach that analyses migration flows, its volume and characteristics as a result of linkages between areas of origin and destination which vary over time (Kritz 1995; Kritz et al. 1992; Mabogunje 1970). Such general approaches evidently lack medium range concepts that explain important phenomena such as the migration industry, transnational mobility or the linkages between globalisation and migration. However, the formulation of new theoretical concepts demands more research and is thus a long-term task. Especially in the broad field of undocumented, irregular or illegal flows of migration we need more and deeper knowledge before we can draw nomothetic conclusions.

Notes

1 This chapter is based on a more elaborate State of the Art Report written jointly by the following members of IMISCOE's cluster A1: Maria I. Baganha, Andreas Breinbauer, Michael Collyer, Jeroen Doomernik, Rob van der Erf, Heinz Fassmann, Sonia Gsir, Martin Hofmann, Michael Jandl, Natalia Kovaleva, Albert Kraler, Gustav Lebhart, Matthias Neske and Ursula Reeger. The full version is published on www.imiscoe.org.

2 Only ten countries were considered. Figures for 1981 and 1991 in OECD 1994 and Baganha 1996.

3 Liberal in the sense that 'migration policy' was not aimed at restricting entry of aliens but rather at ensuring a sufficient supply of (cheap) labour.

4 Article 16(2) of the Constitution simply read: 'Politically persecuted [persons] enjoy the right to asylum'.

5 The principles of a European migration policy have been defined in the 1999 Tampere Summit following the objectives stated in Amsterdam.

6 UNHCR (United Nations High Commissioner for Refugees), ILO (International Labour Organisation) and IMP (International Migration Policy Programme). The latter is an interagency activity that aims to strengthen the migration-management capacity.

7 IOM (International Organisation for Migration), OECD (Organisation for Economic Cooperation and Development), OSCE (Organisation for Security and Cooperation in Europe) or ICMPD (International Centre for Migration Policy and Development).

8 For example, the IOM has a Migration Policy Research Programme (MPRP) that among other things aims to provide policy guidance on migration issues for governments.

9 IGC (Intergovernmental Consultations on Asylum and Migration in Europe, North America and Australia), the Budapest Process in Europe and later the CIS Conference Process in Russia, the Puebla Process or Regional Conference on

Migration between North and South America, the Manila Process in Asia, the
Migration Dialogue for Southern Africa and the Dakar Declaration in West Africa.

10 In Austria, for example, family members of Austrians/EEA citizens now constitute
the overwhelming majority of long term immigrants admitted to the country (88 per
cent in 2003). While the policy of restricting long-term labour migration has been
extraordinarily effective, overall immigration numbers are steadily on the rise, partly
because of the increasing number of naturalisations and family reunions of
Austrians/EEA citizens.

11 Criticism of the transnational approach is widespread. A common issue raised is that
migrant transnationalism is nothing new (Portes 1996) and that what today is called
transnationalism can be found throughout history.

12 UNITED, a European network against nationalism, racism, fascism and in support
of migrants and refugees, monitors migrant deaths since 1993. Up to January 2004,
the network has documented 4,591 deaths, who for instance drowned in the
Mediterranean Sea, the Strait of Gibraltar, suffocated in trucks or committed suicide
in Europe's detention centres. Many more deaths are thought to remain unreported
(see: www.united.non-profit.nl/).

13 See, for example, the Council Directive of 28 November 2002 defining the
facilitation of unauthorised entry, transit and residence (2002/90/EC); the Council
Framework Decision of 28 November 2002 on the strengthening of the penal
framework to prevent the facilitation of unauthorised entry, transit and residence
(2002/946/JHA); the Communication from the Commission to the European
Parliament and the Council in view of the European Council of Thessaloniki on the
development of a common policy on illegal immigration, smuggling and trafficking
of human beings, external borders and the return of illegal residents, COM (2003)
323 final, Brussels, 3.6.2003; as well as the Presidency Conclusions – Thessaloniki,
19 and 20 June 2003, 11638/03 3, available at ue.eu.int.

14 It should be noted that researchers tend to use varying definitions of what they would
consider to constitute human smuggling. Moreover, even if they confine themselves to
those cases where the state would define this type of assistance a crime, it should be
kept in mind that this may well change over time (before the early 1990s, human
smuggling was rarely considered a crime at all in Western Europe).

Literature

Al-Ali, N. & K. Koser (eds.) (2002), *New Approaches to Migration. Transnational communities and the transformation of home.* London: Routledge.
Aronowitz, Alexis A. (2001), 'Smuggling and Trafficking in Human Beings: The Phenomenon, the Markets that Drive it and the Organisations that Promote it', *European
Journal on Criminal Policy and Research* 9 (2): 163-195.
Baganha, M. (1996), *Immigrants Integration in the Informal Economy: The Portuguese Case*
(1st Report). Coimbra: CES.
Basch, L., N. Glick-Schiller & C. Szanton-Blanc (1994), *Nations unbound: Transnational
projects, postcolonial predicaments, and deterritorialized nation-states.* Utrecht: Gordon
and Breach Publishers.
Bean, C., P. Bernholz, J.-P. Danthine & E. Malinvaud (1990), *European Labour Markets: a
Long-run View.* Brussels: CEPS.
Bilger, V., M. Hofmann & M. Jandl (forthcoming), 'Human Smuggling as a Transnational
Service Industry. Evidence from Austria', *International Migration.*
Brochmann, G. (1999), *Mechanisms of migration control.* Oxford: Berg.

Doomernik, J. (2004), 'Migration and security. The wrong end of the stick?', in C. van den Anker (ed.), *The political economy of new slavery*: 37-52. Houndmills: Palgrave.

Doomernik, J. & D. Kyle (2004), 'Introduction', *Journal of International Migration and Integration* Special Issue: Organized Migrant Smuggling and State Control: Conceptual and Policy Challenges 5 (3): 265-272.

Efionayi-Mäder, D., M. Chimienti, J. Dahinden & E. Piguet (2001), *Asyldestination Europa. Eine Geographie der Asylbewegungen*. Zürich: Seismo.

Faist, T. (1998), 'Transnational social spaces out of international migration: Evolution, significance and future prospects', *Archive Européene Sociologique* 39: 213-247.

Faist, T. (2000), *The volume and dynamics of international migration and transnational social spaces*. Oxford: Clarendon.

Geddes, A. (2000), *Immigration and European integration. Towards fortress Europe?* Manchester: Manchester University Press, European Policy Research Unit Series.

Ghosh, B. (1998), *Huddled Masses and Uncertain Shores. Insights into Irregular Migration*. The Hague: Martinus Nijhoff Publishers.

Guiraudon, V. & C. Joppke (2001), 'Controlling a new migration world', in V. Guiraudon & C. Joppke (eds.), *Controlling a new migration world*, 1-127. London: Routledge.

Harris, J. R. & M. P. Todaro (1970), 'Migration, unemployment and development: a two sector model', *American Economic Review* 60: 126-142.

Hesseling, R. & A. Taselaar (2001), 'Asielmigratie en mensensmokkel', *Tijdschrift voor Criminologie* 32 (4): 340-349.

IOM (2003), *World migration 2003. Managing migration – challenges and responses for people on the move*. Volume 2 – IOM World Migration Report Series. Geneva.

Jordan, B. & F. Düvell (2002), *Irregular migration: Dilemmas of Transnational Mobility*. Cheltenham: Edward Elgar.

Klekowski von Koppenfels, A. (2001), 'Informal but effective: Regional consultative processes as a tool in managing migration', *International Migration* 39 (6): 61-84.

Koser, K. & C. Pinkerton (2002), *The Social Networks of Asylum Seekers and the Dissemination of Information About Countries of Asylum*. London: Home Office. Research Development and Statistics Directorate.

Koser, K. (1997), 'Social Networks and the Asylum Cycle. The Case of Iranians in the Netherlands', *International Migration Review* 31 (3): 591-611.

Kritz, M. M. (1995), *Population growth and international migration: is there a link?* The International Center for Migration, Ethnicity and Citizenship, the New School for Social Research. Migration Policy in Global Perspective Series. Occasional Paper 1.

Kritz, M. M., L. L. Lim, & H. Zlotnik (eds.) (1992), *International migration systems: A global approach*. Oxford, United Kingdom: Clarendon Press.

Lavenex, S. & E. Uçarer (eds.) (2002), *Migration and the externalities of European integration*. Lanham, MD: Lexington Books.

Lee, E. S. (1966), 'A theory of migration', *Demography* 3 (1): 47-57.

Liempt, I. van (2004), 'De sociale organisatie van mensensmokkel. Het beeld van mensensmokkel als grootschalige georganiseerde misdaad genuanceerd', *Amsterdams Sociologisch Tijdschrift* 31 (1): 38-60.

Liempt, I. van & J. Doomernik (forthcoming), 'Migrant's agency in the smuggling process. The perspectives of smuggled migrants in the Netherlands', *International Migration*.

Mabogunje, A. (1970), 'Systems approach to a theory of rural-urban migration', *Geographical Analysis* 2 (1): 1-18.

Massey, D., J. Arango, G. Hugo, A. Kouaouci, A. Pellegrino & E. Taylor (1998), *Worlds in Motion. Understanding International Migration at the End of the Millennium*. Oxford: Clarendon Press.

Massey, D. S., J. Durand & N. J. Malone (2003), *Beyond Smoke and Mirrors. Mexican Immigration in an Era of Economic Integration.* New York: Russell Sage Foundation.

Meyers, E. (2000), 'Theories of international immigration policy – A comparative analysis', *International Migration Review* 34 (4): 1245-1282.

Morrison, J. (1998), *The cost of survival. The trafficking of refugees to the UK.* London: the refugee council.

Nadig, A. (2002), 'Human smuggling, national security and refugee protection', *Journal of Refugee Studies* 15 (1): 1-25.

Neske, M (forthcoming), 'Human smuggling to and through Germany', *International Migration.*

Neske, M. & J. Doomernik (forthcoming), 'Comparing Notes: Perspectives on Human Smuggling in Austria, Germany, Italy and the Netherlands', *International Migration.*

OECD (eds.) (1994), *Trends in International Migration.* Geneva: OECD.

Piore, M. J. (1979), *Birds of passage: Migrant labour in industrial societies.* Cambridge: Cambridge University Press.

Portes, A. (1996), 'Transnational communities: Their emergence and significance in the contemporary world-system', in R. P. Korzeniewidcz & W. C. Smith (eds.), *Latin America in the world economy.* Westport, Conn.: Greenwood.

Salt, J. (2000), 'Trafficking and Human Smuggling: A European Perspective', *International Migration* 38 (1): 32-56.

Salt, J. & Stein, J. (1997), 'Migration as a business: The case of trafficking', *International Migration* 35 (4): 467-494.

Salt, J. & J. Hogarth (2000), 'Trafficking and Human Smuggling in Europe: A Review of the Evidence', in IOM (ed.), *Migrant Trafficking and Human Smuggling in Europe. A review of the evidence with cases from Hungary, Poland and Ukraine*, 11-163. Geneva: International Organization for Migration.

Sjaastad, L. A. (1962), 'The costs and returns of human migration', *Journal of Political Economy* 705: 80-93.

Stark, O. (1991), *The migration of labor.* Cambridge: Basil Blackwell.

Staring, R. (2001), *Reizen onder regie. Het migratieproces van illegale Turken in Nederland.* Amsterdam: Het Spinhuis.

Staring, R. (2004), 'Facilitating the Arrival of Illegal Immigrants in the Netherlands: Irregular Chain Migration versus Smuggling Chains', *Journal of International Migration and Integration* 5 (3): 273-294.

Todaro, M. P. (1976), *Internal migration in developing countries.* Geneva: International Labour Office.

Vertovec, S. (2004), *Trends and impacts of migrant transnationalism.* Oxford: Compas.

Vogel, D. (2002), 'Ausländer ohne Aufenthaltsstatus in Deutschland. Methoden zur Schätzung ihrer Zahl', in E. Minthe (ed.), *Illegale Migration und Schleusungskriminalität.* Wiesbaden: Eigenverlag der Kriminologischen Zentralstelle e.V.

Vogler-Ludwig, K. (ed.) (1994), *Medium-Term Employment Forecasts by EU Regions and Sectors of Industry 1991-1997.* Munich: ERECO.

Widgren, J. (1994), 'Multilateral cooperation to combat trafficking in migrants and the role of international organizations', discussion paper presented at the *Eleventh IOM Seminar* 'International response to trafficking in migrants and the safeguarding of migrants rights', Geneva.

3. Migration and Development: Causes and Consequences

Richard Black[1], Xiang Biao, Michael Collyer,
Godfried Engbersen, Liesbeth Heering and Eugenia Markova

1. Introduction

With some notable exceptions, academic and policy attention for international migration has focused to a far greater extent on countries of destination than on countries of origin. Research projects have been motivated primarily by concerns of receiving societies, funded by agencies in destination countries and based on data collected on the receiving side. But it is clear that migration studies cannot do without in-depth understanding of the sending context. In turn, a relative knowledge gap in this area has become particularly salient in the beginning of the 21st century as various receiving countries in Europe are increasingly acknowledging the importance of the 'partnership with the countries of origin' in devising migration policies (Communities 2000).

In this context, this chapter is focused on work on migration from a developing or sending country perspective. Until relatively recently, research evidence was largely negative about the relationship between migration and development. On the one hand, migration was often seen as a product of poverty; whilst at the same time, international migration and rural-urban migration within developing countries alike were seen as draining human capital from poor areas, creating or reinforcing dependence, and undermining regional development strategies in sending areas. In turn, despite some reviews in the early to mid-1990s that took a more critical stance (Papademetriou and Martin 1991; Durand and Massey 1992; Taylor et al. 1996) and the emergence of the 'new economics of labour migration' as a theoretical approach that seeks to explain why poor households *invest* in migration (Stark and Lucas 1988; Stark 1991) rather than acting out of desperation or dependence, public policy towards migration within the development field remained sceptical at best.

However, in the last few years, several new reviews have been carried out, which not only have taken a more positive stance towards the relationship between migration and development, but have started to influence development policy as well. From the academic side, influential overviews have been provided by Skeldon (1997) and Massey et al. (1998). Impacts on policy have also been increasingly evident, especially where reviews have been funded by development cooperation agencies. For example, a study for the Royal Danish Ministry of Foreign Affairs and the Danish International Development Agency (DANIDA) on the 'migration-development nexus' (Van Hear and Nyberg-Sørensen 2003), has been widely disseminated, helping to challenge the simplistic view that poverty 'causes' migration, in turn reinforcing poverty. Rather, Van Hear and Nyberg-Sørensen note that migration is increasingly seen as a viable 'livelihood strategy' by poor people, whilst poverty reduction can also make it easier for individuals to move. Their review also examines the complex interconnections between international mobility, poverty and conflict, with case studies of Somalia, Afghanistan and Sri Lanka highlighting how refugees overseas send significant sums in remittances not only to family at home, but also to relatives living in refugee and displaced persons camps.

Other European development cooperation agencies have followed suit, commissioning research studies and reviews, and/or funding new research to translate research insights into policy. One of the larger studies to emerge to date was funded by the Swedish Ministry of Foreign Affairs (Lucas 2005) and focuses on case studies of migration to the EU, the movement of contract workers to the Persian Gulf from South and Southeast Asia, the 'brain drain' to North America and the migration transition in East Asia. Together with a parallel review by Ramamurthy (2003) on brain drain, remittances and labour market impacts in source countries, this work suggests that the benefits of migration for sending areas can be substantial, though they are highly context-dependent.

The UK's Department for International Development (DFID) has also supported work in this area, drawing on evidence of the increasingly important role played by migrant remittances in poor peoples' livelihoods (De Haan 2000). Here, in addition to funding a major research centre,[2] regional reports have been commissioned on migration and poverty in Asia (Skeldon 2003; Waddington 2003), sub-Saharan Africa (Black 2004) and the Middle East and North Africa (Al-Ali 2004). An interesting overview of the field from a policy perspective was also provided by a recent report of the UK's House of Commons International Development Committee (House of Commons 2004), which argues that there are important opportunities for the UK government – and other northern countries – to enhance the positive benefits of migration for the poor, whilst minimising its risks and costs. In turn, interest has also spread to international organisations, notably the World Bank (Maimbo and Ratha 2005; Caglar and Schiff 2006).

One major reason for this renewed interest of development cooperation agencies in the field of migration is emerging evidence on the
scale of remittances, which at over $100 billion each year are already
around twice the global total of development assistance (Black 2003b).
However, a plethora of reviews of the field that have emerged in the
last few years, including for the UN Population Division (Skeldon
2004), the International Organisation for Migration (Hugo 2003; IOM
2003) and by the Global Commission on International Migration
(GCIM 2005), whose report includes a chapter on migration and development, stress a number of other important dynamics beyond remittances that are significant and worthy of policy attention. For example,
Sriskandarajah (2005) suggests that we need to move not only 'beyond
remittances', but also 'beyond brain drain' and 'beyond simple models',
to acknowledge the varied impacts of growing mobility on sending
areas.

Our purpose here is not to duplicate these existing efforts to synthesise a complex research and policy field, but to highlight two themes of
research within the IMISCOE network, as well as interesting routes for
further research. This more limited aim highlights the contribution of
European researchers to the field, as well as suggesting opportunities
for collaborative European work to advance the debate on migration
and development. In the sections below, we first consider research that
seeks to explain the determinants and patterns of migration. Secondly
we will turn to material on the extent and use of remittances and return migration. This represents only a sub-set of issues relating to migration and development, but is a useful starting point for entering the
debate. The final section then concludes with reflections both on migration policy and on research gaps.

Research on the patterns and determinants of migration within IMI-
SCOE has essentially followed two theoretical and methodological approaches.[3] The first is a demographic and sociological one, as exempli-
fied by the large-scale survey undertaken at the Netherlands Interdisciplinary Demographic Institute (NIDI). This approach aims to identify
individual variables, through statistical analysis, that determine migration behaviour. During the period 1995-1999, NIDI conducted surveys
in five migrant-sending countries (Egypt, Ghana, Morocco, Senegal
and Turkey) and two migrant-receiving countries (Italy and Spain). The
project led to a large database containing information on migration histories and destinations, household economic situations, remittances,
social and demographic characteristics, networks, intentions for future
migration and attitudes/opinions on migration. In each sending country, over 1,500 interviews were conducted, covering both migrants and
non-migrants (Schoorl et al. 2004). A similar approach is taken in re-

cent work at Sussex that has used existing sample surveys to explore
the multiple determinants of migration choice in Albania (Reilly et al.
2004).

In comparison, the second approach is anthropological and aims to
present patterns and histories of migration in a more holistic way
through in-depth observation and qualitative analysis. The approach
has three key characteristics:

- First, it sees migration as just *one* aspect of migrants' lives and emphasises that migration is strongly embedded in the local institutions of the sending community;
- Second, the approach is actor-centred and seeks to reveal the migrants' point of view. Such an approach may explain for instance
  why places that seem to be unlikely destinations for outsiders often
  attract sizable migrant flows for various reasons;
- Third, the approach has a historical dimension: contemporary patterns of migration are often indicative of established historical connections between sending and receiving countries.

An example of such an anthropological approach to studying migration
is the four-year ethnographic research on migration from Fujian province in China conducted by COMPAS, which describes 'the connections between the total sum of social institutions and practices in areas
of origin, transit and destination that produce and sustain a particular
flow of migrants' (Pieke et al. 2004: 19). Findings from this research
have illustrated how one community had resumed its emigration after
a long break, whilst another without any tradition of out-migration (internal or international) suddenly embarked on migration to diverse
destinations (Pieke 1998; Pieke 1999).

Following this second approach, Xiang's work (forthcoming) on
skilled migration from India details how resources are mobilized and
various institutions are utilised or set up to facilitate emigration. His
research identifies the marriage market, education institutes and (extended) family networks, along with the migration brokerage system,
as strategic sites for the social production of emigration. Similar concerns, albeit with variations in approach, exist across the IMISCOE network. For example, in her work on Bangladesh, Gardner (1995) has
used ethnographic methods to show how economic and social inequalities have shaped, but have also been redefined by international migration to Britain and the Gulf.

Despite the different approaches, these research initiatives share important substantive concerns, which are also linked to major debates in
migration studies. In the following section we identify five main factors which are an important part of why people do, or indeed do not,
migrate.

2. Determinants and patterns of migration

Poverty, Inequality and migration

An important issue in migration studies is the extent to which a poverty threshold effect exists, meaning that the poorest (measured in terms of perceived poverty or relative deprivation) either do not intend or are not able to migrate. This is currently a widely accepted assumption in migration studies, and NIDI's research in Senegal, especially in the rural Tuba area, confirms this effect. However, the same study suggests that in other countries the poorest *are* migrating. In Egypt and Morocco, where the surveys included a question on relative deprivation, the perception of being worse off than other households was found to stimulate migration intentions (Schoorl et al. 2004). Meanwhile, Rogaly and Rafique's (2003) research in eastern Indian shows that being landless is a clear driving force for out-migration, though their study deals with seasonal mobility rather than international migration. The work of Pieke et al. (2004) suggests that income levels do not have a determining effect on migration decisions and behaviour: well-off and poor members of a community both migrate. Xiang (2000) found that in the same village in southeast China, while out-migration started with more capable members of one clan, less well-off members were pioneer migrants for another clan. The difference was found to lie in the structures of the two clans rather than income differentiation. It seems clear that migration is not simply caused by poverty, but exactly how income levels affect migration decisions in different contexts remains to be explored. The tendency to focus on 'homogeneous' streams of migrants may also obscure the fact that migrants must negotiate complex webs of dependency and reciprocity with resource-rich individuals such as their employers. These webs may be as restrictive as they are enabling.

The role of networks

'Network' has been a key word in the literature on migration since the 1980s and the notion that emigration, once started, would become self-sustaining with its own autonomy due to migrants' networks has been well-established. The NIDI project again provides fresh material on this: while network effects turn out to be important in Ghana and Egypt, in Senegal and Morocco they appear much less significant (Van Dalen et al. forthcoming). In fact, for men in Morocco, the presence of relatives abroad even decreases their intention to emigrate (Heering et al. 2004). Pieke's work also pays much attention to networks, but it does not take networks for granted. Rather it reveals how new networks are created and how old networks are reproduced, sustained and turned to serve the needs of different groups (old and new migrants, local officials and those left behind). The case stories demonstrate how migrants consciously as well as accidentally transnationalise their networks (Pieke et al. 2004).

Xiang (forthcoming) argues that networks are important, not in themselves, but in that they bridge macro socio-economic situations with individual migrants. Furthermore, based on recent observation of migration from southeastern China, he proposes a hypothesis of 'network failure' (Xiang 2004). It is suggested that the perpetuation of irregular emigration from the region, particularly the deception and exploitation associated with it, is not because migrants' networks are strong, but because of the opposite, namely migrants' networks are too weak compared to professionalised and institutionalised human smuggling networks. Therefore, attempts to dismantle the migrants' networks or even to criminalise entire emigrant communities may be counterproductive.

In explaining why networks do not appear important, the NIDI team turns to the concept of 'migration culture', which in their survey is operationalised as migration history (Van Dalen et al. forthcoming). Heering et al. (2004) define the 'culture of migration' as a culture where migration is considered to be the only way to improve one's standard of living; that is, those who stay are believed to be losers, and those who leave are winners (Heering et al. 2004). Interestingly, it is found that in Morocco, networks affect women's migration decisions but not men's, and that at the same time the existence of a migration culture importantly promotes migration intentions for men, but not for women.

Pieke et al. (2004: 48) also agree that a historically informed cultural explanation, as well as an understanding of structural opportunities and constraints, is necessary in order to understand why people move about the globe. A major feature of this culture is a discourse on migration as a dominant strategy to enable social mobility. This discourse prescribes what constitutes success, as well as ignoring other local strategies that are not considered an option (Pieke et al. 2004: 194). They also argue that this culture of migration 'renders current emigration patterns unintelligible in terms of a narrow cost-benefit analysis'. For example, the NIDI project reported a fairly sizeable group of youngsters who were neither working nor looking for work, but reported that they spent their time and energy in looking for ways to migrate, as they were convinced there were no alternatives for them in Morocco (Schoorl 2002). A culture of migration changes the formula of the potential migrants' decision making process and thus the concept is critical for deeper understanding of emigration dynamics.[4]

The role of the state

It has been widely recognised that migration is as much about state sovereignty and policies as it is about the mobility of people. IMISCOE researchers have conducted various projects aimed at detailing connections between state interventions and migration dynamics particularly in sending countries. In line with Zolberg's argument (1983) that the formation of 'new states' was one of the root causes of current refugee migrations, Kraler (forthcoming; 2004) links refugee flows in Africa to state formation. His work demonstrates that the processes of colonisation and decolonisation were crucial in producing large numbers of migrants and refugees.

Pieke et al. (2004) argue that increasing emigration from China should be understood against the background of the rise of China's position in the world system at the macro-level as well as the efforts of local administration. They identify specific mechanisms through which the state plays a role in migration. In one community with a long emigration tradition, the local administration had sought donations from overseas communities and accorded the diaspora great honour, which highlights emigration as the best, even the only, avenue to true wealth, power and success. In contrast, in another village without established overseas communities, the local government from the county level down to the village 'engineers' emigration by providing information, simplifying procedures and other means (Pieke et al. 2004: 53-60). Curiously, local government's 'engineering' of emigration coincides with a low prevalence of professionalised illegal emigration brokers, and it may be worth investigating whether there are any links between the two.

Xiang's research on the emigration regime of China (Xiang 2003a) and his comparative study on emigration schemes from China and India (Xiang 2003b) suggests that active measures often yield unintended consequences but laissez-faire policies tend to work better. For example, in China the relaxation of exit controls (which Xiang calls 'individualization of emigration management') has increased the volume of emigration, but strict regulations on labour exports, though aimed at forbidding illegal migration, may have contributed to exactly such irregularity. State policies must have synergies with market mechanisms to ensure desirable policy outcomes and their sustainability.

Lacroix (2004) calls attention to local politics in understanding the impacts of migration on sending communities. Emigrants' village development associations have made significant contributions to the development of southern Morocco. These associations have flourished not only because of emigrants' efforts, but also because they provide new sources of power for local elites who have been excluded from the formal administration since the 1970s. They reclaim their status based on the position of being 'in-between' the state and the migrant community. This again shows that migration is deeply embedded in local institutions and intertwines with other phenomena.

Gender differences in migration intentions

Gender differences in migration intentions are also a crucial element of migration patterns (Van der Erf and Heering 2002; Van Dalen et al. forthcoming). One of the more robust findings of work in this area is that there is a significant difference in migration intentions between men and women, with men more likely to wish to emigrate from the study countries than women. The NIDI research, referred to above, suggests that these differences are much more pronounced in Morocco and Egypt than in Ghana and Senegal, possibly reflecting gender norms that are influenced by Islam in the former two countries. For both men and women, economic reasons (such as unemployment or insufficient income or more generally the desire for an improved standard of living) dominate over family and other reasons like education, adventure etc. in the wish to migrate. However, women's motives appear to be more diverse than those of men. Women more often mentioned family-related reasons than men – reflecting the higher number of women than men accompanying or following their spouse abroad. Meanwhile, women may also see independent migration as a way out of their traditional dependence on men and their obligations to male kinsmen (Heering et al. 2004; Schoorl et al. 2004). In Morocco, women with a paid job who judged their financial situation negatively were found to have the highest migration intentions of any group (Heering et al. 2004).

A more detailed analysis of the NIDI data reveals a number of interesting correlations. For example, higher financial expectations and lower anticipated job search costs were found to be statistically significantly associated with having the intention to migrate in all four countries, but this effect was stronger for women than for men. Meanwhile, more educated women, at least in Egypt and Ghana, were found to be much more set on emigration than less educated women and much more so than higher educated men. In contrast, in Ghana, no relationship was found between the intention to migrate and educational attainment amongst men, whilst in Egypt, the correlation was much weaker for men. This reinforces the conclusion that women may see migration as a way to achieve more independence, especially in Egypt, where migration of women is strongly frowned upon (Schoorl et al. 2004; Van Dalen et al. forthcoming).

3. Remittances and return – determinants and effects

The previous section has considered some of the main current debates in terms of the determinants of migration, but a key factor influencing migration decisions is also the intended outcome of this decision for many sending communities – the receipt of remittances and eventual return. Remittances from migrant workers can be broadly defined as transfers in cash and kind to households back in the country of origin. Even without the problem of 'in kind' transfers, measuring remittance flows worldwide or even for a particular country still remains a somewhat tricky task. To a great extent, the ease of measurement is determined by migrant workers' choice between the formal banking system and other, informal channels when remitting their earnings. When predominantly informal channels are used for these transfers, government has no direct access to the foreign exchange and government policy may be constrained. Further, when the true magnitude of remittances from nationals abroad remains imprecisely known, the result may be a distorted view of macroeconomic impacts (Choukri 1986).

The significance of unrecorded remittance flows is only now becoming apparent. The big change came in 2002-03, when a re-examination of how the flow of money from migrant workers was calculated showed that differences in definitions from country to country were keeping much of the funds out of the headline numbers (Ratha 2003). On a global basis, the reworking of the numbers came up with a total of as much as $80 billion for 2002. For 2003, some reports put the figure at $140 billion.[5] That could well still be a sizeable underestimate, partly because the moneys transferred through informal channels are not included. A recent IMF study estimated that such informal transfers of remittances could amount to $10 billion per annum (El-Qorchi et al. 2003).[6] However, others have cautioned that such estimates are excessive (cf. Rosenzweig 2004).

As estimates of global remittances by migrant workers have risen – Ratha's figures suggest that they now exceed global development assistance and are on a par with net foreign direct investment in the developing world – it is not surprising that the phenomenon is of growing interest to development policymakers. One major question that has emerged amongst policymakers is how to maximize the beneficial impact of remittances on development and especially on poverty reduction and the achievement of the Millennium Development Goals (Black 2003b).

This section reviews existing knowledge on migrant remittance behaviour paying special attention to contributions to the literature by IMISCOE researchers. It is organised around four main questions: why and how much do migrants remit; how are migrant remittances used and what are the effects; what are the specific impacts of migration and remittances on gender relations within the family; and what is the role of return migration in the development process?

Remittances: quantity and motivation

At a micro-level, there is an impressive body of literature that endeavours to understand remitting behaviour and migrants' motivations to remit. It distinguishes three main motives: altruism, exchange and co-insurance.

- *Altruism.* Becker (1974) was amongst the first economists to model altruistic behaviour in the context of household, arguing that the utility of one household member, the 'donor', is positively affected by the well-being of another household member, 'the receiver'. The basic prediction derived is that an increase in the income gap between 'the donor' and 'the recipient' increases the probability and the size of the transfers whereas a reduction in the income gap has the opposite effect.
- *Exchange.* Another conceivable motive is that of exchange between household members. Cox (1987), relying on the idea of exchange, formalises a model where private transfers are treated as payments for services rendered. The model predicts that an increase in the income of the donor is associated with an increase in both the probability and size of transfer. However, if the recipient's income increases the probability of transfer decreases, and as the opportunity cost of providing the service increases, the transfer, depending on the elasticities of demand for and supply of recipient's services, may end up being higher or lower than before the change of the income. Thus, a negative correlation between the likelihood of transfer and recipient's income is consistent with both motives (i.e. altruism and exchange), whereas a positive correlation between the size of transfer and recipient's income is consistent with exchange only.
- *Co-insurance.* Lucas and Stark (1985) have proposed a theory of migrants' motivations to remit, known as *Tempered Altruism or Enlightened Self-Interest.* The theory views remittances as part of inter-temporal, mutually beneficial contractual arrangements between the migrant and the household in the origin area. Such contractual arrangements are based on insurance and investment and they are voluntary and, hence, must be self-enforcing. Considerations for self-enforcement can be mutual altruism but also the aspiration to inherit, the desire to return home and the need to have reliable agents to assist in the accumulation and maintenance of assets. Lianos (1997) attempts a critique of that theory suggesting that remittances should be understood as the result of a rational agent's beha-

viour acting freely but constrained by his loyalty and commitment to his family. Moreover, remittances are related to different circumstances of the migrant. The objective of the migrant and his decisions will determine the share remitted.

Poirine (1997) has proposed an alternative approach based on the notion that informal financial markets function within families, in which remittances represent repayments on an informal loan agreement. The would-be migrants receive loans to invest in human capital before migrating and remittances constitute the payback of these loans to the family. Later on, emigrants continue to remit, though not to repay the loan but to finance the education of the next cohort of migrant members of the family.

Empirical analysis of migrant remitting behaviour provides support for both altruism and exchange motives. Johnson and Whitelaw (1974) and Banerjee (1984), analysing internal migration remittances in Kenya and India respectively, provided evidence for altruistic motives. In contrast, Lucas and Stark (1985) and Hoddinott (1994) utilising data respectively from Botswana and Kenya found support for exchange motives. Merkle and Zimmermann (1992) analysing remittance and saving behaviour of immigrants in Germany found evidence for exchange motives as well. However, later work (see Stark 1991; Brown 1997; Secondi 1997; de la Brière et al. 2002) suggests that different remittance motivations should not be considered mutually exclusive. Germenji et al. (2000), using data from a rural household survey in Albania in 2000, provide little evidence of altruism while the evidence for exchange is stronger.

Turning to work by researchers at IMISCOE institutions, Liu and Reilly (2000), using data on male migrant workers, drawn from the Jinan Municipality in Shandong province, China, in the summer of 1995, estimate remittance functions. Their results fail to provide evidence of altruistic behaviour while evidence for exchange and co-insurance theories is mixed. Migrant earnings proved the most robust determinant of the level of remittance and the remittance/labour income (wage) elasticity calculated is found to be at the top end of the range of estimates obtained in the literature.

Markova and Sarris (2002), utilising individual data sets on Bulgarian migrants in Greece, found that immigrants who transfer money – either regularly or sporadically – do not have any other family members residing in a third country and have a more 'cohesive' family unit; they are married and larger shares of their families reside in Bulgaria. The larger the share of family members in Bulgaria, the larger the share of income transferred. Migrant women were found to remit more, whilst remittances were shown to be part of a family strategy.

The notion that remittances form part of a family strategy is echoed in findings from a project undertaken at the University of Sussex on 'Transnational Migration, Return and Development in West Africa' (TRANSREDE). Amongst returnees to Ghana and Côte d'Ivoire, those most likely to have remitted money whilst abroad, and to have done so on a more regular basis, were already married prior to emigrating. They also maintained higher levels of contact with relatives at home and spoke of remittances in terms of an obligation to them, a finding which lends further weight to the 'exchange' hypothesis outlined above. The project concludes with the suggestion that migration be considered not so much as a means for the migrant to combat poverty, but for their parents or children to do so (Black et al. 2003).

Lacroix (2004) has studied the determinants of remittances of Moroccan rural migrants in France, based on migrants' own perceptions and experiences. His results show that explanations of remittances are directly linked to explanations of migration. As far as migrants are concerned, their departure is a means to achieve a personal project and improve their social status; for the household, it allows diversification of income sources; for the community, it is a way to find elsewhere the resources to sustain its own reproduction, including the reproduction of its socio-political order. The money sent to the family or given during the summer visit home is considered a duty rather than a gift.

Groenewold and Fokkema (2002) analyse data on migrant-sending households in Egypt, Morocco and Turkey based on the large-scale NIDI dataset referred to above. Their work seeks to determine why some households receive remittances whereas others do not, and they conclude that emigrant characteristics, especially employment status in the host country, are the most important determinants of remittances. Emigrants' commitment to their household was higher when the migrant was male and married. Poorer households received less than richer households.

Remittances are now well recognised as part of an informal familial arrangement that goes well beyond altruism, with benefits in the realms of mutual insurance, consumption smoothing and even alleviation of liquidity constraints.

Use and effects of remittances

Not only are remittances critical to the foreign exchange position of many migrant-sending countries, they are also vital to the consumption and investment behaviour of migrant households themselves. At the household level, a longstanding literature has suggested that remittances are often put to 'unproductive' uses – satisfying basic consumption, buying medicines, building a house for the migrant's retirement or spending on 'conspicuous consumption' in festivals and funerals as well as daily life. Such expenses, though, can have a number of multiplier effects in the local economy (Russell and Teitelbaum 1992). Black et al. (2003) show that even highly qualified returnees to Ghana and Côte d'Ivoire sent remittances whilst abroad primarily to supply the basic subsistence needs of parents and siblings.

More 'productive' use of remittances is usually considered to involve investments in small-scale enterprises concentrated in the retail and services sectors (Van Doorn 2002). Here, policy measures to encourage the productive use of remittances include preferential conditions to import equipment or to access capital goods, business counselling and training services and entrepreneurship programmes (ibid.). However, evidence from Ghana produced by Black and Castaldo (2005) suggests that more attention might be paid to the work experience and social networks that migrants are able to build up whilst away as factors promoting entrepreneurial activity.

At a macro-level, the short-run effects of remittances have been analysed mainly within the framework of trade-theoretic models (Djajic 1986; McCormick and Wabha 2000). At the same time, a series of studies have demonstrated the growth potential of migration in the context of capital market imperfections, with remittances allowing members of households at the middle-to-bottom end of the wealth distribution to migrate (Lucas 1987; Rozelle et al. 1999). For example, Groenewold and Fokkema (2002) found that receipt of remittances had a positive net effect on emigration intentions of potential emigrants in Morocco where remittances were interpreted as indicators of emigrants' financial success abroad. In the cases of Egypt and Turkey, the effects of remittances on the development of emigration intentions actually reflected the quality of interpersonal relationships between receivers (potential emigrants) and senders of remittances.

One interesting strand of literature has been concerned with the impact of remittances on inequality at origin. For instance, Adams (1989) found that international migration, through remittances sent back, tends to worsen economic inequality in rural Egypt, while the same author found neutral effects in rural Pakistan (1992). In the case of rural Mexico, Taylor and Wyatt (1996) showed that remittances were distributed almost evenly across income groups, hence inducing a direct equalising effect in terms of economic inequality. For a small coastal city in Nicaragua, Barham and Boucher (1998) found that remittances actually increased income inequality, although this conclusion was dependent on imputing the lost domestic earnings of remitters, rather than viewing remittances as an exogenous transfer for migrant households.

The effect of migration on inequality is not limited to the economic sphere. Research in Morocco by Lacroix (2004) highlights how the transfer of money is seen as subversive to the social order (e.g. local villagers were resistant to 'improvements' in infrastructure brought by remittances). Evidence on the effects of migration on these and other aspects of inequality – including social and political inequality – in sending societies, has recently been reviewed by Black et al. (2005).

Migration, remittances and gender relations

One way in which migration and remittances affect home societies is that they influence gender relations in particular and family life more generally. For example, Venier (2003) focuses on migrants as main actors of social and territorial transformations in Kerala, South India. From localities of high emigration, known as 'Gulf pockets', the increase of migration flows in the 1990s has entailed a large spatial diffusion in the state itself. More than a million people from Kerala are directly involved in migration and one in every eight married women has a husband in the Gulf. Focusing on the roles and responsibilities of the wives of male emigrants who left to work in the Gulf, Venier observes that women generally gain autonomy when their husbands are migrants, in terms of household management (including what remittances are spent on), as well as increased activities outside the house. Migrant couples in the research communicated on a regular and intense basis via mail and telephone. The improved level of education throughout the state of Kerala has also facilitated more equal communication between spouses.

Venier also found that migrant families invest more in the education of their children and in particular their daughters than non-migrant families. This investment of the migration benefits in the next generation gives an opportunity to reach a better socio-economic status through marriage. As a result of household and state investment in the education of girls, women are now on average better educated than men (and women of migrants better educated than their spouses). These investments in education are partly paid back by higher dowry prices. International migration has in this context contributed, and still contributes, to raising the level of education of the population, as well as maintaining the structure of dowry as a means to ensure returns on investment in girls' education and even increasing the amount payable. Dowry values have increased tremendously and the financial part of the dowry has gained importance in the total dowry bundle. At the same time, as working conditions and revenues in the Gulf area have deteriorated, it has become much more difficult to raise the resources for dowries. The marriage market has changed as a result of these developments with a more prominent role for financial and educational value that is transferred to establish the alliance between families. However, other research has shown different patterns: for example, work by Gamburd (2000) in Sri Lanka shows how young women migrate to the Gulf independently in order to raise money for their own dowries. An overview of other relevant literature is provided by Waddington (2003b).

Migration, return and development

Remittances represent one form of transfer back to sending communities, but they are not the only form. First, it is important to consider transfers of social and human capital, as well as financial capital in analysing the impact on home communities (Ammassari and Black 2001). In addition, each of these forms of capital may be taken back as migrants return, rather than being 'sent' from abroad. Indeed, in the Copenhagen Consensus papers on migration, one of the few things on which all three authors agree is that return is beneficial to emigration countries – although this conclusion might be called into question (Black and Gent 2004).

One example of how public policy might usefully try to harness the transferred capital of returning migrants is provided by Venier (2003), who reports how Kerala, after the housing boom and transformation of the land market in the 1980s, saw a rise in the number of small industries and the development of services such as banking, education and health in the 1990s as migrants returned from the Gulf. Each of these areas – small and medium enterprises, health and education – represents a potentially fertile sector in which public policy could intervene to assist returnees (Tiemoko 2004), especially where these new facilities are oriented towards the population as a whole, rather than simply the returnees.

However, work on return to West Africa suggests that migration, remittance and return represent family strategies in which it may be relatively difficult for public policy to intervene in order to increase the beneficial impact of remittances and return on poverty and inequality (Black and Castaldo 2005). Meanwhile, a salutary reminder of the difficulties faced is provided by Lacroix (2004), who reports that it is mostly retired emigrants who return to southern Morocco. It is rare that migrants of working age would return for good. He highlights the failure of a French government initiative to co-finance small-business projects in West Africa. In particular, returnees would not participate in projects set up on the condition that they could not subsequently return to Europe.

4. Outlook on future research

In this review we have highlighted research by IMISCOE researchers in two key themes – the determinants and patterns of migration and migration consequences, especially linked to remittances. There is certainly complementarity in the research findings, but there are also a number of issues within these themes that remain to be further explored. These include particularly the role of networks, the nature of links between internal and international migration and the concept of a 'culture of migration'. As to the role of networks, we have seen contradictory findings on how they generate or facilitate migration and its proliferation. Important questions for future research remain here, including: under what conditions does emigration as a choice and practice influence others in the population and locality to migrate, and under what conditions does it not? And what are the patterns of mechanisms of the spreading?

Second, in terms of the links between internal and international migration, Pieke et al. (2004: 23) have argued that 'migrants often consider international and internal migration alternatives to each other, or use one to support or generate the capital for the other.' Their work also demonstrates how international migration networks were created through internal migration and how international migration in turn increases internal migration. In Morocco, improved access to education brings about a shift from external to internal migration (Van der Erf 2003). In Albania, remittances from international emigration have often provided the finance for family members to move from the countryside to major cities (King and Vullnetari 2003). More work is needed to establish whether such mechanisms are contingent or structural.

Third, the concept of migration culture helps explain certain migration behaviours that cannot be explained by conventional notions. But the concept needs to be (1) better operationalised, so that it can be compared across contexts and be both verified and falsified; (2) better analysed (e.g. to identify when and how a community produces a culture of migration); (3) elaborated in terms of its policy implications.

Meanwhile, the wider debate on migration and development also encompasses much more than these themes – not least the growing circulation of skilled workers within a global labour market, the increasing significance of irregular migration and the emerging phenomenon of transnationalism. The issue of global circulation of skilled workers has clear consequences for sending countries, but is dealt with elsewhere in this volume, and for this reason will not be touched on here. However, the other two issues do deserve mention, not least because they are often not seen through a sending country lens.

Firstly, the irregular nature of much movement to Europe over recent years has important implications for development that are still in the process of being unravelled. Three key themes emerge of significance to development and developing countries: first, the growing unplanned nature and irregularity of migration; second, the impact of policies of control around Western welfare states and labour markets; and third, the rise of trafficking and smuggling. It is generally assumed that irregular movement is in the interests of neither migrant nor sending or receiving countries, since it often involves dangerous conditions of travel and work, exploitation and high risks. Yet the consequences of elevated risk for patterns of movement, levels of remittances and commitment to development in home countries have rarely been measured, whilst we know little about the effects of regularisations of migrant workers, or indeed the criminalisation of certain types of migration on outcomes for sending areas.

Secondly, transnational activities of migrants and their associations should be scrutinized for their development potential. Its impact may not only be traced along direct economic or political lines, but can also be linked to changing identities and the juxtaposition of national and transnational forms of belonging – which in turn affect the determinants of further migration. In this sense, understanding transnationalism is central to the project of understanding migration more generally. In our case, the IMISCOE network has started to focus on one particular country (Morocco) and area (North Africa) to explore, in close collaboration with researchers from that country/region, its impact by focusing on:

1. Influences on integration. This theme beholds a diachronic, divergent comparison of Moroccan migrants in the variety of EU destination countries, particularly focusing on the different generations of migrants to assess differences between 1960s labour migration and current migrants.

2. Sending country context. Within this theme, migration and significant political, economic, social and cultural processes within Morocco are linked. This will include an assessment of the diverse range of conditions influencing migration, the effects of migration on these conditions and attempts to alter them with the aim of influencing migration patterns.

3. Transnational links and processes. This theme concerns an assessment of the transnational links sustained by Moroccans residing abroad on the individual, associational and national-institutional level.

Finally, as a more general note, the field of study that we are in here asks for a conscious effort to develop comprehensive methodologies.

Work has been done on this, for example by Groenewold and Bilsborrow (forthcoming) who summarise the methods and research design of the survey, particularly their stage-wise sampling method, and by Pieke et al. (2004: 21) who detail the multi-sited ethnographic research process and the lessons learned on how to better grasp migration which becomes increasingly transnational in scope and fluid in nature. However, as Black (2003a) has pointed out, Europe does not have an initiative similar to the 'Mexican Migration Project' in the US, which has provided for Mexico-US migration a substantial longitudinal database that combines breadth and depth of information on migrants and their sending communities (Massey et al. 1994).

In this context, the IMISCOE network arguably has a unique position to build on its mix of quantitative and qualitative approaches to migration and development. Both approaches are valuable, but where they can be combined, this can lead to greater research strength. Only when we examine variables of statistical significance in real contexts and link them to other factors can we make full sense of these variables. At the same time, in-depth observation needs statistical data to generate conclusions with more general significance. The importance of such large-scale and integrated data for devising evidence-based policies has been increasingly recognised.

Notes

1 Corresponding author at Sussex Centre for Migration Research, University of Sussex, Falmer, Brighton, BN1 9SJ, UK. The authors would also like to thank Mark Thomson and Clare Waddington for their useful comments on an earlier draft.
2 The Development Research Centre on Migration, Globalisation and Poverty at the University of Sussex is funded by a five-year grant from DFID.
3 We realise that several other theoretical and methodological approaches exist in the literature on migration and development. In addition to the 'New Economics of Labour Migration' approach mentioned above, these include migration systems theory (Kritz et al. 1992); Appleyard's trilogy on emigration dynamics (Appleyard 1998), as well as work by African and Asian scholars: (Abella 1993; Adepoju 2000; Aguilar 1999; Go, 1998; Gonzalez 1998) and the work of Philip Martin (Martin 1991; Martin and Straubhaar 2002; Martin and Taylor 2001). The theory of the migration transition is worth examining here too (Amjad 1996; Lim 1996; Zelinsky 1971).
4 For another description of the culture of migration, see: Kandel and Massey (2002) on Mexican migration.
5 http://news.bbc.co.uk/1/hi/business/3516390.stm (retrieved on 22 March 2004).
6 Focusing on the *hawala* system of informal transfers, this IMF study of 15 countries estimated that about $35 billion per annum of remittances was transmitted through informal channels in the early 1980s, falling to $10 billion per annum in more recent years (El Qorchi et al., 2003). The decline was attributed to the disappearance of the black market exchange premiums in many developing countries in the 1990s.

Literature

Abella, M. (1993), 'Labor mobility, trade and structural change: the Philippine experience'. *Asia and Pacific Migration Journal* 2(3): 249-68.

Adams, R. (1989). 'Workers' Remittances and Inequality in Rural Egypt.' *Economic Development and Cultural Change* 38(1): 45-71.

Adams, R. H. (1992). 'The impact of migration and remittances on income inequality in rural Pakistan.' *Pakistan Development Review* 31(4): 1189-1203.

Adepoju, A. (2000). 'Issues and recent trends in international migration in sub-Saharan Africa.' *International Social Science Journal* 165: 383-94. Geneva: IOM, pp.133-162.

Aguilar, F.V. (1999). 'The triumph of instrumental citizenship? Migrations, identities and the nation-state in Southeast Asia.' *Asian Studies Review* 23(3): 307-36.

Al-Ali, N. (2004). 'The Relationship between Migration within and from the Middle East and North-Africa and Pro-Poor Policies.' *Livelihoods Connect: Migration and Poverty Reduction Policy.* London, Department for International Development.

Amjad, R. (1996). 'Philippines and Indonesia: on the way to a migration transition?' *AsiaPacific Migration Journal* 5(2-3): 339-66.

Ammassari, S. and R. Black (2001). 'Harnessing the Potential of Migration and Return to Promote Development.' *Migration Research Series.* Geneva, IOM.

Appleyard, R. (1998). *Emigration Dynamics in Developing Countries.* Aldershot: Ashgate

Banerjee, B. (1984). 'The Probability, Size and Uses of Remittances from Urban to Rural Areas in India.' *Journal of Development Economics* 82(6): 1063-1093.

Barham, B. and S. Boucher (1998). 'Migration, Remittances, and Inequality: Estimating the Net Effects of Migration on Income Distribution.' *Journal of Development Economics* 55(2): 307-331.

Becker, G. S. (1974). 'A Theory of Social Interactions.' *Journal of Political Economy* 82(6): 1063-93.

Black, R. (2003a). 'Breaking the Convention: researching the 'illegal' migration of refugees to Europe.' *Antipode* 35(1): 34-50.

Black, R. (2003b). 'Soaring Remittances Raises New Issues,' *Migration Information Source.* http://www.migrationinformation.org/feature/display.cfm?ID=127.

Black, R. (2004) 'Migration and Pro-Poor Policy in Africa.' Brighton: Development Research Centre on Migration, *Globalisation and Poverty Working Paper no. C6.*

Black, R. and A. Castaldo (2005). 'Migration, return and entrepreneurship: the case of West Africa.' *SSRC-IOM-ESRC Conference on Migration and Development Within and Across Borders: Concepts, Methods and Policy Consideration,* New York.

Black, R. and S. Gent (2004). 'Defining, Measuring and Influencing Sustainable Return: The Case of the Balkans.' *Working Papers.* Brighton, Development Research Centre on Migration, Globalisation and Poverty. WP-T7.

Black, R., C. Natali and J. Skinner (2005). 'Migration and inequality.' *Background Paper for the World Development Report 2006.* Washington DC, World Bank: http://siteresources.worldbank.org/INTRANETSOCIALDEVELOPMENT/Resources/Migration_Inequality_Black_et_al.pdf.

Black, R., R. Tiemoko and C. Waddington (2003). *International migration, remittances and poverty: the case of Ghana and Côte d'Ivoire,* World Bank.

Böhning, R. (2004). 'Population: Migration. Opponent's Paper.' *Copenhagen Consensus Opponent Note.* B. Lomborg. Copenhagen, Copenhagen Consensus 2004: 11.

Brown, R. (1997). 'Estimating Remittance Functions for Pacific Island Migrations.' *World Development* 25(4): 613-626.

Caglar, Ö. and M. Schiff (2006). *International migration, remittances and the brain drain.* Washington DC, World Bank.

Choukri, N. (1986). 'The Hidden Economy: A New View of Remittances in the Arab World.' *World Development* 14(6): 697-712.

Communities, C. o. t. E. (2000). *Communication from the Commission to the Council and the European Parliament: On a community migration policy*. Brussels, COM.

Cox, D. (1987). 'Motives for Private Transfers.' *Journal of Political Economy* 95(3): 508-46.

De Haan, A. (2000). 'Migrants, livelihoods and rights: the relevance of migration in development policies.' London, DFID *Social Development Working Paper no. 4*.

De la Brière, B., A. de Janvry, S. Lambert and E. Sadoulet (2002). 'The Roles of Destination, Gender, and Household Composition in Explaining Remittances: An Analysis for the Dominican Sierra.' *Journal of Development Economics* 68(2): 309-28.

Djajic, S. (1986). 'International Migration, Remittances and Welfare in a Dependent Economy.' *Journal of Development Economics* 21: 229-34.

Durand, J. and D. S. Massey (1992). 'Mexican migration to the United States: a critical review.' *Latin American Research Review* 27(1): 3-42.

El-Qorchi, M., J. F. Wilson and S. M. Maimbo (2003). 'Informal funds transfer systems: an analysis of the Hawala system' *A Joint IMF-World Bank Paper. Occasional Paper 222*. Washington DC, International Monetary Fund.

Gamburd, M. R. (2000). *The Kitchen Spoons' Handle: Transnationalism and Sri lanka's migrant housemaids*. Ithaca, Cornell University Press.

Gardner, K. (1995). *Global Migrants Local Lives*. Oxford, Clarendon Press.

GCIM (2005). *Migration in an interconnected world: New directions for action*. Geneva, Global Commission on International Migrations.

Germenji, E., Beka, I., and Sarris. A., (2001): 'Estimating Remittance Functions for Rural-Based Albanian Emigrants,' *working paper*, ACE research project P97-8158-R: Microeconomic Analysis of Farm Restructuring in Central and Eastern Europe

Go, S. (1998). 'The Philippines: a look into the migration scenario in the nineties.' In OECD (ed.) *Migration and Regional Economic Integration in Asia*. Paris: OECD, 145-54.

Gonzalez, J.L. (1998) *Philippines labour migration: critical dimensions of public policy*. Singapore: Institute of Southeast Asian Studies.

Groenewold, G. & R. Bilsborrow (2004), 'Design of samples for international migration surveys: methodological considerations, practical constraints and lessons learned from a multi-country study in Africa and Europe,' *Paper for the Population Association of America 2004 General Conference*, Boston, Massachusetts.

Groenewold, G. and T. Fokkema (2002). *Receipt of remittances and their effect on emigration intensions in Egypt, Morocco, Turkey*. Amsterdam, Netherlands Interdisciplinary Demographics Institute (NIDI).

Heering, L., R. van der Erf and L. van Wissen (2004). 'The Role of Family Networks and Migration Culture in the Continuation of Moroccan Emigration: a Gender Perspective.' *Journal of Ethnic and Migration Studies* 30(2): 323-337.

Hoddinott, J. (1994). 'A model of migration and remittances applied to Western Kenya.' *Oxford Economic Papers* 46(3): 459-476.

House of Commons (2004). 'Migration and Development: How to make migration work for poverty reduction.' *Sixth Report of Session 2003-04*, Volume 1. London, International Development Committee.

Hugo, G. (2003). 'Migration and Development: A Perspective from Asia.' *IOM Migration Research Series*, no. 14. Geneva, International Organization for Migration.

IOM (2003). *Labour Migration in Asia: Trends, challenges and policy responses in countries of origin*. Geneva, International Organization for Migration.

Johnson, G. and W. Whitelaw (1974). 'Urban-Rural Income Transfers in Kenya: An Estimated Remittances Function.' *Economic Development and Cultural Change* 22(3): 473-479.

Kandel, W. and D.S. Massey (2002). 'The Culture of Mexican Migration: A Theoretical and Empirical Analysis.' *Social Forces* 80(3): 981-1004.

King, R. and J. Vullnetari (2003). 'Migration and Development in Albania.' *Working Papers*. Brighton, Development Research Centre on Migration, Globalisation and Poverty.

Kraler, A. (forthcoming). *Ruanda und die Universalisierung der Nationalstaatsform [Rwanda and the Universalization of the Nation-State].* Globale Prozesse, Lokale Formen. S. Khittel. Vienna, Löcker.

Kraler, A. (2004). 'Staatsbildungsprozesse, Migration und Identität in der Großen Seenregion. Afrikas [State Formation, Migration, and Identity in the Great Lakes Region].' *Graduate Conference 'Powi04. Neue Impulse für die Politikwissenschaft in Österreich'/ Powi04*, New Institute of Advanced Studies, Vienna.

Kritz, M.M., L.L. Lim and H. Zlotnik (1992). *International Migration Systems: a Global Approach*, Oxford, Clarendon.

Lacroix, T. (2004). 'Espace transnational et territoires: les réseaux marocains du développement.' *Geography*. Poitiers, Université de Poitiers.

Lianos, T. (1997). 'Factors Determining Migrant Remittances: The Case of Greece.' *International Migration Review* 31(1): 72-87.

Lim, L.L. (1996). 'The migration transition in Malaysia.' *Asia and Pacific Migration Journal.* 5(2-3).

Liu, Q. and B. Reilly (2000). 'The private income transfers of Chinese rural migrants: some empirical evidence from Jinan.' *Discussion Papers in Economics, DP57.* University of Sussex.

Lucas, R. (1987). 'Emigration to South Africa's mines.' *American Economic Review* 77(3): 313-30.

Lucas, R. and O. Stark (1985). 'Motivations to Remit: Evidence from Botswana.' *Journal of Political Economy* 93(5): 901-918.

Lucas, R. E. (2005). *International Migration and Economic Development: Lessons from Low-income Countries.* London, Edward Elgar.

Maimbo, S. M. and D. Ratha (2005). *Remittances: development impact and future prospects.* Washington DC, World Bank.

Markova, E. and A. H. Sarris (2002). 'Remitting and Saving Behavior of Bulgarian Immigrants in Greece.' *Discussion Paper, no. 34.* University of Athens.

Martin, P. (1991). *The unfinished story: Turkish labour migration to Western Europe.* Geneva: International Labour Office

Martin, P. and Straubhaar, T. (2002). 'Best practices to reduce migration pressures.' *International Migration.* 40(3): 5-21.

Martin, P. and Taylor, J.E. (2001). 'Managing migration: the role of economic policies.' In Zolberg, A.R and P.M. Benda (eds.) *Global migrants, global refugees: problems and solutions.* New York and Oxford: Berghahn, 95-120.

Massey, D. S., J. Arango, G. Hugo, A. Kouaouci, A. Pellegrino and J. E. Taylor (1998). *Worlds in Motion – understanding International Migration at the End of the Millenium.* Oxford, Oxford University Press.

Massey, D. S., L. Goldring and J. Durand (1994). 'Continuities in Transnational Migration: An Analysis of Nineteen Mexican Communities.' *American Journal of Sociology* 99(6): 1492-1533.

McCormick, B. and J. Wabha (2000). 'Overseas unemployment and remittances to a dual economy.' *Economic Journal* 110: 509-534.

Merkle, L. and K. Zimmermann (1992). 'Savings and Remittances: Guest Workers in West Germany.' In: K. Zimmermann. *Migration and Economic Development.* Berlin, Springer-Verlag. 55-75.

Papademetriou, D. G. and P. Martin (1991). *The Unsettled Relationship: Labor Migration and Economic Development*. New York, Greenwood.

Pieke, F. N., P. Nyiri, M. Thunø and A. Ceccagno (2004). *Transnational Chinese: Fujianese Migrants in Europe*. Stanford, Stanford University Press.

Pieke, F. P. (1998). 'At the margins of the Chinese world system: The Fuzhou diaspora in Europe.' *Project proposal as part of the Transnational Communities Programme*.

Pieke, F. P. (1999). 'Introduction: Chinese Migrations Compared.' In: *Internal and International Migration: Chinese Perspectives*. F. Pieke and H. Mallee. Richmond, Surrey, Curzon Press.

Poirine, B. (1997). 'A Theory of Remittances as an Implicit Family Loan Arrangement.' *World Development* 25(4): 589-611.

Rahman, M. (2000). 'Migration as Status Enhancement: A Study of Bangladesh Workers in Singapore,' *www.gradnet.de*

Ramamurthy, B. (2003). 'International Labour Migrants: Unsung Heroes of Globalisation.' *SIDA Studies* 8. Stockholm: Swedish International Development Agency http://www.sida.se/shared/jsp/download.jsp?f=SidaStudies_NO_8.pdf.

Ratha, D. (2003). 'Workers' remittances: an important and stable source of development finance.' *Global Development Finance: Striving for Stability in Development Finance*. Washington, DC, World Bank.

Reilly, B., J. Litchfield and A. Castaldo (2004). *Who is at risk of migrating from Albania? Evidence from the Albanian Living Standards Measurement Survey 2002*. New Perspectives on Albanian Migration and Development, Korce, Albania.

Rogaly, B. and A. Rafique (2003). 'Struggling to save cash: seasonal migration and vulnerability in West Bengal, India.' *Development and Change* 34(4): 659-682.

Rosenzweig, M. R. (2004). 'Copenhagen Opposition Paper on Population and Migration.' *Copenhagen Consensus Challange Paper*. Copenhagen: Copenhagen Consensus. http://osp.stanford.edu/files/Opponent_Note_-2-Migration.pdf.

Rozelle, S., J. E. Taylor and A. d. Brown (1999). 'Migration, Remittances and Agricultural Productivity in China.' *American Economic Review* 78(2): 245-50.

Russell, S. and M. S. Teitelbaum (1992). *International Migration and International Trade*. Washington DC, World Bank.

Schoorl, J. (2002). *Emigration: who moves and who stays? The case of Morocco, Ghana, and Senegal*. The Netherlands, Ministry of Foreign Affairs.

Schoorl, J., E. Spaan, L. Heering, H. van Dalen and G. Groenewold (2004). *Poverty and international migration intentions in Africa: the case of Egypt, Morocco, Ghana and Senegal*. New York, UNFPA.

Secondi, G. (1997). 'Private Monetary Transfers in Rural China: Are Families Altruistic.' *Journal of Development Studies* 33(4): 487-511.

Skeldon, R. (1997). *Migration and Development: a Global Perspective*. Harlow: Addison Wesley Longman.

Skeldon, R. (2003). 'Migration and migration policy in Asia: a synthesis of selected cases.' *Migration, Development and Pro-Poor Policy Choices in Asia*. London, Department for International Development.

Skeldon, R. (2004). *Beyond remittances: other dimensions in the relationship between migration and development*. New York, Population Division of the United Nations.

Sriskandarajah, D. (2005). 'Migration and development: a new research and policy agenda.' *World Economics* 6(2): 141-46.

Stark, O. (1991). *The Migration of Labor*. Boston, MA, Blackwell.

Stark, O. and R. E. Lucas (1988). 'Migration, remittances and the family.' *Economic Development and Cultural Change* 31: 191-96.

Taylor, J.E. and T.J. Wyatt (1996). 'The shadow value of migrant remittances, income and inequality in a household farm economy.' *Journal of Development Studies* 32(6): 899-912.

Taylor, J.E., J. Arango, G. Hugo, A. Kouaouci, D.S. Massey and A. Pellegrino (1996). 'International migration and national development.' *Population Index* 62(2): 181-212.

Tiemoko, R. (2004). *Understanding the opportunities for, and challenges to migrants' investments in Côte d'Ivoire and Ghana*. Migration and Development in Ghana, Accra.

Van Dalen, H.P., G. Groenewold and J. Schoorl (forthcoming). 'Out of Africa: what drives the pressure to emigrate?' *Journal of Population Economics*.

Van der Erf, R. and L. Heering (2002). *Moroccan migration dynamics: prospects for the future*. Geneva, International Organisation for Migration.

Van der Erf, R.F. (2003). *Internal and External Migration in Morocco, Turkey and Senegal: a Comparative Report*. Amsterdam, Dutch Ministry of Foreign Affairs.

Van Doorn, J. (2001). *Migration, remittances and small enterprise development*. Geneva, International Labor Organization.

Van Doorn, J. (2002). 'Migration, remittances and development.' *Labour Education Online* 129(4): http://www.ilo.org/public/english/dialogue/actrav/publ/129/8.pdf.

Van Hear, N. and N. Nyberg-Sørensen (2003). *The Migration-Development Nexus*. Geneva, International Organisation for Migration.

Venier, P. (2003). 'Travail dans le Golfe Persique et développement au Kérala. Les migrants internationaux, des acteurs au coeur des enjeux sociaux et territoriaux.' *'Geography*. Poitiers, Université de Poitiers.

Waddington, C. (2003a). *International Migration Policies in Asia: a Synthesis of ILO and other literatures on policies seeking to manage the recruitment and protection of migrants, and facilitate remittances and their investment*. Migration Development and Pro-Poor Policy Choices in Asia, Dhaka: Bangladesh, RMMRU-DFID.

Waddington, C. (2003b). 'Livelihood outcomes of migration for poor people.' *Working Papers, T1*. Brighton, UK, Development Research Centre on Migration, Globalisation and Poverty.

Xiang, B. (2000). *A Village beyond Borders: the Life History of 'Zhejiang Village' in Beijing (Kuayue Bianjie de Shequ-Beijing 'Zhejiang Cun' de Shenghuo Shi)*. Beijing, Three-joints Books (Sanlian Shudian).

Xiang, B. (2003a). 'Emigration from China: the sending country's perspective.' *International Migration* 41(3): 21-48.

Xiang, B. (2003b). 'Market, state and networks: A comparison of labour emigration schemes of India and China.' *Third International Convention of Asia Scholars (ICAS3)*, National University of Singapore.

Xiang, B. (2004). 'A hypothesis of 'network failure.' *5th Conference of the International Society for the Study of Chinese Overseas*, Elsinore (Helsingør), Denmark.

Xiang, B. (forthcoming). *Global 'Body Shopping': A New International Labour System in the Information Technology Industry*. Princeton, New Jersey, Princeton University Press.

Zelinksy, W. (1971). 'The hypothesis of the mobility transition.' *Geographical Review* 61(2): 219-49.

Zolberg, A. (1983). 'The Formation of New States as a Refugee-Generating Process.' *Annals, American Academy of Social Science* 467(May): 24-38.

4. Migrants' Citizenship: Legal Status, Rights and Political Participation

*Rainer Bauböck, Albert Kraler, Marco Martiniello
and Bernhard Perchinig[1]*

Citizenship has emerged only recently as an important topic of research on migration and migrant integration. Before the late 1980s there was little connection between migration research and the legal literature on nationality laws or political theories and sociological analyses of citizenship in a broader sense. In traditional overseas countries of immigration immigrants' access to citizenship and eventual naturalisation was taken for granted as a step in a broader process of assimilation, while in Europe the largest immigration contingents had emerged from the recruitment of guest workers who had been invited to stay only temporarily and were never perceived as future citizens.

Both expectations were eventually undermined when the dynamics of the migration process interacted with political developments to generate more inclusive conceptions of citizenship. Family reunification turned guest workers into settled immigrants. Many among these, however, maintained strong ties to their countries of origin. For these migrants, retaining the nationality of origin was a natural choice both for its instrumental value as a bundle of rights and for its symbolic value as a marker of ethno-national identity. At the same time, the rights of permanent residents in major democratic receiving states were upgraded in many areas or even equalised with those of citizens. Finally, more and more countries of immigration abandoned the consensus in international law that those who naturalise have to renounce their previous nationality and a growing number of sending countries also accepted multiple nationality among their expatriates. All these developments have blurred the previously bright line separating aliens from citizens. While some observers welcomed these trends as heralding a new cosmopolitan era in which state-bound citizenship would eventually be overcome, others were concerned about migrants' multiple loyalties, their apparent free ride on citizenship rights without corresponding duties and about the political mobilisation of ethnic or religious identities.

1. Three core concepts

In this chapter we trace the main steps in these developments and highlight areas of agreement and controversy among researchers. We have identified three analytical concepts that provide common reference points for our analyses.

The first among these concepts is a society's *political opportunity structure*. This concept has been widely used in research on migrants' political behaviour and activities, including voter turnout and representation in political bodies, membership in political parties and organisations, lobbying, public claims-making and protest movements. A political opportunity structure consists of laws that allocate different statuses and rights to various groups of migrants and formally constrain or enable their activities, of institutions of government and public administration in which migrants are or are not represented, of public policies that address migrants' claims, concerns and interests or do not, and of a public culture that is inclusive and accepts diversity or that supports national homogeneity and a myth of shared ancestry. In describing all these elements of a political system as an opportunity structure we emphasise that migrants are not only objects of laws, policies and discourses but also agents who pursue their interests individually or collectively. The point of analysing a political opportunity structure is to identify institutional incentives and disincentives that help to explain migrants' political choices and strategies. This need not imply that these choices are always rational ones or that they generally achieve their goals.

A second core concept is *political integration*. Integration in a broad sense refers to a condition of societal cohesion as well as to a process of inclusion of outsiders or newcomers. Integration in the latter sense is generally regarded as a two-way interaction between the institutions of a 'receiving society' and those who gain access that will also result in changing the institutional framework and the modes of societal cohesion. Integration thus brings together the two perspectives on opportunity structures under the umbrella of the more normatively accentuated concept of societal cohesion. The concept of integration is open for both transitive and intransitive use. On the one hand, political integration is an aspect of a broader process of structural integration. In this sense it refers to access to political status, rights, opportunities and representation for immigrants and to an equalisation of these conditions between native and immigrant populations. On the other hand, political integration is also about migrants' activities and participation and their acceptance of the laws, institutional framework and political values that 'integrate' a political system. The political integration of immigrants can be broken down into four dimensions: political rights, identification, norms and values, and participation. The more rights they enjoy, the more they identify with the society where they live, the more they share its political values and norms, and the more they participate and are represented in the political system, the better integrated they are.

Research on migrants' political integration focuses on the post-migration stage in the receiving society. Circular migration patterns, immigrants' links to their countries of origin, and these countries' policies towards their expatriates may be taken into account as external factors but are generally regarded as obstacles for integration. This is a serious limitation that can be overcome by expanding research towards transnational arenas and activities. *Political transnationalism* is thus the third core concept that informs our approach to the migration-citizenship nexus. Studies on migrant transnationalism challenge the separation between migration and integration stages. Research on political transnationalism has focused mostly on migrants' political identities and activities in relation to their countries of origin. However, the concept applies also to the status of external citizenship and to sending country policies vis-à-vis emigrant communities and the destination state. Finally, transnational citizenship has been interpreted as a broader transformation of political membership in migration contexts. This is most visible in the proliferation of multiple nationality but pertains also to the separation of citizenship rights from formal citizenship status and the emergence of a residential citizenship for foreign nationals in democratic immigration countries (Bauböck 1994).

2. Citizenship status, rights and obligations

Citizenship is a very old concept that has undergone many transformations. Since the times of ancient Athenian democracy its core meaning has been a status of membership in a self-governing political community. Today, citizenship has acquired many other meanings ranging from the legal status of nationality to the virtues of the 'good citizen' who contributes to the community. In this section, we will focus on a broad political conception of citizenship that refers to individual membership, rights and participation in a polity. In migration contexts, citizenship marks a distinction between members and outsiders based on their different relations to particular states. Free movement within state territories and the right to readmission to this territory have become a hallmark of modern citizenship. Yet in the international arena citizenship serves as a control device that strictly limits state obligations towards foreigners and permits governments to keep them out of, or remove them from, their jurisdiction. A migration perspective therefore highlights the boundaries of citizenship and political control over entry and exit as well as the fact that foreign residents remain in most countries deprived of the core rights of political participation.

Nationality as a filter for regulating migration

From an international perspective, citizenship is a sorting device for allocating human populations to sovereign states. The basic principle in international law pertaining to citizenship is self-determination. Apart from very few constraints, states are free to determine under their own laws who their citizens are. Such self-determination inevitably generates conflicts when international migration produces large numbers of expatriates living outside their states of origin and of foreign nationals in destination countries. A major area of research is to study how norms of international law and domestic state law and practices in this area have changed in response to migration. Trends and causes for convergence with regard to rules for the acquisition and loss of nationality and the toleration of multiple citizenship will be discussed in the following section. Here we want to emphasise how the determination of nationality is important for state capacities in regulating migration flows. Democratic states are committed to free emigration, but all sovereign states claim a right to control their borders. In this respect, citizenship operates as a filter in two basic ways. First, states are obliged to (re)admit their own nationals to their territory. These include nationals born abroad who have inherited their parents' citizenship. Second, states may impose specific restrictions on certain nationals (e.g. through visa requirements) while opening their borders for others (such as European Union citizens migrating to other member states).

Several states (among others Israel, Italy, Japan, Germany, Greece, Spain and Portugal) have also adopted preferences for foreign nationals whom they consider as part of a larger ethnic nation or as cultural and linguistic relatives who will more easily integrate in the destination country. With some notable exceptions (e.g. Thränhardt 2000; Levy & Weiss 2002; Münz & Ohliger 2003; Joppke 2005), ethnic immigration preferences are a rather neglected topic in comparative migration research. This may partly be due to the fact that co-ethnic immigration does not fit well into dominant migration theories that focus on economic push and pull factors and on the sociology of migration networks. From these perspectives, it is not easy to understand why states would encourage the immigration of co-ethnics who crowd out other migrants with better skills and – in the German, Israeli and Japanese cases – are sometimes not even familiar with the destination state's language. There is also a normative puzzle, which has not been fully explored, concerning the legitimacy of such distinctions. In the 1960s and 1970s, the exclusion of particular ethnic and racial groups from immigration was abandoned in the US, Canada and Australia and it is also generally regarded as illegitimate in today's European immigration states. The question of whether preferential admission on similar grounds, which is still widespread and potentially growing, also amounts to discrimination is disputed and requires further clarification. Migration research must be combined with studies of nation-building and nationalism for explaining the persistence of such preferential treatment as well as for evaluating it.

Membership, ties and belonging

There is an emerging literature on modes of belonging that focuses on migrants' constructions of their own identities in relation to different places, groups and countries (e.g. Christiansen & Hedetoft 2004; Rummens 2003; Sicakkan & Lithman 2005). Seen from a different angle, such affiliations may be called ties or stakes. The notion of migrants' social, cultural, economic and political ties focuses our attention less on identities and more on social relations and practices that structure individual lives and can be directly observed.[2] Such ties may be called 'stakes' once we consider them as linking individual interests with those of other persons and communities, including large-scale political communities.

Of these three modes of affiliation, 'belonging' is the most flexible and open-ended one. Migrants may not only develop a sense of belonging to several societies, regions, cities, ethnic and cultural traditions or religious and political movements; they can also feel to belong to imagined communities located in a distant past or future. Modes of belonging will, however, not be purely subjective since they always refer to some socially constructed entity and are shaped by discourses within these about who belongs and who does not. Migrating between distinct societies also creates multiple social ties and political and economic stakes. Different from a sense of belonging, these ties and stakes express how migrants' opportunities structurally depend on their affiliations.

Citizenship is a more discriminating concept than both ties and belonging because it is a status of membership granted by an established or aspiring political community. Citizenship is neither a purely subjective phenomenon (as is a sense of belonging) nor is it objective in the sense that it can be inferred from external observation of a person's social circumstances and activities. Citizenship is instead based on a quasi-contractual relation between an individual and a collectivity. In contrast with belonging and ties, membership is also a binary concept that marks a boundary between insiders and outsiders. This boundary may be permeable or impermeable, it may be stable or shifting, and it may be clearly marked or become somewhat blurred. But it is always recognisable as a threshold. If you cross it, your status, rights and obligations in relation to a political community change as a consequence.

These considerations point to two different tasks for research. There is an agenda for empirical research on 'misalignments' (Sicakkan & Lithman 2005; Hampshire 2005) between citizenship, ties and belonging. And there is a task for comparative as well as normative legal and political analysis of political institutions and practices to examine how migrants' multiple and shifting affiliations are taken into account in determining their membership status (see e.g. Castles & Davidson 2000).

Rights and duties

In a famous lecture the British sociologist T. H. Marshall (1949/1965) identified civil, political and social rights as three dimensions of citizenship. Marshall's analytical model has raised interesting questions for migration research. A first question concerns foreign nationals' access to the three bundles of rights. Even irregular migrants can formally claim certain basic rights of civil citizenship that are considered human rights, e.g. due process rights in court or elementary social rights such as emergency health care or public schooling for their children. On the one hand, these rights are obviously precarious since they effectively depend on a right to residence and because most states of immigration accept only few constraints on their discretionary powers of deportation and expulsion of migrants in irregular status. On the other hand, regularisation measures have been frequent in all Mediterranean EU states and have also been occasionally implemented in traditional immigration states, such as France or the USA.

Immigrants in regular status have access to additional rights. On the civil rights dimension, freedom of speech, association and assembly was strongly restricted for foreign nationals in most democratic countries before World War II. There are remaining limitations in certain states concerning political activities, e.g. public demonstrations or the right to form political parties and to sit on their boards. However, by and large, core civil rights have been extended to legal foreign residents, again with the important exception of migration-related rights such as protection against expulsion, the right to return from abroad, and family reunification in the country of residence.

On the social citizenship dimension, in democratic states with a longer history of immigration, there is nowadays comparatively little legal exclusion of foreign nationals in the provision of public education, health and housing and from financial benefits such as social insurance payments in cases of unemployment, sickness, work accidents or retirement. The pattern is very different in needs-based and means-tested public welfare systems where foreign nationals are frequently excluded or receive reduced benefits. The rationale behind this discrimination is that immigrants are supposed to be either self-supporting or to be supported by their sponsors. In contrast with virtually all other citizenship rights, inclusion of migrants into social citizenship is also not an irreversible process. In the 1990s, legal residents in the US and in Australia were deprived of welfare benefits (Aleinikoff 2000; Zappala & Castles 2000).[3] In a broader conception of social citizenship, one should include not merely legal equality of public entitlements but also protection against discrimination in employment, housing, education and health. The anti-discrimination directives of the European Union have obliged member states to expand and harmonise their policies in this area without, however, covering discrimination on grounds of third country nationality. An even more substantive conception of social citizenship would look at unequal rates of poverty or opportunities for upward social mobility. In this respect, the gaps in achieving full social citizenship for immigrants are obviously still very large.

Political participation and representation is the dimension of citizenship from which foreign nationals remain generally excluded. However, even in this area we find patterns of partial inclusion. Currently non-citizen voting rights in political elections exist, or are explicitly provided for in the national constitution without having been implemented, in 45 democracies (Bauböck 2005). Often such alien franchise is only granted to citizens of specific countries or is limited to regional and local elections. Active voting rights in national elections for all immigrants with a certain period of residence exist in Chile, New Zealand, Uruguay and Malawi. In Europe, Ireland, the UK and Portugal grant voting rights in national elections to privileged categories of nationals. Another significant European development is the emergence of a 'residential citizenship' with voting rights at municipal level disconnected from nationality in 14 of the 25 EU states. Additionally, all EU citizens residing in another member state enjoy the franchise in local and European Parliament elections. This development may be interpreted as a gradual emancipation of local citizenship from nation-state citizenship, with the former becoming more open than the latter for the inclusion of immigrants (see Aleinikoff & Klusmeyer 2002, chapter 3).

Comparative analyses of the rights of foreign nationals that go beyond documenting legal developments are still rare. A comprehensive and reliable set of standardised indicators for citizenship inclusion of migrants could be of great importance for researchers and policymakers alike. Ideally, these indicators should be applied to a large sample of countries and updated each year. This would permit not only ranking countries but also measuring convergence and divergence across time as well as progress with regard to equality and inclusion within each country and for specific sets of rights.

Measuring is not explaining, but it must be the basis for testing various explanatory hypotheses suggested by Freeman (1998), Guiraudon (1998), Guiraudon and Lahav (2000) and Hansen (2002) among others. These include the influence of migrant lobby and advocacy groups, a judiciary relatively insulated from politics, path dependency of rights accumulation within a particular constitutional framework and the nature of 'policy arenas' where decisions are exposed to the public or made behind closed doors and in a consensual or competitive setting. Hypotheses about such factors have been used to explain the general expansion of rights for foreign residents, as well as the specific differences and time lags between countries and different types of rights. We may need to consider other factors when analysing recent backlashes in several European countries where political imperatives of immigration control and assimilation have spilled over into restrictions of rights of settled foreign residents, e.g. with regard to family reunification.

Comparative studies on migrants' access to citizenship and rights as foreign residents will allow testing of two widespread assumptions that we may call the convergence and liberalisation hypotheses. The former claims that citizenship policies of democratic countries of immigration are moving closer to each other. This might be explained as a result of, first, spontaneous policy transfers through learning from successful examples, second, integration into international and supra-national institutions, such as the Council of Europe and the European Union, which then develop a harmonisation agenda with regard to citizenship policies and, third, globalisation that increases interdependencies between states, limits their sovereignty and exposes them to similar immigration flows from a growing diversity of origins. The liberalisation hypothesis assumes furthermore that such convergence is towards more liberal standards of inclusion. This direction has been attributed either to the emergence of a global human rights discourse (Soysal 1994) or to the growing impact of constitutional courts that share interpretations of legal norms across national boundaries (Joppke 2001). The convergence and liberalisation hypotheses have so far been generally defended based on anecdotal evidence from a limited number of case studies. A much more comprehensive and methodologically sophisticated approach would be needed.

While there are many studies on 'denizenship' rights (Hammar 1990), less research has been carried out on other forms of 'quasi-citizenship' that are not based on residence but on special bilateral relations with other states or on cultural and ethnic preferences for certain immigrants. The most prominent example of this is, of course, EU citizenship. Other cases include Commonwealth citizens in the UK, Nordic citizens in the Nordic states and Latin Americans in the Iberian Peninsula.

Liberal theories of citizenship from World War II to the 1980s prioritised rights over duties. More recently, republican and communitarian discourses have re-emphasised moral obligations and responsibilities as well as legal duties of citizenship. Are there specific patterns how these apply to non-citizen immigrants? Duties of education and paying taxes or social security contributions are not attached to nationality but to residence, income and employment. By contrast, military and jury service are generally regarded as linked to citizenship status since these duties have historically been at the very core of ancient and early modern notions of citizenship. Even this is, however, not a universal pattern. Although international law does not allow forcing foreign nationals into the army, permanent residents in the US would be liable to perform military service if the government decided to reintroduce the draft.

Citizenship duties are thus applied to migrants in a less gradual and differentiated way than citizenship rights. Yet receiving countries have periodically asserted a specific obligation of immigrants to assimilate or integrate and have used the naturalisation process as an occasion for asserting a duty of loyalty that remains at best implicit for native citizens. Austria, Denmark, Germany, Finland, the Netherlands and Sweden have introduced integration courses for newcomers that consist mainly of language training with some additional practical orientation and information on the legal and political system of the receiving country. The trend in this area is towards mandatory participation for wider categories, higher fees and stiffer penalties for failing to participate or to pass the exam. Government institutions in the states concerned have commissioned comparative studies on the experience in other countries or evaluation reports where such programmes have been in place for some time (e.g. Entzinger 2004; Michalowski 2004). There is also a new political theory literature that addresses the normative question whether or how immigrants should have to learn the language of the receiving society (Kymlicka & Patten 2003). What is missing so far are policy analyses that explain this new orientation in the integration policies of European states.

3. Access to nationality

Migrants' access to nationality has been studied from various perspectives. A first research agenda compares variations in legal rules for acquisition at birth or through naturalisation and their practical implementation over time and across countries. This can be done from a perspective of positive law, from a political science view that seeks to explain policy decisions and outcomes, or from a normative perspective that considers how principles of equality, inclusion or freedom of choice apply to this policy domain. A second set of research questions focuses on migrants' preferences and decisions concerning naturalisation. What are their motives and how are their choices shaped by policies and structural incentives? How can we explain variations in the propensity to naturalise over time and between different migrant groups? What are the impacts of naturalisation for migrants' opportunities in the wider society and for patterns of economic, social and cultural integration? These questions generally require sociological approaches and quantitative methods of statistical analysis as well as qualitative research on motivations.

Comparing naturalisation regimes

With regard to the former set of questions, there are a number of comparative legal, historical and political case studies of smaller or larger samples of countries. What has been missing so far are systematic comparisons of legal rules that allow for more rigorous testing of the convergence and liberalisation hypotheses by going beyond contextual analyses of individual countries. As far as attempts to explain citizenship policies are concerned, there are two contrasting sets of hypotheses. One affirms that citizenship policy is not merely one aspect of a general migrant integration policy but expresses different conceptions and traditions of national identity. An alternative hypothesis suggests that citizenship, even more so than other areas of migrant integration policy, is a lawyers' rather than a politicians' domain. According to this view, convergence has its roots in an 'epistemic community' of legal scholars and judges who use similar approaches even when starting from divergent constitutional traditions (Galbreath 2004). In order to be able to test hypotheses of this kind we need not only more precise data that allow for an international comparison of laws and their implementation, but we need also additional studies on the policy making process that explore the arenas and networks of actors involved.

Existing comparative analyses (e.g. Hansen & Weil 2001a) and data collected in a recent project (Bauböck et al. 2006) show that there is still a remarkable diversity between European nationality laws concerning conditions for acquisition of citizenship by birth as well as by naturalisation. To the extent that there is convergence, it appears to be rather slow. This is, on the one hand, due to a lack of EU competency for harmonisation or setting of minimum standards. On the other hand, policy imitation across countries seems to be also less developed than in other areas of integration policy.

Migrants' choices of legal status and their consequences

When we consider the second set of questions, there is, first, a problem with statistical data on naturalisation, of which there are four types: (1) Administrative data on naturalisation, i.e. naturalisation statistics, which in most Western countries provide breakdowns for gender, age and former nationality; (2) census data, which would be a very reliable and rich source but unfortunately rarely contain information on naturalisation and naturalised persons; (3) population registers that may contain information on naturalised persons and can sometimes (e.g. in the Nordic countries) be linked to a variety of other data sets containing socio-economic indicators, which makes them particularly useful for answering the question of whether naturalisation improves socio-economic opportunities; (4) survey data, which may provide additional information on topics often not covered by official statistics, such as the migrants' intention to naturalise, their expectations about citizenship acquisition and whether toleration of dual nationality changes their propensity to naturalise (see Council of Europe 1995; Eurostat 2002).[4]

The most often used indicators for measuring citizenship acquisition are naturalisation rates, i.e. numbers of naturalisations in a given year divided by the foreign population at the beginning of the year. These are in fact demographic transition rates that measure the decline of the foreign population through naturalisation. Often they are, however, interpreted as indicators for either the restrictiveness or generosity of nationality laws, or for the propensity of different migrant groups to acquire citizenship. While both factors obviously influence naturalisation rates, these are also determined by a number of other variables, such as net immigration rates that inflate the denominator. Where data on immigration cohorts (i.e. those arriving in the same year) are available, these can be used for rough estimates of numbers of persons eligible for naturalisation. Naturalisation rates are also hard to compare between *ius soli* and *ius sanguinis* regimes because the native-born second and third generations will be counted as foreign population in the latter, but will also be more likely to naturalise and can thereby increase the numerator, too (see Waldrauch & Çinar 2003).

Turning to migrants' motivations for naturalising, one must take into account institutional factors in countries of residence and origin as well as characteristics of migrant groups eligible for naturalisation. Legal obstacles or incentives for naturalisation are not only to be found in nationality laws and decrees for their implementation, but also in the regulation of the status of foreign nationals in the country of residence and of expatriates as defined by the sending state. For example, reforms that deprive resident foreigners of some of their rights to social welfare or to family reunification have often triggered a rush towards naturalisation. The impact of rules in the country of origin depends largely on the toleration of multiple nationality in the receiving state. If naturalisation requires renouncing a previous citizenship, then a loss of external rights to inheritance or property in land and, most importantly, the right to readmission, may act as an important deterrent. One must, however, also consider that, in a world with huge economic inequalities and large zones of great political instability, the citizenship of wealthy and democratic states has a strong instrumental value. There is empirical evidence that migrants from crisis-ridden regions holding a Western citizenship are more likely to take the risks of return than their counterparts with a lesser legal status (Fink-Nielsen et al. 2004; Kibreab 2003).

Among the characteristics of migrants themselves that influence their decision to naturalise are the time of residence, socio-demographic characteristics such as sex, age, occupational status and place of birth (in country or abroad) as well as future migration plans, knowledge about naturalisation options and the presence of emotional, social or family ties to the country of residence and country of origin (see Diehl & Blohm 2003). Such decisions are also not purely individual ones, but are often taken collectively within a family and they may be strongly influenced by attitudes within an ethnic community. Whether a desire for political participation in the country of residence is a relevant motive will depend on the political opportunity structure in a broad sense (i.e. not merely on the right to vote, but on the expected representation of migrants' interests).

An emerging issue of research, little studied so far in Europe but with important pioneering studies in the US and Canada, is the question of whether the acquisition of citizenship has a positive impact on the naturalised person's socio-economic integration. In Europe, detailed datasets (with longitudinal data) that permit an in-depth analysis of socio-economic consequences of naturalisation matching North American research are available only in Scandinavia, the Netherlands and Belgium.[5] One of the main issues is how to interpret empirical results that often show naturalised immigrants in better socio-economic positions than non-naturalised ones in the same migration cohort. The question is whether this outcome is a consequence of the change of status or of a process of self-selection (Rallu 2004). Is naturalisation the cause of upward mobility or are those migrants with a greater potential for upward mobility also more likely to naturalise?

Qualitative studies with in-depth interviews or focus groups can shed some light on questions that are difficult to answer on the basis of statistical data. They can, on the one hand, explore migrants' knowledge, instrumental motives and emotional attitudes towards naturalisation, and, on the other hand, compare experiences of discrimination or social mobility between those who have naturalised and those who have not (see Wunderlich 2005).

4. Transnational and external citizenship

Relations between migrants and countries, regions or local communities of origin have been at the centre of studies on transnational migration. In its broadest sense, this term signals a paradigm change in migration research from a traditional approach of regarding migration as a unidirectional movement that ends with settlement and assimilation in the destination society. Transnational migration studies emphasise instead: that migration is often a process of going back and forth several times between different countries, that even immigrants who are long-term residents may retain strong ties to countries of origin and participate in these countries' developments, e.g. by sending home remittances, and that also sedentary populations who never migrate themselves participate in transnational networks and activities when they are linked to migrants through family and ethnic networks. The Oxford-based transnational communities project, led by Steven Vertovec, and several other scholars (e.g. Glick Schiller et al. 1995; Pries 1997; Faist 2000; Portes 2001; Levitt 2001; Nyberg-Sørensen & Olwig 2002; Guarnizo 2003) have established migrant transnationalism as an important and growing field of theoretical and empirical research.

Claims about the importance of this phenomenon are, however, disputed by scholars who emphasise, on the one hand, that transnationalism is not a historically new phenomenon[6] and, on the other hand, that active involvement in transnational practices may be quite limited among first generation migrants and will gradually fade away over subsequent generations.

Political theorists who have combined the concepts of transnationalism and citizenship have interpreted the term transnationalism in a somewhat broader sense than most of the sociological and anthropological literature (Bauböck 1994, 2003; Kleger 1997). Transnational citizenship refers not only to migrants' political activities directed towards their countries of origin but also to institutional changes and new conceptions of citizenship in states linked to each other through migration chains. Transnational citizenship may be described as overlapping memberships between separate territorial jurisdictions that blur their political boundaries to a certain extent. This phenomenon includes external citizenship rights in states of origin, denizenship and cultural minority rights in states of migrant settlement, and multiple nationality. Empirical research in this field ought to study, on the one hand, how migrants combine or choose between various political identities and statuses and, on the other hand, how the policies of the states involved impact on each other.

External citizenship policies of sending states

While there is a substantial body of theoretical literature of empirical case studies on migrants' access to rights in destination countries, much less attention has been devoted to external citizenship rights that migrants enjoy in their countries of origin. These include minimally the right to return and to diplomatic protection. Sending states differ with regard to property rights concerning inheritance and property in land, which are of particular importance for migrants who want to keep their return options open. Finally, external citizenship may also include certain welfare benefits, cultural support and the right to vote. A growing number of sending states have introduced absentee ballots and some (among them Colombia, France, Italy and Portugal) have even reserved seats in parliament for the expatriate constituency (Itzigsohn 2000; Bauböck 2005). Long-distance voting raises a number of normative problems. Should expatriates be represented in parliaments whose legislation will not apply to them? Should they have a vote even if they have not been exposed to public debates about the candidates and issues (López-Guerra 2005)? A stakeholder approach to citizenship may allow affirmative answers for those migrants whose ongoing ties to their 'homelands' involve them deeply in its present political life and future destiny.

Many sending states have also set up specialised administrative entities dealing with nationals, and sometimes also former nationals, abroad. This is often an explicit acknowledgement of the valuable contributions external citizens make to the national economy through their remittances and to the state more generally, but it is also motivated by efforts, in particular in more authoritarian states, to keep a certain level of control over emigrants. From the perspective of both migrants and the state, the maintenance of external citizenship ties may also reflect broader symbolic and cultural concerns. Sending governments often encourage citizens abroad to retain their citizenship and transmit their nationality to their descendants. Other states do not even permit their citizens to renounce their nationality. Both policies contribute to the increasing incidence of dual nationality. In several Mediterranean and Eastern European countries a conscious effort is often made to re-establish links with relatively old migrant diasporas abroad, mainly by facilitating and encouraging the reacquisition of citizenship (see on Poland Górny et al. 2004).

External citizenship poses several tasks for future research. How do citizenship policies of sending and receiving states interact with each other? Why and how do states encourage their citizens abroad to retain their nationality? Which rights and duties of citizenship are deterritorialised and linked to external citizenship? The lack of comparative and normative studies on external citizenship rights is a major gap in current research. Closing it is also important from a 'receiving state' perspective since sending-state policies in this area are a major factor determining immigrants' choices between return migration, permanent settlement as foreign residents and naturalisation.

Multiple citizenship

In international law, multiple nationality is not a new concern. What has dramatically changed since the mid-1980s is the previously widely accepted doctrine that this phenomenon is an evil to be avoided as far as possible. This traditional view rested on several assumptions. From a domestic perspective all states were assumed to have an interest in the undivided loyalty of their citizens and from an international perspective overlapping membership was regarded as source of conflict between states. Second, dual nationality was also seen as detrimental for the individual concerned since it could lead to the imposition of multiple obligations such as military service or to a lack of diplomatic protection in the country of second citizenship. Conversely, the accumulation of rights in several countries was regarded as an unfair privilege not enjoyed by the native 'singular' citizens. Finally, dual citizenship was seen as an impediment to immigrant integration by encouraging attachment to a foreign country and culture of origin (Hansen & Weil 2002: 7). In recent years there has been a new academic interest in dual nationality (e.g. Hammar 1985; Martin & Hailbronner 2003; Hansen & Weil 2001b; Faist et al. 2004; Howard 2005) stirred by empirical evidence about the growth of the phenomenon, by new legislation in a number of states that abandoned renunciation requirements as a condition for naturalisation and by public debates in other countries. There are clear signs of increased toleration of dual nationality notwithstanding the fact that token opposition to dual nationality has remained widespread.

A major part of the phenomenon is due to dual acquisition of nationality at birth by children born in mixed marriages or in countries with ius soli provisions. The more controversial mechanism is the retaining of a previous nationality in naturalisations. While the legal and normative arguments pro and contra multiple nationality have been extensively stated, there is still a lack of hypotheses and comparative research on the conditions under which dual nationality is likely to be accepted and on the driving forces behind changes of citizenship policy. From the available evidence, however, it seems that the explicit acceptance of dual nationality in Europe is very much driven by native elites and emigrant citizens, and involves immigrant groups mainly as clients rather than as actors.

The impact of sending state policies on dual citizenship has been generally neglected. Sending states may contribute to the proliferation not merely through ius sanguinis rules, but also when they either refuse to release persons who naturalise abroad or when they encourage them to retain or reacquire their previous citizenship. The opposite impact may be expected when countries of origin make expatriation less costly in terms of procedures, fees and loss of rights, as Turkey did in 1995. Such effects may, however, be largely offset by emotional attachments and by instrumental advantages of holding two passports.

There is little quantitative evidence on dual nationality. Even the plausible claim that this phenomenon is increasing is hard to document since states generally register only their own citizenship. Occasionally, multiple nationality is included in census or survey data, but reliable statistics would have to be international rather than national ones.

5. Migrant citizenship in the European Union

There is abundant research on the impact of European integration on migration and refugee policies. Social scientists have been fascinated by the question how a supra-national union of states engaged in building an area of free movement deals with member state prerogatives in determining the admission and rights of third country nationals. And the EU has channelled research funding towards such questions since these were deemed of great political relevance for the Commission's projects. A lot of ink has also been spilled on the question of whether citizenship of the Union formally introduced in the Maastricht Treaty represents a move towards new postnational or cosmopolitan conceptions of citizenship or is, instead, nothing more than a symbolic sweetener for the ongoing transfer of sovereignty towards a largely unaccountable European bureaucracy. These two topics have, however, rarely been linked systematically by asking how citizenship at the European level has affected the status of third country nationals.

There are three major research tasks in this area. A first one concerns the evolution of EU citizenship itself as essentially a bundle of rights for internal migrants within the Union who are nationals of a member state. A second issue concerns the access of third country nationals to this status, and a third is about the benefits of a general harmonisation of fundamental rights and anti-discrimination policies for third country nationals and about the emergence of an alternative status of residential or civic citizenship for long-term resident third country nationals disconnected from their nationality.

The evolution of Union citizenship

The roots of Union citizenship can be traced back to the 1970s when Community politicians first began to discuss 'European identity'. Initial concepts merely included student mobility, the exchange of teachers and the harmonisation of diplomas. A broader approach emerged at the 1973 Copenhagen summit where the European Commission suggested to introduce a 'passport union' as well as 'special rights' for citizens of member states (Wiener 1997). In 1975 the Heads of Government of Belgium and Italy for the first time proposed to enfranchise all Community nationals on the local level. The Commission's technical report on special rights went even further by stating that these 'first and foremost' imply 'the rights to vote, to stand for election and to become a public official at local, regional and national levels' (Connolly et al. 2005: 6-8). In the 1980s, the prevailing political paradigm changed towards economic integration and the rights associated with freedom of movement. This new focus pushed political participation to the background of debates on European Union citizenship. It was only in 1992 that the Treaty of Maastricht established citizenship of the Union as one of the three pillars of European political union in Article 8-8e (now Art. 17-22) of the EC Treaty.

These provisions created a new type of citizenship that departs in significant ways from the well-known pattern of nested citizenship in federal states, whose nationals are both citizens of a constituent unit (a province, region, canton or state) and of the larger federation. Apart from the right to vote in European Parliament elections, EU citizenship is of little significance for persons living within a member state whose nationals they are. The main beneficiaries are internal migrants who take up residence in another member state. Union citizens possess civil, social and political rights (and duties) with regard to the nation-state whose nationality they hold and they enjoy residential and social rights, but not the full range of political rights, vis-à-vis a second member state in which they reside. Voting rights are only granted at local and European levels but not for national elections in another member state. Furthermore, rights of Union citizenship, particularly the right of residence, may still be revoked in case of a threat to public order. Third country nationals enjoy social rights, providing that they are members of the labour force, but few other rights comparable to those of Union citizens and no political rights at all. Thus the current form of Union citizenship, although extending the rights of Union citizens in other member states, has not overcome the boundaries of state-based nationality. On the contrary, it has cemented the clear divide between nationals, Union citizens from another member state and third-country nationals. It is also remarkable that the content of rights attached to EU citizenship has remained unchanged since 1992 although the drafting of the Charter of Fundamental Rights and of the Constitutional Treaty had provided ample opportunities for redefining and expanding it.

Whereas the strategies of political actors involved in the making of European migration policies have been studied to some extent (Favell 2001, Geddes & Guiraudon 2002, Guiraudon 2001, 2003), research on the politics of European citizenship policy is still quite limited. This research gap contributes to the low level of visibility of the issue in the public discourse on European integration. In particular, too little attention has been devoted to the role of the European Court of Justice (ECJ) in the development of Union citizenship. In a 2001 decision the ECJ stated that 'Union citizenship is destined to be the fundamental status of nationals of the member states, enabling those who find themselves in the same situation to enjoy the same treatment in law irrespective of their nationality, subject to such exceptions as expressly provided for'.[7] This could indicate that, in the absence of consensus at the political level, the ECJ's interpretation of Union citizenship might trigger a further evolution of the concept. A similar development occurred in the past with regard to the expansion of rights of Community workers towards rights attached to residence in another member state. For the time being, however, EU citizenship still is like a glove turned inside out: 'It cannot act within the territory of nationality but only outside it though it purports to express citizen rights' (Guild 2004: 14).

As no reporting procedure has been implemented, there is no comprehensive information available on how citizens of the Union make use of their political rights. With regard to elections to the European Parliament, the available data show a significantly lower turnout of Union citizens living in a second member state as compared to nationals of this state. There are no data on turnout rates for municipal elections available, but the low number of non-nationals elected to municipal councils reported to the Commission clearly shows that Union citizens are not well represented in local councils (Connolly et al. 2005: 16).

Access to Union citizenship and member state nationality

One peculiar feature of Union citizenship is that the institutions of European polity to which this membership refers have no power to confer or withdraw the status. The Amsterdam Treaty stated that 'Citizenship of the Union shall complement and not replace national citizenship' (now Art. 17 TEC). The former is therefore directly derived from the latter. Moreover, the member states' nationality laws, which indirectly regulate the acquisition and loss of EU citizenship, fall outside Union competence and differ dramatically from each other (Preuss et al. 2003). In the Micheletti and Chen cases the ECJ has stated that the competence of each member state to lay down the conditions for the acquisition and loss of nationality must be exercised with due regard to Community law.[8] However, this reservation has not had a major impact so far (cf. Guild 1996: 45; De Groot 2003: 19). As long as member states continue to hold the sole right to regulate acquisition and loss of citizenship, they can even undermine Union policies with regard to the integration of immigrants by raising the requirements for naturalisation.

From a theoretical and normative perspective, the elements and dynamics of this peculiar European architecture of citizenship have been evaluated differently and there is still need for conceptual debate and clarification in this area. It has been suggested that Union citizenship should be fully disconnected from member state nationality, or should at least be directly accessible for third country nationals who have resided in the Union for a certain number of years (Migrants Forum 1996). Some researchers have gone further in proposing that at the level of member states, too, immigrants should be turned into citizens automatically without having to naturalise (Rubio-Marín 2000; Kostakopoulou 2003). One way of clarifying these issues is to distinguish the *linkage* between Union citizenship and member state nationality (i.e. each Union citizen is a national of a member state and vice versa) from the mode of *derivation* (of Union citizenship from member state nationality instead of other way round) and from *inequality* in conditions of acquisition and loss (of Union citizenship because of the lack of harmonisation of nationality laws). Rejecting any of these elements in the present architecture has specific implications for reform that need to be spelled out.[9]

Civic citizenship and European rights for third country nationals

While the EU has failed to use its own citizenship as an instrument for political integration of third country nationals, it has to a certain extent embraced the alternative option of harmonising the legal status and rights of long-term third country nationals. The 1998 Amsterdam Treaty opened this possibility by bringing migration under Community competence. In 1999 the Tampere European Council outlined this agenda by stating that long-term resident third country nationals should enjoy 'rights and obligations comparable to those of EU citizens', that their legal status 'should be approximated to that of member states' nationals' and they should be granted in their country of residence 'a set of uniform rights which are as near as possible to those enjoyed by EU citizens' (Presidency Conclusions, Tampere European Council 15 and 16 October 1999). Although this conclusion was weaker than the initial draft, which had used the term *equal* rights, against the background of widespread legal discrimination against third country nationals in most member states, this was still a fairly strong statement. The Commission took up the ball by drafting directives on admission of third country nationals for employment, on family reunification and the legal status of long-term residents. Due to considerable resistance from several member states, the former proposal was shelved while the latter two directives were adopted in substantially watered down versions.

In 2000, the Commission introduced the new concept of civic citizenship: 'The legal status granted to third country nationals would be based on the principle of providing sets of rights and responsibilities on a basis of equality with those of nationals but differentiated according to the length of stay while providing for progression to permanent status. In the longer term this could extend to offering a form of civic citizenship, based on the EC Treaty and inspired by the Charter of Fundamental Rights, consisting of a set of rights and duties offered to third country nationals' (COM (2000) 757 final: 21). In a later communication the Commission specifically included under this heading local voting rights for third-country nationals. It also outlined for the first time European standards for member state's nationality laws by suggesting that 'naturalization should be rapid, secure and non-discretionary' and that for second and third generation immigrants 'nationality laws should provide automatic or semi-automatic access' to citizenship (COM (2003) 336 final: 22). Civic citizenship is described as a status that helps immigrants to settle successfully but also as 'a first step towards acquiring the nationality of the member state concerned' (ibid: 23). Proposals along similar lines had been previously made by academic researchers, e.g. Philippe Schmitter's suggestion to introduce a European denizenship (Schmitter 2000).

While civic citizenship has so far remained an aspiration more than a manifest development, immigrants have gained important civic rights through European legislation with regard to protection against discrimination. By introducing a new Article 13 into the TEC, the Treaty of Amsterdam for the first time supplied the European Union with competence in the field of fighting discrimination based on 'race' and ethnic origin (Bell 2002a, b; Geddes & Guiraudon 2002; Liegl et al. 2004: 13-17). This change was achieved after the European Parliament and NGOs campaigning for migrants' rights (Chopin & Niessen 2001) had exerted pressure. Despite previous deferments by some member states, the Council agreed in 2000 on two directives implementing measures against discrimination based on ethnic origin – the Racial Equality Directive[10] and the Employment Equality Directive[11]. The adoption of these directives was ironically accelerated by the inclusion of the extreme right-wing Freedom Party into government in Austria and the subsequent diplomatic ostracism against Austria, which convinced European governments that they had to take a stance against ethnic and racial discrimination (Tyson 2001).

Although they differ in scope – discrimination outside working life is only prohibited with regard to 'race' and ethnic origin – both directives provide protection against four different forms of discrimination: direct and indirect discrimination, discriminatory harassment, and instruction to discriminate. The protection against discrimination conferred by the directives applies to all persons who are on the territory of one of the EU member states, irrespective of their nationality (Liegl et al. 2004: 9). Despite the reluctance of the member states to implement the directives, it is likely that decisions of the ECJ will eventually harmonise the protection against racial discrimination and discrimination based on ethnic origin.

The exclusion of discrimination based on nationality and the different scope of protection in the two directives are major weaknesses of EU anti-discrimination regulations. Future research will have to examine the usage of the concept of indirect discrimination at European and member state levels and its potential to also prevent discrimination based on nationality of migrants from outside the EU. Furthermore, thorough studies on the adequacy and efficiency of the implementation system will be necessary to develop clear criteria for evaluating the quality of anti-discrimination systems (Perchinig 2003).

There is rather broad agreement among political and legal theorists on normative arguments in favour of civic citizenship and comprehensive protection against discrimination. More controversial debates about affirmative action for specifically disadvantaged groups of immigrants have not yet been fully addressed at European level. There is, however, a clear need for further studies of the European policy making process with regard to rights for third-country nationals, whose lack of political representation in the member states means that they have little leverage in the European arenas as well.

6. Political participation

Citizenship is not merely a legal status and a bundle of rights and duties, but refers also to the active involvement and passive representation of citizens in politics. In many EU countries, large numbers of immigrants first arrived in the 1960s and 1970s as 'guest workers' who were not regarded as potential citizens. Their task was to contribute to building the economy, but not to interfere with their hosts' political affairs. This has changed, at least in those European countries that have already witnessed several waves of immigration in the past five decades. Here, political mobilisation, participation and representation of ethnic immigrant minorities have become topical issues, especially at the local and city levels.

Participation, mobilisation and representation

Political participation is the active dimension of citizenship. It refers to the various ways in which individuals take part in the management of collective affairs of a political community. Studying political participation must not be restricted to conventional forms such as voting or running for elections, as is often the case in political science. It also covers political activities such as protests, demonstrations, sit-ins, hunger strikes, boycotts, etc. These less conventional and extra-parliamentary forms of political participation generally presuppose the formation of a collective actor characterised by a shared identity and some degree of organisation through a mobilisation process. In the context of non-conventional participation, *political mobilisation* refers to this process of building collective identity and agency. By contrast, in conventional participation, mobilisation occurs within a previously structured set of political institutions. In general terms, participation can be individual or collective in both types of arenas. An individual may stage a hunger strike and ethnic mobilisation may turn the individual act of voting into a collective action. In other words, while the focus is usually on individual participation in conventional arenas and on collective mobilisation in non-conventional ones, these distinctions must be kept open for all possible combinations.

In modern democracies, political power is usually exercised by persons whose legitimacy to govern has its source in free and competitive elections. Through their vote, citizens mandate these persons to govern on their behalf. *Political representation* refers to this legitimation process and its results, i.e. the relation between representatives and their constituency. While the institutions of representative democracy are broadly endorsed in European societies, there are still important controversies over the meaning of the concept that are highly relevant for the representation of immigrant ethnic, racial or religious minorities. For some theories, the role of citizens is restricted to electing representatives whom they trust and to recall them when their trust is betrayed. For others, representatives are not free to decide as they think is best, but are bound to defend the interests of their voters even against their own convictions. A third position goes a step further and argues that representative bodies such as parliaments should also mirror the social composition of the electorate in terms of stable identities such as gender, class or ethnicity. Although this latter demand for 'descriptive representation' has been generally rejected by political theorists (e.g. Pitkin 1967), some have argued for 'affirmative representation' for specifically disadvantaged groups under conditions of pervasive discrimination and lack of trust between groups (Phillips 1995; Mansbridge 2001).

Migrants' political opportunities

As has been pointed out above, in contrast with civil liberties and many social welfare entitlements, political participation rights are still significantly attached to the legal status of nationality. However, European Union citizenship and the introduction of local voting rights independent of nationality in currently 12 of the 25 member states (as well as in Norway and in four Swiss cantons) illustrate a gradual decoupling at the municipal level. In many countries where there is no local franchise for third-country nationals, cities have experimented with consultative bodies. These are either appointed by the municipal authorities, or composed of delegates of immigrant associations, or emerge from elections in the migrant communities. Political scientists have generally criticised the idea of special consultative bodies because of their limited influence and because even elected bodies entrench the democratic disparity through setting up separate electoral constituencies and representative bodies for citizens and non-citizens. However, recently, a new initiative from the Council of Europe has put the promotion of these institutions again on the table (Gsir & Martiniello 2004). There are hundreds of consultative bodies for immigrants across Europe. The idea of the Council of Europe is to develop a manual of common principles and guidelines that could be used by cities interested in creating such bodies.

In national elections immigrants still have to pass through the gate of naturalisation in order to achieve equal representation in nearly all countries. From a democratic perspective, it is clearly problematic to exclude long-term residents, who will be fully subjected to the laws and have a stake in the future of the society, from representation in the making of these laws. The question that is still disputed among theorists is whether this deficit should be overcome by facilitating and encouraging the naturalisation of immigrants or by extending voting rights also to foreign nationals.

A second research task is to study the institutional avenues, incentives and obstacles for political participation and representation of those migrants who do enjoy equal political rights. These include formal and legal aspects, such as different systems of automatic or voluntary voter registration, rules for drawing and revising constituency boundaries and proportional or majoritarian electoral systems, as well as informal elements such as the numbers and political orientation of parties, styles of political campaigning and the openness of a public political culture for ethnic diversity and the immigrant voice. While there have been studies in Europe and the US on how these institutional features affect participation and representation of women or of African Americans, so far there has been very little systematic comparative research on the political opportunity structures for immigrants in Europe.

Migrants' political behaviour

The third task is to examine and explain variations in migrants' political behaviour within a given opportunity structure. The oldest conjecture in this field may be called the migrant quiescence thesis (Martiniello 1997). It assumes that migrant groups have special characteristics that explain why they tend to be politically less involved than native citizens. This hypothesis has been argued from contrasting sides of the political spectrum. Some Marxist scholars regarded migrant workers only as a labour force imported to undermine the collective mobilisation of native workers and assumed that these workers were primarily interested in achieving short-term economic goals. On the other side, we find culturalist explanations that regard migrants as shaped by pre-modern and non-democratic values of their societies of origin and with little experience and interest in democratic politics. Both approaches have obvious weaknesses in their underlying premises that either deny migrants' agency or ignore their exposure and adaptation to the destination society through the very process of migration itself. They are also flawed in being selective with regard to supporting empirical evidence. In many cases, such as emigration from Spain and Greece during dictatorship, migrant workers were actually politicised in their country of origin before their departure and migration was a way to escape authoritarian regimes. Furthermore, both explanations confuse quiescence or passivity with apolitical attitudes. When avenues of political participation are restricted, passivity can be a transitional waiting position for better days and future opportunities for participation. Finally, immigrants may often participate more effectively outside the conventional arenas of representative democracy in unions and other interest organisations or by forming their own associations.

Where there are sufficient opportunities, the extent to which immigrants and their offspring seize them depends on several variables such as: their political ideas and values, their previous involvement in politics (including experiences in the country of origin), the degree of 'institutional completeness' of the immigrant ethnic community, the vision they have of their presence in the country of residence as permanent or temporary, their feeling of belonging to the societies of settlement and origin, their knowledge of the political system and institutions, the social capital and density of immigrant associational networks,[12] plus all the usual determinants of political behaviour such as level of education, linguistic skills, socio-economic status, gender, age or generational cohort.

Recent research on immigrants' social capital has shown that the research on this question has often been strongly shaped by specific national themes and paradigms and has rarely used a broad comparative perspective. In France, there is extensive research on the second-generation immigrants' extra-parliamentary mobilisation in the 1980s and on the *sans-papiers* movement of the 1990s (Simeant 1997; Wihtol de Wenden 1988). Very recently the religious-political mobilisation during the debate on secularism and the ban of ostentatious religious signs in public schools has drawn much attention. Only a few authors have also focused on the political representation of immigrants (e.g. Geisser 1997 on immigrant local councillors). In the UK, the issue of the electoral power of ethnic minorities as well as the political colour of each ethnic minority is discussed in all elections. Historically, West Indians and Asians were largely pro-Labour but recently their votes have become a little more evenly distributed across parties. The representation of minorities in elected assemblies has also been rather extensively studied (e.g. Anwar 1986; Geddes 1998; Saggar 1998). In the Netherlands and in Scandinavia there have been precise studies on the electoral behaviour of immigrants (e.g. Tillie 1998; Fennema & Tillie 2001; Soininen 1999). Swedish studies tried to explain the decline of immigrant voter turnout in local elections over the past decade. The Dutch research team linked migrant participation in local elections to data about the density of their associational networks and found positive correlations between these variables. This group has recently organised a comparative study of immigrant participation in ten European cities that tests the social capital approach in a broader setting.

Transnational political participation

With a few notable exceptions (e.g. Østergaard-Nielsen 2003) research on migrants' transnational political participation is rather underdeveloped in Europe. In this field the task is, first, to study the political opportunity structure for political participation in the country of origin. This includes the dimensions of legal rights for expatriates already discussed above (to retain or reacquire citizenship status, to cast votes in elections and to special representation) and sending countries' policies towards this group. These may either try to strictly control political activities abroad and to channel them towards support for a current regime, or regard emigrants as an irrelevant group that has cut its ties with the homeland, or, alternatively, encourage them to stay connected and get involved in the political process (Bauböck 2003). In the latter category we find not only sending country governments, but also political parties and candidates in elections that sometimes carry their campaigns abroad to mobilise absentee ballots or to collect campaign funds among those who have no voting rights.

Migrants' political orientations towards their country of origin may, however, also be fundamentally opposed to a present regime. Just as governments try to control emigrants, so rebels try to recruit fighters and supporters among diasporas. Migrants who have at least partly political motives for leaving their country often show highly divergent attitudes. Some groups want to disconnect themselves as fully as possible and are more ready to assimilate in their host country than other immigrants. This was a typical pattern among refugees from Communist Central and Eastern Europe who settled in the US during the Cold War. Others, however, maintain a much stronger commitment towards their country of origin because they conceive of themselves as diasporas with an aspiration to return. Involvement in 'homeland politics' that may persist across several generations is often fuelled by unresolved conflicts about national self-determination.

The broad range of variation between both sending state attitudes towards expatriates and migrant groups' orientations towards their countries of origin calls for systematic comparative studies that go beyond the description of single cases. This is a broad field for future research.

It is also of great importance for societies of immigration. Ultimately, political transnationalism is not merely about an external relation between migrants and homelands, but about the broader opportunity structure for migrant political activity that emerges from the interaction between institutions and policies in sending and receiving states. Understanding this mutual impact and growing interdependence may be crucial for promoting the political integration of immigrants in the country of settlement but also for resolving festering political crises and promoting democratic transitions in many source countries.

7. Conclusions

We have identified large gaps in research on migrants' citizenship and a number of promising avenues for a future research agenda. In the most general way our main tasks can be described as follows: (1) to compare institutions and policies of citizenship that respond to migration within and across countries; (2) to assess the consistency of these responses with legal norms, their legitimacy in terms of political norms and their consequences and effectiveness in achieving policy goals; (3) to study the impact of migration on changes of institutional arrangements and policies; and (4) to analyse migrant attitudes, ties and practices with regard to citizenship: their sense of belonging to political communities, their involvement in different polities through social, economic, cultural and political ties, their choices with regard to alternative statuses of citizenship, their use of rights and their political activities.

This research agenda emerges from our focus on the three core concepts explained in section 1.

1. Research that focuses on institutional *opportunity structures* for political participation must be combined with analyses of social capital generated within migrants' associations and networks. Furthermore, two alternative perspectives on opportunity structures should be more systematically linked to each other. Some regard these structures as explanatory 'independent variables' while others focus instead on their change over time or their variation across countries, regions and cities. This latter approach includes not only institutionalist approaches but also normative political theories, comparative law and political discourse and policy making analyses. Combining the two perspectives helps to understand feedback loops, i.e. changes in an opportunity structure as a result of migrants' political choices and activities. Such interactions between structure and agency have been at the centre of much contemporary sociological theory, but making these relevant for empirical research

requires bringing together researchers who work predominantly within one of the two perspectives.

2. *Immigrant political integration* is a major concern in public discourses in many European states, where it is generally interpreted as a need to strengthen immigrants' identification with their host societies, their assimilation in linguistic and cultural terms and their acceptance of democratic core values and norms. The other crucial dimensions of political integration, i.e. access to political status, rights and opportunities and incentives for political participation tend to be neglected or even overtly rejected. The concept of integration has unavoidable normative overtones even when used in academic research. These normative aspects of integration should always be made explicit and they may sometimes for good reasons be challenged. For an unbiased research agenda it is important to reject a nationalist perspective, from which immigrants raise an integration problem whenever they do not fit a preconceived definition of national community. At the same time, we have to be aware that immigrant exclusion and social marginalisation may breed forms of political radicalism and religious fanaticism that create serious threats for democratic polities. In Europe, political integration has yet another meaning that refers to the pooling or transfer of state sovereignty within the European Union. As we have discussed in this chapter, the significance of Union citizenship and the direct impact of European integration on citizenship policies of the member states are quite limited. However, there is a nascent European citizenship regime that has historically emerged from rights of free movement for nationals of the member states and now hesitantly embraces the harmonisation of legal status, rights and integration policies for third country nationals.

3. We have suggested that the emerging research field of *political transnationalism* should similarly combine two perspectives by analysing not merely migrants' political activities across international borders, but also the transformation of policies and political institutions in both receiving and sending countries in response to migrants' transnational ties. While a transnational research perspective transcends a focus on integration in the receiving society, it can also be used to broaden the notion of political opportunity structures so that it includes states of origin as well as transnational migrant networks and geographically dispersed diasporic communities.

Studying these phenomena requires a plurality of methods and multidisciplinary perspectives. Research within the IMISCOE network can be classified into two main groups of research questions and methodological approaches: (1) comparative studies and normative theories of political institutions, laws and policies; and (2) quantitative and qualitative case studies of migrants' attitudes and behaviour and their participation in mainstream or minority organisations and movements.

The topic of migration and citizenship is at the heart of many public debates and public policy making. It is not necessarily the task of academic research to intervene in these debates and to give advice to policymakers. But sound theory-guided arguments and solid empirical evidence can certainly help to improve the quality of media discourses and of decision making. The IMISCOE network aspires to contribute to this task by bringing together researchers from various disciplines and countries and offering a platform for dialogue between researchers, journalists and policymakers.

Notes

1   This chapter is a summary compiled by Rainer Bauböck from a longer co-authored report published separately on the IMISCOE website at: www.imiscoe.org.
2   Along similar lines, Glick Schiller (2003) and Glick Schiller and Levitt (2004) distinguish between transnational ways of belonging and ways of being, with the latter referring to actual social relations and practices rather than to identities associated with these.
3   In the US, some of the initial decisions in the 1996 welfare reform that deprived permanent residents of federal welfare benefits were subsequently reversed or compensated by state-based welfare.
4   The German Socio-Economic Panel may be cited as an example for such a survey.
5   See Scott (2004) and Bevelander and Veenmann (2004) for European case studies based on relatively comprehensive data. Kogan's (2003) comparative analysis of the consequences of naturalisation for ex-Yugoslavs in Austria and Sweden shows that research on the 'economics of citizenship' can to a certain extent also be done on the basis of more limited data.
6   This claim is broadly supported by historical research on migration, e.g. Hoerder (2002) and Moch (1992).
7   Grzelczyk vs. Centre public d'aide sociale d'Ottignies-Louvain-la-Neuve, C-184/99 ECR 2001, I-6193.
8   Micheletti vs. Delegacion del Gobierno en Cantabria, C-369/90, ECR 1992, I-4258; Chen v. Secretary of State for the Home Department, C-200/02, ECR 2004, I-3887.
9   See Bauböck (2004) for an argument that affirms the former two elements as adequate for the present stage of political integration in the Union while rejecting the latter as not only detrimental for the integration of immigrants but also devaluing the meaning of citizenship at the level of the Union.
10   Council Directive 2000/43/EC of 29 June 2000 implementing the principle of equal treatment between persons irrespective of racial or ethnic origin.
11   Council Directive 2000/78/EC of 27 November 2000 establishing a general framework for equal treatment in employment and occupation.
12   Using a social capital approach, Fennema and Tillie have argued that dense associational networks within ethnic groups enhance political trust and participation (Fennema & Tillie 2001, 2004; Jacobs & Tillie 2004; Heelsum 2004).

Literature

Aleinikoff, A. T. (2000), 'Between Principles and Policies: U.S. Citizenship Policy', in A. T. Aleinikoff & D. Klusmeyer (eds.), *From Migrants to Citizens. Membership in a Changing World*, 119-174. Washington, DC: Carnegie Endowment for International Peace.

Aleinikoff, A. T. & D. Klusmeyer (eds.) (2002), *Citizenship Policies for an Age of Migration*. Washington, DC: Carnegie Endowment for International Peace.

Anwar, M. (1986), *Race and Politics. Ethnic Minorities and the British Political System*. London: Tavistock.

Bauböck, R. (1994), *Transnational Citizenship. Membership and Rights in International Migration*. Aldershot: Edward Elgar.

Bauböck, R. (2003), 'Towards a political theory of migrant transnationalism', *International Migration Review* 37 (3): 700-723.

Bauböck, R. (2004), 'The Shape of a New Species. Citizenship and Territorial Borders in the EU Polity', in S. Puntscher Riekmann, M. Latzer & M. Mokre (eds.), *The State of Europe. Transformations of Statehood from a European Perspective*, 170-195. Campus: Frankfurt.

Bauböck, R., E. Ersbøll, K. Groenendijk and H. Waldrauch (2006), *Acquisition and Loss of Nationality. Policies and Trends in 15 European states*, Amsterdam: Amsterdam University Press, forthcoming.

Bauböck, R. (2005), 'Expansive Citizenship: Voting Beyond Territory and Membership,' *Political Science and Politics*, 38 (4): 683-687.

Bell, M. (2002a), *Anti-Discrimination Law and the European Union*. New York: Oxford University Press.

Bell, M. (2002b), 'Combating racism through European laws: a comparison of the Racial Equality Directive and Protocol 12', in I. Chopin & J. Niessen (eds.), *Combating Racial and Ethnic Discrimination. Taking the European Legislative Agenda further*, 7-34. London etc.: Commission for Racial Equality etc. www.migpolgroup.com.

Bevelander, P. & J. Veenmann (2004), 'Naturalization and Immigrants' Employment Integration in the Netherlands', paper presented at the conference 'Immigrant ascension to citizenship: recent policies and economic and social consequences', *International conference organised under the auspices of the Willy Brandt Guest Professorship's Chair International Migration and Ethnic Relations (IMER)*, Malmö University, 7 June 2004.

Castles, S. & A. Davidson (2000), *Citizenship and Migration. Globalization and the Politics of Belonging*. London: Routledge.

Chopin, I. & J. Niessen (eds.) (2001), *The Starting Line and the Incorporation of the Racial Equality Directive into the National Laws of the EU Member States and Accession States*. London etc.: Commission for Racial Equality etc. www.migpolgroup.com.

Christiansen, F. & U. Hedetoft (eds.) (2004), *The Politics of Multiple Belonging. Ethnicity and Nationalism in Europe and East Asia*. Aldershot: Ashgate.

Connolly, A., S. Day & J. Shaw (2005), 'The contested case of EU electoral rights', forthcoming in R. Bellamy, D. Castiglione, J. Shaw (eds.), *Making European Citizens*. London: Palgrave. www.law.manchester.ac.uk/staff/jo_shaw.htm.

Council of Europe (1995), *Measurement and indicators of integration*. Strasbourg: Council of Europe.

De Groot, G. R. (2003), 'Loss of Nationality. A Critical Inventory', in D. A. Martin & K. Hailbronner (eds.), *Rights and Duties of Dual Nationals. Evolution and Prospects*, 201-299. The Hague: Kluwer Law International.

Diehl, C. & M. Blohm (2003), 'Rights or Identity? Naturalization Processes among "Labour Migrants" in Germany', *International Migration Review* 37: 133-161.

Entzinger, H. (2004), *Integration and Orientation Courses in a European Perspective. Expert report written for the Sachverständigenrat für Zuwanderung und Integration.* www.bafl.de/template/zuwanderungsrat/expertisen_2004/expertise_entzinger.pdf.

Eurostat (2002), *The social situation in the European Union 2002.* Luxembourg: Eurostat.

Faist, T. (2000), *The Volume and Dynamics of International Migration.* New York: Oxford University Press.

Faist, T., J. Gerdes & B. Rieple (2004), 'Dual Citizenship as a Path-Dependent Process', *International Migration Review* 38 (3): 913-944.

Favell, A. (2001), 'Integration policy and integration research in Europe: a review and critique', in A. T. Aleinikoff & D. Klusmeyer (eds.), *Citizenship Today. Global Perspectives and Practices,* 349-399. Washington, DC: Carnegie Endowment for International Peace.

Fennema, M. & J. Tillie (2001), 'Civic community, political participation and political trust of ethnic groups', *Connections* 23 (2): 44-59.

Fennema, M. & J. Tillie (2004), 'Do immigrant policies matter? Ethnic civic communities and immigrant policies in Amsterdam, Liege and Zurich', in: R. Penninx, K. Kraal, M. Martiniello, S. Vertovec, *Citizenship in European Cities, Immigrants, Local Politics and Integration Policies,* Ashgate, Aldershot: 85-106.

Fink-Nielsen, M., P. Hansen & N. Kleist (2004), 'Roots, Rights and Responsibilities. Place-making and Repatriation among Somalis in Denmark and Somaliland', *Stichproben. Wiener Zeitschrift für kritische Afrikawissenschaften* 7.

Freeman, G. P. (1998), 'The Decline of Sovereignty? Politics and Immigration Restriction in Liberal States', in C. Joppke (ed.), *Challenge to the Nation-State. Immigration in Western Europe and the United States,* 86-108. Oxford: Oxford University Press.

Galbreath, D. J. (2004), 'International Sources of Domestic Policy: Europe and Latvia in the context of minority rights', paper presented at the *European Consortium for Political Research* joint sessions workshop on 'International Organisations and Policy Implementation', Uppsala Universitet, 13-18 April 2004.

Geddes, A. (1998), 'Race Related Political Participation and Representation in the UK', *Revue Européenne des Migrations Internationales* 14 (2): 33-49.

Geddes, A. & V. Guiraudon (2002), 'Anti-discrimination Policy: The Emergence of an EU Policy Paradigm amidst Contrasted National Models', paper presented at the workshop *Opening the Black Box: Europeanisation, Discourse, and Policy Chang',* Oxford, 23-24 November 2002.

Geisser, V. (1997), *Ethnicite Républicaine.* Paris: Presses de Sc.Po.

Glick Schiller, N. (2003), 'Transnational Theory and Beyond', in D. Nugent & V. Joan (eds.), *A Companion to the Anthropology of Politics.* Malden, MA: Blackwell.

Glick Schiller, N. & P. Levitt (2004), 'Conceptualizing Simultaneity: A Transnational Social Field Perspective on Society', *International Migration Review* 38 (3): 1002-1039.

Glick Schiller, N., N. Basch & C. Blanc-Szanton (1995), 'From Immigrant to Transmigrant: Theorizing Transnational Migration, *Anthropological Quarterly* 68 (1): 48-63.

Górny, A., A. Grzymała-Kazłowska, P. Koryś & A. Weinar (2005), 'Selective tolerance? Regulations, Practice and Discussions Regarding Dual Nationality in Poland', *International Migration Review* 39 (3) (forthcoming).

Gsir, S. & M. Martiniello (2004), *Local consultative bodies for foreign residents – a handbook.* Strasbourg: Council of Europe Publishing.

Guarnizo, L. (2003), 'The Economics of Transnational Living', *International Migration Review* 37 (3): 666-699.

Guild, E. (1996), 'The legal framework of citizenship in the European Union, in D. Cesarani & M. Fulbrook (eds.), *Citizenship, Nationality and Migration in Europe,* 30-57. London etc.: Routledge.

Guild, E. (2004), *The emerging Constitution of the European Union: Citizenship, Justice and Security*. Brussels: European Commission, DG EAC – Jean Monnet Project. europa. eu.int/comm/education/programmes/ajm/people_culture/contributions/elspeth_-guild_en.pdf.

Guiraudon, V. (1998), 'Citizenship Rights for Non-Citizens: France, Germany, and the Netherlands', in C. Joppke (ed.), *Challenge to the Nation-State. Immigration in Western Europe and the United States*, 272-318. Oxford: Oxford University Press.

Guiraudon, V. (2001): 'The EU "garbage can": Accounting for policy developments in the immigration domain', paper presented at the *2001 conference of the European Community Studies Association*, Madison Wisconsin, 29 May-1 June 2001.

Guiraudon, V. (2003), 'The constitution of a European policy domain: a political sociology approach', *Journal of European Public Policy* 10 (2): 263-282.

Guiraudon, V. & G. Lahav (2000), 'A Reappraisal of the State-Sovereignty Debate. The Case of Migration Control', *Comparative Political Studies* 33 (2): 163-195.

Hammar, T. (ed.) (1985), *European immigration policy: a comparative study*. Cambridge: Cambridge University Press.

Hammar, T. (1990), *Democracy and the Nation State. Aliens, Denizens and Citizens in a World of International Migration*. Aldershot: Ashgate.

Hampshire, J. (2005), *Citizenship and Belonging. Immigration and the Politics of Demographic Governance in Post-war Britain*. Basingstoke: Palgrave.

Hansen, R. (2002), 'Globalization, Embedded Realism, and Path Dependence. The Other Immigrants to Europe', *Comparative Political Studies* 35 (3): 259-283.

Hansen, R. & P. Weil (eds.) (2001a), *Towards a European Nationality. Citizenship, Immigration and Nationality Law in the EU*. Basingstoke: Palgrave.

Hansen, R. & P. Weil (2001b), 'Introduction: Citizenship, Immigration and Nationality: Towards a Convergence in Europe?', in R. Hansen & P. Weil (eds.), *Towards a European Nationality. Citizenship, Immigration and Nationality Law in the EU*, 1-24. Basingstoke: Palgrave.

Hansen, R. & P. Weil (2002), 'Dual Citizenship in A Changed World: Immigration, Gender and Social Rights', in R. Hansen & P. Weil (eds.), *Dual Nationality, Social Rights and Federal Citizenship in the U.S. and Europe. The Reinvention of Citizenship*, 1-15. New York etc.: Berghahn Books.

Heelsum, A. van (2004), 'Political participation and civic community of ethnic minorities in four cities in the Netherlands', *Politics*, vol. 25 (1): 19-30.

Hoerder, D. (2002), *Cultures in Contact: World Migrations in the Second Millennium*. Durham: Duke University Press.

Howard, M. (2005), 'Variation in Dual Citizenship Policies in the Countries of the EU', *International Migration Review* 39 (3): 697-720.

Itzigsohn, J. (2000), 'Immigration and the Boundaries of Citizenship: The Institutions of Immigrants' Political Transnationalism', *International Migration Review* 34 (4): 1126-1154.

Jacobs, D. and J. Tillie (eds.) (2004), 'Social Capital and Political Integration of Migrants', Special Issue of *Journal of Ethnic and Migrations Studies*, vol. 30, no. 3.

Joppke, C. (2001), 'The Legal-Domestic Sources of Immigrant Rights', *Comparative Political Studies* 34 (4): 339-366.

Joppke, C. (2005), *Selecting by Origin: Ethnic Migration in the Liberal State*. Cambridge, MA: Harvard University Press.

Kogan, I. (2003), 'Ex-Yugoslavs in the Austrian and Swedish Labour Markets: The Significance of the Period of Migration and the Effect of the Acquisition of Citizenship', *Journal of Ethnic and Migration Studies* 29 (4): 595-622.

Kostakopoulou, D. (2003), 'Why Naturalisation?', *Perspectives on European Politics and Society* 4 (1): 85-115.

Kibreab, G. (2003), 'Citizenship Rights and Repatriation of Refugees', *International Migration Review* 37 (1): 24-73.

Kleger, H. (ed.) (1997), *Transnationale Staatsbürgerschaft*. Frankfurt/Main: Campus.

Kymlicka, W. & A. Patten (eds.) (2003), *Language Rights and Political Theory*. Oxford: Oxford University Press.

Levitt, P. (2001), *The Transnational Villagers*. Berkeley, CA: University of California Press.

Levy, D. & Y. Weiss (eds.) (2002), *Challenging Ethnic Citizenship. German and Israeli Perspectives on Immigration*. Oxford: Berghahn.

Liegl, B., B. Perchinig & B. Weyss (2004), *Combating Ethnic and Religious Discrimination in Employment. From the EU and International Perpective*. Brussels: European Network Against Racism. www.enar-eu.org.

López-Guerra, C. (2005), 'Should Expatriates Vote?' *Journal of Political Philosophy* 13 (2): 216-234.

Mansbridge, J. (2001), 'What Does a Representative Do? Descriptive Representation in Communicative Settings of Distrust, Uncrystallized Interests, and Historically Denigrated Status', in W. Kymlicka & W. Norman (eds.), *Citizenship in Diverse Societies*, 99-123. Oxford: Oxford University Press.

Marshall, T. H. (1965), 'Citizenship and Social Class', in T. H. Marshall, *Class, Citizenship, and Social Development. Essays by T. H. Marshall*. New York: Anchor Books.

Martin, D. A. & K. Hailbronner (eds.) (2003), *Rights and Duties of Dual Nationals: Evolution and Prospects*. The Hague: Kluwer Law International.

Martiniello, M. (1997), 'Quelle participation politique?', in M.-T. Coenen & R. Lewin (eds.), *La Belgique et ses immigrés – Les politiques manquées*, 101-120. Bruxelles: De Boeck Université.

Michalowski, I. (2004), *An Overview on Introduction Programmes in Seven European member states*. The Hague: Adviescommissie voor Vreemdelingenzaken.

Migrants' Forum (1996), 'Proposals for the Revision of the Treaty on European Union at the Intergovernmental Conference of 1996', *The Forum Series* 2.

Moch, L. P. (1992), *Moving Europeans. Migration in Western Europe since 1650*. Urbana: Indiana University Press.

Münz, R. & R. Ohliger (eds.) (2003), *Diasporas and Ethnic Migrants: Germany, Israel and Post-Soviet Successor States in Comparative Perspective*. London: Frank Cass.

Nyberg Sørensen, N. & K. F. Olwig (eds.) (2002), *Work and Migration – Life and Livelihoods in a Globalizing World*. London: Routledge.

Østergaard-Nielsen, E. (2003), *Transnational Politics. Turks and Kurds in Germany*. London: Routledge.

Perchinig, B. (2003), *Politische und rechtliche Rahmenbedingungen für betriebliche Antidiskriminierungspolitik in ausgewählten Ländern*. Studie im Auftrag des Europäischen Zentrums für Wohlfahrtspolitik und Sozialforschung für das EQUAL-Projekt 'Gleiche Chancen im Betrieb'. www.euro.centre.org/equal.

Phillips, A. (1995), *The Politics of Presence*. Oxford: Oxford University Press.

Pitkin, H. F. (1967), *The Concept of Representation*. Berkeley: University of California Press.

Portes, A. (ed.) (2001), 'New Research and Theory on Immigrant Transnationalism', Special Issue, *Global Networks* 1 (3).

Preuss, U. K., M. Everson, M. Koenig-Archibugi & E. Lefebrvre (2003), 'Traditions of Citizenship in the European Union', *Citizenship Studies* 7 (1): 3-14.

Pries, L. (ed.) (1997), *Transnationale Migration. Soziale Welt*. Sonderband 12. Baden-Baden: Nomos.

Rallu, J. L. (2004), 'Access to citizenship and integration of migrants: Lessons from the French case', paper presented at the *twelfth conference of the Australian Population Association*, Canberra, 15-17 September 2004. www.acsr.anu.edu.au/APA2004.

Rubio-Marín, R. (2000), *Immigration as a Democratic Challenge. Citizenship and Inclusion in Germany and the United States*. Cambridge: Cambridge University Press.

Rummens, J. A. (2003), 'Conceptualising Identity and Diversity: Overlaps, Intersections, and Processes', *Canadian Ethnic Studies* 35 (3): 10-25.

Saggar, S. (ed.) (1998), *Race and British Electoral Politics*. London: UCL Press.

Schmitter, P. (2000), *How to Democratize the Union – and Why Bother*. Lanham, MD: Rowman and Littlefield.

Scott, K. (2004), 'The Economics of Citizenship. Is there a Naturalization Premium?', paper presented at the conference '*Immigrant Ascension to Citizenship: Recent Policies and Economic and Social Consequences*', International conference organised under the auspices of the Willy Brandt Guest Professorship's Chair International Migration and Ethnic Relations, Malmö University, 7 June 2004.

Sicakkan, H. & Y. Lithman (eds.) (2005), *Changing the Basis of Citizenship in the Modern State. Political Theory and the Politics of Diversity*. Lewiston, NY: Edwin Mellen Press.

Simeant, J. (1997), *La cause des sans-papiers*. Paris: Presses de Science Po.

Soininen, M. (1999), 'The "Swedish Model" as an institutional framework for immigrant membership rights', *Journal of Ethnic and Migration Studies* 25 (4): 685-702.

Soysal, Y. (1994), *Limits of Citizenship. Migrants and Postnational Membership in Europe*. Chicago etc.: University of Chicago Press.

Thränhardt, D. (2000), 'Tainted Blood: The Ambivalence of "Ethnic" Migration in Israel, Japan, Korea, Germany and the United States', *German Policy/Politikfeldanalyse* 3. spaef.com/GPS_PUB/vin3.html.

Tillie, J. (1998), 'Explaining Migrant Voting Behaviour in the Netherlands. Combining the Electoral Research and Ethnic Studies Perspective', *Revue Européenne des Migrations Internationales* 14 (2): 71-95.

Tyson, A. (2001), 'The Negotiation of the European Community Directive on Racial Discrimination', *European Journal of Migration Law* 3: 111-229.

Waldrauch, H. & Dilek Çinar (2003), 'Staatsbürgerschaftspolitik und Einbürgerungspraxis in Österreich', in H. Fassmann & I. Stacher (eds.), *Österreichischer Migrations- und Integrationsbericht. Demographische Entwicklungen – Sozioökonomische Strukturen – Rechtliche Rahmenbedingungen*, 261-283. Klagenfurt/Celovec: Drava.

Wiener, A. (1997), 'Making sense of the new geography of citizenship: Fragmented citizenship in the European Union', *Theory and Society* 26: 529-560.

Wihtol de Wenden, C. W. (1988), *Les immigrés et la politique*. Paris: Presses de la Fondation Nationale des Sciences Politiques.

Wunderlich, T. (2005), *Die neuen Deutschen. Subjektive Dimensionen des Einbürgerungsprozesses*. Stuttgart: Lucius & Lucius.

Zappala, G. & S. Castles (2000), 'Citizenship and Immigration in Australia', in A. T. Aleinikoff & D. Klusmeyer (eds.), *From Migrants to Citizens. Membership in a Changing World*, 32-81. Washington DC: Carnegie Endowment for International Peace.

5. Migrants' Work, Entrepreneurship and Economic Integration

Michael Bommes and Holger Kolb

1. Introduction

Although economic issues have not been the centrepiece of migration research in the last decades,[1] quite an amount of scientific material, literature and empirical data from different theoretical starting points has been accumulated dealing with topics of economic integration. The aim of this chapter is to provide a 'state of the art' by sifting the milestones of the existing literature focusing on economic approaches, and to structure them in a way that allows us to identify strengths and weaknesses of economic as well as non-economic approaches to the field of work, entrepreneurship and economic integration.[2]

In a first step we develop a heuristic framework that serves as the vantage point allowing us to distinguish and organise the types of conceptualisations and different theories dealing with economic integration. Secondly, the centrepiece of this report then reviews approaches and theories treating the (three) topics listed in the title.

In doing so the economy and economics take centre stage.[3] This does not imply that only economists can do proper research in this field. It just implies that any analysis (regardless of its disciplinary background) has to rely on some kind of analytical scheme that connects the different approaches to economic approaches and to the general theoretical discussions in this field. The status of this report therefore is a reflexive one: discussion of the dominant economic topics and methodologies in this research area that any disciplinary or interdisciplinary approach in this field should be aware of. Issues related to work, entrepreneurship and economic integration are of major importance for any migration research effort, even if this does not imply that one needs to be an economist to do research in this field.

2. Economic integration – a heuristic frame

Any operationalisation of the meaning of 'work, entrepreneurship and economic integration' should start from what economists have made available already. The economists Thomas Bauer, John Haisken-DeNew and Christoph Schmidt have recently provided a systematic review and classification of economic migration research (Bauer et al. 2004). The authors identify three broad lines of research: The first line is dedicated to the analysis of factors determining the decision to migrate; the second line concentrates on the economic performance of immigrants in the destination countries; the third line focuses on the impact of immigration on the economy and especially its macroeconomic effects in the destination countries (Bauer et al. 2004: 5-6).

Such a descriptive classification indeed allows us to cover most of the relevant literature of economic migration research. In this chapter we choose a different approach: We will try to order and describe the existing approaches and their different theoretical and definitional assumptions systematically in relation to an explicit understanding of 'economic integration'. In order to do this it is appropriate to start from some very basics of economic theory. In such theory the price mechanism is regarded as the most decisive precondition for the effective and efficient allocation of resources and the maximum provision of goods and services. Prices are important for processes of market clearing, for the information of the market participants about the relative scarcity of certain goods and services, for the coordination of supply and demand and for the sanctioning of those who are not willing to pay. The function economic theory assigns to the price mechanism can be taken as a valuable first heuristic hint for a simple operationalisation of our central term 'economic integration': We define economic integration as the general ability to pay and the effort to gain this ability by either selling services or goods. Seen in this way, every action in the realm of the economy is formally reduced to the question if an individual is willing or able to pay for goods and services and to secure the reproduction of this ability.[4] Definitions, such as the 'ability to pay' and 'the capacity of maintenance of this ability', are rather technical and the concomitant 'balancing of the individual budget restriction with the utility maximising combination of goods and services' is certainly a very abstract conceptualisation of economic integration. But applied to migration research they allow for modifications and re-specifications (e.g. the 'ability to sustain oneself'). Functional equivalents like social transfers and welfare state arrangements which bypass market mechanisms can be easily grasped in this frame.

Starting from this definition[5] it becomes clear that the two terms 'work' and 'entrepreneurship' describe the most relevant options of obtaining the 'ability to pay'. Economic integration therefore functions as the umbrella term for work and entrepreneurship. Relying on work individuals sell their manpower as a factor of production and obtain wages in return. Self-employment means combining production factors

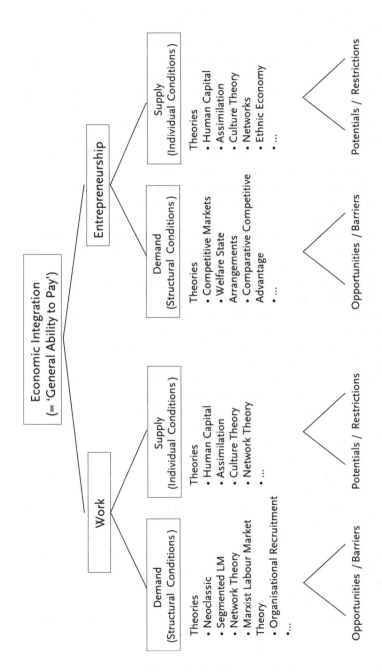

Graph 1. Heuristic scheme for mapping theoretical approaches

as a tool to gain revenues. Both strategies aim at economic integration in the sense defined above.

Based on the heuristic approach outlined above we try to map the field by summarising the most relevant research approaches. The two modes of economic integration of migrants in the most general sense, i.e. work or entrepreneurship, can be further differentiated if we distinguish socio-structural and individual conditions of work or entrepreneurship. Research approaches focus primarily either on socio-structural or individual conditions of work and entrepreneurship. This applies to both economic and non-economic approaches in migration research.

The general differentiation between socio-structural and individualistic approaches (in recent years often labelled 'rational choice') can be applied to both work and self-employment. Structural theories identify the demand/supply mechanism and its structural peculiarities as the economic core condition, whereas from the perspective of individualistic approaches, structural conditions are conceptualised as constraints or opportunities for individual action.

Under the heading of structural theoretical approaches variants derived from the neoclassical paradigm, segmentation theories, Marxist considerations and network theories can be subsumed. Under individualistic approaches, human capital considerations and assimilation theories are the most relevant ones. The same classification can be applied to the field of 'entrepreneurship': 'economic integration' via self-employment can be analysed either from a structural or from an individual point of view. In the first case, structural conditions of the market and its inherent incentives, opportunities and barriers are investigated and interpreted as the decisive parameters for the performance and success of entrepreneurship. In the second case, the question of what the individual (migrant) entrepreneur is able to supply, his specific abilities and equipment can be regarded as crucial to assess investment and self-employment.

In the next section we first discuss approaches dealing with 'work', i.e. conditions of integration in the labour market. Most of the research has concentrated on this side of 'economic integration'. More than 90 per cent of the active population receive income by entering so-called dependent employment relations. This applies to all Western industrial countries. 'Work' therefore refers to the most relevant strategy in the past and the future for individuals to secure their 'economic integration'. This holds true also for the overwhelming majority of the migrant population.[6] For this reason the bulk of research on 'economic integration' of migrants concentrates on the labour market focusing either on the structural conditions of markets or on the capacity of individuals to match the requirements of these markets.

The section on 'entrepreneurship' will be much briefer. The theoretical contributions from political economy and the body of economic literature on 'entrepreneurship' as the second principal option of economic integration are much smaller than on 'work'. In the survey of Bauer, Haisken-DeNew and Schmidt comments on entrepreneurship are completely absent. In contrast, the social scientists Rath and Kloosterman ascertain that 'immigrant and ethnic entrepreneurship' has become a 'recurrent theme at international conferences run by anthropologists, historians, sociologists and geographers' (Kloosterman & Rath 2003), however without referring to economists.[7] One reason for this is certainly the fact that the overwhelming majority of the foreign population in all countries studied enter dependent employment relations and only a relatively small percentage act as entrepreneurs (Rath 2002: 4). This disequilibrium of research, however, may also be based in the internal division of labour of the academic discipline of economics, i.e. the sub-disciplinary differentiation between political economy on the one hand, dealing mainly with the conditions and constraints of the allocation of scarce resources, and business studies on the other hand, focusing on organisational and technical decision making processes in companies. Within economic theory, the discussion of internal structures of enterprises and entrepreneurship are therefore mainly ceded to the subfield of business studies, which so far has done little research on migrant entrepreneurship. Economic studies focusing on the individual preconditions of successful or failing migrant entrepreneurship are largely missing as well.

The internal division of labour between the economic sub-disciplines has also some effects on economic research related to work. In much of the research the focus is on labour markets. 'Work', however, is defined more broadly as the successful entrance of membership roles in organisations and the acceptance of the social expectations combined with these membership roles. Economic research on 'work', as labour market research, leaves out to a large extent these organisational conditions of economic integration.[8] However, this is not unique for economic research: Other social science disciplines also tend to neglect both organisations as a main site of integration and the large research tradition of organisational research. We note this here as one major desideratum concerning 'work, entrepreneurship and economic integration'.

A final note: Some of the theories referred to in the next sections have not received much attention in migration research so far. It seems however to us that they have some potential to be made fruitful for the analysis of processes of migration and integration.

3. Mapping work

Structural approaches

The oldest, most traditional and prominent economic theoretical approach in migration research is based on the *neoclassical paradigm*, originally developed by Alfred Marshall (1890/1920) and Leon Walras (1877/1965).[9] According to this approach the economy is not primarily regarded as a closed and self-contained system, but rather as a method of optimisation applicable to the whole society. For an assessment of the neoclassical paradigm in migration theory it is useful to differentiate between macro- and micro-analytical approaches (Kalter 1997: 16; Massey et al. 1993).[10]

Already Ravenstein's early work on the 'laws of migration' (Ravenstein 1885), developed on the basis of census data at the end of the 19th century, can be traced back to this approach. The most general proposition of the neoclassical approach is that migration is an effect of disequilibria on the labour market or generally spoken of market failure and imperfect factor allocation. Existing wage differentials between the labour markets of two different countries induce incentives to migrate. Migration as a special mode of factor reallocation leads to the re-establishment of the equilibrium on the labour market: 'International immigration of income-maximising persons is simply another way of ensuring that factor prices are equalised across countries.'[11]

An interesting modification of this concept has been proposed by Todaro (1980). He argues that the decision to migrate should not only be derived from existing, immediate wage differentials. It is rather based on the comparison of the expected and anticipated future incomes in the destination and the home country. The larger the planning interval in which the different possible incomes can be compared, the bigger the probability that the wages that can be obtained in urban regions exceed the income that can be earned in rural regions. This is even true in the case of a possible intermediate unemployment in urban regions. Migration thus can also be a rational decision in the case of rising unemployment, because 'the greater the difference in economic opportunities between urban and rural regions, the greater the flow of migrants from rural to urban areas.' (Todaro 1980: 377)

The arguments of neoclassical authors on the micro-level depart from the same theoretical starting points and differ only by emphasising the individual cost-benefit calculation (Sjastaad 1962). Individuals seek to maximise their benefits and migrate to those places where they expect the biggest returns: 'Individuals migrate because it is in their benefit [...] to do so.' (Borjas 1989: 457).[12] The decisive mechanism steering the migration decision is the market. The immigration market coordinates the allocation of migrants (in technical terms: the production factor labour) to different countries dependent on variables like economic conditions in the home and destination country, immigration policies and individual characteristics of the migrants like age, gender, skills and family relations (Borjas 1988).

Neoclassical approaches dominate economic migration theory particularly in the USA. There has been an intensive debate between two neoclassical economists, George Borjas and Julian Simon, about the implications of immigration for the USA for a few years (Borjas 1990; Simon 1989).[13] Borjas argues that increasing immigration leads to some kind of dilution of the stock of human capital of American society. In his view this leads to a growing concentration of wealth and poverty and, in between, to a shrinking middle class. Contrary to Borjas one of the leading 'admissionists', Simon, claims an 'economic advancement for the community' induced by additional migration, because 'immigrants work harder, save more, have a higher propensity to start new business, and are more likely to innovate' (Simon 1989: 103-104).[14] This debate is by no means finished. It demonstrates, however, the productivity of the neoclassical migration theory initiating competitive and innovative debates about the meaning of empirical findings.

An important modification of the pure neoclassical model has been proposed by the 'New Economics of Migration', Oded Stark being its main proponent. This approach modifies the level of analysis. Not the individual actor, but his or her family are conceptualised as the decisive unit of decision (Mincer 1978). According to this approach labour migration is not so much a direct effect of wage differentials between certain regions or countries, but rather the result of the failure of existing markets for capital and insurances (Stark 1991; Stark & Taylor 1991). Due to the brittleness of markets for certain goods, families have to rely on other resources: 'It is here the rural-to-urban migration by the most suitable family member – a mature son or daughter (especially if educated) – comes into the picture. In bypassing the credit and insurance markets [...] migration facilitates the transformation; it succeeds in doing this via its dual role in the accumulation of investment capital [...], usually generating significant urban-to-rural flows of remittances, and, through diversification of income resources, controlling the level of risk' (Stark 1991: 11). The 'New Migration Economics' interprets migration as a collective strategy of capital accumulation of the relevant household. It can be regarded as a strategy of 'portfolio diversification' (Stark 1991: 48) which allows the minimisation of risk by its diversification (Massey et al. 1993: 439; Mahmood & Schömann 2002: 4; Spaan 1999). This approach can be considered as one of the most coherent enhancements of the neoclassical approaches.

The neoclassical paradigm has been confronted with much criticism and sometimes even hostility. The precursors of this approach have been the main targets of Marx's trenchant attacks on the 'bourgeois science' and his 'Marxist' followers have recurrently identified other neoclassical approaches as an outcome of the ideological blind spots of this 'bourgeois science'.

Marxist labour market approaches have been influential in one way or another in different versions of migration and economic research. For instance segmentation theories (see below) inherit Marxist assumptions although there are also non-Marxist approaches.[15] In particular, the labour migration of the 1960s and 1970s induced new research efforts of Marxist theorists due to the general revival of Marxism in the social sciences as an effect of '1968'. In the Marxist tradition, labour migration is seen as a phenomenon that visualises the relevant core structures of capitalist societies. Thus Marxist approaches have never been economic in a strict disciplinary sense but conceptualised migration rather in a frame that was understood as a theory of society, i.e. the modern capitalist society.

Labour migration is seen as a special facet of the international relations of exploitation and inequality, a case of empirical evidence for the reality of international class relations.[16] On the one hand, Marxist approaches employ a similar understanding of economic integration as has been proposed in the introductory section: In capitalist societies individuals are forced to sell their labour power on markets as a commodity in order to gain 'the ability to pay' for the necessary means of reproduction. Since the entrance of markets is conceptualised as a relation of exploitation, economic integration in capitalist societies refers to a 'social scandal': Exploitation, is the basis for the emergence and reproduction of social inequality conceptualised as class differences. The modern society is hence defined as a capitalist class society.

Marxist approaches reserve 'integration' in its positive meaning in the end for a societal situation which does not rely on exploitation structurally built into the capitalist market relations. These approaches have therefore often seen an extra need to explain why and how these relations of exploitation are reproduced even by the exploited themselves. This is explained by an internal division of the working classes based on the internationally unequal relations of exploitation which privilege certain segments of the class in the advanced societies and create internal hierarchies. Inside of the richer countries the role of ideologies is seen as central and several approaches refer to nationalism and racism (Balibar & Wallerstein 1991).

Since the collapse of socialism in Eastern Europe, Marxist approaches have lost ground, not only in the discipline of economics[17]. This should not however be taken as an indicator of the complete irrelevance of this tradition. Several elements and assumptions of this tradition have found their place in approaches which operate under different names and they can be traced in the work of quite a number of still highly relevant approaches as will be seen when we turn now to labour market segmentation theories.

Among the most influential approaches that take issue with the neo-classical assumptions discussed above are *segmentation theories*, most prominently developed and formulated by Michael J. Piore. Segmentation theories put a strong emphasis on the structural dimension, especially the demand side of the labour market.[18] They reject the neoclassical assumption that migration will lead to a general equilibrium on the labour market. Instead they assume a strong segmentation of the labour market into a secure primary[19] and an instable, insecure but flexible secondary labour market that functions 'only as residuum for those employees that do not match the criteria required' (Lärm 1982: 175). In a broader sense segmentation theories can be counted as a type of institutionalist approach (Richter 2003; Keller 1993: 241).[20] The demand for labour is anchored in the structural traits of the labour market which are the basis for the continuous requirement of temporary immigration in the secondary labour market (Haug 2000: 3). In this view, the permanent demand for labour is not dependent on the conjunctural cycle but closely interrelated with the economic structure of advanced industrial economies.

Further differences between this approach and the neoclassical paradigm are based in the different conceptualisations of market relations. Segmentation theories do not regard wages as the only relevant parameter, which determines the supply-demand relationship. Factors like status and prestige are seen as equally relevant and have been integrated into the theoretical model. This assumption is derived from the observation that, even in the case of labour shortages, wages cannot easily be enhanced because such enhancements would endanger existing hierarchies (Lebhardt 2002: 13). According to segmentation theories the entry in specific labour market segments thus proves to be connected with specific restrictions based on different labour conditions and earnings (Sengenberger 1987: 52).

The importation of foreign labour is regarded as a functional substitute for the deficit of flexibility, which results from the structure of segmented labour markets. Foreign workers provide this flexibility since they are regarded as those who work for lower wages and do not enter the existing hierarchies and the relations of status and prestige linked with them (Parnreiter 2001: 60). They constitute their own underclass separated from the other segments of the labour market.[21] These lower segments of the labour market are not attractive for indigenous workers who can escape from them based on status and prestige provided by education and welfare transfers. The workforce in these segments consists mainly of labour migrants since for this group the option to

earn money is the main decisive parameter. They disregard other factors like reputation and status and are perceived as suitable candidates
for these kinds of positions, because they plan to return home after
having earned a certain amount of money. Immigrants are therefore
perceived as 'target earners' (Piore 1979, p. 95)[22] who have a rather instrumental relationship with their job. They separate their social role
and their economic role and thus are willing to accept work and working conditions that are not accepted from the indigenous population.
Especially Piore constructs a close relationship between social status
and the identity of the labourer. Migrants that remain in the host country are in that perspective 'failing migrants'. It is an effect of the role of
the migrant in the economic system of the destination country which
is based on the presupposed aim of temporary stay (Hillmann 1997:
13).

The structural demand for such a type of labour in advanced industrial economies leads to the emergence and stabilisation of a dual economy characterised by a capital-intensive primary segment and a labour-
intensive secondary segment. Labour in the primary sector is regarded
as human capital and is similar to capital seen as a factor of production
and investment. Labour in the secondary segment is mainly low skilled
and treated as substitutable. Migrants are restricted to these segments
of the labour market and behave like 'birds of passage'. International
migration is thus the result of the joint recruitment efforts of governments and companies in advanced industrial economies: 'Recruitment
[...] explains why one region develops significant out-migration, and another, essentially comparable in terms of income, transportation costs,
culture, and labour-force characteristics, never does so.' (Piore 1979:
24).[23]

Segmentation theories draw their empirical evidence from the state
programmes of foreign labour recruitment in the 1960s and 1970s.[24]
According to segmentation theories this demand for foreign labour
was not an effect of different wage levels or different purchasing power
parities but of the structural demand of the economy (Massey et al.
1993: 444): 'It is the employers, not the workers, and the jobs, not the
incomes, that are strategic.' (Piore 1979: 19). Price elasticity of the factor labour in that segment plays a minor role, wages do not react to
changing relations of shortages and remain low because of the institutional arrangements on segmented markets.[25]

We conclude this section with a few remarks on limitations of segmentation theories. The most prominent approaches of Piore, Edwards
and Sengenberger have been developed in a historical context, which at
least in Europe was characterised by prosperity and the extension of
the welfare state. From a contemporary perspective, segmentation theories appear to be time- and context-bound approaches with a limited

applicability under changing contextual conditions. The arrangements, which these theories point to, have been under growing pressure during the 1980s and 1990s. Under conditions of globalisation, gained status and prestige on labour markets erode even if this happens to a non-homogenous degree and in different ways on various parts of labour markets. These changes affect wage levels, the stability and permanence of employment, i.e. the standardised models of employment relations (Castells 1996: 268) on the one hand, and the social chances to refuse labour inappropriate to the claimed status that was politically backed up by the extended welfare states on the other hand.[26] Thus migration in Europe must be interpreted for several reasons as one element in this process of erosion of status rights or (in the words of Esping-Anderson 1993) the recommodification of the labour force – contrary precisely to Piore's assumption that international migration consolidates them:

1. Labour migrants of the 1960s and 1970s settled more and more and were by no means the 'birds of passage' as they had been conceptualised by segmentation theories – and in this way these theories failed already empirically. These migrants settled and became denizens, i.e. they gained access to most civil, political and social rights formerly restricted to citizens (Hammar 1989). In this same process, they became part of the labour population with a high risk of unemployment and a high propensity to become welfare receivers – based on their status as denizens. Linked with the failure of large parts of the second and third generations in the education systems and their reduced chances of employment, this provided the context for current political debates in nearly all European countries on the risks and costs of failing social integration of migrants.

2. The labour migrants were no 'birds of passages' indeed but labour market segmentation has been reproduced precisely on this ground: European welfare states spent large amounts of their budgets for the sustenance of the unemployed part of the indigenous and resident migrant population parallel to the employment of migrants on a seasonal or contract basis. These forms served to restrict the further growth of denizens and to secure the return of these successive migrants, i.e. to preserve their status as 'birds of passage'. European welfare states have attracted migrants for about 25 years parallel to the financing of a high level of unemployment. Under the conditions of globalisation and international competition, welfare states have more and more lost this capacity to pay for the reproduction of status and therefore this arrangement seems currently to come to an end linked with two correlated tendencies: a) the emergence of differentiated migrations and migration policies allowing for the widely approved complementary immigration of highly

skilled persons[27] and for seasonal migrations and contract labour on a strongly regulated basis whereas the permanent immigration of low skilled workers is largely disapproved. The backside of this is the growth of irregular migrations (Bommes 2006); b) the deregulation of labour markets and the lowering of welfare standards and status rights. This can be interpreted as a process of deinstitutionalisation of status and prestige, i.e. of precisely those structures which have been identified by segmentation approaches as characteristic for 'advanced industrial societies'. In this sense they become 'postindustrial societies'.

We interpret these recent developments as an instructive context for a comparative discussion of neoclassical and segmentation approaches: Neoclassical approaches gain new evidence precisely in the context of the recent restructurings of labour markets and welfare states. Globalisation – certainly a much too general catch-all term – refers to the enforcement of market mechanisms in global horizons of reference and its effect is the restriction of the political capacity of the welfare state to secure status and prestige because national welfare states have to take into account economic conditions beyond the scope of their territorially limited sovereignty.

Network approaches have gained prominence during the last two decades in many academic fields and various scientific disciplines (Emirbayer & Goodwin 1994; Trenzzini 1998; Weyer 2000). In the field of economics the transaction cost theory can be regarded as the most influential theoretical approach dealing with characteristics and elements of network theory. For migration research the transaction cost approach has gained relevance especially in the field of highly skilled migration. Many recent studies have pointed in the case of highly skilled migration to a rising share of intra-organisational movements (Wolter 1997; Salt 1988, 1992; Kolb 2004; Ford 1992; Straubhaar & Wolter 1997; Peixoto 2001).[28] Transaction costs are taken into consideration as a decisive factor since it seems that: 'the internal provision of goods and services displays the most efficient institutional arrangement. This is because in this case it is possible to save ex-ante transaction costs and to effect flexible adjustments of the conditions of production.' (Ebers & Gotsch 1993: 231).[29] This type of labour turnover costs contradict the neoclassical presumption of perfect markets (March 1990: 3). Lower costs of searching, decision, bargaining, control and handling are seen as structural advantages of internal labour allocations in comparison to external recruitment.[30] 'Large organisations require individuals able to offer more general management skills across many different divisions or locations. Often these skills are more specific to the organisation than they are to any one task or responsibility [...]. Individuals can find their skills applicable within the internal labour market of their employing organisation but *relatively unsaleable outside'* (Ford 1992: 3).[31] Internal labour market allocation often results in a higher degree of commitment to the company and – derived from that – in decreasing recruitment, screening and training costs (see Layard et al. 1991: 153 and Gould & Findlay 1994: 22).[32] Continuous flows of highly skilled executive personnel lead according to the interpretation of Edström and Galbraith to an increasing identification of these employees with their company. And because of the regular company internal mobility, international network structures among executive employees emerge. Both elements allow the reduction of control mechanisms and the conversion to a more decentralised and more efficient mode of management (Edström & Galbraith 1979; Galbraith & Edström 1976).[33]

Economic research stressing the relevance of networks can further be found in studies which deal with the emergence of so-called clusters, which are defined as a 'set of actors and interactions' (Berwert et al. 2004).[34] The main line of argument here is that successful enterprises use networks as mechanisms of trust building and absorption of insecurity with the result of the emergence and stabilisation of trust. These approaches are dealing with problems of resource recruitment. They have not, however, been explicitly dealing with issues of international migration.

We conclude this section on network approaches with a rather general methodological remark on the different and often ambivalent status of network concepts used in the literature. This concept has gained a central role in many studies of different disciplines trying to explain the size, stability and continuity of international migration on labour markets and the resulting social structures (Gurak & Caces 1992; Faist 2000, Massey 1998, Vertovec 2001). At the same time networks have become an element of the social semantics of self-description of modern society. A systematic complexity and imprecision arises from this multiple prominence of the network concept: the network approach refers on the one hand to a method which is claimed to be generally applicable to the formal analysis of social structures. To explain social actions it is epistemologically assumed that any action is socially embedded (Granovetter 1985).[35] Seen in this way networks define the final social reality, i.e. they are a non-contingent social phenomenon (Tacke 2000). The aim of this type of network research is the analysis of the formal structures of networks, meanwhile a comprehensive research tradition.[36] On the other hand, migration research barely links with this type of research and its frequently criticised formalism and there is a simple reason for that: In the field of migration research networks are conceptualised as remarkable, i.e. contingent phenomena. Net-

works are therefore referred to as only one among other socio-structural conditions of modern society. Social networks have gained prominence precisely for the reason that they affect more or less all of the
various differentiated realms of society. Accordingly, policy, entrepreneur, administration, innovation as well as migration networks have
become the subject of research (Marsh 1998; Heidling 2000; Ladeur
1993; Kowol & Krohn 1995). One problem of this type of research is,
however, that these networks are identified by reference to the realms
in which they are seen as relevant. In other words, they are identified
by giving them a name. Therefore in many cases it remains pretty un-
clear what kind of social structure precisely the term network refers to.
Thus it also remains open which socio-structural developments allow
networks to gain so much impact, as is proposed by recent network
studies. Migration research based on network approaches therefore
needs to answer at least the three following questions: What precisely
is referred to by the term network? Which social contexts trigger the
emergence, reproduction and stabilisation of networks? Why do networks gain the structural importance often fairly generally ascribed to
them? (Bommes & Tacke 2005, 2006). These kinds of questions can
serve as a reflexive device in research making use of network concepts.

Individualistic Approaches

Human capital theories can be regarded as the most influential and relevant approaches on the individual level. Using the microeconomic
frame of migration theory they attend to a question that in the macro
perspectives is left unanswered: Why do some individuals migrate,
while most others do not? (Taylor & Martin 2002). Human capital theories depart from the assumption that individual actions are based on
rational decisions and expectations.[37] Migration is seen as the result of
the aim to guarantee an optimal provision with economic goods and
services. The main difference between the macro- and microeconomic
approach is its focus: the latter centres the analysis on the individual
and his or her endowment with human capital. This version thus dis-
penses with aggregated rates and ratios:[38] Migration must be regarded
'as an investment increasing the productivity of human resources, an
investment which has costs and which also renders returns' (Sjaastad
1962: 83). Human capital theory in the tradition of Gary Becker (1975)
[39] summarises the stock of knowledge, abilities and characteristics of
an individual that influences his or her productivity. Human capital is
accumulated via education and training and therefore also depends on
the environmental conditions of investment (training facilities, aspirations of parents and siblings, unemployment rate, infrastructure).[40]
Becker differentiates between two forms of human capital. General hu-

man capital is applicable in many places, occupations and jobs. This generalised knowledge is made accessible by institutionalised apprenticeship systems and training programmes, study courses or on-the-job-training. Specific human capital is bound to contexts such as a certain employer, occupation or sector and is acquired by company internal training and work experience. Here linkages can be found between the micro-analytical approach and transaction cost theory. Transaction cost advantages of internal personnel allocations are closely linked to the advantages of specific human capital accumulation. Company internal transfers allow for both the coordination of transaction cost minimisation with specific human capital allocation and the maintenance of a symbiotic relation between the interests of the company and the interests of the employee.[41] Seen in this way, highly skilled migration is not exclusively based on patterns of demand, but also displays an element of supply.[42]

Human capital theory has been used to describe the position of migrants on labour markets in various respects. It is a very common approach to explain the underprivileged position of labour migrants on labour markets (see for example Kalter & Granato 2004, Seifert 1995; Schlotböller & Van Suntum 2002; Lang 2004). Many of the studies on highly skilled migration in the last two decades (Salt 1983; Salt & Findlay 1989) display important features of human capital theory. Mobility and stays abroad are explained as necessary steps in the human capital accumulation process, seen as a sequential process of career building driven by efforts of upward mobility. For many multinational companies temporary employment abroad has become institutionalised as a requirement in the process of career development.[43] In this context the differentiation between company-specific and generalised human capital is applied (Becker 1975).[44]

Human capital approaches also play an important role in studies on ethnic entrepreneurs. Self-employment is regarded then as a sequence in a long-term investment process in the stock of human capital. This may, however, be a theoretically induced optimistic reading of what may also be interpreted in many cases as a resort to the last remaining option.

Assimilation as a concept in migration research is barely used in the economic context and is rather present in discussions about appropriate strategies of governmental 'integration policies'.[45] The focus of assimilationists dealing with issues of migrant economic integration, however, is mainly on the dynamic development of the relative wage position of different migrant workforces in the country of destination (Bauer et al. 2004: 25; Bauer & Zimmermann 2002). Assimilation in this context refers to the relative income distances generated by dependent work in relation to the indigenous work population. Interestingly, since Chiswick's groundbreaking study (Chiswick 1978; see also Mincer 1974; Borjas 1985) *economic assimilation theory* largely relies on the human capital framework introduced above (Bauer et al. 2004: 25) and often identifies a direct correlation between the amount of human capital accumulation of immigrants and the degree of income gaps between immigrants and natives.[46] Current assimilation studies largely underline the importance of the compatibility of individual skill profiles and human capital portfolios with the requirements of the destination country. A growing wage gap between immigrants and natives is interpreted as an empirical indicator for the declining quality of immigrants and it is argued that one precondition for successful assimilation strategies is the reliance on selection procedures based on labour market oriented criteria (Bauer et al. 2000). Such strategies are, for example, employed in countries like Canada and New Zealand, but more recently also in the Czech Republic.[47]

4. Mapping entrepreneurship

Entrepreneurship is the second option of economic integration as explained above. Also here, different approaches for the analysis of the conditions and results of this type of integration focus either on the socio-structural or the individual level. For reasons, which we have briefly discussed before, however, the theoretical contributions from political economy and the body of economic literature is much smaller than on 'work'. Individualistic approaches are largely absent and it seems that economic literature on entrepreneurship has largely not been applied to the field. Instead, we find sociological and anthropological approaches dealing with 'ethnic economies' relying on network and social capital approaches.

Structural Approaches

As for socio-structural conditions, the analysis of *welfare state arrangements* has been on the agenda of research. George Borjas (1999) put the discussion of the degree of welfare dependency of immigrants on par with the other main topics of economic migration research, i.e. immigrant labour market performance and its impact on labour markets and fiscal systems. However, most studies find comparatively little evidence for the alleged connection of immigration and welfare state generosity.[48] Welfare state regulations, however, are also discussed from a different perspective. From a neoclassical point of view welfare arrangements are political interventions in markets which cause market failure as a consequence of misallocation. In particular, social security schemes are seen as the equivalent to some kind of minimum wages.[49] According to the theory of marginal productivity, the process of recruitment of labour exhibits a diminishing marginal productivity. The optimal amount of labour is hired when the productivity of the marginal labourer equals the cost of his or her recruitment (marginal productivity of labour equals the wage). Unemployment indicates that the real wage rate surmounts the real marginal productivity and only wage rate flexibility is able to restore full employment.[50] Any introduction of minimum wages therefore disrupts the labour market equilibrium and 'discriminates' (Bender et al. 1999: 3) jobs and work opportunities of a marginal productivity below these minimum wages. Welfare state arrangements impede the creation of jobs with lower wages because of the absence of a corresponding labour supply. Countries which cut off the employment of the least productive labour – via a minimum wage, trade union resistance to downward wage mobility or other forms of labour market inflexibility – certainly increase the productivity per person employed or per work hour – but at the expense of total output and indeed of unemployment. At the same time, this is the context for the emergence of informal labour markets and irregular migration providing the labour supply for employment on these markets (Schneider 2000; Enste & Schneider 2006).

Correspondingly, ethnic entrepreneurship may become relevant in this context. Welfare benefits are often restricted to citizens or longtime residents. Other immigrants are not or only partially included in different social security schemes. They may enter jobs and occupations that cannot be filled with workers from the indigenous population[51] or alternatively set-up new businesses. This may be interpreted in a more optimistic sense like in human capital theory (see above) or as a kind of 'forced entrepreneurship' (Bommes 2004; Watson et al. 2000). Faced with unemployment, entrepreneurship may have become a functional equivalent of wage labour, rather involuntarily chosen.

The concept of *mixed embeddedness* was explored quite recently by Robert Kloosterman and Jan Rath (2001) in order 'to combine agency and structure perspectives' (Kloosterman & Rath 2003: 8) and to overcome the neoclassical assumption that opportunities occur and entrepreneurs just seize them, which these authors see as oversimplified. Their approach rejects especially the neoclassical premises of market transparency and economically rational, profit-seeking actors and falls back on the results of Esping-Anderson's seminal work (Esping-Anderson 1993, 1999: 135). Adapting his conclusion of a strong correlation between the rigidities of labour markets (indicating for newcomers obstacles to enter) in advanced economies and the incidence of (non-agricultural) self-employment, Kloosterman and Rath depart from the assumption that divergent postindustrial employment trajectories are linked with patterns of resource provision either through markets, states or families. Economies are moulded by these patterns and from these emerge different opportunity structures for migrant entrepreneurship. Based on this conceptualisation a whole set of formal and informal institutions are taken into account, 'institutions mediating between aspiring entrepreneurs and concrete openings to start a business' (Kloosterman & Rath 2003: 9). This approach can be read as a demand side approach, which supplements supply side approaches often dominating the analysis of immigrant entrepreneurship.

Studies on *ethnic niches and ethnic businesses* have been mainly conducted by sociologists and social anthropologists. These studies often underline the importance of social networks[52] and social capital. Various authors highlight the role of community networks as a vital resource (Zhou 1992; Portes 1987; Light & Bonacich 1988; Waldinger 1996). They apply some of the findings of mainstream economic sociology such as the work of Granovetter (1995) to the study of ethnic entrepreneurship. Many depart from the assumption that ethnicity is used by the immigrants themselves as a tool for economic advancement within an enclave. Entrepreneurs that are active in those 'ethnic economies' are characterised by four central attributes: Their horizontal and vertical networks are placed in the same ethnic group; they rely on employees and customers of the same origin; trade creditors belong to the same ethnic community or come from the same country; additionally unpaid family work seems to be of particular importance.[53] In this view ethnic enclaves often function as catalysts for certain immigrant groups to accelerate economic integration in the host society (Portes & Bach 1985). Challenging the assimilationist assumptions these studies of ethnic economies underline the importance of ethnic and cultural capital.[54] Ethnic niches are perceived as a fruitful starting point for immigrant integration into the society of the host country and as a kind of pre-phase of assimilation (Zhou 1992). According to a case study, ethnicisation is one decisive feature in the ongoing transformation processes in New York's fast-food industry, and ethnicity must be regarded as one basic category of work force organisation in this sector (Parker 1996). In the same line many authors underline the significance of 'ethnic solidarity'.

Others are, however, much more doubtful if strategies of ethnic solidarity will be successful in the long run (Sanders & Nee 1987; Kim 1996). It should also be noted that approaches influenced by network theories are more and more criticised in recent years. On the one hand the critique points to theoretical problems (the mixed embeddedness approach criticises the one-sidedness of social network approaches and the negligence of wider politico-economical aspects – Kloosterman, Van der Leun & Rath 1999), on the other hand, assimilation theorists claim that assimilation understood as the reorientation of entrepreneurial behaviour to the expectations of the market environment is the decisive condition for the success of enterprises. According to assimilationists the most promising strategy for economic integration based on entrepreneurship is the adoption of the entrepreneurial principles of the indigenous population. Similarly some studies emphasise that many ethnic entrepreneurs do not act in a so-called 'ethnic economy' but try to penetrate the same market niches as their native competitors.[55]

5. Conclusion

In the preceding paragraphs we have argued that the theoretical and empirical mainstream of the academic discipline of economics are of major relevance for the topic of migration and integration. In particular, economic approaches embrace theoretically elaborated discussions about labour market participation and the importance and impact of dependent employment. The theoretical spectrum ranges from the internally highly differentiated neoclassical paradigm to various Marxist approaches, segmentation theories and network approaches mainly employed in transaction cost theories. There is also quite a conceptual potential in economics to be applied to the second mode for economic integration, i.e. entrepreneurship. But here, at first glance, economics are surprisingly not present to the same extent as in the case of work. In this field of ethnic entrepreneurship economics do not display a specific, self-contained empirical and theoretical concern. Instead social sciences like social anthropology, sociology, and social geography dominate in this field. This leaves us with a kind of two-fold conclusion concerning disciplinary approaches in the field of economic integration in migration research.

1. Economic approaches dealing with work have a long tradition in migration research and feature an impressive theoretical and empirical sophistication. In this field, non-economic social science approaches have a complementary status, but a valuable one. This has been discussed in relation to three fields of research. a) Some of the limits of segmentation theories seemed to be due to the time and context dependency of this approach. This indicated the necessity to take into account the specific socio-historical context in which this approach had been developed. b) Economic theory in general has barely developed a sufficient understanding of the interrelation be-

tween organisational rationality and labour market outcomes
(Bommes & Geddes 2004; Bommes & Tacke 2001). Organisations
as the site of employment seem to be strikingly absent from labour
market research. c) The short discussion of the transaction cost theories pointed to some major methodological and theoretical problems of network approaches which also seem to be ignored in economic research (Tacke 1999).

2. Contrary to work, non-economic social sciences dominate in the
field of entrepreneurship. Correspondingly, theories derived from
(political) economics in this field are rather absent in research. Instead, social anthropological approaches of mixed embeddedness
and ethnic enclaves are employed. The reason for this intra-disci-
plinary disequilibrium of economics is due to the disciplinary internal division of labour referred to above. There is no doubt that
many studies on entrepreneurship exist (see among others De Wit
1993 and Kirzner 1973). Entrepreneurship and entrepreneurs have
played a major role within economic theory-building from the start.
The classic theorist Jean-Baptiste Say already conceptualised entrepreneurship as the combination and coordination of productive services (Say 1819). Joseph Schumpeter, another key figure, empha-
sised the entrepreneurial function of innovation (Schumpeter
1961). The application of this economic knowledge of entrepreneurship to the case of ethnic entrepreneurship, however, appears to be
non-existent. And it seems that the (mainly anthropological) work
in this area does not employ this knowledge since it is driven by
the master paradigm of migration research, i.e. social integration
(Bommes 1999: chapter 1). Therefore, entrepreneurship seems to
attract the attention of migration research so far mainly for the reason that it is welcomed as a strategy to increase autonomy of migrants (Kotkin 1992; Saxenian 1999; Light & Roach 1996). Opponents stay in the same frame even if they interpret migrant entrepreneurship rather as the backside of the trap of lacking
opportunities on the labour market (Aldrich et al. 1984; Rath
2002). It remains a task for future research to make systematic use
of the available theoretical and methodological knowledge within
economics to the specific interests of migration research in the field
of migrant entrepreneurship.

'Work, entrepreneurship and economic integration' – the title of this
chapter and of the research cluster in IMISCOE – circumscribes a
broad field of research, which will not and cannot be covered as a
whole by a single research group. For the organisation of future research in the IMISCOE cluster this chapter serves as a reflexive device.
Starting from the specific interests of members and initial discussions,

the work of the coming years concentrates on the following areas: 1) Economic and other social science approaches in migration research tend to proceed separately without clarifying potential methodological and theoretical interrelations. Based on this observation two conferences have been organised bringing together economists, sociologists, political scientists and anthropologists to discuss similarities and differences of methodological and theoretical approaches.[56] 2) A research project on the dynamic relations between illegal migration, the informal economy and the development of knowledge and control organisations of states is currently prepared. This research project requires a combination of sociological, political science and economic approaches in order to account for the dynamic interrelations between the informal economy, the emergence and reproduction of migration networks and political efforts of knowledge and control production. 3) Several members of the cluster deal with various aspects of migration of highly skilled persons including ICT-specialists, medical doctors and managerial staff. Migration of the highly skilled points to a change of conditions of mobility which indicates a transformation of this type of migration based on the enlargement and institutionalisation of international labour markets. 4) 'Migration and socio-economic development' has been extensively discussed as another important field of research involving especially the economic and social impact of migrant communities or 'diasporas' on their regions of origin. In order to explore the field an empirical pilot project was started by a small research group on the social, economic and political relations of three migrant groups in Germany (Serbs, Egyptians, Afghans) to their home regions.[57]

Notes

1   This claim finds empirical evidence in the National Survey of Immigration Scholars (NASIS). This survey analyses the social, academic and ethnic background of immigration scholars as well as their research interests. 33 per cent of all scholars surveyed categorised themselves as sociologists, 28 per cent as historians and 12 per cent as anthropologists. Only 9 per cent were grouped as economists or political scientists. See Rumbaut 1999. Sociology and anthropolgy dominate in migration research. Both disciplines have a long tradition in dealing with issues of migration and integration. In sociology the Chicago School dealt with problems of assimilation and ethnic relations. See the early pathbreaking study of Thomas & Znaniecki (1858, first 1918/1921) and Park 1950. For the assimilation approach currently returning on the agenda (Brubaker 2002) see Gordon 1964.
2   The title of this chapter serves at the same time as the title of one research cluster of the IMISCOE network. It has been produced in this context and is based on two workshops which discussed: 1) the contents to be included in this report and 2) an early version of this chapter.

3   A clarification may be helpful here: Studies of the economy may involve many
    disciplines of the social sciences. We can distinguish disciplinary differentiated
    approaches analysing the economy on the one hand, and economics as a general
    methodological approach seeking to analyse all sorts of phenomena, not just
    economic ones. In this paper we concentrate on disciplinary differentiated economic
    approaches actually or potentially relevant for the analysis of the relation between
    migration and economic integration.

4   His or her willingness is, of course, dependent on the relevant marginal utilities.
    Formally spoken individuals chose the consumption bundle so as to maximise the
    utility subject to the budget constraint, taking prices and income as fixed.

5   A conceptual clarification may be useful here: The formal concept of economic
    integration employed here does not imply any assumptions about the forms and the
    strengths or weaknesses for *social* integration. For example, economic integration
    may be based on political inclusion or exclusion. It may support or erode familial re-
    lations, etc.

6   In Germany, for example, a little bit more than 3 million foreigners are active in the
    labour market. More than 2.73 million work as wage labourers or employees, only
    300,000 as self-employed entrepreneurs. The share of entrepreneurs in most
    European countries has grown in the 1990s, albeit at different rates in different
    countries, but this growth has leveled out in recent years. See in this context also the
    remark of Portes and Rumbaut that 'entrepreneurial minorities are the exception in
    both turn-of-the-century and contemporary migrations' (Portes & Rumbaut 1996: 21).

7   The same applies to the attempt of Egbert 2003 to summarise 'theoretical
    approaches of entrepreneurship of ethnic minorities'. Although published in an
    economic journal, he mainly relies on sociological literature.

8   Sociologically seen, the success or failure to enter membership roles pre-structures
    the social options of individuals in all kinds of other realms of life mediated by their
    so-called client-roles. For the differentiation between membership and client roles
    see Stichweh 1996; on the relevance of organisations for the distribution of social
    resources and social inequality, see Bommes 2001; on the meaning of 'labour' as a
    medium of inclusion for organisations constituted by markets see Bommes & Tacke
    2001.

9   And was followed by regular modifications, e.g. by Joan Robinson 1933, Edward
    Chamberlain 1933, Josef Schumpeter 1911 and Friedrich August von Hayek 1968.

10 See also Peixoto, differentiating between the 'individualistic standpoint' and
    'structural standpoint'; Peixoto 2000: 1, 2, 7.

11 Borjas 1989: 459; similar Straubhaar & Fischer 1996, Straubhaar 1988. Critical on
    these assumptions for example the Nobel prize winner Robert Solow 1990 who
    argues that the labour market cannot adequately be analysed in economic terms,
    because he also sees it driven by motives of fairness.

12 At this point certain possible linkages to human capital theory become visible. The
    decision to invest in his or her own human capital is based on the expectation to
    enhance the returns.

13 Similar to Borjas also Bouvier (1992); and for the German context Sinn, Flaig,
    Werding, Munz, Düll & Hofmann (2001) and Straubhaar (1997). Supporting
    Simon's position see Russel (1986).

14 See also George Gilder, characterising immigration restrictions as 'economically self-
    destructive'; Gilder 1981: 67, 1984: 54.

15 For the Marxist version see Piore 1979, for the non-Marxist see Sengenberger 1987.

16 The most relevant studies in this context are Piore 1979; similar Castells 1975. See
    also Castles & Kosack 1973, Castles 1987, Nikolinakos 1972, Balibar & Wallerstein
    1991, Sassen 1988; a late and sophisticated version: Bader 1995. See also Potts 1988.

For a more systematic discussion of the role of the Marxist tradition in migration research see Bommes 1999.

17 See Berger 1987, 1990, complaining about the early abandoning of the class paradigm in migration research. For one of the most recent Marxist approaches, see Bader 1995.

18 See for example Piore 1979: 33ff., Biller 1989, Sengenberger 1979: 15, Doehringer & Piore 1971. As a special approach within segmentation theory see also the approach of the radical economics, Edwards 1979. See also Edwards, Reich & Gordon 1975, Piore 1975: 125-150. Edwards himself reacted to the at that time to the seminal work of Braverman 1974, based on Baran & Sweezy 1973.

19 In the classical work of segmentation theory the primary sector consists of a series of internal markets. See Doehringer & Piore 1971. See also the alternative interpretation of the school of the radical economists, Edwards 1979; Edwards, Reich & Gordon 1975.

20 See for an introduction in institutionalist approaches Brandes & Weise 1991.

21 In this context Hoffmann-Nowotny coined the frequently used term 'substratification', see Hoffmann-Nowotny 1973.

22 The 'target earning' described by Piore is, however, not only characteristic for foreign workers. It also applies to housewives and adolescents occupied at lower income levels. The features of these groups and their position on the labour market are – to a lesser extent – comparable to those of migrants with respect to formability and availability in the labour market as well as susceptibility to manipulation and control. See also Elwert 2002: 14.

23 See for Germany also Szydlik 1990.

24 Among others see Bade 1994.

25 The version of segmentation theory of Piore relies on a neo-Marxist analytic frame which is compatible to world system approaches that attracted some attention. Most relevant in this context, Wallerstein 1974, 1979. More recent Sassen 1988, 1996 and Altvater & Mahnkopf 1999. For a discussion of the relation between world society, the world system approach and globalisation see also Stichweh 1995 and Luhmann 1997.

26 Esping-Anderson (1993, 1999) calls this the decommodification of labour markets.

27 See for a comparative report McLaughlan & Salt 2002.

28 See also the volume by Bommes, Hoesch, Hunger & Kolb 2004.

29 Translation by the author.

30 'Labor Turnover Costs' are the centrepiece of the argumentation of Lindbeck & Snower 2002. The argumentation follows the theoretical tradition of the transaction cost theory of Coase (1937) and Williamson (1975). For a definition of transaction costs see Picot 1993.

31 In this context see also the differentiation between an 'industrial subsystem' which requires a high degree of company internal knowledge and the 'craft subsystem' where knowledge can be substituted rather easily. See among others Osterman 1984: 167.

32 See also for the particularities of internal labour markets the microeconomic study of Hennart 1986.

33 For the role of trust see also Granovetter 1985. Rudolf Stichweh claims some kind of trade-off between rising globality which results in a loss of control and the set-up of ethnic company-based enclaves that restrict globality. See Stichweh 1998: 58-59. Edström and Galbraith (1979) underline the advantages of setting up enclaves. See also the case study about the American company Eli Lily by Malnight 1995.

34 See for the most prominent application Porter 1985.

35 This can well be interpreted as an 'anti-categorically' motivated assumption as Emirbayer has convincingly argued.
36 Compare for this e.g. Burt 1982 and for an overview see Trenzini 1998.
37 The theory of rational expectations concerning the behavior of market participants has mainly been developed by Lucas Jr. 1972. For a summary see Lucas Jr. 1987.
38 The difference between neoclassical approaches which we have classified as structural approaches, and human capital theory may therefore be further characterised as follows: human capital theory takes the neoclassical assumptions as a model of action in order to explain individual behaviour. The neoclassical approach reconstructs economic macro-structures as the result of individual actions. The first approach employs the model with the aim to forecast individual action. The second approach presupposes this model of action and interprets economic macro-results deviating from model expectations as the effect of some kind of intervening factors which then need to be identified and explained.
39 Becker's work also activated a new appraoch of dealing with issues of personnel policy in business administration. Human resource management is a new field of management and becomes more and more a part of the curricula in business administration. See Wiskemann 2000 and Cronenberg, Funk & Djarrahzadeh 1993.
40 Ebenrett, Hansen & Puzicha 2003 state that there is a clear and significant correlation between the cognitive abilities (understood as human capital) of youngsters and location factors like unemployment, lower incomes and training facilities. This is the reinvention of an insight that can be found in the classical investigation by Jahoda, Zeisel & Lazarsfeld 1975.
41 Case studies can be found in Wolter 1997, Ford 1992, Kolb 2004 and Wolter & Wolburg 1996.
42 See in this context the studies of King & Shuttleworth 1995, Chen 1995 and Li, Findlay, Jowett & Skeldon 1996.
43 See for the case of the car manufacturer Volkswagen Posth 1990: 378. See Senn, Rohde, Ahrens & Bargmann 2003: 113 who assess in their position as HR managers of the Volkswagen corporation the mobility of their employees in a geographical as well as professional sense as 'self-conception'. See also Peixoto 2001: 1041.
44 The interconnectedness of human capital investment, employment abroad and promotion and career development is confirmed in many more recent studies; Mahmood & Schömann 2002 and Rell & Weiß 2001: 17. Sami Mahroum identifies 'highly skilled globetrotters'; Mahroum 1999. Stalker and Amit-Talai mention as further important incentives of abroad stays the options to improve the individual income level and a certain degree of adventuresomeness, see Stalker 2000, Amit-Talai 1998 and Tzeng 1995.
45 The term 'integration' is the focal point of a huge arsenal of other terminologies. Very popular in migration research are approaches of incorporation and of inclusion which have mainly been developed in response to the concept of assimilation. For incorporation see Castles 1987 and Soysal 1994, for inclusion Miles & Thränhardt 1995, Faist 1995, Mackert 1998. The main differences between these labels are their normative basics. See Bade & Bommes 2004.
46 See for the USA Borjas 1999, for Great Britain Hatton & Price 1999, for Sweden Ekberg 1994 and Edin, LaLonde & Aslund 2000, for Austria Winter-Ebmer 1994, for Germany Dustmann 1993, Schmidt 1997. In a comparative perspective, Werner 1994 and Bauer, Lofström & Zimmermann 2000. In a sociological context similar approaches can be identified: Kalter & Granato 2004, Kristen & Granato 2004.
47 For an overview see Sachverständigenrat für Zuwanderung und Integration 2004.
48 See for example Levine & Zimmermann 1999, Blank 1988, Meyer 1998. For Germany see Fertig & Schmidt 2001.

49 This is true for the *Sozialhilfe* (social aid) in Germany. Real minimum wage regulations exist in France, the USA and Great Britian.

50 Many studies emphasise that flexibility of the real wage is not given and that adjustment to lower wage rates do not occur. See for example Jacoby 1990: 33. See in this context also the recommendation of Boswell & Straubhaar (2004: 7), to combat illegal labour migration by 'lowering the costs of hiring regular workers'.

51 An example for this is the German farming industry. About 300,000 work permits are granted per year mostly for workers from Middle and Eastern Europe; see Sachverständigenrat für Zuwanderung und Integration 2004: 131.

52 In various studies Waldinger e.g. emphasises that the economic integration of immigrant entrepreneurs is a network-driven process that is only barely influenced by conjunctural changes. See among others Waldinger 1996, Waldinder & Lapp 1993.

53 Paternalistic employer-employee-relations are also reported by Light 1972 and Bonacich 1973.

54 For an interesting study on the interfaces of human capital theory and ethnic capital see Borjas 1992. Borjas assumes that ethnicity acts as an externality in the human capital accumulation process.

55 See for a case study on Turkish female entrepreneurs Hillmann 1999. See also Hillmann & Rudolph 1997. For an early study on ethnic businesses and the food sector see Light 1972.

56 A special issue of the Journal of Ethnic and Migration Studies is currently prepared, edited by Christina Boswell and Peter Mueser. An edited volume on 'Migration Research in Economics and the other Social Sciences' is prepared by Holger Kolb, Clemens Esser and Henrik Egbert.

57 This project is jointly conducted by IMIS and the HWWA (directed by Michael Bommes and Tanja El-Cherkeh).

Literature

Aldrich, H. E., T. Jones & D. McEvoy (1984), 'Ethnic Advantage and Minority Business Development', in R. Ward & R. Jenkins (eds.), *Ethnic Communities in Business: Strategies for Economic Survival*. Cambridge: Cambridge University Press.

Altvater, E. & B. Mahnkopf (1999), *Grenzen der Globalisierung: Ökonomie und Ökologie und die Politik der Weltgesellschaft*. Münster: Westfälisches Dampfboot.

Bade, K. J. (1994), *Ausländer – Aussiedler – Asyl: Eine Bestandaufnahme*. Munich: Beck.

Bade, K. J. & M. Bommes (2004), 'Einleitung', in Bade, K.J. & M. Bommes (eds.), *Migration – Integration – Bildung. Grundfragen und Problembereiche* (IMIS-Beiträge 23), Osnabrück: IMIS, 7-20.

Bader, V. (1995), *Rassismus, Ethnizität, Bürgerschaft. Soziologische und philosophische Überlegungen*. Münster: Westfälisches Dampfboot.

Balibar, E. & I. Wallerstein (1991), *Race, Nation, Class. Ambiguous Identities*. London: Verso.

Baran, P. A. & P. M. Sweezy (1973), *Monopoly Capital: An Essay on the American Economic and Social Order*. Harmondsworth: Penguin Books.

Bauer, Th., M. Lofström & K. F. Zimmermann (2000), 'Immigration Policy, Assimilation of Immigrants and Native's Sentiments towards Immigrants: Evidence from 12 OECD-countries', *Swedish Economic Policy Review* 7 (2): 11-53.

Bauer, Th. & K .F. Zimmermann (2002), *The Economics of Migration. International Library of Critical Writings in Economics*. Cheltenham: Elgar.

Bauer, Th.K., J. P. Haisken-DeNew & Ch.M. Schmidt (2004), 'International Labor Migration, Economic Growth and Labor Markets. The Current State of affairs'. *RWI Discussion Paper* 20: Essen.

Becker, G. (1975), *Human Capital. A Theoretical and Empirical Analysis with Special Reference to Education.* New York/London: Columbia Univ. Press.

Bender, St., H. Rudolph & U. Walwei (1999), 'Staatliche Zuschüsse zur Sozialversicherung hinter der 630 DM-Grenze', *IAB-Kurzbericht* (8): 3.

Berwert, A., P. Vock & M. Tiri (2004), *Cluster in der schweizerischen Volkswirtschaft und im Espace Mittelland – Identifikation, Analyse und Diskussion aufgrund von Input-Output-Daten.* Center for Science and Technology Studies 8: Bern.

Biller, M. (1989), *Arbeitsmarktsegmentation und Ausländerbeschäftigung. Ein Beitrag zur Soziologie des Arbeitsmarktes mit einer Fallstudie aus der Automobilindustrie.* Frankfurt a.M./New York: Campus.

Blank, R. (1988), 'The Effect of Welfare and Wage Levels on the Location Decision of Female Households', *Journal of Urban Economics* 24 (2): 186-211.

Bommes, J. (1999), *Migration und nationaler Wohlfahrtsstaat. Ein differenzierungs-theoretischer Entwurf.* Wiesbaden: Westdeutscher Verlag.

Bommes, M. (2001), 'Organisation, Inklusion und Verteilung. Soziale Ungleichheit in der funktional differenzierten Gesellschaft', in V. Tacke (ed.), *Organisation und gesellschaftliche Differenzierung*, 236-258. Wiesbaden: Westdeutscher Verlag.

Bommes, M. (2004), 'Erarbeitung eines operationalen Konzeptes zur Einschätzung von Integrationsprozessen und Integrationsmaßnahmen'. *Gutachten für den Sachverständigenrat für Zuwanderung und Integration.* Osnabrück/Nürnberg: Bundesamt für Migration und Flüchtlinge.

Bommes, M (2006), Illegale Migration in der modernen Gesellschaft – Resultat und Problem der Migrationspolitik europäischer Nationalstaaten, in: J. Alt & M. Bommes (eds.): *Illegalität. Grenzen und Möglichkeiten der Migrationspolitik.* Wiesbaden: VS Verlag.

Bommes, M., K. Hoesch, U. Hunger & H. Kolb (eds.) (2004), *Organisational Recruitment and Patterns of Migration. Interdependencies in an Integrating Europe* (IMIS-Beiträge, No. 25). Osnabrück.

Bommes, M. & A. Geddes, 'Conclusion', in M. Bommes, K. Hoesch, U. Hunger & H. Kolb (eds.), *Organisational Recruitment and Patterns of Migration. Interdependencies in an Integrating Europe* (IMIS-Beiträge, No. 25). Osnabrück, 279-297.

Bommes, M. & V. Tacke (2001), 'Arbeit als Inklusionsmedium moderner Organisationen', in V. Tacke (ed.), *Organisation und gesellschaftliche Differenzierung*, 61-83. Opladen: Westdeutscher Verlag.

Bommes, M. & V. Tacke (2005), 'Systems and Networks: Competing Theories or Complementary Social Structures?', in D. Seidl & K.H. Becker (eds.), *Niklas Luhmann and Organisation Studies*, 282-304. Copenhagen: Copenhagen Business School Press.

Bommes, M. & V. Tacke (2006), 'Das Allgemeime und das Besondere des Netzwerks', in B. Hollstein & F. Straus (eds.), *Qualitative Netzwerkanalyse*, forthcoming. Wiesbaden: VS Verlag.

Bonacich, Th. (1973), 'A Theory of Middleman Minorities', *American Sociological Review* 38: 583-594.

Borjas, G.J. (1985), 'Assimilation, Changes in Cohort Quality, and the Earnings of Immigrants', *Journal of Labor Economics*, October: 463-489.

Borjas, G.J. (1988), *International Differences in Labor Market Performance of Immigrants.* Kalamazoo: University of California.

Borjas, G.J. (1989), 'Economic Theory and International Migration', *International Migration Review* 23 (3): 457-485.

Borjas, G.J. (1990), *Friends or Strangers. The Impact of Immigrants on the U.S. Economy.* New York: Basic Books.

Borjas, G.J. (1992), 'Ethnic Capital and Intergenerational Mobility', *Quarterly Journal of Economics* 107: 123-150.

Borjas, G.J. (1999), 'The Economic Analysis of Immigration', in O. Ashenfelder & D. Card (eds.), *Handbook of Labor Economics*, 1679-1769. Amsterdam: Elsevier.

Boswell, Ch. & Th. Straubhaar (2004), 'The Illegal Employment of Foreigners in Europe', *Intereconomics* 39 (1): 7.

Bouvier, L.F. (1992), *Peaceful Invasions. Immigration and Changing America.* Lanham: Center for Immigration Studies.

Brandes, W. & P. Weise (1991), 'Arbeitsbeziehungen zwischen Markt und Hierarchie', in W. Müller-Jentsch (ed.), *Konfliktpartnerschaft. Akteure und Institutionen den industriellen Beziehungen*, 11-30. München-Mering: Hampp.

Braverman, H. (1974), 'Labor and Monopoly Capital. The Degradation of Work in the Twentieth Century'. New York: Monthly Review Press.

Burt, R.S. (1982), *Toward a Structural Theory of Action. Network Models of Social Structure, Perceptions and Action.* New York: Academic Press.

Castells, M. (1975), 'Immigrant Workers and Class Struggles in Advanced Capitalism: The Western European Experience', *Politics and Society* 5: 33-66.

Castells, M. (1996), *The Rise of the Network Society. The Information Age.* Oxford: Blackwell.

Castles, S. (1987), *Migration und Rassismus in Westeuropa.* Berlin: Express Ed. Castles, S. & G. Kosack (1973), *Immigrant Workers and Class Structure in Western Europe.* London: Oxford University Press.

Chamberlin, E.H. (1969), *The Theory of Monopolistic Competition* (1933). Cambridge, Mass.: Harvard University Press (first published 1933).

Chen, S. J. (1995), 'Migrant Selectivity and Returns to Skills: the Case of Taiwanese Immigrants in the United States', *International Migration* 33 (2): 251-271.

Chiswick, B. (1978), 'The Effects of Americanization on the Earnings of Foreign Born Men', *Journal of Political Economy* 86: 897-921.

Coase, R. (1937), 'The Nature of the Firm', *Economica* 4: 386-405.

Cronenberg, A.G., J. Funk & M. Djarrahzadeh (eds.) (1993), *Internationalisierung als Herausforderung für das Personalmanagement.* Stuttgart: Schäffer-Poeschel.

Doehringer, P. & M. J. Piore (1971), *Internal Labor Markets and Manpower Analysis*, Lexington: Heath.

Dustmann, C. (1993), 'Earnings Adjustments of Temporary Migrants', *Journal of Population Economics* 6: 153-168.

Ebenrett, H. J., Hansen, D. & K. J. Puzicha (2003), 'Verlust von Humankapital in Regionen mit hoher Arbeitslosigkeit', *Aus Politik und Zeitgeschichte* 6-7: 25-31.

Ebers, M. & W. Gotsch (1993), 'Institutionenökonomische Theorie der Organisation', in A. Kieser (ed.), *Organisationstheorien.* Stuttgart: Kohlhammer.

Edin, P.A., R. LaLonde & O. Aslund (2000), 'Emigration of Immigrants and Measures of Immigrant Assimilation: Evidence from Sweden'. Paper presented at the *Swedish Economic Council's conference on: The Assimilation of Immigrants in the Labor Market*, Stockholm, 13 March 2000.

Edström, A. & J.R. Galbraith (1979), 'Transfer of Managers as a Coordination and Control Strategy in Multinational Organizations', *Administrative Science Quarterly* 22: 248-263.

Edwards, R. (1979), *Contested Terrain: The Transformation of the Workplace in the Twentieth Century.* London: Heinemann.

Edwards, R., M. Reich & D. M. Gordon (eds.) (1975), *Labor Market Segmentation.* Lexington, MA: Heath.

Egbert, H. (2003), 'Theoretische Ansätze zum Unternehmertum ethnischer Minderheiten', *Wirtschaftswissenschaftliches Studium* 12: 700-706.

Ekberg, J. (1994), 'Economic Progress of Immigrants in Sweden from 1970 to 1990: A Longitudinal Study', *Scandinavian Journal of Social Welfare* 3: 148-157.

Elwert, G. (2002), 'Unternehmerische Illegale. Ziele und Organisationen eines unterschätzten Typs illegaler Einwanderer', *IMIS-Beiträge* 19: 7-20.

Enste, D., & F. Schneider (2006), 'Schattenwirtschaft und irreguläre Beschäftigung: Irrtümer, Zusammenhänge und Lösungen', in J. Alt & M. Bommes (eds.), *Illegalität: Grenzen und Möglichkeiten der Migrationspolitik, 35-59*. Wiesbaden: VS Verlag.

Esping-Anderson, G. (1993), *The Three Worlds of Welfare Capitalism*. Cambridge: Polity Press.

Esping-Andersen, G. (1999), *Social Foundations of Postindustrial Economies*. Oxford: Oxford University Press.

Emirbayer, M. & J. Goodwin (1994), 'Network Analysis, Culture, and the Problem of Agency', *American Journal of Sociology* 99: 1411-1454.

Faist, Th. (1995), *Social Citizenship for Whom? Young Turks in Germany and Mexican Americans in the United States*. Aldershot: Avebury.

Faist, Th. (2000), *The Volume and Dynamics of International Migration and Transnational Social Spaces*. Oxford: Clarendon.

Fertig, M. & Ch. Schmidt (2001), 'Aggregate-level Migration Studies as a Tool for Forecasting Future Migration Streams', in S. Djajic (ed.), *International Migration – Trends, Policies and Economic Impact*. New York: Routledge.

Ford, R. (1992), *Migration and Stress among Corporate Employees*. London: University College Dissertation.

Galbraith, J.R. & A. Edström (1976), 'International Transfer of Managers: Some Important Policy Considerations', *Columbia Journal of World Business* 11: 44-55.

Gilder, G. (1981), *Wealth and Poverty*. New York: Basic Books.

Gilder, G. (1984), *Spirit of Enterprise*. New York: Simon and Schuster.

Gordon, M. (1964), *Assimilation in American Life*. New York/Oxford: Oxford University Press.

Gould, W.T.S. & A.M. Findlay (1994), 'Refugees and Skilled Transients: Migration between Developed Societies in a Changing World Order', in idem (eds.), *Population, Migration and the Changing World Order*. Chichester: Wiley.

Granovetter, M.S. (1985), 'Economic Action and Social Structure: The Problem of Embeddedness', *American Journal for Sociology* 91 (3): 481-510.

Granovetter, M.S. (1995), 'The Economic Sociology of Firms and Entrepreneurs', in A. Portes (ed.), *The Economic Sociology of Immigration. Essays on networks, Ethnicity and Entrepreneurship*. New York: Russel Sage Foundation.

Gurak, D.T. & F. Caces (1992), 'Migration Networks and the Shaping of Migration Systems', in M. Kriz, L. Lim & H. Slotnik (eds.), *International Migration Systems, 150-176*. Oxford: Clarendon.

Hammar, T (1989), State, Nation and Dual Citizenship, in: R. Brubaker (ed.): *Immigration and the Politics of Citizenship in Europe and North America, 81-95*. Lanham/New York: University Press of America.

Hatton, T.J. & W. Price (1999), 'Migration, Migrants and Policy in the United Kingdom'. *IZA Discussion Paper 81*. IZA, Bonn.

Haug, S. (2000), 'Klassische und neuere Theorien der Migration'. *MZES Arbeitspapier Nr. 30*. Mannheim: Arbeitspapiere – Mannheimer Zentrum für Europäische Sozialforschung.

Hayek, F. (1968); Der Wettbewerb als Entdeckungsverfahren, in: F. Hayek (ed.): *Freiburger Studien – Gesammelte Aufsätze, 249-265*. Tübingen: Mohr Siebeck.

Heidling, E. (2000), 'Strategische Netzwerke. Koordination und Kooperation in asymmetrisch strukturierten Unternehmensnetzwerken', in J. Weyer (ed.), *Soziale Netzwerke*, 111-133. München/ Vienna: Oldenbourg.

Hillmann, F. (1997), 'This is a Migrant's World: Städtische ethnische Arbeitsmärkte am Beispiel New York City', *Discussion Paper FS I 97-103*, Wissenschaftszentrum Berlin für Sozialforschung.

Hillmann, F. (1999), 'Türkische Unternehmerinnen', *WZB-Mitteilungen* 84: 21-24.

Hillmann, F. & H. Rudolph (1997), 'Redistributing the Cake? Ethnicisation Processes in the Berlin Food Sector'. *WZB-Working Paper*. WZB FS I: 97-101.

Hoffmann-Nowotny, H. J. (1973), *Soziologie des Fremdarbeiterproblems*. Stuttgart: Enke.

Jacoby, S.M. (1990), 'Sticky Stories: Economic Explanations of Employment and Wage Rigidity', *The American Economic Review* 80 (2): 33.

Jahoda, M., Zeisel, H. & P. F. Lazarsfeld (1975), *Die Arbeitslosen von Marienthal. Ein soziographischer Versuch über die Wirkungen langandauernder Arbeitslosigkeit*. Frankfurt a. M: Suhrkamp (first published 1938).

Kalter, F. (1997), *Wohnortwechsel in Deutschland*. Opladen: Leske und Budrich.

Kalter, F. & N. Granato (2004), 'Sozialer Wandel und strukturelle Assimilation in der Bundesrepublik. Empirische Befunde mit Mikrodaten der amtlichen Statistik', in K.J. Bade & M. Bommes (eds.), *Migration – Integration – Bildung. Grundfragen und Problembereiche* (IMIS-Beiträge 23). Osnabrück: 61-81.

Keller, B. (1993), *Einführung in die Arbeitspolitik: Arbeitsbeziehungen und Arbeitsmarkt in sozialwissenschaftlicher Perspektive*. Munich/ Vienna: Oldenbourg.

Kim, D.Y. (1996), 'The Limits of Ethnic Solidarity: Mexican and Ecuadorian Employment in Korean-owned Businesses in NYC'. *Working paper*, Department of Sociology, Center for Urban Research, CUNY.

King, R. & I. Shuttleworth (1995), 'The Emigration and Unemployment of Irish Graduates: The Export of Highly-skilled Labour from the Periphery of Europe', *European Urban and Regional Studies* 2 (1): 21-40.

Kirzner, I. (1973), *Competition and Entrepreneurship*. Chicago/London: University of Chicago Press.

Kloosterman, R.C., J. P. van der Leun & J. Rath (1999), 'Mixed Embeddedness, Migrant Entrepreneurship, and Informal Economic Activities', *International Journal of Urban and Regional Research* 23(2): 253-267.

Kloosterman, R. & J. Rath (2001), 'Immigrant Entrepreneurs in Advanced Economies: Mixed Embeddedness further Explored', *Journal of Ethnic and Migration Studies* 27 (2): 189-201.

Kloosterman, R. & J. Rath (2003), *Immigrant Entrepreneurs. Venturing Abroad in the Age of Globalization*. Oxford: Berg.

Kolb, H. (2004), *Einwanderung zwischen wohlverstandenem Eigeninteresse und symbolischer Politik. Das Beispiel der deutschen Green Card*. Münster: Lit.

Kotkin, J. (1992), *Tribes: How Race, Religion, and Identity Determine Success in the New York Global Economy*. New York: Random House.

Kowol, U. & W. Krohn (1995), 'Innovationsnetzwerke. Ein Modell der Technikgenese', in J. Halfmann (ed.), *Technik und Gesellschaft*. Jahrbuch 8: Theoriebausteine der Techniksoziologie, 77-105. Frankfurt a.M./New York: Campus.

Kristen, C. & N. Granato (2004), 'Bildungsinvestitionen in Migrantenfamilien', in K.J. Bade & M. Bommes (eds.), *Migration Integration Bildung. Grundfragen und Problembereiche* (IMIS-Beiträge 23). Osnabrück.

Ladeur, K. H. (1993), 'Von der Verwaltungshierarchie zum administrativen Netzwerk', *Die Verwaltung* 26: 7-165.

Lärm, Th. (1982), *Arbeitsmarkttheorie und Arbeitslosigkeit: Systematik und Kritik arbeitsmarkttheoretischer Ansätze*. Frankfurt a.M.: R.G. Fischer.

Lang, G. (2004), How Different are Wages from Wage Potentials? Analysing the Earnings Disadvantage of Immigrants in Germany. *Volkswirtschaftliche Diskussionsreihe (256)*. Augsburg: Universität Augsburg.

Layard, R., St. Nickell & R. Jackman (1991), *Unemployment – Macroeconomic Performance and the Labour Market*. Oxford: Oxford University Press.

Lebhardt, G. (2002), 'Internationale Migration. Hypothesen, Perspektiven und Theorien', Demographie heute. *Vorträge – Aufsätze – Forschungsberichte (19)*. Humboldt-University Berlin.

Levine, Ph.B. & D. J. Zimmermann (1999), 'An Empirical Analysis of the Welfare Magnet Debate Using the NLSY', *Journal of Population Economics* 12 (3): 391-409.

Li, F.L.N., A. M. Findlay, A. J. Jowett & R. Skeldon (1996), 'Migrating to Learn and Learning to Migrate: A Study of the Experiences and Intentions of International Student Migrants', *International Journal of Population Geography* (2): 51-67.

Light, I. (1972), *Ethnic Enterprises in America*. Berkeley: University of California Press.

Light, I. & E. Bonacich (1988), *Immigrant Entrepreneurs: Koreans in Los Angeles*. Berkeley: Univ. of California Press.

Light, I. & E. Roach (1996), 'Self-Employment: Mobility Ladder or Economic Lifeboat', in R. Waldinger & M. Bozorgmehr (eds.), *Ethnic Los Angeles*. New York: Russel Sage Foundation.

Lindbeck, A. & D. J. Snower (2002), 'The Insider-Outsider Theory: A Survey', *IZA Discussion Paper* (534). Bonn: Institute for the Study of Labor.

Lucas Jr., R. E. (1972), 'Expectations and the Neutrality of Money', *Journal of Economic Theory* (4): 103-124.

Lucas Jr., R. E. (1987), *Models of Business Cycles*. Oxford: Blackwell.

Luhmann, N. (1997), *Die Gesellschaft der Gesellschaft*. Frankfurt a.M.: Suhrkamp.

Mackert, J. (1998), *Kampf um Zugehörigkeit. Nationale Staatsbürgerschaft als Modus Sozialer Schließung*. Opladen: Westdeutscher Verlag.

Mahmood, T. & K. Schömann (2002), 'Die Determinanten der Migrationsentscheidung von IT-Hochschulabsolventen aus Pakistan: Empirische Befunde zum Design einer deutschen "Green Card"', *Discussion Paper FS IV 02-03*, Wissenschaftszentrum Berlin.

Malnight, Th.W. (1995), 'Globalization of an Ethnocentric Firm: An Evolutionary Perspective', *Strategic Management Journal* 16: 119-141.

March, J. G. (1990), *Entscheidung und Organisation*. Wiesbaden: Gabler.

Marsh, D. (ed.) (1998), *Comparing Policy Networks*. Buckingham: Open University Press.

Marshall, A. (1920), *Principles of Economics*. London: Macmillan (first published 1890).

Massey, D.S. et al. (1993), 'Theories of International Migration: A Review and Appraisal', *Population and Development Review* 19 (3): 431-466.

Massey, D.S. (1998), *Worlds in Motion. Understanding International Migration at the End of the Millenium*. Oxford: Clarendon.

McLaughlan, G. & J. Salt (2002), *Migration Policies Towards Highly Skilled Foreign Workers*. Report for the Home Office. London.

Meyer, B (1998), *Do the Poor Move to Receive Higher Welfare Benefits?* Mimeo: Northwestern University.

Miles, R. & D. Thränhardt (eds.) (1995), *Migration and European Integration. The Dynamics of Inclusion and Exclusion*. London: Pinter.

Mincer, J. (1974), *Schooling, Experience and Earnings*. New York: Columbia University Press.

Mincer, J. (1978), 'Family Migration Decision', *Journal of Political Economy* 86: 749-773.

Nikolinakos, M. (1972), *Politische Ökonomie und Gastarbeiterfrage. Migration und Kapitalismus*. Reinbek bei Hamburg: Rowohlt.

Osterman, P. (1984), 'White Collar Internal Labour Markets', in P. Osterman (ed.), *Internal Labor Markets*. Cambridge: The MIT Press.

Park, R.E. (1950), *Race and Culture*. Glencoe: Free Press.

Parker, J. (1996), *Labor, Culture, and Capital in Corporate Fast Food Restaurants Franchises: Global and Local Interactions Among an Immigrant Workforce in New York*. New York: PhD Thesis at the Dept. of Sociology, City University of New York, Graduate Center.

Parnreiter, Ch. (2001), 'Die Mär von den Lohndifferentialen. Migrationstheoretische Überlegungen am Beispiel Mexikos', *IMIS-Beiträge* (17): 55-89.

Peixoto, J. (2000), 'Migration, Labour Markets and Embededdness: The Social Constraints of the International Migration of Labour'. *SOCIUS Working Paper (4)*. Universidade Técnica de Lisboa.

Peixoto, J. (2001), 'The International Mobility of Highly Skilled Workers in Transnational Corporations: The Macro and Micro Factors of the Organizational Migration of Cadres', *International Migration Review* 35 (4): 1030-1053.

Picot, A. (1993), 'Organisation', in: M. Bitz, K. Dellmann, M. Domsch & H. Egner (eds.), *Vahlens Kompendium der Betriebswirtschaftslehre*, 101-174. Münster: Vahlen.

Piore, M. J. (1975), 'Notes for a Theory of Labor Market Stratification', in R. Edwards et al. (eds.), *Labor Market Segmentation*, 125-150. Lexington MA: Heath.

Piore, M. J. (1979), *Birds of Passage. Migrant Labor in Industrial Societies*. Cambridge, MA: Cambridge University Press.

Porter, M. E. (1985), *Competitive Advantage. Creating Superior Performance*. New York: Free Press.

Portes, A. (1987), 'The Social Origins of the Cuban Enclave Economy of Miami', *Sociological Perspectives* 30: 340-72.

Portes, A. & R. L. Bach (1985), *Latin Journey: Cuban and Mexican Immigrants in the U.S.* Berkeley: University of California Press.

Portes A. & R. Rumbaut (1996), *Immigrant America. A Portrait*. Los Angeles: University of California Press.

Posth, M. (1990), 'Internationale Personalentwicklung bei Volkswagen', *Betriebswirtschaftliche Forschung und Praxis* 42 (5): 369-378.

Potts, L. (1988), *Weltmarkt für Arbeitskraft. Von der Kolonisation Amerikas bis zu den Migrationen der Gegenwart*. Hamburg: Junius.

Pries, L. (1996), 'Transnationale Soziale Räume. Theoretisch-empirische Skizze am Beispiel der Arbeitswanderungen Mexiko-USA', *Zeitschrift für Soziologie* 49 (1): 135-150.

Rath, J. (2002), 'Needle Games: Mixed Embeddedness of Immigrant Entrepreneurs', in J. Rath (ed.), *Unravelling the Rag Trade. Immigrant Entrepreneurship in Seven World Cities*, 1-22. Oxford: Berg.

Rath, J. (ed.) (2002), *Unravelling the Rag Trade. Immigrant Entrepreneurship in Seven World Cities*. Oxford: Berg.

Ravenstein, E. G. (1885), 'The Laws of Migration', *Journal of the Royal Statistical Society* 48: 167-277.

Richter, R (2003), *Neue Institutionenkonomik: eine Einführung und kritische Würdigung*. Tübingen: Mohr Siebeck.

Robinson, J. (1976), *The Economics of Imperfect Competition*. London: Macmillan (first published 1933).

Rumbaut, R. (1999), 'Immigration Research in the United States. Social Origins and Future Orientations', *American Behavioral Scientist* 42 (9): 1285-1301.

Russel, S. St. (1986), 'Remittances from International Migration. A Review in Perspective', *World Development* 41 (6): 677-696.

Sachverständigenrat für Zuwanderung und Integration (2004), *Migration und Integration – Erfahrungen nutzen, Neues wagen*. Berlin.

Salt, J. (1983), 'High Level Manpower Movements in Northwest Europe and the Role of Careers: An Explanatory Framework', *International Migration Review* 17 (4): 633-652.

Salt, J. (1988), 'Highly-Skilled International Migrants, Careers and Internal Labor-Markets', *Geoforum* 19 (4): 387-399.

Salt, J. (1992), 'Migration Processes among the Highly Skilled in Europe', *International Migration Review* 26 (2): 484-505.

Salt, J. & A.M. Findlay (1989), 'International Migration of Highly-skilled Manpower: Theoretical and Developmental Issues', in R. Appleyard (ed.), *The Impact of Migration on Developing Countries*, 159-180. Paris: OECD.

Sanders, J. M. & V. Nee (1987), 'Limits of Ethnic Solidarity in the Enclave Economy', *American Sociological Review* 52: 745-767.

Sassen, S. (1988), *The Mobility of Labor and Capital. A Study in International Investment and Labor Flow.* Cambridge: Cambridge University Press.

Sassen, S. (1996), *Losing Control. Souvereignty in an Age of Globalization.* New York: Columbia University Press.

Say, J. B. (1819), *Traite d'économique politique.* Paris: Calmann-Lévy Éditeur.

Saxenian, A.L. (1999). *Silicon Valley's New Immigrant Entrepreneurs.* San Francisco: Public Policy Institute of California.

Schlotböller, D. & U. van Suntum (2002), *Arbeitsmarktintegration von Zuwanderern. Einflußfaktoren, internationale Erfahrungen und Handlungsempfehlungen.* Gütersloh: Bertelsmann Stiftung.

Schmidt, Chr. (1997), 'Immigrant Performance in Germany: Labor Earnings of Ethnic German Migrants and Foreign Guest-Workers', *Quarterly Review of Economics and Finance* 37: 379-397.

Schneider, Fr. (2000), 'Shadow Economies: Size, Causes, and Consequences', *Journal of Economic Literature* 38 (1): 77-114.

Schumpeter, J. (1961), *The Theory of Economic Development.* New York: Oxford University Press (first published 1911).

Seifert, W. (1995), *Die Mobilität der Migranten. Die berufliche, ökonomische und soziale Stellung ausländischer Arbeitnehmer in der Bundesrepublik.* Berlin: Sigma.

Sengenberger, W. (1979), 'Zur Dynamik der Arbeitsmarktssegmentierung', in: Ch. Brinkmann, J. Kühl, R. Schultz-Wild & W. Sengenberger (eds.), *Arbeitsmarktsegmentation – Theorie und Therapie im Lichte der empirischen Befunde*, BeitrAB 33, 1-44. Nürnberg: Institut für Arbeitsmarkt- und Berufsforschung.

Sengenberger, W. (1987), *Struktur und Funktionsweise von Arbeitsmärkten.* Frankfurt a.M.: Campus.

Senn, J.F., C. Rohde, I. Ahrens & M. Bargmann (2003), 'Arbeitsmarktpolitische Instrumente auf dem betriebsinternen Arbeitsmarkt', in H. Klein-Schneider (ed.), *Interner Arbeitsmarkt. Beschäftigung und Personalentwicklung in Unternehmen und Verwaltungen*, 108-123. Frankfurt a.M.: Bund.

Simon, J.L. (1989), *The Economic Consequences of Immigration.* Oxford: Basil Blackwell.

Sinn, H.W., G. Flaig, M. Werding, S. Munz, N. Düll & H. Hofmann (2001), 'EU-Erweiterung und Arbeitskräftemigration: Wege zu einer schrittweisen Annäherung der Arbeitsmärkte', *Ifo-Beiträge zur Wirtschaftsforschung*, Bd. 2, ifo Institut München.

Sjastaad, L. A. (1962), 'The Costs and Returns of Human Migration', *Journal of Political Economy* 70: 80-93.

Solow, R. M. (1990), *The Labor Market as a Social Institution.* Oxford: Basil Blackwell.

Soysal, Y. (1994), *Limits of Citizenship. Migrants and Postnational Membership in Europe.* Chicago/London: Univ. of Chicago.

Spaan, E. (1999), *Labour Circulation and Socio-economic Transformation. The case of East Java.* The Hague: NIDI Report.

Stark, O. (1991), *The Migration of Labor.* Cambridge: Blackwell.

Stark O. & E. J. Taylor (1991), 'Migration Incentives, Migration Types: The Role of Relative Deprivation', *The Economic Journal* 101: 1163-1178.

Stichweh, R. (1995), 'Zur Theorie der Weltgesellschaft', *Soziale Systeme* 1: 29-45.

Stichweh, R. (1996), 'Professionen in einer funktional differenzierten Gesellschaft', in A. Combe & W. Helsper (eds.), *Pädagogische Professionalität. Untersuchungen zum Typus pädagogischen Handelns*, 49-69. Frankfurt a.M.: Suhrkamp.

Stichweh, R. (1998), 'Migration, nationale Wohlfahrtsstaaten und die Entstehung der Weltgesellschaft', in M. Bommes & J. Halfmann (eds.), *Migration in nationalen Wohlfahrtsstaaten. Theoretische und vergleichende Untersuchungen*, 49-61. Osnabrück: Universitätsverlag Rasch.

Straubhaar, Th. (1988), *On the Economics of International Labor Migration*. Bern/Stuttgart: Haupt.

Straubhaar, Th. (1997), 'Ost-Erweiterung der EU und Migration aus Ost- nach Westeuropa. Zu große Hoffnung hier, zu starke Ängste dort und zu wenig gelernt aus der Erfahrung der EG-Süderweiterung', in W. Zohlnhöfer (ed.), *Osterweiterung der Europäischen Union*. Berlin: Duncker & Humblot.

Straubhaar, Th. & P. A. Fischer (1996), *Migration and Economic Integration in the Nordic Common Labour Market*. Copenhagen: Nordic Council of Ministers & Nordic Council.

Straubhaar, Th. & A. Wolter (1997), 'Globalisation, Internal Labour Markets and the Migration of the Highly Skilled', *Intereconomics. Review of International Trade and Development* 32 (4): 174-181.

Szydlik, M. (1990), *Die Segmentierung des Arbeitsmarktes in der Bundesrepublik Deutschland. Eine empirische Analyse mit Daten des sozioökonomischen Panels, 1984-1988*. Berlin: Sigma.

Tacke, V. (1999), 'Wirtschaftsorganisationen als Reflexionsproblem. Zum Verhältnis von Neuem Institutionalismus und Systemtheorie', *Soziale Systeme* 5: 55-81.

Tacke, V. (2000), 'Netzwerk und Adresse', *Soziale Systeme* 6: 291-320.

Taylor, J. E. & Ph.L. Martin (2002), 'Human Capital: Migration and Rural Population Change', in B.L. Gardner & G.C. Rausser (eds.), *Handbook of Agricultural Economics.*, New York: Elsevier Science.

Thomas, W. I. & F. Znaniecki (1858, first 1918/1921), *The Polish Peasant in Europe and America*. New York: Dover.

Todaro, M. P. (1980), 'Internal Migration in Developing Countries: A Survey', in R.A. Eastelin (ed.), *Population and Economic Change in Developing Countries*, 361-401. Chicago: University of Chicago Press.

Trenzzini, B. (1998), 'Konzepte und Methoden der sozialwissenschaftlichen Netzwerkanalyse. Ein aktueller Überblick', *Zeitschrift für Soziologie* 27: 378-394.

Vertovec, S. (2001), 'Transnational Social Formations'. *Working Paper* '01-06n. Princeton University, The Center for Migration and Development. Princeton.

Waldinger, R. (1996), *Still the Promised City? African-Americans and New Immigrants in Post-Industrial New York*. Cambridge, MA: Harvard University Press.

Waldinger, R. & M. Lapp (1993), Back to the Sweatshop? Or Ahead to the Informal Sector?, *International Journal of Urban and Regional Research* 17: 6-29.

Wallerstein, I. (1974), *The Modern World System, Capitalist Agriculture and the Origins of the European World Economy in the Sixteenth Century*. New York: Academic Press.

Wallerstein, I. (1979), *The Capitalist World Economy, Essays*. Cambridge: Cambridge Univ. Press.

Walras, R. (1965), *Elements of Pure Economics or The Theory of Social Wealth*. London: Allen and Unwin (first published 1877).

Watson, R., K. Keasey & M. Baker (2000), 'Small Firm Financial Contracting and Immigrant Entrepreneurship', in J. Rath (ed.), *Immigrant Businesses: The Economic, Political and Social Environment*. Basingstoke/New York: Macmillan.

Werner, H. (1994): 'Integration ausländischer Arbeitnehmer in den Arbeitsmarkt. Deutschland, Frankreich, Niederlande, Schweden', in *Die Integration ausländischer Arbeitnehmer in den Arbeitsmarkt*, Nürnberg. Beiträge zur Arbeitsmarkt- und Berufsforschung (178): 85-187.

Weyer, J. (ed.) (2000), *Soziale Netzwerke. Konzepte und Methoden der sozialwissenschaftlichen Netzwerkforschung*. Munich/Vienna: Oldenbourg.

Williamson, O. (1975), *Markets and Hierarchies. Analysis and Antitrust Implications*. New York: Free Press.

Winter-Ebmer, R. (1994), 'Motivation for Migration and Economic Success', *Journal of Economic Psychology* 15: 269-284.

Wiskemann, G. (2000), *Strategisches Human Resource Management und Arbeitsmarkt*. Baden-Baden: Nomos.

Wit, G. de (1993), 'Models of Self-Employment in a Competitive Market', *Journal of Economic Surveys* 7 (4): 367-397.

Wolter, A. (1997), *Globalisierung der Beschäftigung. Multinationale Unternehmen als Kanal der Wanderung Höherqualifizierter innerhalb Europas*. Baden-Baden: Nomos.

Wolter, A. & M. Wolburg (1996), 'Die Wanderung Höherqualifizierter als Trend der Europäischen Binnenmigration – eine empirische Untersuchung am Beispiel der IAB-Beschäftigtenstichprobe', Europa-Kolleg Hamburg, *Diskussionspapier 2*.

Zhou, M. (1992), *New York's Chinatown: The Socioeconomic Potential of an Urban Enclave*. Philadelphia: Temple Univ. Press.

6. Social Integration of Immigrants with Special Reference to the Local and Spatial Dimension[1]

Olivier Asselin, Françoise Dureau, Lucinda Fonseca, Matthieu Giroud, Abdelkader Hamadi, Josef Kohlbacher, Flip Lindo, Jorge Malheiros, Yann Marcadet and Ursula Reeger

1. Introduction

This chapter deals with the social dimension of integration processes of immigrants. The organisation of work units within IMISCOE defined the social dimension as distinct from the political, the economic and the cultural/religious dimension which are treated in the two preceding and the following chapter respectively. This field is a vast one covering a significant amount of research in the past decades. In surveying the literature on social integration we will focus specifically on its local and spatial expressions for reasons that we will unfold in the next pages.

In the first section, we discuss some of the conceptual issues related to the term 'integration' and its use in the academic and policy fields. We discuss the notion of integration as a general sociological concept and propose to use the social environment, in which individuals and groups form interdependencies, as the special unit of study. Focusing on spaces as the locus of developing interdependencies, we emphasise the spatial dimension of immigrants' social integration processes.

Section two focuses specifically on the spatial dimensions of integration. It reviews the relationships between the characteristics of the housing market and their implications in terms of socio-ethnic segregation, emphasising the spatial dimension of social integration. Immigrants' and ethnic minorities' geographical placement and the extent of their mobility condition their access to urban resources (e.g. housing, education, health, jobs and different kinds of goods and services). We discuss the basic concepts of ethnic segregation as well as its advantages and disadvantages by drawing on contemporary literature. The main determinants of residential segregation and the manner in which they are explained and conveyed in the literature are surveyed. Finally, we discuss the issue of accessibility to urban resources, as a spatial expression of social integration and its measurement.

In the third and final section, we seek to synthesise the key ideas and conclusions of the previous sections and present a number of proposals for future lines of research.

2. From assimilation to integration and back again

If the current use of the concept of integration in social sciences and policy when dealing with immigrant settlement is relatively recent, the associated notions of assimilation, acculturation and accommodation have a longer history.

The classical assimilationist approach finds its roots in the 1920s Chicago School of Sociology, led by Park and Burgess. Park has become well-known for his theory of the race relations cycle and is seen as one of the founding fathers of what is often called 'assimilation theory'. However, even in the name of the theory, which conceives a sequence of contact, competition, accommodation and, in the end, assimilation, it is clear that the focus of analysis is on the relations between people, especially between immigrants and native inhabitants of urban spaces (Park 1950). The ecological emphasis, taking the social environment as the unit of analysis, and the interest in the life world of actors[2] – stressing the importance of meaning and motives – is another prominent feature in the work of Park and others of the Chicago School. Contrary to what often is believed, these early theorists on migration and integration understood that assimilation, however 'apparently progressive and irreversible', would proceed best if immigrants could keep their own pace in adapting to life in the new country, building on their existing attitudes and memories. Also, Park and his collaborators regarded assimilation essentially as a two-way process in which the sharing of experiences and history in the longer term would incorporate people of different origins in a communal life, achieving 'a cultural solidarity sufficient at least to sustain a national existence' (Park 1930).

The concept of 'straight-line assimilation' was introduced at the end of the Second World War by Warner and Srole in their *Social Systems of American Ethnic Groups* (1945).[3] All groups in American society, they contended, would evolve towards the same existing universal culture of reference: the American way of life. However, the authors conceived of great differences in the pace in which this one-sided process of adaptation would come about. Warner and Srole invoke cultural distance (the Anglo-conformity gap) and even racial categorisation to explain the differential speed of assimilation they observe and predict.

In 1964, Milton Gordon coined some extremely influential notions in the subsequent scientific and public discourse on the integration of immigrants in his *Assimilation in American Life*. Although he did not develop a theory of assimilation in the proper sense, he did codify the process with a rigour formerly unheard of and identified several dimensions, for some of which he posited time-sequential relations. Acculturation, or the mastery of English and the adoption of some core behavioural patterns, values and goals, is a process that typically preceded incorporation into the status groups of the middle class. Gordon discriminates between extrinsic and intrinsic traits. The extrinsic traits are the ones required to engage in fruitful interaction with the host society; these are also the ones that can be easily accepted by the immigrants themselves. Gordon seems to have had membership of the most important contemporary religious streams in mind when thinking of acculturation. Using the traditional image of the melting pot, he judges it probable that 'American society has come to be composed of a number of "pots," or subsocieties, three of which are the religious containers marked Protestant, Catholic, and Jew, which are in the process of melting down the white nationality background communities contained within them.' Those three pots, he continued, 'are tending to produce, with somewhat different speeds, products which are culturally very similar, while remaining structurally separate.' So, though a prerequisite, acculturation is, according to Gordon, not a *sufficient* condition for further socio-economic integration. He considers that assimilation in all domains of life will only happen if immigrants and their descendants are accepted, and are willing to join the primary groups within the host society (Price 1969). Entry into the socio-economic mainstream and subsequent internalisation of intrinsic traits will only follow suit if immigrants and their descendants join these primary groups. Gordon calls this *structural assimilation*. Somewhat along the lines of Warner and Srole, Gordon also formalised and developed the concept of the *melting pot*, as a possible social outcome of the assimilation process, if the groups in presence were strong enough: in the final stage, a new culture would emerge as a kind of fusion of elements coming from the different groups, eventually with an Anglo-Saxon group dominating. Although Gordon's hypothetical formulations suggest a full-blown theory, his concepts are not always clearly enough defined (What is precisely the difference between intrinsic and extrinsic traits? What are primary groups?), and how suppositions on diachronic sequences should be understood in causal terms is not clear either.

Almost simultaneously, empirical evidence urged other authors to severely criticise the ideas of the 'melting pot' and 'straight-line assimilation'. For instance, in *Beyond the Melting Pot*, Glazer and Moynihan (1963) discuss the position of several immigrant groups (including African-Americans, then still referred to as 'Negroes') and observe that, although all these 'ethnicities' have become American in so many respects, they have not 'melted' together with the (Anglo-American) 'old stock' into the mainstream. Although the authors, in their exposé on the different groups, highlight the different pace of upward mobility between them, Glazer and Moynihan's most central point is that, in the socio-economic and political context of New York, all groups have an interest in keeping, developing and claiming their ethnic origin, while at the same time becoming very American. A different direction was followed by Gans (1979, 1996), who posited the 'bumpy line theory' (socio-economic decline for the second generation was very well possible) and questioned Warner and Srole's assumption of a positive relationship between acculturation and social mobility, by stating that acculturation might, in fact, be connected to downward, not upward, mobility.

From here, it is only a small step to the notion of segmented assimilation, introduced by Portes and Zou (1993). The development of this idea is based on the recognition that immigrants are incorporated in different strata of the host society. They, or rather their descendants, may join the middle class by a process of – often intergenerational – upward social mobility. Others and their descendants may, however, link up with disadvantaged societal strata, because, for instance, they have come to live with them in adjacent neighbourhoods, and children take over the oppositional frame of reference of their disappointed peers from these disadvantaged groups. The third possibility is not so much assimilation in yet another stratum or segment of society, but a strategy to keep the influence of the disadvantaged groups and their disillusioned behaviour at bay. These groups create their own self-supporting communities and networks, and find their way upward in the host society by developing their own economic niches.

The aforementioned reference to Portes and Zou points to the trend towards the recovery of the assimilation concept, in both North America and Europe. In the first case, the long-standing experience of immigration to the United States, marked by diverse public discourses, policies and 'integration' practices, has led to a progressive shrinking of socially relevant differences between groups, which makes the *process* of assimilation a legitimate subject of (comparative) research and analysis. As far as Europe is concerned, the comeback of the term 'assimilation' is associated with a growing fear that, without staunch policy measures, immigrants and their descendants will *not* integrate and will pose a serious danger to the cohesion of European societies. After having stressed the contested character of the concept of assimilation especially in Europe, Heckmann (2004) observes a growing awareness that minority formation among migrants is leading to and reinforcing ethnic stratification, which lends support to positions and policies that are critical of cultural pluralism and multiculturalist principles. He gives the examples of the Netherlands, Great Britain and Germany where –

nationally different – manifestations of multiculturalist thought are giving way to policies of assimilation, materialised, for instance, in so-
called 'integration programmes'.

The convergence of, on the one hand, European public and political
interest in the concepts of assimilation and integration, and the renewed, chiefly American, attention for the concept in the social scientific debate, on the other, seems to have almost opposing causes. This
should make us all the more cautious about using these concepts. Studies on immigration and integration processes that are informed by
policy goals often eclipse what is going on in the lives of immigrants.
Policy discourse and policy measures still assume a more or less linear
path of 'integration' (the Warner and Srole model), ignoring that the
complex interplay of acculturation, identification, social status and concrete interaction patterns of individuals may produce many 'outcomes'.
Additionally, keeping with this perspective, assimilation is frequently
assumed to be a 'one-sided' concept, based on the principle that only
newcomers change with time, independent of the paths they take. The
truth is that the large numbers of immigrants having settled in Europe
have caused significant changes in their receiving societies.

3. Defining integration: a proposal

Following this brief historical overview of the construction and meaning of the concept of assimilation and its comeback in the policy and
academic fields in the last years, we now turn to the definition of the
concept of integration that we want to adopt and operationalise.

This task is a difficult one in view of the generality, indefiniteness
and even imprecision that are associated with the use of concepts such
as integration and assimilation. First of all, it is not clear what they
mean in concrete terms: the measuring stick, the point of reference, is
often indicated with vague vocabulary like 'the society in general', 'the
mainstream', or 'the middle class'. These reference units are only va-
guely circumscribed – being socio-demographic entities, their character
and size have changed and will continue to change in the course of
time (Alba & Nee 2003). Secondly, without explicit qualifications, concepts like assimilation and integration not only cover different dimensions of behaviour and experience, they pertain to a multitude of social
fields as well. Behavioural and experiential dimensions can be identified regarding socio-economic position and status, interaction, and
identification. And these positions/dimensions should be distinguished
in several social sub-fields such as education, housing, spatial mobility
and health. Using these general concepts, outside the context of those
dimensions and social fields, does not help us to distinguish between

processes and their causes. Finally and perhaps most importantly, these terms do not only refer to a process, but to the end-stage as well. This is the way they are used in public *and* academic discourse and many scholars find it difficult to get away from the normative dimension, not only referring to the processes as desirable but also accepting their appropriateness as self-evident.

Viewed as a process, the concept of integration indicates on the one hand the further strengthening of relations within a social system and, on the other hand, relating additional actors or groups to an existing social system and its core institutions (Heckmann 2004: 4). The second meaning is the one attached to the concept when it is used within migration and ethnic studies. Leaving aside the problem of how we should understand core institutions and their definition, we have good reasons to focus on the connotation of integration within the framework of a system approach. Firstly, since we will concentrate on the development of interdependencies between individuals and groups in certain territorial spaces, we should approach our subject matter as a relational issue and not as a feature of a category or group of actors. Secondly, perceiving of integration as the development of interdependencies in a given environment offers the opportunity to identify different 'levels' at which relations may develop.

If we define integration as *the process in which people and their activities become intertwined in social life and form mutual interdependent relations of some form and to a certain degree*, we are describing i) a multilevel and ii) a multidimensional process.

Let us first examine *the different levels of scale* on which processes (in all different dimensions) can be analysed. In concentrating on the *space* in which individuals and groups interact, we take the spatial focus to be an opportunity *and* a challenge, and we assume that the analysis of integration at the local (urban) scale must be intertwined with other scales of analysis (the regional, the national and even the supra-national), due to the nature of the migration phenomenon and also to the scope of action of the individual and institutional actors more directly involved in the process. The influence of large-scale processes within the local and national society, as well as of global processes, should not be disregarded.

In specific terms, we can distinguish the micro-, meso- and macro-level. The micro-level treats the more or less consciously motivated interaction between individuals, as well as their attitudes towards each other and towards the institutions that rule inside subgroups and the social environment as a whole.[4] The meso-level concerns the development of institutions within (sub-)groups and (institutional) relations between groups and institutions in the social environment, as a consequence of arising interdependencies (be they conflictive or cooperative) between (groups of) newcomers and native inhabitants. Processes on the macro-level are mostly not the product of goal-orientated action of individuals or groups locally; people generally do not feel to have command over them and they are often felt to intrude on the life of individuals and groups. However, instances of initiatives to guide or confront these processes in a creative and effective way, individually or collectively, have been identified in many places, although interaction patterns unwind in ways unexpected by most parties involved.[5] The differential distribution of power in society, and in the social environment under study, is of overriding importance here.

The processes we identify on the micro-, meso- and macro-levels are not mutually independent. As we have seen, they also transgress the boundaries *we* have drawn around our locus of research. This is the case with processes on all three levels. Besides being multidimensional, the chains of interdependency are, socially *and* spatially, extensive.

Immigrant integration is often seen as resulting from the interplay between structural factors in the receiving society ('structure of opportunity', 'allocation processes') and purposive behaviour of immigrants (informed by 'cultural' characteristics, especially when they are referred to as a group or ethnic category). When focusing on the interaction of processes on different levels, it is inevitable that we combine concepts that refer to these different vantage points. We should however be careful not to assign volitional or 'culture-inspired' concepts only for understanding the behaviour, position and orientation of (relative) newcomers and reserve the more structural-processual terms for everything immigrants and their offspring encounter in 'the receiving society'. The often extended and tight networks of immigrants, for instance, generate 'domestic' structures of constraint and opportunity that cannot be conceived of as purposive behaviour or as consolidated by cultural transmission only (Lindo 1995).

Concerning the *analytical dimensions* that might best describe the developing entanglement within and between categories of actors in a certain space, we have taken Esser (2001) as a departure point. He proposes four dimensions of, what he calls, social integration: acculturation, positioning, interaction and identification (Esser 2001: 16).[6] He defines social integration as 'the inclusion [of individual actors] in already existing social systems'.[7] However, since we propose a relational focus, and the social environment in which (groups of) people interact as the unit of analysis, we need to define these four dimensions in a relational way.

We take '*acculturation*' to refer to the acquisition, development and mutual transmission of knowledge and competences, and the degree

and way in which these are variably distributed in the social environment under study. Acculturation is emphatically not restricted to the
process of acceptance of practices that brings one ahead in the world; it
refers in equal measure to the borrowing of practices that commonly
are seen as, for instance, anti-social, unhealthy or detrimental to upward mobility.[8] Neither should it be conceived as a taking-over of complete behavioural or ideational codes. Often bits and pieces are mutually borrowed and reworked in a creative way, to produce a certain
consistency with 'traditional' patterns, thus becoming transformed in
the process into something different from either the borrowing or the
lending 'culture'.

Positioning refers to the process of occupying different positions in
society, and of gaining, maintaining, defending or losing access to resources that are relevant for the position of an individual or a group,
especially in the substantive domains of education, income, housing,
mobility and health.

One specific positioning variable that has not been given much attention[9] is of great importance when concentrating on a concrete social
environment as locus of analysis. This is the opportunity for (groups
of) actors to access various resources that are, in their nature, to a
greater or lesser degree dispersed within the space under study.[10] The
spatial constellation of relevant resources conditions its access. We propose to regard it as a resource in itself (albeit a relational one) as its
quality is obviously variable. *Geographical positioning,* as we propose to
call it, has two derivatives, *geographical mobility* and *geographical accessibility,* which can both be regarded as resources as well. Differential mobility (real or virtual, associated with the use of communication technologies) of individuals, groups and places leads to inequalities in access to resources, especially in an increasingly mobile society. On the
other hand, if the key urban social resources of a certain place display
a high accessibility pattern (due to an efficient location, a good public
transport system or a well-planned road infrastructure), inequalities of
access decrease. In summary, equal and easy access to housing, work,
education, health and leisure facilities – to name the most important
resources – presupposes the possibility to overcome the obstacle of the
geographical dispersion of these resources.

Interaction is a third dimension, and obviously connected to the
others. The relational character of this dimension is evident. We can
discern many different kinds, in terms of intensity, multi- or single-
strandedness, positive versus negative emotive content, institutional
context, social environment, formal or informal communication, intra-
versus intergroup character, individual opposed to collective exchanges,
gender make-up, and contacts across or within generations. Interaction

has many sides, and space is lacking to highlight all of the relevant aspects.

We should, however, not forget that interaction in which a local population is involved is not confined to the particular urban spaces on which our comparative inquiries focus. Natives and newcomers alike often develop, both formally and informally, significant relationships with others outside research contexts, and the impact of these relationships should be taken into consideration.

Identification comprises acts and feelings of belonging besides representational processes and mutual stereotyping, and has individual as well as collective aspects. Having broadened the scope of the dimension in this way, we will have to take into account the public discourses on 'integration' that prevail locally and which might have come to constitute a more or less dominant part of the 'local identity'.

The conceptual framework for the study of societal integration developed here will serve as a tool for more systematic empirical research in which the local and spatial dimension are taken as a starting point. In the next section we will specifically review what the literature on the spatial aspect of integration may contribute.

4. Residential segregation, housing market and immigrants

The concept of segregation

'Residential segregation is a fundamental feature of urban landscapes' (Kaplan & Holloway 1998). It is a phenomenon that occurs with such frequency across divergent historical and geographical settings that we may be tempted to think that segregation is either ubiquitous (and thus not problematic) or necessary (and thus amenable to facile interpretation). 'There is not a spatial segregation, but there are multiple segregations' (Barbosa 2001: 17). Indeed, residential segregation is a multidimensional concept (Johnston et al. 2002: 216). Because segregation is a very specific phenomenon – to the particular groups involved, to the individual contexts within which it occurs, to the historical timing of the encounters which produce and sustain it and to the scale within which it is observed – attempts to understand segregation as an ubiquitous phenomenon are frustrated by its tremendous diversity (Kaplan & Holloway 2000).

One basic problem arises from the fact that a Babel of languages concerning segregation-related terminology can be observed in the literature. The terms 'spatial segregation', 'socio-spatial segregation', 'housing segregation', 'residential segregation', 'ethnic (residential) segregation' and 'social segregation' are often mixed, sometimes used in one and the same sense but sometimes also with different meanings without being defined exactly.

What does 'segregation' really mean? Definitions presented in several recent studies vary from 'the residential separation of groups within a broader population' (Özüekren & Van Kempen 1997: 22) to 'the spatial translation of social inequality' (Fassmann 2002: 14). It embraces not only a spatial but also a temporal dimension. Segregation refers both to the processes of social differentiation and to the spatial patterns that result from such processes, which are usually located at the urban scale. Factors playing a role in the context of ethnic residential segregation of immigrants include: socio-economic status, the status of migrants on the housing market, discriminatory mechanisms within a society, the handling of migrant families by public housing authorities, legislative frameworks and last but not least ethnic affiliation demonstrated by the migrants themselves.

A group is considered to be completely mixed when its members are distributed uniformly relative to the rest of the population. The greater the deviation from this uniformity, the larger the degree of segregation (Johnston 2000). Spatial segregation exists when some areas show over-representation and other areas show an under-representation of members of a certain ethnic or social group. In most popular uses, the term is applied only to situations in which disadvantaged groups occupy circumscribed territories (Brun & Bonvalet 1998: 319-326; Dangschat 2000a: 209215; Grafmayer 1994).

Broadly speaking, spatial segregation is generated through the interplay of three opposing spatial forces (Massey 1984): 1) concentration, 2) dispersion and 3) succession. The concentration of ethnic groups is rooted in the spatial differentiation of the urban economy, in housing market mechanisms and reinforced by the nature of immigrants and immigration. Dispersion is driven by socio-economic mobility and acculturation, and is based on the fact that a differentiated urban economy distributes resources and opportunities unevenly in space, encouraging immigrants to move in order to improve their position in society. While succession is driven by immigration, it is strongly influenced by conditions in the larger urban economy. If immigration coincides with a period of metropolitan expansion, then residential changeover is very rapid, as socially mobile classes vacate neighbourhoods, leaving them for arriving immigrants. If immigration occurs during a time of economic stagnation, migrants pile up in established enclave areas because succession is slow. Succession is also dependent upon the relative amount of capital employed in economic production and the extent to which it is spatially concentrated, in addition to the cost and availability of urban transportation.

Labelling concentration areas: Ghetto versus ethnic enclave

One of the most controversial terms used for the contemporary 'segregation landscape' is 'ghetto'. From the Jewish diaspora in medieval Europe to the Black experience in the post-Fordist American metropolis, the concept of the ghetto has historically designated a spatial environment bound by confinement and seclusion.

All ghettos are segregated, but not all segregated areas are ghettos. Thus, residential segregation is a necessary but not a sufficient condition for ghettoisation (Wacquant 2004: 6). Based on Boal's (1999) analysis of the processes and patterns of intra-urban ethnic segregation, four types of migrant 'spatialised' communities can be classified: 1) areas of assimilation-pluralism, where the host society is a large element in the local population, but does not form a majority; 2) mixed minority areas, shared by two or more ethnic groups; 3) polarised areas, with one minority group substantially encapsulated, forming at least 60 per cent of the population; 4) ghettos, which are characterised by a high degree of concentration of one minority group. In addition, a large share of the total minority population lives in this area.

The ghetto may according to Boal (1981) be either voluntarily embraced or negatively enforced. Most authors, however, see the latter mechanism as the dominant one. A hegemonic group wishing to separate itself from its perceived inferiors will attempt to enforce segregation upon the lower group (Lemon 1991; Massey & Denton 1993). The urban ghetto constitutes an extreme form of spatial segregation. A ghetto can be defined as an 'institutionalised residential district that is almost exclusively the preserve of one ethnic or cultural group' (Johnston 2000). 'Institutionalised' means that the inhabitants did not choose their residential area themselves but were to some degree coerced by society. This coercion may be direct (for instance by law) or indirect (by subtle discrimination) (Özüekren & Van Kempen 1997: 23). Not every area inhabited by an ethnically, racially or religiously defined group is a ghetto. The involuntary aspect is a very important dimension. Without the aspect of coercion, the area is more appropriately described as an ethnic enclave (ibid.).

Marcuse (2001: 3) makes a comparable distinction: A ghetto is an area of spatial concentration used by forces within the dominant society to separate and to limit a particular population group, externally defined as racial, ethnic or foreign, held to be, and treated as, inferior by the dominant society. An enclave, on the other hand, is an area of spatial concentration in which members of a particular population group, self-defined by ethnicity or religion or otherwise, congregate as a means of protecting and enhancing their economic, social, political and/or cultural development (ibid.). According to Peach (2001), one has to distinguish between ghettos and ethnic enclaves on the basis of the following differences (see Table 6.1).

Table 6.1 *Ghetto versus ethnic enclave*

Ghetto	Ethnic enclave
Dually segregated: a large majority of a minority group lives in it; a large majority in it belongs to a certain minority	Dually diluted: only a minority of the group resides in it; they form only a minority of the population of the area associated with the group
Negative	Positive
Enforced	Voluntary
Expanding	Residual
Real	Symbolic
Threatening	Touristic
Permanent	Temporary

Source: Peach (2001: 13), modified.

Politicians and the media frequently use the term 'ghetto' indiscriminately with respect to the situation in Europe. The term evokes negative connotations and indeed polarises more than can be substantiated by the factual situation (Ellingsen 2003: 9). 'So far, in European societies, few ghettos can be found [...]. The fear [of ghettoisation] is based on the idea that a sequence of events may happen which is regarded as unwanted. That sequence is: increasing spatial segregation will lead to increasing separation of different social and ethnic classes and population categories; in its turn, that will produce ghetto-like developments and will finally result in the disintegration of urban society' (Fortuijn et al. 1998: 367).

Housing segregation in Western European cities is almost nowhere as strong for minorities as it is for Blacks in American cities. There are a few examples in which 80 to 90 per cent of an area's population is of one minority (Huttman 1991: 21). Whereas the segregation index for African Americans in the United States is about 81 (Lucassen 2004: 9), the highest levels in Western Europe are about 68 (Bangladeshis in London) and for most groups below 50 (ibid.).

Frequently, policy making strategies considered ghettos a bad urban component. One justification for this lies in the presumption that involuntary allocation of space to any group is undesirable in a democratic society. Another one relies on the desirability for diversity, for mixing, for open interchange and communication, among population groups in a democratic society (Marcuse 2001: 3), processes that are apparently more limited in the socio-spatial boundaries of the ghetto.

Interestingly enough, segregation of elite migrants is never classified as a problem (Kohlbacher & Reeger 1999). There is evidence from a lot of European cities that some elite migrant populations manifest high levels of segregation. Glebe's (1986) study on the Japanese in Düsseldorf, White's (1998) analysis on the Japanese in London or Malheiros' (2001) discussion on the case of British in Lisbon are good examples of this.

Measuring residential segregation and its limits

There is a substantial literature on methodological problems of measuring segregation (see for example Cortese et al. 1976; Stearns & Logan 1986; Waldorf 1993; Wong 1998). Most studies of socio-spatial segregation use either one or both of two main technical approaches: 1) mapping where members of the various groups live in a city and 2) computing indices that show the degree of residential separation.

One critical point is that both methods can only give some indication of the degree of concentration for different groups – and, as a corollary, its degree of separation from other groups (Johnston et al. 2002: 210). A large number of techniques, differing not only in mathematical formulae but also in conceptualisation of segregation itself exist (see Peach 1981). Three basic concepts for the measurement of segregation can be distinguished: 1) measures of evenness:[11] index of segregation, index of dissimilarity, Gini-coefficient; 2) measures of exposure/isolation between social and ethnic groups; 3) measures of clustering.

An important methodological issue in segregation analysis is the designation of an appropriate reference group. Many studies of segregation proceed by examining selected groups to a) 'all others'; or b) some key reference group.

The first approach has been used in the numerous dissimilarity index or exposure index studies that use group-versus-non-group measures. In the exposure framework, this is commonly termed the 'isolation' index. The second option – the use of one key group – implies that such a particular comparison is meaningful or appropriate. Thus, the social distance of a group from the culturally dominant group would be captured by the pairwise segregation index and applications using, for example, Turks versus autochthones.

Numerous indices of segregation have been developed over the years. The most popular and widely used of it are the indices of Duncan and Duncan (1955a, 1955b) and the index of Taeuber and Taeuber (1965). The segregation index expresses the percentage of people from a certain social or ethnic group that would have to move to different neighbourhoods to make that group non-segregated. The Taeuber and Taeuber index of segregation is based on block data. The formula for computing the index is based on the proportion of households of a specific group in a given block in relation to the proportion of this minority or migrant group in the city as a whole (see also Saltman 1991: 2

ff.). The Duncan and Duncan segregation index is one-half the sum of the absolute values of the differences between the respective distributions, taken area by area within a city. It is computed between one group and all other groups combined (compare White 1983, 1986 and Wong 1998). The value of the segregation index is influenced by the size of the spatial units used in the calculation (Jones 1991: 183; Lee 1977; Peach 1987: 43-45). The size of the populations in analysis may also influence the results of the indices. Large population groups tend to display smaller segregation values because their group members have a higher probability of diffusion (in statistical terms) than individuals part of small population groups (being composed by few people, the probability of finding them scattered throughout several geographical sub-units is, naturally, smaller).

The index of dissimilarity (ID)[12] compares the residential location of pairs of groups (e.g. group A versus group B; A versus C; B versus C, etc.) according to their proportion in the total population of the community. It gives a measure of the net percentage of one population that would have to relocate in order to produce an equally distributed (nonsegregated) population. The higher the index is, the greater the degree of segregation. Frequently, the results of the dissimilarity indices computed for all pairs of key groups settled in certain metropolitan or urban regions are presented in a matrix that allows to compare which groups display similar spatial distribution patterns and which groups display very different distributions. Indices of evenness will be computed for a multi-group analysis rather than the traditional two-group analysis.

Reliance on the single measure of segregation index was strongly criticised by Lieberson (1980, 1981) who pointed out that a given level of the segregation index means very different things to majority and minority groups. In order to assess asymmetrical experiences, Lieberson proposed to use so-called P* indices of isolation/exposure that give the closest measure of the degree of spatial segregation. This measure of isolation has come into more general use since the 1980s. Unlike ID, it is an asymmetrical measure. It recognises that the degree of exposure of a small group to a large group is different from the exposure of the large group to the small group. Unlike ID, its use has tended to be descriptive rather than analytical in correlation regressions. In their subsequent use (e.g. Jones 1983; Robinson 1980), these have come to be known as exposure, isolation or interaction indices. They measure the chances that members of an ethnic group have of encountering, in their neighbourhood, a member of another ethnic group. Like segregation indices, the value of P* indices is influenced by the scale of the neighbourhoods used in the calculation. These effects of scale, however, are not as straightforward as those of segregation indices. If a scale change brings along an increase in chances of interaction within the group, then it follows that its chances of interactions with other groups must, in aggregate, be decreasing.

Given the diversity of the migrant population in European metropolitan areas, it is necessary to compute multi-group indices, extending beyond the conventional two-group approach. Thus efforts have been directed toward modifying segregation methods to capture the multi-ethnic milieu (Reardon & Firebaugh 2003; Wong 1998). Still, there is an important task here. The availability of improved measures, data management techniques and the rapidly evolving conceptualisation of ethnicity and metropolitan residence (ethnic pluralism) converge to argue for a view on residential patterns that is at once comprehensive and revealing the pattern of that ethnic residential mosaic. A method should be developed that incorporates detailed ethnic diversity and provides a descriptive summary measure of the segregation of an ethnic group with reference to the panoply of all groups.

Determinants of residential segregation

A rich empirical literature has focused on the underlying causes of segregation and measuring the consequences of segregation. Researchers have attempted to measure the extent to which segregation can be explained by differences in income, wealth and education. A related strand in the literature has explored whether segregation is driven by housing preferences of households as they make their residential location decisions or by some form of centralised discrimination. Others like Sarre et al. (1989: 39) see many factors at work stating that segregation and 'ethnic disadvantage in housing stems from a combination of cultural choices, economic differences, institutional policies and practices, and racial or cultural discrimination'. Most of the housing segregation literature has focused on residential preferences (e.g. Clark 1991, 1992; Farley et al.1994) and the geographic mobility of individuals that underlies segregation (Massey et al.1994; South & Crowder 1997, 1998).

Segregation in any particular place for any particular group results from a complex interplay of forces ranging in scale from the local to the global. Any reasonable account should be able to understand whether the choices and constraints experienced are due to global forces, national forces, regional forces, local forces or even neighbourhood dynamics (Kaplan & Holloway 2000).

Only empirical research can answer the question concerning the causes of socio-spatial segregation. Most explanations of segregation are based on three hypotheses:

- A range of discriminatory private practices and public policies that restrict housing opportunities for specific groups and serve to create and perpetuate segregated housing. It is argued that these policies and practices, and individual prejudices and stereotypes, are primarily responsible for the formation of ethnic ghettos and for the persistence of segregation in urban housing markets (Massey 2001; Massey & Denton 1988, 1993; Yinger 1995). Discrimination means treating groups differentially, which may be economically motivated (Yinger 1995), whereas exclusion is an institutionalised policy that prevents minorities from locating in specific areas (Anas 2004: 8).
- A second explanation focuses on economic status arguing that the spatial concentration of ethnic groups reflects their financial status. Since some ethnic groups in general have higher incomes and control more wealth than others, they have more choices in the housing market (Becker 1957; Clark 1986). Although segregation by income does not necessarily imply spatial segregation, the two are in practice strongly correlated (Anas 2004: 2). In the context of socio-economic explanations of socio-spatial segregation, European researchers usually point out that immigrants' socio-economic status does not allow them to enjoy housing comparable to that of the native population (Friedrichs & Alpheis 1991; Huttman 1991: 33).
- Individual choice, arguing that most households generally prefer to live in culturally homogeneous neighbourhoods. The housing market, from this perspective, reflects the freely chosen preferences of buyers who make their voluntary decisions in a free market (Glazer 1975; Thernstrom & Thernstrom 1997). This may be valid for the US situation but does not fit for the segmented housing markets in most European metropolises.

Although each of these approaches is relevant in explaining segregation in European cities, in each metropolis a different mixture of factors is responsible for the specific local segregation patterns. A significant problem arises therefore, when observations and data from various cities are conflated. One must not overlook the specificity of the national and local history and institutional context.

While the basic facts of segregation are well documented, there is less investigation into the experiences of the groups that suffer the consequences of segregation. Most of the research on segregation is done from a scientific distanced perspective or with a normative orientation towards the political claim for mixed housing areas. In most cases, the perspective of migrants themselves living in more or less segregated areas is completely neglected. Do they prefer to settle in mixed residential areas, or is it advantageous for them to live more segregated? In which stage of the integration process do they evaluate segregation positively?

One of the few studies that tried to provide answers to these questions was done in Vienna by Fassmann et al. (2004). The inquiry, including more than 400 Turks, former Yugoslavs, Poles and Germans living in the Austrian capital, showed clear divergences in the evaluation of segregated housing between the various migrant groups due to different valuations attributed to factors such as cultural and religious traditions, mutual support, nostalgia for home or practices of mobility.

Evaluation of segregation: advantages and problems

Since the days of the Chicago School, the relation between segregation and integration or assimilation has been vividly discussed. The same structural differentiation of society that makes segregation possible also may lead to its demise through spatial assimilation. The driving forces behind spatial assimilation are acculturation and socio-economic mobility. In Western societies, acculturation implies an achievement-orientated outlook that reinforces the link between social and spatial mobility. Many scholars and politicians assume that high levels of social and/or ethnic segregation, which often go hand-in-hand with high levels of ethnic concentration, will obstruct integration and participation in society. Thus, segregation may generate negative intra-ethnic features. Pronounced ethnic residential segregation is usually conceived of as a failure of integration policies (Ellingsen 2003: 7). Growing up in a purely ethnic environment may slow down assimilation, putting the residents at a disadvantage. Positive peer effects may be absent in segregated schooling. Spatial isolation can have adverse economic effects such as difficulties in acquiring jobs.

The study by Duncan and Lieberson (1959) was of long-lasting importance, demonstrating an inverse correlation between high ethnic segregation indices and modest assimilation levels of immigrants based on their residential distribution in urban areas. Since that analysis, many social scientists (e.g. Massey & Denton 1993; Peach 1981) have maintained that residential patterns are valid indicators of assimilation or integration in general.

Concentration is felt to hamper the social mobility of those with a weak social position and/or low skills, particularly immigrants of non-Western origin. Although these ideas may have some validity in contexts where extremely high levels of social and ethnic segregation exist, they are hardly tested in contexts with more moderate levels of segregation and stronger welfare states (compare Dangschat 2002; Fassmann 2002). In these cases, the idea that spatial segregation of immigrant groups is associated with a lack of integration is far from proven.

Furthermore, in contexts such as that of the European city, where a diversity of ethnic groups frequently mix in the same (or neighbouring) quarter, segregation levels tend to be lower and the relationship between spatial concentration and integration levels is even less clear.

Table 6.2 *The relationship between ethnic segregation and assimilation*

Phase	Relation between immigrants and the society in country of destination	Housing areas	Ethnic segregation
1	Immigration	Ethnic residential quarters	Extremely high
2	Competition (or conflict) for housing areas, labour market positions and social status	Ethnic residential quarters	Extremely high
3	Accommodation	Initial phase of moving out of social climbers	Medium level
4	Assimilation	Ethnic residential quarters disappear, perfectly assimilated migrants are moving	Disappeared

Source: Fassmann (2002: 18).

Several authors have identified both advantages and disadvantages to the residential segregation of migrant groups (Cutler & Glaeser 1997; Van Kempen & Özüekren 1998: 1632-1635). Among the negatives are counted: delayed or obstructed integration, difficulties in providing proper municipal services and school facilities, dissatisfaction among the non-immigrants in the area and social conflicts, delinquency and deterioration of the built environment. Among the positives are: intra-ethnic support, a sufficiently large grouping to enable a supportive minority network, and ethnic business and institutions.

Often segregation is seen exclusively as 'bad' or derogatory (Brun & Bonvalet 1998: 322; Grafmayer 1994) and associated with social injustices (Harvey 1997) but, as a matter of fact, socio-spatial segregation is not necessarily a problem *per se* for the whole urban society or for the migrants in particular. There is a high probability that it will become problematic if the most disadvantaged groups are placed in residential areas where their living conditions become further aggravated (Dangschat 2002).

'Segregation has become an issue of public debate. In this debate, segregation has an outspoken negative connotation and is predominantly focussed upon the ethnic dimension. The black ghetto in American cities symbolises the cumulation of the miseries of modern Western societies' (Fortuijn et al. 1998: 367) .[13] Many social scientists of residential segregation throughout the 20th century saw it as a negative feature of urban life – as a result of socio-economic processes which condemned members of minority ethnic groups to live in relatively deprived housing areas where, for a variety of reasons, their life chances were lower than average. But such attitudes were largely founded on the experience of African-Americans in US cities, where hyper-segregation is still the norm (Johnston et al. 2002: 231). Hyper-segregation, which Massey and Denton (1989, 1993) associate with five characteristics of ethnic minority residential patterns (uneven distributions, lack of exposure to others, concentration, centralisation and clustering), may well indicate social exclusion[14] – members of a group are virtually confined to enclaves/ghettos and as a consequence are being denied equal opportunities, not only economically but also more widely with regard to social justice and citizenship.

This contrasts, however, with the situation for many other immigrant groups in the US and for the situation in European cities in general. Thus, in some recent studies, segregation has been interpreted in a positive sense (compare Johnston et al. 2002), especially in the broader context of integration (Alba & Nee 1997). Spatial segregation is indeed not always a problem. The possibility for migrants of the same origin to communicate easily is the major advantage. Communication opens up the possibility for the continued existence of culture-specific manners and customs, not those of the mainstream society (Özüekren & Van Kempen 1997: 23). Indeed some segregation, indicative of pluralism, may bring positive benefits to a society, allowing those members of groups who wish to retain their identities by living in relatively culturally exclusive areas while participating fully in other aspects of urban life, and also providing a base-area within which business and employment opportunities can be developed (see Bolt et al. 1998; Galster et al. 1999).

A typical local government policy against residential segregation in European metropolises has been dispersal but this strategy remains a vividly debated issue. The social mix principle is often interpreted in a biased way. No one knows how to define it exactly. A common definition of an 'ideal social and ethnic mix' is really impossible, because of the locally diverging composition of the migrant population and the differences in the main determinants of segregation in different cities. What can be observed is that social mixing is applied when it regards the unattractive, devalorised neighbourhoods but that it is no more referred in cases of attractive districts (Sala Pala 2003: 12). In summary, there are researchers who find dispersal policies positive and others who criticise them and approve the more recent policies of improving poor housing areas, often inhabited both by migrants and natives (compare Arin 1991; Mik 1991).

Socio-spatial segregation and the housing market

Understanding the experiences of the various actors in urban housing markets can help to explain the phenomenon of segregation and to stimulate current political debates (Kohlbacher & Reeger 2002; Kohlbacher & Schwab 2002). The residential location decision of each household is a choice that is based on a set of housing possibilities available in the market. Each household's valuation of choice characteristics varies with its own characteristics, such as income, education, ethnicity, employment status and household composition. The spatial distribution of households is determined by the structure of the housing market (segmentation, spatial distribution and availability of flats), discrimination mechanisms in the housing market, direct preferences for the ethnic affiliation of one's neighbours (e.g. preferences on the part of recent immigrants to live with other immigrants of the same ethnic background) and preferences for ethno-specific aspects of neighbourhood qualities (e.g. ethnic infrastructure like groceries, mosques, etc.). Whether the effects of the interactions of household ethnicity and neighbourhood ethnic composition are the result of preferences or discrimination remains an often unanswerable question.

The housing market and socio-spatial segregation are strongly interwoven through contextual as well as individual factors. This contextual framework differs between countries and even between cities within the same country. These determinants are also changing through time. Locational differences and historical developments set the stage for the current housing conditions of all households that operate within a housing market. The contextual developments constitute a framework within which preferences and resources of households and the structure of the supply-side of the housing market play a role (Özüekren & Van Kempen 1997). In explaining the structure of the housing market as a determinant of ethnic residential segregation in Western Europe, the role of the state deserves close examination. Differences between countries concerning segregation emerge with respect to the role of the state. Market barriers may have an enormous influence on the spatial segregation patterns of immigrant groups. For instance, in the case in Vienna, accessibility rules with respect to different segments of the housing stock can be seen as one of the most important factors in explaining the residential patterns of Turks and Yugoslavs (Kohlbacher & Reeger 2002, 2003).

Contemporary state of the art of segregation-related research in Europe

In discussing the main issues in the residential segregation research above we have remarked some specific differences between the US and

European traditions. First of all, such studies started much earlier in the US and they initially focused particularly on African-Americans. Classical authors of racial segregation with emphasis on the Black minority are: Drake and Cayton (1945), Duncan and Duncan (1957), Taeuber and Taeuber (1965) and Massey and Denton (1993). Later Massey and Denton (1987, 1989) also did research on segregation patterns of Hispanics and Asians. More recently, an innovative analysis was made by Rehn (2002), measuring segregation in melting-pot suburbs.

Secondly, many American researchers on housing segregation are race relations specialists, whereas most of the European scientists are specialists on urban issues, housing experts, sociologists or geographers who are interested in spatial relations;

Thirdly, the focus in American literature is more on measurements of dissimilarity or effects of race relation laws and other integration efforts, whereas European research focus on residential patterns, often documented by maps, housing types, housing conditions and housing market affairs (see Huttman 1991: 26).

Fourthly, apart from such differences of timing, of groups involved and methods used, US and European cities do differ in their institutional build-up, leading to different results. Within Western European metropolitan areas, some degree of socio-spatial segregation between immigrants and the autochthonous population is usual whereas a complete residential mix can hardly be found (Özüekren & Van Kempen 1997: 22). Ethnic segregation in European cities tends to occur more on the level of houses and blocks; it more seldom occurs at the scale of city districts (White 1987; Kohlbacher & Reeger 2003), as it is in the USA.

In view of this specific situation in Europe it is worthwhile to look at the development of research, particularly comparative research, on European cities. Peach (1975) and Peach et al. (1981) were among the first to make a general and comparative analysis of European metropolises. Recent work by Peach (1996, 1997, 1999; Peach & Rossiter 1996) suggests that similar socio-cultural processes and spatial outcomes as in the US operate more generally among Western cities. A broad investigation on social exclusion and its spatial manifestations in European Cities was made by Madanipour et al. (1998). Van Kempen and Özüekren (1997) dedicated a study to housing and urban segregation of Turkish migrants all over Europe. Body-Gendrot and Martiniello (2000) studied the dynamics of social integration and social exclusion at the neighbourhood level. Musterd and Ostendorf (1998) presented a detailed overview about the impact of the welfare state upon urban segregation. Fortuijn et al. (1998) investigated many aspects of international migration and ethnic segregation and their impact on urban areas in Europe. As Wessel (2000a, b) points out, the potential for socio-economic and ethnic segregation now is larger in most EU countries than some decades ago.

In addition to these cross-comparative studies, there is now an extensive bulk of literature on segregation for all metropolises of the European countries. From John Rex's (1981) almost classical study about segregation in British cities, where he identifies the social solidarity advantages that result for migrant communities of living close to each other, to the articles by Peach (1996), discussing the question of ghettos in Britain, or Simpson (2004) on racially segregated residential patterns of Northern UK cities, the scientific production on this topic made by British scholars is very abundant. But also outside the UK academia, an enormous amount of research on segregation of immigrants and their housing patterns has been developed, including the works of Andersson (1998), Blom (1999), Hansson (1998), Lindén and Lindberg (1991) and Wessel (2000a) for the Scandinavian cities. As far as Germany and Austria are concerned, several ethnic groups and cities have been scrutinised (Berlin: Schulz 2002; Hamburg: Grabowski et al. 2002; Vienna: Bockstefl et al. 1996; Dangschat 2000b; Fassmann & Münz 1996; Giffinger 1998; Giffinger & Wimmer 2002; Kohlbacher & Reeger 2002; Leitner 1982). The same holds for the Benelux metropolises (Amersfoort & De Klerk 1987; Kesteloot & Meert 2000; Kesteloot & Van der Haegen 1997; Kesteloot et al. 2001; Musterd and Ostendorf 1996; Peleman 2002; Perchinig 2002). For France, studies have been developed by Guillon and Noin (1996), Lévy and Brun (2000), Menanteau (1994), Merlin (1999), Pinson (1992), Simon (1998) and Stébé (1999), several of them addressing the particular case of spatial concentration of immigrants in the urban peripheries (la banlieu).

The new immigrant metropolises of the Mediterranean countries of the EU have also been the subject of recent research that relate segregation patterns of minority groups with the specificities of migration and the particularities of national welfare states, namely on issues of housing market policy (Arbaci 2004 – cross-comparative research with several metropolises; Fonseca et al. 2002 – Lisbon Metropolitan Area; King & Iosifides 1999 – Athens; Malheiros 2000 and 2002 – cross-comparative with an emphasis on Lisbon; Tosi & Lombardi 1999 – Milan).

In the new EU member states in Central and Eastern Europe, the situation with respect to segregation is quite different from Western Europe. The degree of segregation and inequality under socialism was less than under capitalism (Smith 1989). In most post-socialist cities there were and still are neighbourhoods with concentrations of Roma population that are similar to American ghettos. These are areas with high ethnic and poverty concentration. There is a strong social stigma attached to these residential neighbourhoods and their residents (Wacquant 1999). Despite the relatively reduced number of foreigners settled in most of Eastern and Central European metropolises, socio-residential segregation gained increasing importance in these cities, in the last years (Andrusz et al. 1996, Sailer-Fliege 1999; Vesselinov 2004). Changes in the socio-spatial structures of Prague were studied by Sykora (1999) and the changing housing market and its impact on segregation in Warsaw and in Poland in general was analysed by Tasan (1999) and by Weclawowicz (1996).

'Accessibility to urban resources' as a spatial expression of social integration

As we have made clear in the first section of this chapter, the issue of location and access to urban resources is crucial to the multidimensional concept of integration defined in the first pages of this state of the art. Therefore, by privileging a spatial entry point into the issue of integration, it is important to point out that, in large cities where functional specialisation intensifies, mobility becomes a condition for access to facilities, employment, etc. Yet spatial mobility is deeply discriminatory. In such a context, it is even more necessary today than in the past to keep in mind the diversity and global nature of spatial practices and usage of the city, beyond its residential practices. While the geography of social areas becomes more complex, leading to the multiplication of spatial proximities between social classes, the spatial distribution of urban resources is increasingly unequal and mobility becomes an increasingly powerful filter for access to them. It is therefore essential to pose the question of access to spatial mobilities (international, residential and daily) for different categories of the population, as conditions for access to place-specific urban resources in the areas of health, education and housing.

How can we understand access to place-specific urban resources by various populations? A first step is considering that access to place-specific urban resources by various populations is determined by 1) the location of resources in urban space; 2) accessibilities between places within a city as defined by the transportation system; and 3) access to mobility by various categories of the population.

Individuals can inhabit the same place without living in the same city, as their income differentials translate into differences in access to mobility. While some may master metropolitan space, others are restricted to their homes. This puts into question the social mixing spatial policies that are all too often considered the panacea for resolving social problems in several cities. Significant inequalities are even present in households: despite living in the same place, the members of the household do not all dispose of the same resources in terms of mobility. For example, living in a peripheral urban area situated outside of public transport networks does not mean the same thing for a husband using his car and for his wife who is left to get around on foot.

The issue at hand is, in essence, to envision spatial mobility as a resource and to question the extent of access to mobility by international migrants and other urban inhabitants at different time scales: daily mobility (access to work, services, facilities, social and family relations) and residential mobility (moving from one residence to another, moving within a city or between cities within the same country, etc.).

Socio-spatial configurations are the object of continual change. Whether programmed or 'spontaneous', these changes are characterised by three elements:

- *Space*: An example of this is the creation of a housing offer geared towards a specific population (a gated residential community, a rehousing building for populations taken out of precarious housing conditions, etc.); but the degradation of a neighbourhood due to filtering (selective abandonment by certain populations) can also contribute to the concentration of more disadvantaged populations.
- *Relationships between places*: Accessibilities between places in a city can be suddenly put into question. This is the case when a new motorway or subway line has been created, leading to a reduction in the distance-time ratio and introducing new kinds of connectivity. This is also the case when automobile imports have been liberalised, leading to a saturation of the existing road network and tangibly increasing the distance-time between places within a city.
- *Time*: Urban rhythms condition access to spatial resources. For this reason, changes made to public transport or service schedules may facilitate or discourage access to them for certain population groups. Being able to master time is an important condition for being able to master urban resources. This is why some local public authorities have started to think and to act not only in space (the connection between places) but also along urban temporalities.

Without even changing their residence, inhabitants' access to the city can be profoundly modified. The term 'access' brings individual inhabitants to the fore, be they residents, users or simply people that frequent these areas. With their practices, acts and usages, they provide themselves with 'access' to a certain number of resources. This encourages us to consider the individual as a spatial actor. It is important to assess the spatial practices of diverse individuals and to understand how their usages produce spatialities via an approach focused on individuals' roles in situations and their values (Lévy & Lussault 2000).

It is also important to identify methodological approaches that enable the measurement of the accessibility to urban resources. Accessibility is a tool that can be used in spatial analysis whose variation allows us to measure the degree of exclusion of certain areas and, thus, of their inhabitants to local resources. While we should not reject qualitative approaches on the access to resources (observation of discrimination and racism in daily life, for example, that may limit or block access to a certain resource), the use of accessibility can bring us new, complementary information as a quantitative tool of measurement of socio-spatial segregation.

Such a measurement implies beginning with a starting place, a trajectory and a destination: an individual leaves one location in order to access another. Accessibility corresponds, therefore, to a relationship in a given space between population distribution and resource distribution, separated by a distance greater than or equal to zero (Grasland 1998). This distance may be measured in kilometres (Euclidian) but may also correspond to distance-time or distance-cost (Johnston 2000). In that way, the transport system to which an individual is restricted for his/her trajectory should equally be considered, characterised by the structure of the network, the quality of the infrastructure, topographic constraints, restrictions in force, technical characteristics of vehicles, traffic variability and, in the case of public transport, the schema of service (network, frequency, schedules) and vehicle fuel rates (Chapelon 2004). These different elements interact with one another, making for variation in time and space of the degree of accessibility to spatial resources.

In analysing accessibility, we can also consider the relationship between the distribution of the population groups and the resources they need (for example, between the residential distribution of immigrant populations and the distribution of education and health services). An analysis of the needs can be done, according to the desired proximity of resources (Smith 1980), that allows for the creation of a measurement tool between desired distance and effective distance. This can be completed by the use of threshold of tolerable distance (Thériault et al. 2003). A multivariate analysis of resources can also help to determine what resources are more or less important in residential choices, and then to relativise the variations of accessibility (Knox 1995). Moreover, we should integrate the population information, in order to understand which populations live in the areas in which accessibility to resources is weak. It becomes then possible to analyse the socio-demographic conditions of populations in order to determine the relationship between their needs and accessibility to resources.

Finally, the trajectory itself should be equally taken into consideration, given that the duration and cost vary in accordance with the mode and system of transport available. The idea here is to consider mobility as a resource, and to analyse the lack of access to mobility as a cause of exclusion. Indeed, access to mobility differs for instance in function with the individual's access to various modes of transport: travelling by car, public transport or by foot does not require the same abilities and budget. That access is by consequence a factor of exclusion, especially when considering women, children and the elderly, who are more often touched by that lack of mobility (Moseley 1978).

5. Research gaps and future strategies

The debate on the key notion of integration led to the critical discussion of American perspectives on assimilation since the 1920s Chicago School as well as to the context that has led to its recovery in the late 1990s (the neo-assimilationist perspective) in political and academic discourse, as an opposition to the notions of multiculturalism and cultural pluralism that have framed social insertion policies in the 1980s and '90s in countries such as the Netherlands or Sweden.

Departing from the general sociological notion of integration as the process in which people and their activities become intertwined in social life and form mutual interdependent relations of some form and to a certain degree, we must assume a relational focus on the social environment in which individuals and groups interact. The focus of research should not be any category or group of people but rather the relations of interdependences between individuals and groups and their development over time, within the spatial framework of a certain place.

In order to make the concept operational, we could start with the dimensions of social integration identified above and chose a set of indicators that might be associated with each of them. The development of this process should take into consideration:

– the different process levels: 1) purposeful behaviour of individuals, 2) collective behaviour between and within formal and informal groups and 3) the 'invisible hand' of institutional developments that often transgress the horizons of the life-world of individuals and face-to-face groups;
– the relevance of the context as expressed in xenophilia and xenophobia, in the regulatory mechanisms allowing the participation of foreigners in the different fields of social life – labour market, housing market, political sphere, etc., not only at the local level but also at the national and international one;
– the need to incorporate a clear spatial dimension in the concept of integration. This could be based on three issues: 1) the discussion of access to urban resources, 2) the analysis of the role of immigrants in the process of production and transformation of urban spaces and 3) the exploration of the relationship between (spatial) segregation and (social) integration. This could complement the more clas-

sical perspective of integration (socially-orientated – based on the ideas of social relations, participation in society) with another one, centred on the notion of 'construction of place', encompassing physical production, social practices and relations, identities and symbolic meanings.

Using the analytical tools outlined above and taking into account the conceptual queries expressed throughout this chapter as well as the researchers' interests and the research suggestions, the following themes or domains are considered priorities:

Housing and segregation

Firstly, a common methodology to analyse spatial segregation in European cities, associating classic segregation indices with measures of neighbourhood interaction and accessibility to urban resources (especially in the domains of education and health) should be developed. A set of cities (from Northern, Central and Southern Europe, including both older and newer cities of immigration) will be selected in order to test the methodology, framed in common research denominators. The comparative analysis of the recent evolution of the socio-ethnic segregation patterns will take the specific housing, planning, social and immigrant policies developed in each city into consideration. Immigrants will be considered an element of the urban dynamics and not a mere product of the interaction of external elements.

Secondly, a neighbourhood-level approach should be implemented with the purpose of identifying the perspective of several population groups (immigrants and non-immigrants) in relation to spatial concentration, segregation and group interaction. Experimental research conducted in Vienna, Lisbon and Amsterdam seems to point to low levels of group interaction in certain neighbourhoods as well as to divergent perspectives in relation to the perception and the meaning of the spatial concentration of immigrant groups. This research package aims to create a methodology that combines diverse techniques with the purpose of identifying the different meanings attributed by the various groups living in the same neighbourhood, to spatial concentration and group interaction.

Thirdly, processes of social and spatial mobility of the second generation also deserve a deeper analysis. Because immigrants' descendants face specific problems (in terms of housing mobility, social progression, representation, etc.) and the issues of spatial and social mobility are frequently interwoven, this issue should be subject to specific methodological approaches.

Education

Here we want to contribute to the neighbourhood-level approach by in-corporating a specific methodology geared towards the analysis of spa-tial accessibility to education resources. The notion of 'spatial accessi-bility' must be broadly defined so as to include the tangible elements (e.g. distance to housing concentrations, organisation of transport sys-tems, etc.) as well as the intangible ones corresponding to the percep-tion of the integration pathways and institutional prejudice, the quality of teaching, namely in terms of language training, the perception of group relations at school.

Health

Health and health care systems and their accessibility are another basic domain that should be studied within the approach we have outlined above. The international-comparative study of health and health care for immigrants is still in an early stage. Initiatives in this field should start at the basic level of surveying health conditions, health care sys-tems and practices in different countries and cities in a comparative analysis to develop specific methodology for an in-depth local analysis later.

Notes

1   An extensive and detailed version of this state of the art report is available as a full
     IMISCOE report: M.F. Fonseca and J. Malheiros (coord.) (2005), Social Integration
     and Mobility: Education, Housing and Health; IMISCOE Cluster B5 State of the Art
     Report. Lisbon: Centro de Estudos Geográficos, Universidade de Lisboa. In addition
     to the authors of the chapter (a specific section of the larger text), the following
     members of the cluster have also contributed to that report: Haleh Chahrokh
     (ICMPD), Milena Chimienti (SFM/FSM), Panos Hatziprokopiou (SCMR), David
     Ingleby (ERCOMER), Cláudia de Freitas (ERCOMER), Concepción Maiztegui (Univ.
     de Deusto), Ines Michalowski (IMIS), Meghann Ormond (CEG), Rosa Santibáñez
     (Univ. de Deusto), Elisabeth Strasser (ICMPD) and Rick Wolff (IMES). The various
     parts of the State of the Art Report (on education, health and housing) will be
     published as Working Papers on the IMISCOE website.
2   See for instance Park's essay on the marginal man (Park 1928).
3   This is the meaning most people nowadays (opponents and supporters alike) attach
     to assimilation.
4   Heckmann calls this 'social integration' (2004: 4).
5   See Lindo (1999) on a protracted conflict over the establishment of a mosque
     between the council of an Amsterdam borough and a group of Muslims of Turkish
     origin, in the macro-level context of urban renewal to which all local actors respond
     in a purposeful way, without however being able to predict the actual outcomes of
     these multi-stranded and multileveled processes of interaction.

6   See Heckmann (2003) for a comparable distinction in four dimensions.
7   See Esser (2004: 46; author's translation). Esser's distinction between system
    integration and social integration does not only identify separately institutional
    processes on a macro-level, on the one hand, and processes concerning individuals
    and groups (micro- and meso-levels), on the other, but signifies simultaneously the
    difference between 'integration of' and 'integration into'. This seems to be an
    unhelpful fusion of analytical categories, at least for our purposes.
8   See, for instance, Lindo (forthcoming) on the *lifestyle* and *way of life* of street youth of
    mixed origin in the city of Rotterdam, the Netherlands.
9   However, see Asselin et al. (2004) and Giroud (2004).
10 Some resources might even be positioned outside the spatial unit of research.
11 Evenness is the most widely used and fully explored dimension. Evenness refers to
    the differential distribution of two social groups among spatial units in a city
    (Massey & Denton 1993).
12 ID measures the percentage of a population that would have to shift its area of
    residence in order to replicate the distribution of the population with which it is
    being compared (Peach 1981). ID is a measure of unevenness with similar
    characteristics and values to the economists' Gini index.
13 In the volume of Huttman et al. (1991), the international recruited team of authors
    discuss the pros and cons of segregation, dispersal policy and mention the
    advantages of clustering. The positive functions of segregated areas are described,
    giving newcomers a helping hand and finding them housing and jobs (Barou 1988;
    Blanc 1991).
14 For the spatial aspect of social exclusion compare Madanipour (1998). Social
    exclusion in European cities is also analysed in Madanipour et al. (1998).

Literature

Alba, R. & V. Nee (1997), 'Rethinking assimilation theory for a new era of immigration',
    International Migration Journal 31 (4): 826-874.
Alba, R. & V. Nee (2003), *Remaking the American Mainstream. Assimilation and Contempor-
    ary Immigration*. Cambridge: Harvard University Press.
Amersfoort, H. van & L. de Klerk (1987), 'The dynamics of immigrant settlement; Surina-
    mese, Turks and Moroccans in Amsterdam 1973-1983', in G. Glebe & J. O'Loughlin
    (eds.), *Foreign minorities in Continental European cities*, 199-222, Stuttgart: Franz Stei-
    ner Verlag.
Anas, A. (2004), 'Ethnic segregation and ghettos', in R. Arnott & D. McMillen (eds.), '*A
    companion to urban economics*', 94-122. London: Blackwell Publishers.
Andersson, R. (1998), 'Segregation dynamics and urban policy issues in Sweden', *paper
    presented at the Metropolis Inter Conference on 'Divided cities and strategies for undivided
    cities'*, Göteborg, Sweden, 25-26 May 1998. www.international.metropolis.net/events/
    goth/segregation.html
Andrusz, G., Harloe, M. & I. Szelenyi (eds.) (1996), *Cities after socialism: urban and regio-
    nal change in post-socialist societies*. London: Blackwell Publishers.
Arbaci, S. (2004), 'Southern European multiethnic cities and the enduring housing cri-
    sis. Framing the urban and residential insertion of immigrants', *paper presented at the
    ENHR Conference*, Cambridge, 3 July 2004.
Arin, C. (1991), 'The housing market and housing policies for the migrant population in
    West Berlin', in E. D. Huttman, W. Blauw & J. Saltman (eds.), *Urban housing segrega-
    tion of minorities in Western Europe and the United States*, 199-214. Durham/London:
    Duke University Press.

Asselin, O., F. Dureau, M.Giroud, A. Hamadi & Y. Marcadet (2004), 'Mobility and accessibility issues: immigrants and the dynamics of the city', paper presented at the *IMISCOE Cluster B5 Workshop*, IMISCOE Conference in Coimbra, 4-5 December.

Barbosa, E. M. (2001), 'Urban spatial segregation and social differentiation: foundation for a typological analysis'. Lincoln Institute of Land Policy Conference Paper CP01A03 for the *International Seminar on Segregation in the City, Lincoln Institute of Land Policy,* Cambridge, Massachusetts, 26-28 July 2001. www.lincolninst-edu/pubs/dl1595_barbosa.pdf

Barou, J. (1988), 'North African ethnic minorities and urban changes: an historical survey of the Paris region', paper presented at *the International Housing Policy and Urban Innovation Conference Amsterdam.* Amsterdam.

Becker, G. S. (1957), *The economics of discrimination.* Chicago: University of Chicago Press.

Blanc, M. (1991), 'Urban housing segregation of North African immigrants in France', in E. D. Huttman, W. Blauw & J. Saltman (eds.), *Urban housing segregation of minorities in Western Europe and the United States,* 145-154. Durham/London: Duke University Press.

Blom, S. (1999), 'Residential concentration among immigrants in Oslo', *International Migration 37* (3), 617-641.

Boal, F. W. (1981), 'Residential segregation, ethnic mixing and resource conflict', in C. Peach, V. Robinson & S. Smith (eds.) *Ethnic segregation in cities,* 235-251. London: Croom Helm.

Boal, F. W. (1999), 'From undivided cities to undivided cities: assimilation to ethnic cleansing', *Housing Studies* 14 (4): 585-600.

Böcker, A. & D. Thränhardt (2003), 'Erfolge und Misserfolge der Integration – Deutschland und die Niederlande im Vergleich', *Aus Politik und Zeitgeschichte. Beilage zur Wochenzeitung Das Parlament,* 3-11.

Bockstefl, J., N. Hochholdinger, A. Millonig & W. Millonig (1996), *Sozialdynamik und Wohnmilieu in Wien. Zur Analyse und Bewertung städtischer Wohnqualität und städtischer Segregation anhand ausgewählter Wiener Stadtteilgebiete.* Vienna: Institute for Urban and Regional Research of the Technical University Vienna.

Body-Gendrot, S. & M. Martiniello (eds.) (2000), *Minorities in European cities. The dynamics of social integration and social exclusion at the neighborhood level.* Basingstoke: Macmillan.

Bolt, G., J. Burgers & R. van Kempen (1998), 'On the social significance of spatial location: spatial segregation and social exclusion', *Netherlands Journal of Housing and the Built Environment* 13 (1): 83-95.

Brun, J. & C. Bonvalet (1998), 'Logement et division sociale de l'espace', in M. Segaud, C. Bonvalet & J. Brun (eds.), *Logement et habitat: l'état des savoirs,* 319-326. Paris: Editions la Découverte.

Chapelon, L. (2004), *Accessibilité.* Hypergéo, www.hypergeo.free.fr.

Clark, W. A. V. (1986), 'Residential segregation in American cities', *Population Research and Policy Review* 5: 95-127.

Clark, W. A. V. (1991), 'Residential preferences and neighbourhood racial segregation: a test of the Schelling segregation model', *Demography* 28: 1-19.

Clark, W. A. V. (1992), 'Residential preferences and residential choices in a multiethnic context', *Demography* 29: 451-466.

Cortese, C. F., R. F. Falk & J. K. Cohen (1976), 'Further consideration on the methodological analysis of segregation indices', *American Sociological Review* 41: 889-893.

Cutler, D. & E. Glaeser (1997), 'Are ghettos good or bad?' *Quarterly Journal of Economics* 112: 827-72.

Dangschat, J. S. (2000a), 'Segregation', in H. Häussermann (ed.), Großstadt – Soziologische Stichworte, 2nd ed., 209-221. Opladen: Westdeutscher Verlag.

Dangschat, J. S. (2000b), 'Segregation und dezentrale Konzentration von Migrantinnen und Migranten in Wien', in K. Schmals (ed.), Migration und Stadt. Entwicklungen, Defizite, Probleme, 155-182. Opladen: Westdeutscher Verlag.

Dangschat, J. S. (2002), 'Residentielle Segregation – die andauernde Herausforderung an die Stadtforschung', in H. Fassmann, J. Kohlbacher & U. Reeger (eds.), Zuwanderung und Segregation. Europäische Metropolen im Vergleich, 25-36. Klagenfurt: Drava.

Drake, S. C. & H. A. Cayton (1945), Black metropolis: a study of negro life in a northern city. Chicago: University of Chicago Press.

Duncan, O. D. & B. Duncan (1955a), 'A methodological analysis of segregation indices', American Sociological Review 20: 210-217.

Duncan, O. D. & B. Duncan (1955b), 'Residential Distribution and Occupational Stratification', American Journal of Sociology 60: 493-503.

Duncan, O. D. & B. Duncan (1957), The negro population of Chicago. Chicago: University of Chicago Press.

Duncan, O. D. & S. Lieberson (1959), 'Ethnic segregation and assimilation', American Journal of Sociology 64: 364-374.

Ellingsen, W. (2003), Social integration of ethnic groups in Europe. How can concepts of place and territoriality help explain processes, policies and problems of socially integrating different ethnic groups in a European context?. Arbeider fra Institut for Geografi Bergen 255. Bergen. www.nhh.no/geo/Nyesider/GIBframe/GIBfull.pdf/255.pdf

Esser, H. (2001), Integration und Etnische Schichtung. MZES Working Paper no. 40.

Esser, H. (2004), 'Welche Alternativen zur "Assimilation" gibt es eigentlich?', IMIS – Beiträge, 23: 41-59.

European Commission (2003), Communication from the Commission on immigration, integration and employment, (COM (2003) 336), Brussels, 30.06.2003.

Farley, R., C. Steeh, M. Krysan, T. Jackson & K. Reeves (1994), 'Stereotypes and segregation: neighborhoods in the Detroit area', American Journal of Sociology 100: 750-780.

Fassmann, H. (2002), 'Zuwanderung und Segregation', in H. Fassmann, J. Kohlbacher & U. Reeger (eds.), Zuwanderung und Segregation. Europäische Metropolen im Vergleich, 1-13. Klagenfurt: Drava.

Fassmann, H. & R. Münz (1996), 'Between melting pot and ethnic fragmentation: historical and recent immigration to Vienna', in C. C. Roseman, H. D. Laux & G. Thieme (eds.), EthniCity. Geographic perspectives on ethnic change in modern cities, 165-185. London: Rowman & Littlefield Publishers.

Fassmann, H., J. Kohlbacher & U. Reeger (2004), Polen in Wien – Entwicklung, Strukturmerkmale und Interaktionsmuster. ISR-Forschungsbericht 30. Vienna: Verlag der ÖAW.

Fonseca, M. L., J. Malheiros, P. White, N. Ribas-Mateos & A. Esteves (eds.) (2002), Immigration and place in Mediterranean metropolises. Lisbon: Luso-American Foundation.

Fortuijn, J. D., S. Musterd & W. Ostendorf (1998), 'International migration and ethnic segregation: impacts on urban areas', Urban Studies 35 (3): 367-370.

Friedrichs, J. & H. Alpheis (1991), 'Housing segregation of immigrants in West Germany', in E. D. Huttman, W. Blauw & J. Saltman (eds.), Urban housing segregation of minorities in Western Europe and the United States, 116-144. Durham/London: Duke University Press.

Galster, G. C., K. Metzger & R. Waite (1999), 'Neighborhood opportunity structures and immigrants' socio-economic advancement', Journal of Housing Research 10 (1): 95-127.

Gans, H. (1979), 'Symbolic Ethnicity: The Future of Ethnic Groups and Cultures in America', Ethnic and Racial Studies 2 (1): 1-20.

Gans, H. (1996), 'Second-Generation Decline. Scenarios for the Economic and Ethnic Futures of the post-1965 American immigrants', in N. Carmon (ed.), *Immigration and Integration in Post-Industrial Societies. Theoretical analysis and policy-related research*. Basingstoke: Macmillan, 65-85.

Giffinger, R. (1998), 'Segregation in Vienna: impacts of market barriers and rent regulations', *Urban Studies* 35 (10): 1791-1812.

Giffinger, R. & H. Wimmer (2002), 'Segregation von ausländischer Wohnbevölkerung als Barriere der sozialen Integration?', in H. Fassmann, J. Kohlbacher & U. Reeger (eds.), *Zuwanderung und Segregation. Europäische Metropolen im Vergleich*, 209-232. Klagenfurt: Drava.

Giroud, M. (2004), 'A Few (Spatial) Stakes in the Term 'Integration'. Suggestions from the Case of Berriat/St Bruno in Grenoble (France), a Cosmopolitan Area Undergoing Urban Renewal', paper presented at the *IMISCOE Cluster B5 Conference* in Lisbon, 16-17 July.

Glazer, N. (1975), *Affirmative discrimination: ethnic inequality and public policy*. New York: Basic Books.

Glazer, N. & D. Moynihan (1963), *Beyond The Melting Pot*. Cambridge: MIT Press.

Glebe, G. (1986), 'Segregation and intra-urban mobility of a high-status ethnic group: the case of the Japanese in Düsseldorf', *Ethnic and Racial Studies* 9: 432-441

Gordon, M.M. (1964), *Assimilation in American Life. The Role of Race, Religion and National Origins*. New York: Oxford University Press.

Grabowski, W., U. Michel, U. Podszuweit & H. Tietjens (2002), 'Das Tor zur Welt: Zuwanderung und Segregation in Hamburg', in H. Fassmann, J. Kohlbacher & U. Reeger (eds.), *Zuwanderung und Segregation. Europäische Metropolen im Vergleich*, 143-160. Klagenfurt: Drava.

Grafmayer, Y. (1994), *Sociologie urbaine*. Paris: Nathan.

Grasland, C. (1998), *Analyse spatiale des phénomènes sociaux. Chapitre 2: L'accessibilité*. www.grasland.cicrp.jussieu.fr.

Guillon, M. & D. Noin (1996), 'Foreigners in the Paris agglomeration', in C. C. Roseman, H. D. Laux & G. Thieme (eds.), *EthniCity. Geographic perspectives on ethnic change in modern cities*, 77-95. London: Lanham.

Hansson, S. (1998), *The housing segregation of ethnic minorities – the example of Fittja, Sweden*. infogettable.Net/essays/ethnic-segregation/.

Harvey, D. (1997), *Justice, nature and the geography of difference*. Oxford: Basil Blackwell.

Heckmann, F. (2003), 'From Ethnic Nation to Universalistic Immigrant Integration', in: Heckmann, Friedrich and Schnapper, Dominique (eds.), *The Integration of Immigrants in European Societies. National Differences and Trends of Convergence*. Stuttgart: Lucius und Lucius, 45-78.

Heckmann, F. (2004), 'Integration: Conceptual Issues and Definitions', paper presented at the *IMISCOE Cluster B5 Conference* in Lisbon, 16-17 July.

Huttman, E. D. (1991), 'Housing segregation in Western Europe: an introduction', in E. D. Huttman, W. Blauw & J. Saltman (eds.), *Urban housing segregation of minorities in Western Europe and the United States*, 21-42. Durham/London: Duke University Press.

Huttman, E. D., W. Blauw & J. Saltman (eds.) (1991), *Urban housing segregation of minorities in Western Europe and the United States*. Durham/London: Duke University Press.

Johnston, R., J. Forrest & M. Poulsen (2002), 'The ethnic geography of EthniCities', *Ethnicities* 2 (2): 209-235.

Johnston, R .J. (ed.) (2000), *The dictionary of human geography*. Padstow: Blackwell Publishers.

Jones, E. (1991), 'Race and ethnicity in London', in K. Hoggart & D. R. Green (eds.), *London: a new metropolitan geography*, 17-32. London: Edward Arnold.

Jones, T. (1983), 'Residential segregation and ethnic autonomy', New Community 11, 10-22.

Kaplan, D. H. & S. R. Holloway (1998), Segregation in cities. Washington, DC: Association of American Geographers.

Kaplan, D. H. & S. Holloway (2000), 'Contingency and segregation: making sense of a global phenomenon', paper prepared for the Urban Affairs Association Conference, Los Angeles, California, 2000. www.psrv.dl.kent.edu/dkaplan/contingency%20and%20and%20segregation.doc

Kesteloot, C. & H. van der Hagen (1997), 'Foreigners in Brussels 1981-1991: spatial continuity and social change', Tijdschrift voor economische en Social Geografie 88: 105-119.

Kesteloot, K. & H. Meert (2000), 'Segregation and economic integration of immigrants in Brussels', in S. Body-Gendrot & M. Martiniello (eds.), Minorities in European cities. The dynamics of social integration and social exclusion at the neighborhood level, 54-74. Basingstoke: Macmillan.

Kesteloot, D., A. de Turck, C. Vandermotten, P. Marissal & G. van Hamme (2001), 'Structures sociales et quartiers en difficulté dans les régions urbaines belges', Report to Charles Piqué, ministre chargé de la politique des Grandes villes. Brussels.

King, R. & T. Iosifides (1998), 'Socio-spatial dynamics and Exclusion of Three Immigrant Groups in Athens Conurbation', South European Society and Politics, 3 (3): 205-229.

Knox, P. (1995) Urban Social Geography, 3rd edition. Harlow: Longman Scientific & technical.

Kohlbacher, J. & U. Reeger (1999), 'Ethnische Segregation und Fremdenfeindlichkeit in Wien', Mitteilungen der Österreichischen Geographischen Gesellschaft 141: 19-52.

Kohlbacher, J. & U. Reeger (2002), 'Zuwanderung und Segregation in Wien', in H. Fassmann, J. Kohlbacher & U. Reeger (eds.), Zuwanderung und Segregation. Europäische Metropolen im Vergleich, 181-196. Klagenfurt: Drava.

Kohlbacher, J. & U. Reeger (2003), 'Die Wohnsituation von AusländerInnen in Österreich', in H. Fassmann & I. Stacher (eds.), Österreichischer Migrations- und Integrationsbericht, 87-108. Klagenfurt.

Kohlbacher, J. & D. Schwab (2002), 'Ausländer auf dem Wiener Wohnungsmarkt Strukturen, Probleme und aktuelle Entwicklungen', in H. Fassmann, J. Kohlbacher & U. Reeger (eds.), Zuwanderung und Segregation. Europäische Metropolen im Vergleich, 197-208. Klagenfurt: Drava.

Lee, T. R. (1977), Race and residence. The concentration and dispersal of immigrants in London. Oxford: Oxford University Press.

Leitner, H. (1982), 'Residential segregation, socio-economic integration an behavioural assimilation: the case of Yugoslav migrant workers in Vienna', in European Science Foundation (ed.), Cultural identity and structural marginalisation of migrant workers, Human Migration II, 60-78. Strasbourg.

Lemon, A. (ed.) (1991), Homes apart: South Africa's segregated cities. Bloomington, Indiana: Indiana University Press.

Lévy, J.P. & J. Brun (2000), 'De l'extension au renouvellement métropolitain', in F. Dureau et al. (eds.) Métropoles en mouvement: une comparaison internationale, 229-246. Paris: Anthropos – IRD.

Lévy, J & Lussault, M (eds.) (2000), Logiques de l'espace, exprit des lieux. Géographies à Cerisy, 11-57. Paris: Belin.

Lieberson, S. (1980), A piece of the pie: black and white immigrants since 1880. Berkeley: University of California Press.

Lieberson, S. (1981), 'An asymmetrical approach to segregation', in C. Peach, V. Robinson & S. Smith (eds.), Ethnic Segregation in Cities, 61-82. London: Croom Helm.

Lindén, A. L. & G. Lindberg (1991), 'Immigrant housing patterns in Sweden', in E. D. Huttman, W. Blauw & J. Saltman (eds.), Urban housing segregation of minorities in

Western Europe and the United States, 92-115. Durham/London: Duke University Press.

Lindo, F. (1995), 'Ethnic Myth or Ethnic Might? On the Divergence in Educational attainment between Portuguese and Turkish Youth in the Netherlands', in: G. Baumann & T. Sunier (ed.) *De-essentializing Post-Migration Ethnicity: Cohesion, Commitments, Comparison,* 144-164. Amsterdam: SISWO/IMES.

Lindo, F. (1999), *Heilige Wijsheid in Amsterdam.* Amsterdam: Het Spinhuis.

Lindo, F. (forthcoming), 'A Streetcar Named Desire. Lifestyle and Identity of Street Kids in Multi-Ethnic Rotterdam'. To be published in J. Bastos, J. Dahinden & C. Westin, *Immigrant Identity.*

Lucassen, L. (2004), 'Old wine in new bottles? Turks and Poles in Germany and the importance of historical comparisons', paper presented at the *Workshop on the Integration of Immigrants from Turkey in Austria, Germany and Holland, Bogazici University,* Istanbul, 27-28 February 2004. http: www.ces.boun.edu.tr/papers/feb/leo_lucassen_-final_papaer.pdf.

Madanipour, A. (1998), 'Social exclusion and space', in A. Madanipour, G. Cars & J. Allen (eds.), *Social exclusion in European cities: processes, experiences and responses,* 75-89. London: Regional Studies Association & Jessica Kingsley.

Madanipour, A., G. Cars & J. Allen (eds.) (1998), *Social exclusion in European cities: processes, experiences and responses.* London: Regional Studies Association & Jessica Kingsley.

Mahnig, H. (2001), 'Die Debatte um die Eingliederung von Migranten oder was ist das Ziel von Integrationspolitik in liberalen Demokratien?' *Swiss Political Science Review* 7 (2): 124-130.

Malheiros, J. M. (2000), 'Urban Restructuring, Immigration and the Generation of Marginalised Spaces in the Lisbon Region', in R. King, G. Lazaridis & C. Tsardanidis (eds.), *Eldorado or Fortress 'Migration in Southern Europe,* 207-232. London: Macmillan Press.

Malheiros, J. M. (2002), 'Ethni-cities: residential patterns in the Northern European and Mediterranean metropolises – implications for policy design', *International Journal of Population Geography* 8 (2): 107-134.

Marcuse, P. (2001), 'Enclaves yes, ghettos no: Segregation and the state', Lincoln Institute of Land Policy Conference Paper for the *International Seminar on Segregation in the City,* 26-28 July, 2001. http:www.lincolninst.edu/pubs/dl/605_marcuse.pdf

Massey, D. S. (1984), 'Ethnic residential segregation: a theoretical synthesis and empirical review', *Sociology and Social Research* 69 (3): 315-350.

Massey, D. S. (2001), 'Residential segregation and neighbourhood conditions in U.S. metropolitan areas', in N. J. Smelser, W. J. Wilson & F. Mitchell (eds.) *America becoming: racial trends and their consequences,* vol. I, 391-434. Washington, D.C.: National Academy Press.

Massey, D. S. & N. A. Denton (1987), 'Trends in the residential segregation of Blacks, Hispanics, and Asians', *American Sociological Review* 52: 802-825.

Massey, D. S. & N. A. Denton (1988), 'The dimensions of residential segregation', *Social Forces* 67, (3): 281-315.

Massey, D. S. & N. A. Denton (1989), 'Hypersegregation in United States metropolitan areas: black and Hispanic segregation along five dimensions', *Demography* 26 (2): 373-391.

Massey, D. S. & N. A. Denton (1993), *American apartheid: segregation and the making of the underclass.* Cambridge: Harvard University Press.

Massey, D. S., A. B. Gross & K. Shibuya (1994), 'Migration, segregation, and the geographic concentration of Poverty', *American Sociological Review* 59: 425-445.

Menanteau, J. (1994), *Les banlieues.* Paris: Le Monde-Editions.

Merlin, P. (1999), *Les banlieues*. Paris: Presses Universitaires de France.

Mik, G. (1991), 'Housing segregation and policy in the Dutch metropolitan environment', in E. D. Huttman, W. Blauw & J. Saltman (eds.), *Urban housing segregation of minorities in Western Europe and the United States*, 179-198. Durham/London: Duke University Press.

Moseley, J. M. (1979), *Accessibility: the rural challenge*. London: Methuen & Co.

Musterd, S. & W. Ostendorf (1996), 'Ethnicity and the Dutch welfare state: the case of Amsterdam', in C. C. Roseman, H. D. Laux & G. Thieme (eds.), *EthniCity. Geographic perspectives on ethnic change in modern cities*, 121-140. London: Rowman & Littlefield Publishers.

Musterd, S. & W. Ostendorf (eds.) (1998), *Urban segregation and the welfare state. Inequality and exclusion in Western cities*. London/New York: Routledge.

Özüekren, A. S. & R. van Kempen (1997), 'Explaining housing conditions and housing market positions', in A. S. Özüekren & R. van Kempen (eds.), *Turks in European cities: housing and urban segregation. Comparative Studies in Migration and Ethnic Relations 4*, 11-29. Utrecht: Ercomer.

Park, R. E. (1928), 'Human Migration and the Marginal Man', *American Journal of Sociology* 33(6): 881-893.

Park, R. E. (1930), 'Assimilation, Social', in E. Seligsman & A. Johnson (eds.) *Encyclopedia of the Social Sciences*. New York: Macmillan.

Park, R. E. (1950), *Race and Culture*. Glencoe: The Free Press.

Peach, C. (ed.) (1975), *Urban social segregation*. London: Longman.

Peach, C. (1981), 'Conflicting interpretations of segregation', in P. Jackson & S. J. Smith (eds.) *Social interaction and ethnic segregation*. Special Publication of the Institute of British Geographers 12, 19-34. London: Academic Press.

Peach, C. (1987), 'Immigration and segregation in Western Europe since 1945', in G. Glebe & J. O'Loughlin (eds.), *Foreign minorities in continental European cities*, 72-97. Stuttgart: Franz Steiner Verlag.

Peach, C. (1996), 'Does Britain have ghettos?' *Transactions of the Institute of British Geographers* 21 (1): 216-235.

Peach, C. (1997), 'Pluralist and assimilationist models of ethnic settlement in London, 1991,' *Tijdschrift voor economische en sociale geografie* 88 (2): 130-134.

Peach, C. (1999), 'London and New York: contrasts in British and American models of segregation', *International Journal of Population Geography* 5 (4): 319-351.

Peach, C. (2001), 'The ghetto and the ethnic enclave', Lincoln Institute of Land Policy Conference Paper, presented at the *International Seminar on Segregation in the City*, Lincoln Institute, 26-28 July 2001. http\\:www.lincolninst.edu/pubs/dl/610_peach. pdf.

Peach, C. & D. J. Rossiter (1996), 'Level and nature of spatial concentration and segregation of ethnic minority populations in Great Britain, 1991', in P. Ratcliffe (ed.) *Ethnicity in the 1991 Census: Volume Three. Social geography and ethnicity in Britain: geographical spread, spatial concentration and internal migration*, 111-134. London: HMSO.

Peach, C., V. Robinson & S. Smith (eds.) (1981), *Ethnic segregation in cities*. London: Croom Helm.

Peleman, K. (2002), 'The impact of residential segregation on participation in associations: the case of Moroccan women in Belgium', *Urban Studies* 39 (4): 727-747.

Perchinig, B. (2002), 'Einwanderung und Minderheitenpolitik in Amsterdam 1945-2000', in H. Fassmann, J. Kohlbacher & U. Reeger (eds.), *Zuwanderung und Segregation. Europäische Metropolen im Vergleich*, 51-76. Klagenfurt: Drava.

Phillips, D. (1981), 'The social and spatial segregation of Asians in Leicester', in P. Jackson & S. J. Smith (eds.), *Social interaction and ethnic segregation*, 101-121. Oxford: Blackwell.

Pinson, D. (1992), *Des banlieues et des villes*. Paris: Éditions Ouvrières.

Portes, A. & M. Zou (1993), 'The New Second Generation: Segmented Assimilation and its Variants Among Post-1965 Immigrant Youth', *The Annals of the American Academy of Political and Social Sciences* 530: 74-96.

Price, Ch. (1969), 'The Study of Assimilation', in J. Jackson (ed.) *Migration*. Cambridge: Cambridge University Press, 181-237.

Reardon, S. F. & G. Firebaugh (2002), 'Measures of multigroup segregation', *Sociological Methodology* 32 (1): 33-67.

Rehn, S. D. (2002), 'Measuring segregation in melting-pot suburbs: concepts, methods, and a case study', *thesis presented to the Department of Planning, Public Policy & Management of the University of Oregon*. www.darkning.uoregon.edu/nschlossb/PPPM/thesis/thesis.rehn.pdf.

Rex, J. (1981), 'Urban segregation and inner city policy in Great Britain', in C. Peach, V. Robinson & S. Smith (eds.), *Ethnic segregation in Cities*, 25-42. London: Croom Helm.

Robinson, V. (1980), 'Lieberson's Isolation Index: a case study evaluation', *Area* 12: 307-312.

Sala Pala, V. (2003), 'The French "republican integration model"', in practice and in comparative perspective: the political construction and treatment of ethnic minorities housing in France and Britain', Conference Paper for the *ECPR Joint Sessions*, Edinburgh, 28 March-2 April 2003. www.essex.ac.uk/ECPR/events/jointsessions/paperarchive/edinburgh/ws24/salapala.pdf.

Sailer-Fliege, U. (1999), 'Characteristics of post-socialist urban transformation in East Central Europe', *GeoJournal* 49: 7-16.

Saltman, J. (1991), 'Theoretical orientation: residential segregation', in E. D. Huttman, W. Blauw & J. Saltman (eds.), *Urban housing segregation of minorities in Western Europe and the United States*, 1-17. Durham/London: Duke University Press.

Santibáñez, R. & C. Maiztegui (Dirs.) (2004), Jóvenes de Bilbao sin secundaria obligatoria. *Report for the City Hall of Bilbao* (Department of Education, Youth and Sports). Unpublished.

Sarre, P., D. Phillips & R. Skellington (1989), *Ethnic minority housing: explanations and policies*. Aldershot: Avebury.

Schulz, M. (2002), 'Ethnische Segregation im wieder vereinigten Berlin', in H. Fassmann, J. Kohlbacher & U. Reeger (eds.), *Zuwanderung und Segregation. Europäische Metropolen im Vergleich*, 121-142. Klagenfurt: Drava.

Simon, P. (1998), 'Ghettos, immigrants, and integration: the French dilemma', *Netherland Journal of Housing and the Built Environment* 13 (1): 13-32.

Simpson, L. (2004), Statistics of racial segregation: measures, evidence and policy, *Urban Studies* 41 (3): 661-681.

Smith, C. J. (1980) 'Preferred residential distance from different public facilities', in Herbert, D. & Johnston, R.J. (eds.), *Geography and the Urban Environment, v3*. Chichester: Wiley.

Smith, D. (1989), *Urban inequality under socialism: case studies from Eastern Europe and the Soviet Union*. Cambridge: Cambridge University Press.

South, S. J. & K. D. Crowder (1997), 'Escaping distressed neighbourhoods: individual, community, and metropolitan influences', *American Journal of Sociology* 102: 1040-1084.

South, S. J. & K.D. Crowder (1998), 'Leaving the hood: residential mobility between black, white and integrated neighbourhoods', *American Sociological Review* 63: 17-26.

Stearns, L. B. & J. R. Logan (1986), 'Measuring trends in segregation: three dimensions, three measures', *Urban Affairs Quarterly* 22: 124-150.

Stébé, J.-M. (1999), *La crise des banlieues*. Paris: Presses Universitaires de France.

Sykora, L. (1999), 'Changes in the internal spatial structure of post-communist Prague', *GeoJournal* 49: 79-89.

Taeuber, K. & A. Taeuber (1965), *Negroes in cities*. Chicago: Aldine.

Tasan, T. (1999), 'Warsaw under transformation: new tendencies in the housing market', *GeoJournal* 49: 91-103.

Thériault, M. et al. (2003). 'Measuring Accessibility to Urban Services Using Fuzzy Logic within Transportation Geographical Information System', in *10th Annual European Real Estate Conference*. Helsinki. http://www.crad.ulaval.ca/documents/COMSCI/2003/ID1069_ERES_2003_Theriault.pps

Thernstrom, S. & A. Thernstrom (1997), *America in black and white: one nation, indivisible*. New York: Simon & Schuster.

Tosi, A. & Lombardi, M. (1999), 'Spatial Concentration and Mobility in Milan', in Luso-American Development Foundation (ed.), *Proceedings of the International Metropolis International Workshop*, 15-38. Lisbon: Luso-American Development Foundation.

Van Kempen, R. & A. S. Özuekren (1997), 'Introduction', in A. S. Özuekren & R. van Kempen (eds.), *Turks in European cities: housing and urban segregation*, 1-11. Utrecht: Ercomer.

Van Kempen, R. & A. S. Özuekren (1998), 'Ethnic Segregation in Cities: new forms and Explanations in a Dynamic World', *Urban Studies*, 35 (10), 1631-1656.

Vesselinov, E. (2004), *Eastern European cities on the move: new housing and segregation patterns*. Eurex Lecture No. 10. www.shakti.uniurb.it/oldsociodidatticaonline/lessonfiles/courses/59/160/Vesselinov_lecture.pdf.

Wacquant, L. (1999), 'Urban outcasts: stigma and division in the black American ghetto and the French urban periphery', *International Journal of Urban and Regional Research* 17 (3): 366-383.

Wacquant, L. (2004), 'What is a ghetto? Constructing a sociological concept, Berkeley & Paris', in N. J. Smelser & P. B. Bates (eds.) *International Encyclopedia of the Social and Behavioral Sciences*. London: Pergamon Press. www.newschool.edu/gf/soc/faculty/wacquant/papers/ghetto.pdf

Waldorf, B. S. (1993), 'Segregation in urban space: a new measurement approach', *Urban Studies* 30 (7): 1151-1164.

Warner, W.L. & L. Srole (1945), *The Social Systems of American Ethnic Groups*. New Haven: Yale University Press.

Warnes, A. M. (2003), 'The challenge of intra-Union and in-migration to social Europe', *Journal of Ethnic and Migration Studies* 28 (1): 135-152.

Weclawowicz, G. (1996), *Contemporary Poland: space and society*. Westview Press.

Wessel, T. (2000a), 'Social polarisation and socioeconomic segregation in a welfare state: the case of Oslo', *Urban Studies* 37 (11): 1947-1967.

Wessel, T. (2000b), 'Losing control? Inequality and social divisions in Oslo', *European Planning Studies* 9: 889-906.

White, M. J. (1983), 'The measurement of spatial segregation', *American Journal of Sociology* 90 (1): 1008-1018.

White, M. J. (1986), 'Segregation and diversity measures in population distribution', *Population Index* 52: 198-221.

White, P. (1987), 'The migrant experience in Paris', in G. Glebe & J. O'Loughlin (eds.), *Foreign Minorities in continental European cities*, 184-198. Stuttgart: Franz Steiner Verlag.

White, P. (1998), 'The settlement patterns of developed world migrants in London', *Urban Studies*, 35 (10): 1725-1744.

Wicker, H.R. (2003), 'Introduction: migration, politique de migration et recherche sur la migration', in H.-R. Wicker, R. Fibbi & W. Haug (eds.), *Les migrations et la Suisse*, 11-62. Zurich: Seismo.

Wong, D. W. S. (1998), 'Measuring multiethnic spatial segregation', *Urban Geography* 19 (1): 77-87.

Yinger, J. (1995), *Closed doors, opportunities lost: the continuing costs of housing discrimination*. New York: Russell Sage Foundation.

7. Cultural, Religious and Linguistic Diversity in Europe: An Overview of Issues and Trends

Steven Vertovec and Susanne Wessendorf

This chapter considers developments surrounding 'Cultural, Religious and Linguistic Diversity' in Europe in recent years. It has three purposes: (1) to elaborate on the rise of the concepts of diversity and multiculturalism as they have emerged in the academic world and engaged public debate and policy development; (2) to give an overview of the academic literature concerning two key forms of diversity, namely religious and linguistic diversity, and (3) to analyse the recent critical debates on the concepts of multiculturalism and diversity in various national contexts. It is intended to be indicative of the major trends and topics, but does not claim to be exhaustive to the issues or literature.

1. Diversity and multiculturalism

The rise of diversity issues

Alongside the growth of immigrant communities in Europe (as well as in Australia, the USA and Canada) from the 1960s there emerged a growing rejection of policies and public pressure calling for immigrant and ethnic minority assimilation – usually conceived as an expectation that migrants would discard their values and practices and adopt those of the majority society. In various countries and contexts this rejection found voice among politicians, academics and proponents of a broad civic rights movement. Significantly, the rejection of assimilationism was high on the agenda of nascent immigrant and ethnic minority movements and organisations themselves. This arose especially when, in the 1970s, family reunification and strategies toward long-term settlement came to change the nature of what had been previously thought of as mainly temporary, single male immigrant populations. From the 1960s through the 1970s much public discourse in immigrant-receiving societies highlighted notions of tolerance, representation, participation and group/cultural/minority rights – including the freedom to congregate, worship, speak one's own language and engage in other cultural institutions and practices. Campaigns to promote such notions within policy, governance and public awareness came to be described as an emergent 'politics of identity' or 'politics of recognition', regarded by many advocates as a necessary counterpart to anti-racism and anti-discrimination. By the 1980s, many of these concerns around immigrants (now settled and considered ethnic minorities in many countries) and the growing cultural, linguistic and religious diversity they brought to receiving societies led to public measures that were subsumed under the broad rubric of 'multiculturalism'.

Multiculturalism

The discourses of 'multiculturalism' described below became important throughout the public spheres of Australia, North America and Europe in the 1980s. The causes and processes through which the term arose and has been debated are complex and context specific. In each case and context, the ideals and measures associated with multiculturalism have stimulated both positive and negative readings.[1]

People who invoke 'multiculturalism' in a positive manner tend to associate the term with ideals of: tolerance, the right of ethnic minority groups to maintain aspects of cultural heritage and language; equal treatment, equal access and full participation with regard to matters of law, employment, education, social services, economic activity and political representation; rights to collective expression; and commitment by all, regardless of ethnic background, to a constitution or state and its rule of law. People who invoke 'multiculturalism' in a negative way commonly view the agenda as representing ideas and policy measures which threaten core national societal values, such as republican citizenship; therefore, in their eyes, the term represents a recipe for the destruction of national identity and the breakdown of social cohesion (see below).

In any case, it is an illusion to consider 'multiculturalism' as being one philosophy, structure, discourse or set of policy measures. The term is invoked differently to describe a number of discrete – albeit sometimes overlapping – phenomena. In this way multiculturalism can variously be understood as (1) a way of describing the actual make-up of a society; (2) a general vision of the way government and society should orient itself; (3) a specific set of policy tools accommodating minority cultural practices; (4) specially created frameworks of governance allowing for the representation of immigrant and ethnic minority interests, and (5) a variety of support mechanisms and funds for assisting ethnic minority communities to celebrate and reproduce their traditions.

The first usage corresponds to an objective demographic description. In this discourse the term 'multicultural' describes a condition of ethnic diversity, usually following a recent historical period of mass immigration. Here, the presence of people whose origins are in another place is often said to make this or that country a 'de facto multicultural society'.

The second usage implies a broad political ideology. In 1967, the British Home Secretary Roy Jenkins made a famous speech in which he advocated a model of integration 'not as a flattening process of uniformity but of cultural diversity, coupled with equal opportunity in an atmosphere of mutual tolerance.' This view – arising as an alternative to both models of exclusion and of assimilation – could be seen as the foundation of a broad political ideology of multiculturalism. Its general tenets are an acceptance of ethnic pluralism as a long-term feature of society, and a recognition that ethnic minority communities will retain their own languages and cultures. Following such an ideology, politicians' task, then, is to formulate and safeguard these ideals in law and public institutions.

The third meaning refers to concrete elements of socio-political policy. This policy discourse surrounding multiculturalism especially involves: identifying structural factors contributing to discrimination, disadvantage and exclusion (here, based especially on aspects of culture or religion) and formulating and implementing policies which facilitate equality of opportunity and outcome. Ethnic monitoring in employment and public services, too, falls within this kind of discourse. Other key aspects of 'multicultural' policy often include:

a. Accommodation of ethnic minority needs in social services, the health service, legal and judicial systems. Examples include the permission for the ritual slaughter of animals for Muslims and Jews, traditional clothing for Asian girls in schools or Asian women employees, turbans instead of motorcycle helmets or construction-site hard-hats for Sikhs;

b. Provisions, sometimes including state funds, for language training, translation, interpreting facilities (in courts, health care facilities, social services) and linguistic assistance in schools; and for special 'community' workers, centres and organisations;

c. Education, where multiculturalism by way of policy should contribute (1) to raise the self-esteem of the ethnic minority child, and (2) to create the basis for social understanding in the classroom which, it is hoped, will extend beyond this setting once children grow into adulthood.

In a fourth interpretation, multiculturalism leads to institutional restructuring. Once social and political policies were formulated in the name of multiculturalism, local and national institutions had to be created or restructured in order to operationalise policies aimed at fostering or safeguarding ethnic minority equality, access and participation. Foremost among these institutional measures have been:

a. Consultation through providing frameworks within which ethnic minority communities can speak on their own behalf. These have included special advocates for immigrants, liaison units in local government and/or a range of *ad hoc* bodies and other consultative forums for ethnic minority organisations. The traditional roles of all of these councils and boards set up on behalf of migrant minorities have been simultaneously as social welfare advisors, legal watchdogs and policy advocates;

b. Organisation of ethnic minority groups. Associations of immigrants have proliferated throughout countries like the Netherlands and Britain, especially during the 1980s when local government initiatives promoting multiculturalism exhibited a political drive towards pluralistic welfare provision by extending public resources to a range of ethnic groups. In this way, a vision of multiculturalism held sway according to which certain (presumed uni-cultural) communities would be ensured of equality, respect – or at least tolerance – and continuity of tradition by local government financing or other support of specific identity-based organisations; and

c. Training for public sector workers, including social workers, health care practitioners and police. The idea here has been to foster sensitivity to the values and practices of ethnic minorities by teaching about customs. While certainly doing much good (for instance, Muslims are less frequently offered pork on hospital or school menus), the training courses and materials have sometimes amounted to no more than catalogues of 'facts' and gross descriptions of the values and practices of migrant groups. Such collections may serve to further distance ethnic minorities by stressing their 'otherness', rather than serving to underscore their status as co-citizens.

The fifth and most far-reaching interpretation implies active resourcing of cultural expression. In line with the ideal of fostering the maintenance and reproduction of ethnic minority traditions, some multicultural programmes have extended public resources for community cultural activities. In this way, popular festivals, music and dance have come to characterise ethnic minorities and multiculturalism in the eyes of many within the majority population.

Given such a variety of meanings and measures associated with the concept of multiculturalism, it becomes clear that rather than offering sweeping generalisations, both advocates and critics of the notion (see below) need to be much clearer and more specific as to the particular dimensions, policies and frameworks of multiculturalism they are addressing.

Social scientists have discussed cultural diversity mostly in the context of 'multiculturalism' and 'social cohesion'. While some scholars focus on general principles and philosophies of cultural diversity, others focus more concretely on specific aspects of diversity such as religion and language. We will summarise some of the issues in these two key fields of diversity and describe how religious and linguistic diversity is envisioned on a more practical level.

2. Research on religious and linguistic diversity

The debate on religious diversity has been more dominant lately in public discourse than that on linguistic diversity and immigrant-receiving states have shown more inclination towards religious rather than linguistic pluralism. The challenges each of these topics implies for states are different: the state needs to demand linguistic choices, while a separation of church and state is possible and a reality in many liberal nation-states (Kymlicka 1995). According to Joppke and Morawska (2003), 'the accommodation of religious diversity epitomizes the inevitable trend toward de facto multiculturalism in liberal states'. However, this trend has been accompanied by wide academic and public debates and controversies from diverse theoretical and normative perspectives.

Religious diversity[2]

Phenomena such as religious (particularly Islamic) fundamentalism which currently dominate public discussions are also on the forefront of many scientific discourses (Bergmann et al. 1993; Juergensmeyer 2003; Schiffauer 2001). Some observers try to explain and understand the emergence of religious fundamentalism, influenced by and embedded in the political, social and cultural environments of specific national and ethnic contexts (Schiffauer 2001). Others depict 'alien' religions as confrontation of Western liberal 'values' and are concerned with questions whether, for example, diversity is a threat to internal security (Huntington 1998).

But there has also been much engagement in more general, normative considerations regarding religious diversity, especially among political philosophers, legal and political scholars who discuss issues such as the principles of secularism in increasingly plural societies (Kymlicka 1995; Parekh 2000b; Bader 1999; Bauböck et al. 1996). Two of the main themes in these debates are the public manifestation and the institutional recognition of religion. Various scholars (i.e. Bader 1999; Parekh 2000b; S. Ferrari 2004a) criticise the 'exclusion of religious reasons and arguments from public debate and politics in political liberalism' as morally arbitrary and unfair (Bader 2003c). This criticism has been mirrored in research which has shown, for example, that the public manifestations of religion can serve as a crucial force in terms of collective belonging and identity, providing a tool for the management of social problems (Zachary 2003; Schiffauer 2004). Similarly, studies across Europe have shown that the institutional recognition of religious minorities and the official inclusion of religious organisations into negotiations about the governance of diversity have had positive impacts on processes of integration (Sunier 1999; Heitmeyer et al. 1997; Penninx 2000). These studies have demonstrated that in states with official ethnic minorities' policies such as the Netherlands, the recognition of Islamic and other immigrant organisations as potential partners in integration policies fostered positive attitudes of Muslims towards integration and engagement, especially on a local level. In contrast, in a state like Germany with less institutionalised initiatives to engage immigrants, a more inward oriented attitude could be observed (Penninx and Martiniello 2004).

All in all, researchers agree that despite the existence of legal instruments to deal with religious diversity, introduced on the grounds of experiences with other religious communities, the 'Muslim question' poses new challenges to liberal nation-states (S. Ferrari 2004a; Buijs and Harchoui 2003). To tackle these challenges, it is not only state-church relationships that should be addressed but 'the full, reciprocal relationships between society-culture-politics-nation-state and (organized) religions' (Bader 2003c).

Sociologists, social anthropologists, religious studies' scholars and some political scientists have tried to capture these relationships in various empirical in-depth studies in order to gain a better understanding of the conflicts and dilemmas resulting from religious diversity, but also to contribute to successful solutions for the realisation of religious freedom in plural societies.

Studies on religious diversity have concentrated either on one or more religious groups in one nation-state (Cesari 1997; A. Ferrari 2004c; Riccio 2001; Werbner 2002; Niekerk 2000) or in several national contexts (S. Ferrari 2004b; Haddad 2002; Vertovec and Peach 1997; Baumann et al. 2003). An exception to studies focusing on specific collectivities in specific contexts is Baumann's (1996) research that concentrates on an area in suburban London. He looks at how groups from various religious, cultural and linguistic backgrounds engage with each other and negotiate their identities, and how they deal with discourses of people who strongly engage in identity politics on the one hand, and with the local government, on the other.

There has also been increasing research on the transformation of religious groups and religiousness through the migration experience. These studies are particularly interested in processes of religious adaptation to new circumstances and the importance of collective aspects of religious life in the diaspora (Baumann 2000; Baumann et al. 2003; Krause 2004; Pereira Bastos 2001; Werbner 2002; Vertovec and Rogers 1998). Various studies have been looking at the organisational and congregational dynamics of religious communities in the diaspora (Baumann 2000; Lewis 1997; Vertovec 2001), tackling, for example, how religious identities can be transformed and strengthened among second-generation youth participating in religious organisations (Schiffauer 2001, 2004).

There has been increasing interest in comparing the accommodation of different faiths in different societal and national contexts. These studies have, for example, been concerned with how religious freedom is negotiated and how different religions are incorporated into the institutional contexts of the host countries (Allievi 2002; Cattacin 2003; Grillo and Pratt 2002; Heckmann and Schnapper 2003; Kastoryano 2002; Penninx and Martiniello 2004; Pfaff-Czarnecka 2004; Rath et al. 2001). Some scholars have compared states with public policies with a clear separation of church and state (France) and states where there is some state support for religious institutions (Germany, the Netherlands, Belgium) or states where there is a state religion (Britain, Norway) (Kastoryano 2002; Shadid and Koningsveld 2002).

A large body of literature has been concerned with religious claims-making, the politics of recognition and ethnic mobilisation (Cattacin 2003; Statham 2003; Zolberg and Long 1999). Prevalent in these studies are those concerned with Muslim communities and the emergence of new Muslim assertiveness in Europe. This is for example manifested by organisations of young Muslims who help to foster proactive identities of the second generation, or as a new discourse of a common Islamic European identity (Modood 2003; Schiffauer 2004; Vertovec and Rogers 1998).

Whereas most research on religious diversity in Europe has been nationally focused and concerned with specific groups or issues in specific European nation-states, social scientists have recently began to develop a more comparative perspective regarding religious diversity in Europe (Kälin 2000; Schiffauer et al. 2004; Vertovec 1997). Such endeavors are very fruitful for a better understanding on both the institutional frameworks of nation-states and their strategies for the governance of diversity, and the dynamics of religious communities themselves. By comparing specific institutional solutions in different contexts, the uncovering of broader societal implications, for example regarding the value attached to religion or access to religion in public space, can be facilitated. Furthermore, comparative analyses help us to better understand the ways in which religious minorities deal with, for example, authorities and neighbours in different contexts, and what kind of strategies, rationalities and modes of action they use. Compara-

tive, interdisciplinary initiatives could also direct social scientists towards normative considerations concerning religious diversity in Europe. Though less subject to heated public debates, normative considerations as well as concrete institutional measures for immigrant integration have been particularly important in the realm of language.

Linguistic diversity

While modern states can, at least theoretically, take a neutral stand in
regard to religious matters, it is structurally impossible to be similarly
neutral with regard to linguistic diversity. In order for state bureaucracies and services to function for the general public, but also regarding
any kind of provision of information to facilitate participation, there
has to be a standardised language which citizens are able to use (Heath
1983). Also, it is justifiable to require an immigrant to learn another
language, whereas it is rather problematic to ask an immigrant to
change his/her religion. Hence, language assimilation is generally interpreted to be more compatible with liberal values than religious assimilation because the acquisition of language does not prevent people
from freely expressing their moral convictions (Bauböck 2003; Joppke
and Morawska 2003). Discourses on linguistic diversity focus both on
normative questions regarding the governance of linguistic diversity according to principles of liberal states, and on practical solutions in state
and private institutions confronted with the presence of an increasing
variety of languages.

Bauböck (2003) suggests several principles as guidelines for public
policy in various national contexts: *linguistic liberty, assimilation, accommodation* and *recognition*. Since these principles capture the main ideologies and the crucial points of discussion underlying empirical research and debates on the governance of linguistic diversity, they will
be summarised here.

Regarding *linguistic liberty* Bauböck states that liberal democracies
must guarantee the right for immigrants to use their own languages in
both the private and public sphere. Immigrants should not only have
the right to use their languages for shop signs, advertising, private
print or audiovisual media, but also as a medium of instruction in private schools.

Whereas these liberal principles do not oblige the state to actively
promote minority languages, *accommodation* and *assimilation* refer to
the state's tasks and responsibilities. According to Bauböck, especially
for newly arriving immigrants, accommodation of linguistic difference
is often more appropriate than assimilation into one of the official languages. Especially in institutional environments that are experienced
as stressful, such as hospitals or police stations, communication be-

tween immigrants and institutions should be fostered by providing translation and interpreter services, bilingual forms and ballots and information in immigrant languages.

Furthermore, Bauböck suggests that states should enhance linguistic assimilation by promoting the acquisition of the dominant language through public education for both children of immigrants and newcomers. Providing these skills is a public task because the need to earn money prevents many migrants from investing into language acquisition. This is a problem that has been particularly prevalent among post-war European labour migrants who, even after living in the host country for more than thirty years, still have difficulties speaking the dominant language. To prevent a policy which blames migrants for their failure to integrate, public institutions should provide language courses.

Empirically oriented research on linguistic diversity has taken place in two main areas. First, it has been concerned with how immigrants and their children cope with linguistic demands and expectations of the host society and, in the case of immigrant children, with bilingualism. Second, it has focused on the challenges which nation-states and their legal and public institutions face in regard to increasing linguistic diversity (Kaya 2002; Spencer and Di Mattia 2004; Wilson 1999). Discussions surrounding the provision of mandatory or non-mandatory language courses are among the most hotly debated in European discourses on the governance of linguistic diversity, and testing the language abilities of immigrants is getting increasingly important at every stage of the life cycle, beginning with preschool children and leading up to adult applicants for nationality or permanent residence (Mehlem et al. 2004a).

At school level, the programme of international students' assessment (PISA) demonstrated that being of immigrant background still constitutes a disadvantage with respect to school success, thus putting the responsibility on public schools to establish equal chances for every child (Mehlem et al. 2004a). Issues of competence in the host language and of educational measures needed to deal with increasing numbers of immigrant children had already been discussed during the first waves of post-war immigration from post-colonial areas and from Southern Europe during the 1970s and 1980s (Ager 1996; Kühlwein 1978; Twitchin and Demuth 1985; Verma and Bagley 1979; Verma 1989). Out of these debates came a considerable body of both scientific and policy-oriented literature such as the Swann Report (DES, 1985) in Britain, which thoroughly discussed these matters and focused on both internal and external difficulties concerning ethnic minority education. Hence, in contrast to earlier approaches to integrating immigrant children in the educational system, the problem was no longer seen in the migrants and their children alone, but also in the school-system. This argument has also been raised in other contexts such as Germany, where researchers have pointed to the 'institutionalised reproduction of inequality' as a factor for migrants' and their children's underachievement (Radtke and Gomolla 2002). Yet, despite this shift towards a more 'balanced' understanding of linguistic and educational integration barriers and difficulties, today, the old problems still exist and are therefore still subject to a considerable amount of research and literature (for a summary see Reich and Roth 2002).

Regarding linguistic integration of adult immigrants, there have been recent developments towards the introduction of language courses for adult migrants as an obligatory requirement for the right to stay in the country of settlement. In the framework of so-called integration programmes, such courses were established as an obligation for both the state and for the immigrant at the same time (Mehlem et al. 2004b) While some European states have introduced such formal language and integration programmes for new migrants (e.g. the Netherlands, Finland, Denmark, Germany, Austria, Sweden), other states built integration measures into mainstream services (e.g. Italy, Spain) (Spencer and Di Mattia 2004; Westin and Dingu-Kyrklund 2000; Wolf and Heckmann 2003) or put the task on the shoulders of private associations such as NGOs (Italy) (Cingolani, 2004).

According to Bauböck, such linguistic assimilation policies are legitimate only 'when they assume a convergence of public interests and private interests of the immigrants themselves'. Hence, mandatory language courses for adults must be justifiable 'as a form of benign paternalism'. From this point of view, language courses can secure migrants' long-term interests regarding social upward mobility as opposed to short-term interests in earning income in low-skilled jobs. However, the legitimacy of defining such interests 'from above', that is 'without the consent of the migrants themselves', remains questionable.

Whether language courses are mandatory or not, in all national contexts there are important questions concerning their content. While some studies argue that it is crucial to teach the basic skills necessary for everyday conversations, others stress the importance of literacy and writing (Mehlem and Maas 2003).

While acquiring the dominant language is crucial regarding integration on all levels (economic, social, cultural), implicit or explicit issues in debates on the governance of linguistic diversity in schools are also concerned with questions whether teaching only the official language makes sense when most of the pupils have other language backgrounds (Mehlem et al. 2004a). These debates are closely linked to discourses on the politics of *recognition* (Bauböck 2003). Languages do not only have a communicative value, but they are also crucial regarding the ways we see the world and as markers of individual and collective identities. To recognise immigrants as linguistic minorities, some nation-states have, for example, introduced optional courses in immigrant languages in public schools for children of the second and third generation (e.g. Germany, Switzerland, the Netherlands) (Bauböck 2003). In other states, the responsibility for teaching the language of origin has been passed on to the private sector and migrant associations have taken up this task (e.g. Italy) (Cingolani 2004).[3]

The controversies raised in discussions regarding the official institutionalisation of mother tongue teaching are manifold and these have ideological, institutional and practical aspects. They are not new and many of the issues discussed today have already been the subject of debate during the 1970s and 1980s (see for example Dabène et al. 1984; Baker and Jones 1998; Tosi and Leung 1999). However, this earlier discourse in education and other social sciences was dominated by rather contrastive views of cultural and linguistic difference which presented other languages as an obstacle rather than a resource. Today, the one-sided focus on language competence in the official language as a central condition for integration is criticised (Reich 2001) and emphasis is put on inter- or multicultural pedagogy which tries to bridge cultural and linguistic difference and focuses on a more open-minded approach that confronts the needs of pupils to act in multilingual contexts in their everyday lives (Mehlem et al. 2004a).

On an ideological level, there have been debates about whether other languages than the dominant language form part of the nation or whether they 'dismember' the state. This debate is also relevant regarding autochthonous minority languages (France, Belgium) (Caubet 2004; Martiniello 2004; Mehlem et al. 2004a). In fact, in many countries (e.g. Britain, France, Switzerland, Belgium, Sweden, etc.) the frameworks within which immigrant languages are discussed today have been shaped by earlier policy initiatives and ideologies concerning regional minority languages. Hence, already before the increase of linguistic diversity through immigration, most European states had achieved a concordat with regional minorities over the issue of minority languages, and some form of bi- or multilingualism was accepted as part of national unity. However, while autochthonous language communities participate in the welfare state and try to escape national homogenisation, allochthonous communities aim to enter the national social system (Castan 1984; Mehlem et al. 2004a).

A problem for the politics of recognition in the realm of language is that recognition alone does not guarantee the preservation of minority languages and does not necessarily lead to wider value put on multilingualism (Caubet 2004; Dirim and Auer 2004; Mehlem et al. 2004a).

Other important issues concern, for example, which community languages should be funded and supported. In some cases, the target languages are only the official languages of the home countries, whereas the migrants' mother tongue may sometimes be persecuted and suppressed by the nationalist policy of the home country (like Kurdish in Turkey and, although to a lesser extent, Berber in Morocco). Furthermore, the home language can be a non-standard or substandard variety stigmatised by the foreign teachers (like Sicilian and south Italian dialects) (Gogolin 2002; Mehlem et al. 2004a).

Decisions about which immigrant languages should be taught in public institutions are a typical example of mechanisms that tend to 'essentialise minority cultures' because governments need to define the mother tongue of, for example, a Kurdish child from Turkey (Closta et al. 2003; Entzinger 2000). In this context it is difficult not to fall into the trap of essentialism and not to define culture in substantialist terms.

Another controversy surrounds questions such as how far the education of community languages leads to the retreat of the minorities into their communities or encourages social integration beyond the family (Mehlem et al. 2004a).

In some countries, the practical difficulties of mother tongue teaching as well as ideological discourses on definitions of immigrant languages, and the positive or negative outcomes of institutionalised politics of recognition has led to the marginalisation of mother tongue teaching out of the official school curriculum (Sweden, the Netherlands, Norway) (Dingu-Kyrklund 2004b; Entzinger 2003b; Eurydice 2004).[4] This marginalisation, however, also has to be interpreted in the context of increasing budgetary restrictions and the discourses on 'too much diversity'.

All in all, concerns surrounding linguistic diversity have played an important role in the realm of multiculturalism because immigrants' linguistic competences are often used to benchmark the 'success' or 'failure' of integration.

3. The recent debate on multiculturalism and diversity

Multiculturalism as policy and philosophy has received considerable criticism since it came to the fore in the public sphere and in social sciences in the 1970s. Social scientists all over Europe are presently discussing models of the so-called 'new' multiculturalism to overcome the problems of previous models (and ideologies) of cultural diversity. These previous models of multiculturalism have been widely discussed in the social sciences over the past twenty years and there is a considerable body of literature on the subject (see among others Castles 2000; Grillo 1998, 2000; Faist 2000; Gutmann 1994; Goldberg 1994; Kymlicka 1995; Favell 1998; Willett 1998; Parekh 2000).

In a nutshell, multiculturalism represents a kind of corrective to assimilationist approaches and policies surrounding the national incorporation of immigrants (Castles 2000; Grillo 1998; Faist 2000). Most of today's social scientists and policymakers agree on the impracticality and 'outdatedness' of such assimilationist approaches, which has led to a shift towards a greater acceptance of cultural diversity across Europe. However, religious, racial and ethnic 'otherness' are still perceived as threat or challenge in many national contexts, and multiculturalism is associated with many – sometimes divergent, sometimes overlapping – discourses (cf. Blommaert and Verschueren 1998; Vertovec 1998a).

Drawing from various key texts concerned with multiculturalism (Amselle 1998; Baumann 1999; Martiniello 1997; Stolcke 1995; Grillo 1998: 195) outlines some of the key problematics of multicultural theory and practice: (1) multiculturalism's implicit essentialism; (2) the system of categorisation which underpins it; (3) the form that multicultural politics takes; (4) the ritualisation of ethnicity often associated with it; (5) the elision of race (and class) that it appears to entail; and (6) the attack on the 'common core' which it represents. 'Many of these criticisms,' Grillo rightly observes, 'stem from a focus on "culture"' (cf. Amselle 1998). This point is, for example, taken up by Yasmin Alibhai-Brown (2000a) who is critical of what she identifies as consumer or boutique multiculturalism, artistic and style multiculturalisms, corporate multiculturalism and role model multiculturalism. All such minimalist, celebratory and tribal forms of multiculturalism, she claims, tend to 'keep diversity in a box' (ibid.: 42) and may end up doing more harm than good.

Such essentialised understandings of culture have been observed, over the past few decades, in multicultural programmes and frameworks mentioned earlier, for example educational curricula, media images, forums of 'ethnic community leadership', public funding mechanisms, and professional training courses and handbooks (for instance, in police or social services). Scrutiny of the cultural essentialism in multicultural policies and theories has been made in Canada (Kobayashi 1993), Australia (Castles et al. 1988; Hage 1998), Mauritius (Eriksen 1997), the United States (Turner 1993), Germany (Radtke 1994), Sweden (Ålund and Schierup 1991) and Britain (Anthias and Yuval-Davis 1993, Baumann 1996, 1999).

Closely linked to the debates on the dangers of cultural essentialism inherent in multicultural theory and practice are the controversies between liberal pluralists and communitarians, though recent influential theoretical contributions have tried to transcend the opposition between normative multiculturalism and pure individualism (Kymlicka 1995; Parekh 2000; Taylor and Gutmann 1992). Drawing from these theoretical contributions and confronted with the fact that at a descriptive level, all European societies are multicultural (Grillo 2004a; Martiniello 2004; Penninx et al. 2004b) scholars have tried to capture the variety of ways in which different societies and governments perceive and deal with diversity or, in other words, the varieties of 'multiculturalisms'. They have, for example, differentiated between 'de facto' and 'official multiculturalism', distinguishing between a reality in most of today's liberal, immigrant receiving states where multiculturalism is firmly entrenched at the level of individual rights and liberties protected by the constitutions, and the official recognition and protections of immigrants as distinct ethnic groups (Joppke and Morawska 2003).

Grillo (2004a) makes a similar distinction of 'weak' and 'strong' multiculturalism. In 'weak' multiculturalism, cultural diversity is recognised in the private sphere, while a high degree of assimilation is expected of immigrants and ethnic minorities in the public sphere of law and government, the market, education and employment. This is what Entzinger (2000) has called the 'individual approach' to cultural diversity, which is based on ideas of liberal pluralism. In this approach the state has a neutral attitude towards cultural diversity, and it limits public intervention to promoting a better understanding between members of different ethnic and religious groups. Entzinger points out that liberal pluralism often leads to assimilation within two or three generations, which can cause anomie and social exclusion for those who find it difficult to familiarise themselves with the dominant culture. In contrast to the individual approach, advocates of the 'group approach', or, in Grillo's (2004a) terms, 'strong multiculturalism', promote the acknowledgement and institutionalised recognition of cultural differences in the public sphere including political representation (Entzinger 2000). We can observe such differential patterns when comparing immigrant and ethnic minority policies across Europe, particularly on local levels (Cuperus et al. 2003; Ireland 1994; Martiniello 1998b; Penninx et al. 2004a; Soysal 1994; Vertovec 1998).

'Strong' or 'official' multiculturalism has come under pressure in many European countries. The main question is how far states should recognise and support cultural pluralism and how they should define which elements of immigrant cultures are within certain limits defined by the law and socially acceptable (Entzinger 2000). There has been an increasing fear that multiculturalism exacerbates diversity and undermines the common will. In this discourse, multiculturalism is perceived as producing difference and separateness and as being counterproductive to social cohesion. Taken to the extreme, these scholars fear that to move away from the strict principles of universal political citi-

zenship and individual rights is 'the first step down the road to apartheid' (May 1999:15, for a summary of the discourse see Eriksen 2002;
Grillo 2004a).

This problematisation of diversity has long been part of the governance of diversity in those states with immigrant policies based on liberal pluralism and assimilationist ideas, such as France. The French discourse about the 'fear of communitarianism' is one of the most prominent examples and has been illustrated in a large body of literature
concerned with the long-lasting affair of the 'headscarves' (Favell
2001b; Freedman 2004; Silverman 1992; Todd 1994). In this discourse, the role of secularism and *laïcité* in the French conception of
the nation-state became the centre of the debate and led to the establishment of a commission which, in the so-called Stasi report, discussed and reaffirmed the principles of *laïcité* in the public sphere (Stasi 2003). The legal enforcement of secularism, expressed by the ban of
the headscarf, was justified by officials and scholars by 'arguing that to
proclaim publicly and loudly one's private identities is to generate division and conflict in a society' (Bowen 2004:34).

The French debate is paralleled in other European countries by discourses on 'too much diversity' (Britain) (Grillo 2004a), the fear of
'parallel societies' (Germany) (Salentin 2004) or the 'dismembering' of
society (Italy) (Sartori 2002). Even in countries with officially institutionalised multicultural policies, a shift away from group emancipation
towards an emphasis on individual integration is taking place.

The two most prominent examples of this shift away from official
multiculturalism are Sweden and the Netherlands, both countries having had well-established multicultural policies (Entzinger 2003b;
Joppke and Morawska 2003). The Dutch debate cumulated in a newspaper article about the 'multicultural tragedy' by the historian Paul
Scheffer, who stated that an 'ethnic underclass' was emerging, consisting of (particularly Muslim) people who do not feel attached to Dutch
society and who are not willing to integrate (Entzinger 2003b). Such
statements illustrate that anti-diversity writers such as Scheffer or Sartori not only overlook or misrepresent actual policies, but have stereoty-
pical or 'essentialised' views of the ethnic minority groups concerned.

The fear of self-exclusion or 'groupism', publicly expressed by blam-
ing immigrants for non-integration, has probably been one of the most
powerful arguments against multiculturalism in recent years. Yet there
are further 'troubles with multiculturalism' such as those expressed by
Alibhai-Brown (2000a): it is only about 'ethnic minorities'; it has created a sense of white exclusion; its model of representation only deals
with elites; it freezes change and can entrench inequalities; it erects
group barriers; it is seen as 'woolly liberalism'; it has not engaged with
globalisation. Hence, 'multiculturalism is something that black folk do'

(Alibhai Brown 2004:52) According to Kymlicka (2003), this was clearly reflected in the public reactions to the Parekh report on the Future of Multi-Ethnic Britain (2000a) which suggested that British citizens need to rethink what it means to be British. These reactions, on both the left and the right, implicitly or explicitly expressed that 'the idea that multiculturalism might require individuals in the dominant group to re-evaluate (and hence temporarily destabilize) their inherited identities, heroes, symbols and narratives is apparently unthinkable' (Kymlicka 2003:205).

The unthinkable prospect of re-evaluating the concept of *a* national culture and identity is reflected in yet another feature of much multicultural discourse and policy concerned with a bounded nation-building project. Via multiculturalism, Adrian Favell (1998) observes that 'ethnic minorities are offered cultural tolerance, even "multicultural" rights and institutions, in exchange for acceptance of basic principles and the rule of law; they are imagined as culturally-laden social groups, who need to be integrated and individualised by a public sphere which offers voice and participation, transforming them from "immigrants", into full and free "citizens"; they are to become full, assimilated nationals, in a nationstate re-imagined to balance cultural diversity, with a formal equality of status and membership.'

Implicit in this process is what Favell sees as 'an under-theorised, elite re-production of a long-lost idea of national political community; papering over inequality, conflict and power relations with a therapeutical, top-down discourse of multicultural unity' (ibid.). Similarly, Day (2004) points out that although states are: 'all too willing to give the often unwanted and generally meaningless gift of "cultural recognition", multiculturalism as liberal theory and state policy remains staunchly silent on inequalities and injustices that are intimately entwined with the system of states it so desperately wishes to preserve...'

Hence, these scholars are critical of the way such an approach re-appropriates a 'functionalist, Parsonian idea of social integration' purporting to 'unite all classes, and all groups – whether majority or minority – around some singular ideas of national political culture' (Favell 1998).

The premise here is what we might call the 'container model' of the nation-state. In this, social cohesion, cultural belonging and political participation are mutually defined within the geographical and administrative boundaries of the state (cf. Brubaker 1989; Turner 1997; Vertovec 1999b; Faist 2000). This 'container model' persisted despite many social scientists taking a more transnational stance on migration, emphasising the connections between places and the possibilities of belonging and engaging in several national contexts. (Glick-Schiller et al. 1992).

While ideas of cultural and territorial homogeneity of the nation, and the assimilationist approaches to immigrant incorporation built on these ideas were criticised and abandoned in multicultural discourse and policies, the expectation of common attachment to the encompassing nation-state went unchallenged. Hence, although the culturally essentialising model of multiculturalism has recently been rethought, multiculturalism's relationship to the nation-state seems to remain as it was (Vertovec 2001).

Among both advocates and critics, it has been pointed out that ideologies and policies for the recognition or accommodation of cultural, religious and linguistic diversity may, despite good intention, ultimately have negative consequences. This may be due in part or combination to considerations such as the following:

- almost all discourses of multiculturalism entail a kind of 'ethnisation', or a process through which cultural values are presumed to imbue all interests among members of ethnic minority communities (that is, that immigrants are always drawing from an imported 'cultural agenda' rather than, for instance, basing their interests on the fact that they may be co-workers, neighbours, parents);
- political representation or consultation under multiculturalism may amount to a kind of internal neo-colonialism underpinning undemocratic forms of leadership within presumed bounded 'communities';
- these same forms of community consultation may lead to the local state freezing a specific kind of relationship with highly institutionalised minority groups and certain representatives, to the disadvantage of newer or less organised groups or other voices within a group;
- well-meaning multiculturalist policies which local government authorities initiated in the 1980s may work to the disadvantage of minorities by creating conditions of dependency among, and rivalry for state largesse between, ethnic minority groups;
- too much attention to cultural identity can divert attention from other issues of inequality surrounding racism, sexism, class, housing, unemployment, the justice system;
- multicultural policies may have the effect of putting ethnic minority populations into virtual cultural conservation areas like endangered species. In the name of a vague relativism and non-interference with tradition, culturally defined no-go areas have been created among social workers, health care practitioners, police and other workers in the public realm who feel an inability to act because they think it is racist to interfere with 'ethnic cultures'.

In sum, the understanding of 'culture' assumed and prescribed by many multicultural/diversity policies and discourses is one that may distance immigrants and minorities as much as or more than it actually seeks to include them.

'Culture', in the sense entailed in many such measures, is presumed to be something forever distinguishing and separating immigrants and ethnic minorities from the rest of society. A 'multi-cultural' society, in this reasoning, is therefore a pool of bounded uni-cultures, forever divided into we's and they's.

Contra diversity

In recent years throughout Europe there have arisen other critiques of diversity and its accommodation. These critiques or debates *against* diversity have themselves been diverse, but in many ways they share common features. Rather than just a new variation of far right anti-immigrant sentiments, the new critiques have been voiced on both the right and, perhaps surprisingly, left side of the political spectrum. Essentially the critiques commonly voice a fear that multiculturalism or the public recognition of cultural, religious and linguistic diversity will lead to a kind of 'balkanisation' or ethnic separatism marking a breakdown of societal concord. Parallel arguments have been made significantly in public arenas, for instance by Paul Scheffer (2000) in the Netherlands, Giovanni Sartori (2002) in Italy, and Bob Rowthorne (2003) and David Goodhart (2004) in the UK. In these arguments 'too much diversity' disrupts a national identity, breaks down a society's sense of cohesion, dissipates common values and undermines participatory institutions such as the welfare state. What is needed, such commentators urge, is an emphasis on historical continuity, citizenship, national symbols, a return to immigrant cultural assimilation and a kind of enforced integration by way of emphasising a core set of national values over recognising minority specificities.

Why have such calls *contra* multiculturalism arisen of late? Answers to this are possibly many, and are likely specific to the national contexts in which they have arisen, although it is significant that such arguments have risen simultaneously across Europe. The most important of these are the following.

A first argument is the 'failure of integration'. Recent national censuses and other instruments for measuring the socio-economic standing of communities have, in many countries, shown that immigrant groups and ethnic minorities now, at least two or three generations since original migration, tend to show poor levels of education, quality of housing and degree of residential segregation, types of jobs or levels of unemployment and other indicators of low socio-economic attainment or mobility. Some commentators suggest that in the past or even currently, some recent immigrant groups did or do much better than others. Hence these commentators, including those mentioned above, as well as media reporters, claim there has been a 'failure to integrate', and therefore ask the question: Does the 'culture' of poorly attaining groups, which has been underpinned by multicultural policies, actually have something to do with their underachievement? Or, does such culture either lead immigrants to consciously reject the prospects of integration – or indeed is their culture 'unassimilable'? Often the *contra* diversity commentators' answers to such questions suggest 'yes' (while ignoring a range of historical and structural factors, including discrimination, that contribute heavily if not wholly to poor socio-economic standing).

A second argument focuses on specific signs of non-integration of the second generation. Along with the public concern about the kinds of indicators and questions mentioned above, some societies including the UK, France, Germany and the Netherlands have witnessed a kind of moral panic surrounding the place of the so-called 'second generation', marked by interethnic tensions or violence, suspicions and some indicators of criminal activity and public disturbances or indeed riots. Again there are often attempts to explain these issues with reference to 'culture' (here, with 'Islam' usually considered a key mode of culture by way of attitudes, values and practices, rather than as 'religion' in terms of ritual, faith and morality). The viewpoint *contra* diversity sees the call for citizenship, common values and cohesion as the key way to remedy allegedly culture-fueled tensions and problems surrounding young people of immigrant and ethnic minority origin.

A third argument is the threat to security and social cohesion. Although perhaps too many of the world's current problems are being laid upon the events of 11 September 2001, it is certainly not presumptuous to suggest that they play an important contributing role in the turning of the tide *contra* diversity. The 'civilisational logic' wrought by 9/11 – i.e. the Huntingtonian worldview that pits large scale 'culture' vs. 'culture' in a struggle for dominance – is coming to filter people's understanding of what is happening with immigrants and ethnic minorities on the streets of Berlin, Bradford, Rotterdam, Marseille and numerous other settings across Europe. Once more 'Islam' is conceived as the *other* 'culture' or the civilisation most at odds with – and therefore most 'unassimilable' and ultimately threatening – the cohesion of a presumed national society. This ignores the fact that other minority groups such as Jews, Irish or Italians were once perceived as unassimilable, and that the societies of modern nation-states have never been culturally homogenous. Nevertheless, policies and programmes promoting diversity come to be regarded as measures sure to undermine the collective well-being of immigrant receiving societies by supporting values, practices and entire communities which are inherently at odds with these societies. In this view, the majority society is being imagined as linguistic, religious and cultural entity, as much stereotyped as immigrant communities themselves.

The kinds of concerns noted above are not only suggested broadly in newspaper essays, radio phone-ins and television talk shows, but 'concretised' in debates and policy decisions regarding what we might call some of the 'iconic issues' of diversity in our times. It is not surprising that various iconic issues of diversity (purporting to indicate the breakdown of social cohesion) specifically involve Islam. Such iconic issues that are highly visible in public space include Muslim headscarves, the call for separate Muslim schools, the outrageous utterances of certain imams and the presence of young Muslims on lists of terrorist suspects.

The tasks for researchers then is to understand such trends in social processes, public discourse and government policy affecting cultural, religious and linguistic diversity. In the concluding section some of the main lines of inquiry are suggested.

4. Prospects for future research

This brief overview of the debate on multiculturalism leaves us with a conundrum: basing participation, representation and public service on 'culture' can petrify culture and stigmatise people, thereby maintaining or exacerbating conditions of exclusion; yet ignoring 'culture' (and religion and language) can neglect legitimate special needs (based on particular values and practices) and at the same time perpetuate patterns of discrimination and inequality. When looking into the basic premisses of explicit policies in this field we furthermore have to ask the basic question: multicultural or integration policies for whom primarily? For the minorities, as a means of assisting in the reproduction of values and practices and for reaffirming their sense of worth? Or for the majority, as a means of education into the lifeways of the minorities who co-comprise society and may be (or become) fellow citizens? Or for society in the abstract, as a way of fashioning new ways of belonging, participating, living together?

This leads to a general consideration for future research in this domain: comparative assessment of policy development surrounding cultural, religious and linguistic diversity cannot be attempted without a concurrent examination of public attitudes, debates and representations that inform or have an impact upon policymakers' decisions. In

most European nation-states at present, there is a revitalised delibera-
tion on the relationship between national identity and collective values,
challenges of cultural difference, and the purported 'failure of integration' among migrants. This climate of attitude and discourse must be
examined in order to make sense of the policy issues faced by politicians, civil servants, NGOs and community groups today.

With this major principle in mind we still have to set priorities for
research in the wider field. As a consequence of the analysis in this
chapter, and taking into account the special interest and expertise of
the researchers involved, we have identified five special topics for priority.

*Cross-national comparison of the debate on cultural difference and
reassessing multiculturalism*
As we have seen, debates about cultural difference and the rights and
wrongs of different ways of living sometimes thought to be incompatible, are occurring throughout Europe and include diverse voices among
both majority and minority ethnic populations. These debates take
place at many levels (locally, nationally, transnationally) and may be observed in public policy statements, the speeches of politicians and religious leaders, the media and everyday conversations. At the same time
such debates differ in form, intensity and outcome. Focusing on specific issues and situations (e.g. the family), we will ask how the idea of
cultural difference is deployed; what variations occur between countries
and over time; and how such debates are conducted, and perhaps re-
solved.

Analogously, but focusing more explicitly on the use of official vocabulary in governmental policy, a cross-national comparison of the 'reas-
sessment of multiculturalism' will be made. Observers have witnessed
how, in a relatively short time, many governments have been purpose-
fully dropping 'multicultural' from their policy vocabularies. Is there
indeed a common 'sceptical turn' against cultural diversity or 'backlash
against difference' (Grillo 2003a)? If so, what has brought about such
seeming parallel thinking in different societies and political contexts?

Public religion and secular democracy
Comparative research on institutionalised regimes of governance of religious diversity in Europe, their impact on organisation and mobilisation of immigrant minorities (and vice versa), and on their societal and
political incorporation in general, is still in a nascent state, while the
need for a well-informed analysis is extremely high. This is particularly
the case when it comes to variant forms of Islam in European countries and the great variety of national reactions to this religion that is
associated primarily with immigrants. Some of the central topics will

be: (i) Governance of religious diversity and path dependency: making theories and methods fit for comparative studies; (ii) Organizing and representing Islam in Europe; (iii) New religious minorities as 'public religions' in Europe; (iv) Governance of Islam in Europe: from colonialism to post-colonialism.

Legal practice and cultural diversity

Debates and practices of cultural diversity and difference in Europe can be fruitfully studied cross-nationally and empirically by scrutinising the legal frames and practices. Legal frames may determine on the one hand such debates and practices and their (non-)acceptance; on the other hand, once accepted and embedded in the legal system, practices of cultural diversity and difference, may be endorsed and more widely accepted.

Language policy and practices

As indicated earlier in this chapter, language policies and practices in immigration contexts are situated around two axes: the access to the language of the host country as a prerequisite of participation in that society, and the use of other languages, spoken in the country of origin and constituting an integral part of social and cultural practices among migrants. The cross-national study of language policy and practices is crucial, the central issues being those of literacy acquisition on the one hand, and of managing diverse language situations in immigration contexts on the other.

Ethnic minority and immigrants cultural productions as forms of political expression

Central in this theme (and in the following) is the agency of immigrants in the cultural fields and their innovative contribution to society. Here the question is asked to what extent immigrant and ethnic popular cultural productions (music, literature, etc.) can be analysed in terms of political expression and participation, especially at the city level.

Cities of diversity: the spatial nexus

The objective here is to contextualise the cultural dimension in space and in relation to other domains of daily life: the interrelationship of manifestations of religious and cultural diversity in and of urban public spaces on the one hand, and the production and reproduction of social, political and economic relations on the other.

Notes

1   The significance of 'culture' as an analytical concept is much contested and has changed considerably in recent years with the emphasis now on dynamic interpretations (Kuper 1999, Grillo 2003). For present purposes, however, it suffices to say that by 'culture' we understand the different ways of living associated with majority and minority ethnic populations in Europe, which are sometimes thought to be incompatible.

2   The literature on religious diversity draws from a programme of a workshop on 'Accomodating religious diversity' written by Aristide Zollberg. The workshop took place at the Zentrum für interdisziplinäre Forschung in Bielefeld, 2004.

3   For a discussion of the status of immigrant minority languages at home and at school see the UNESCO report on 'Language and Diversity in Multicultural Europe' (Extra and Yagmur 2002).

4   For a detailed overview of the measures of European states regarding the cultural and linguistic integration of immigrant children into schools see the report of the European Commission: Eurydice (2004).

Literature

Ager, D. E. (1996), *Language Policy in Britain and France: the Processes of Policy*. London: Cassell.

Alibhai-Brown, Y. (2000a), *After Multiculturalism*. London: Foreign Policy Centre.

Alibhai-Brown, Y. (2000b), *Who Do We Think We Are?: Imagining the New Britain*. London: Allen Lane.

Alibhai-Brown, Y. (2004), Beyond Multiculturalism. *Diversité Canadienne* 3:51-54.

Allemann-Ghionda, C. (1998), *Multikultur und Bildung in Europa*. Bern, New York: Peter Lang.

Allievi, S. (2002), 'Islam in Italy: Sociology of a Newcomer', in S. Hunter (ed.), *Islam, Europe's Second Religion: the New Social, Cultural, and Political Landscape*. Westport, Conn.: Praeger.

Ålund, A., & C. Schierup. (1991), *Paradoxes of Multiculturalism: Essays on Swedish Society*. Aldershot: Avebury.

Amselle, J. L. (ed.)(1998), *Mestizo Logics: Anthropology of Identity in Africa and Elsewhere*. Stanford: Stanford University Press.

Anthias, F., & N. Yuval-Davis. (1993), *Racialized Boundaries: Race, Nation, Gender, Colour and Class and the Anti-Racist Struggle*. London: Routledge.

Bader, V. (1999), 'Religious Pluralism. Secularism or Priority for Democracy?'. *Political Theory* 22: 597-633.

Baker, C., & S. P. Jones. (1998), *Encyclopedia of Bilingualism and Bilingual Education*. Clevedon: Multilingual Matters.

Bauböck, R. (2003), 'Public Culture in Societies of Immigration,' in R. Sackmann, T. Faist, and B. Peters (eds.), *Identity and Integration. Migrants in Western Europe*. 37-57. Ashgate: Avebury.

Bauböck, R., A. Heller, & A. R. Zolberg. (1996), *The Challenge of Diversity: Integration and Pluralism in Societies of Immigration*. Aldershot: Avebury.

Bauböck, R., and J. F. Rundell. (eds.) (1998), *Blurred Boundaries: Migration, Ethnicity, Citizenship*. Aldershot: Ashgate.

Baumann, G. (1996), *Contesting Culture: Discourses of Identity in Multi-Ethnic London*. Cambridge: Cambridge University Press.

Baumann, G. (1999), *The Multicultural Riddle: Rethinking National, Ethnic, and Religious Identities*. New York, London: Routledge.

Baumann, M. (2000), *Migration – Religion – Integration. Buddhistische Vietnamesen und hinduistische Tamilen in Deutschland*. Marburg: Diagonal.

Baumann, M., B. Luchesi & A. Wilke. (2003), *Tempel und Tamilen in zweiter Heimat: Hindus aus Sri Landa im deutschsprachigen und skandinavischen Raum*. Würzburg: Ergon.

Bergmann, J., A. Hahn & T. Luckmann. (1993), Religion und Kultur. *Kölner Zeitschrift für Soziologie und Socialpsychologie* 33.

Blommaert, J., & J. Verschueren. (1998), *Debating Diversity: Analysing the Discourse of Tolerance*. London: Routledge.

Bowen, J.R. (2004), Does French Islam Have Borders? Dilemmas of Domestication in a Global Religious Field. *American Anthropologist* 106 (1): 44-55.

Brubaker, R. (1989), *Immigration and the Politics of Citizenship in Europe and North America*. Lanham, Md, London: University Press of America.

Buijs, F. J., & S. Harchaoui. (2003), Islamitisch radicalisme en rekrutering in Nederland. Proces. *Tijdschrift voor berechting en reclassering* (Special over terrorisme) 82: 98-109.

Castan, F. (1984), *Manifeste multiculturel et antirégionaliste, 30 ans d'expérience décentralisatrice*. Mounauban: Le Moustier.

Castles, S. (2000), *Ethnicity and Globalization: from Migrant Worker to Transnational Citizen*. London: Sage.

Castles, S., M. Kalantzis, B. Cope & M. Morrissey. (1988), *Mistaken Identity: Multiculturalism and the Demise of Nationalism in Australia*. Sydney: Pluto Press.

Cattacin, S. (2003), *Etat et religion en Suisse: luttes pour la reconnaissance, formes de la reconnaissance*. Berne: Commission fédérale contre le racisme (CFR).

Caubet, D. (2004), *Les mots du bled*. Paris: L'Harmattan.

Cesari, J. (1997), *Etre musulman en France aujoud'hui*. Paris: Hachette.

Cesari Lusso, V. (2001), *Quand le défi est appelé intégration: parcours de socialisation et de personnalisation de jeunes issus de la migration*. Bern, Berlin, etc.: Lang.

Cingolani, P. (2004), 'The Amazing Familiarity of the City. Places, Journeys and Discourses of Nigerian Migrants in Turin and Their Transnational Connections.' *Conference: Pathways of Immigration in Europe*, Università di Trento, 2004.

Closta, C., T. Ostermann, & C. Schroeder. (2003), Die Durchschnittsschule und ihre Sprachen. Ergenisse des Projekts 'Sprachenerhebung Essener Grundschule'. *Elise* 3: 43-139.

Cuperus, R., K. A. Duffek & J. Kandel (eds.) (2003), *The Challenge of Diversity. European Social Democracy Facing Migration, Integration, and Multiculturalism*. Innsbruck, Vienna, München, Bozen: Studien Verlag.

Dabène, L., M. Flasaquier, & J. Lyons. (1984), *Status of migrants' mother tongues*. Strasbourg: European Science Foundation.

Day, R. (2004), Dialogue and Differends: On the Limits of Liberal Multiculturalism. *Diversité Canadienne* 3: 36-38.

DES (Department of Education and Science) (1985), *The Swann Report*. London: Department of Education and Science.

Dingu-Kyrklund, E. (2004), 'Mother-Tongue Instruction for Immigrant Children and Children Belonging to Historical Minorities.' *Unpublished paper prepared for the IMISCOE Cluster B6, 2004.*

Dirim, I., & P. Auer. (2004), *Türkisch sprechen nicht nur die Türken – über die Unschärfebeziehung zwischen Sprache und Ethnie in Deutschland*. Berlin: De Gruyter.

Entzinger, H. (2000), 'The Dynamics of Integration Policies: A Multidimensional Model,' in R. Koopmans and P. Statham (eds.), *Challenging Immigration and Ethnic Relations Politics: Comparative European Perspectives*, 97-118. Oxford: Oxford University Press.

Entzinger, H. (2003), 'The Rise and Fall of Multiculturalism: The Case of the Netherlands,' in C. Joppke and E. Morawska (eds.), *Toward Assimilation and Citizenship; Immigration in Liberal Nation-States*. 59-261. London: Palgrave Macmillan.

Eriksen, T. H. (1997), 'Multiculturalism, Individualism and Human Rights: Romanticism, the Enlightenment and Lessons from Mauritius,' in R. Wilson (ed.), *Human Rights, Culture and Context: Anthropological Perspectives*. 49-69. London: Pluto.

Eriksen, T. H. (2002), *Ethnicity and Nationalism*. London: Pluto.

Eurydice (The Information Network on Education in Europe). (2004), *Integrating Immigrant Children into Schools in Europe*. Euridyce and European Commission.

Extra, G., & K. Yagmur. (2002), *Language Diversity in Multicultural Europe. Comparative Perspectives on Immigrant Minority Languages at Home and at School*. UNESCO.

Faist, T. (2000), *The Volume and Dynamics of International Migration and Transnational Social Spaces*. Oxford: Clarendon Press.

Favell, A. (1998), 'To Belong or not to Belong: the Postnational Question,' in A. Favell and A. Geddes (eds.), *The Politics of Belonging: Migrants and Minorities in Contemporary Europe*. Aldershot: Ashgate.

Favell, A. (2001), 'Integration Policy and Integration Research in Europe: a Review and Critique,' in A. Aleinikoff and D. Klusmeyer (eds.), *Citizenship Today: Global Perspectives and Practices*, 349-399. Washington DC: Brookings Institute/Carnegie Endowment for International Peace.

Ferrari, A. (2004a), *Ecole et religion en Italie, ou de la 'saine laïcité' de l'Etat*. École Pratique des Hautes Etudes.

Ferrari, A. (2004b), *La lotta dei simboli e la speranza del diritto: Laicità e velo musulmano nella Francia di inizio millennio*. Rome: Carocci.

Ferrari, A. (2004c), 'L'islam in Italia: aspetti giuridici di un'integrazione silenziosa.' Marsala.

Ferrari, S. (2004a), *Islam in Europe: An Introduction to Legal Problems and Perspectives* (unpublished paper).

Ferrari, S. (2004b), *The European Pattern of Church and State Relations* (unpublished paper).

Freedman, J. (2004), Secularism as a Barrier to Integration? The French Dilemma. *International Migration* 42:5-27.

Giovannini, G. (1998), *Allievi in classe, stranieri in città. Una ricerca sugli insegnanti di scuola elementare di fronte all'immigrazione*. Milan: Fondazione Cariplo, ISMU, F. Angeli.

Glick-Schiller, N., L. Basch and C. Blanc-Szanton (1992), 'Transnationalism: A New Anaytical Framework for Understanding Migration,' in N. Glick-Schiller, L. Basch and C. Blanc-Szanton, *Towards a Transnational Perspective on Migration*. New York: Academy of Sciences, 1-24.

Gogolin, I. (2002), 'Linguistic and Cultural Diversity in Europe: a Challenge for Educational Research and Practice.' *European Educational Research Journal* 1:123-138.

Grillo, R. (1998), *Pluralism and the Politics of Difference: State, Culture and Ethnicity in Comparative Perspective*. Oxford: Clarendon.

Grillo, R. (2003), 'Racism in Europe: A Backlash against Difference?' *Lecture, University of Western Australia, 2003*.

Grillo, R. (2003), Cultural Essentialism and Cultural Anxiety. *Anthropological Theory* 3: 157-173.

Grillo, R. (2004), *Backlash Against Diversity? Identity and Cultural Politics in European Cities* (Unpublished Paper).

Grillo, R. (2004), 'Diversity, Identity and Cultural Politics in European Cities.' *Lecture, Barcelona, 2004*.

Grillo, R. (2004), Islam and Transnationalism. *Journal of Ethnic and Migration Studies* 30: 861-878.

Grillo, R. (2005) (forthcoming), 'Saltdean Can't Cope': Protests against Asylum-Seekers in an English Seaside Suburb.' *Ethnic and Racial Studies* 28.

Grillo, R., & J. C. Pratt. (2002), *The Politics of Recognizing Difference: Multiculturalism Italian-Style*. Aldershot: Ashgate.

Gutmann, A. (ed.) (1994), *Multiculturalism: Examining the Politics of Recognition*. Princeton: Princeton University Press.

Haddad, Y. Y. (ed.). (2002), *Muslims in the West: From Sojourners to Citizens*. Oxford, New York: Oxford University Press.

Hage, G. (1998), *White Nation: Fantasies of White Supremacy in a Multicultural Society*. Sydney: Pluto Press.

Heath, S. B. (1983), *Ways with Words: Language, Life, and Work in Communities and Classrooms*. Cambridge: Cambridge University Press.

Heckmann, F., & D. Schnapper. (eds.) (2003), *The Integration of Immigrants in European Societies. National Differences and Trends of Convergence*. Stuttgart: Lucius & Lucius.

Heitmeyer, W., J. Müller, & J. Schröder. (1997), *Verlockender Fundamentalismus: Türkische Jugendliche in Deutschland*. Frankfurt a.M.: Suhrkamp.

Huntington, S. P. (1998), *The Clash of Civilizations and the Remaking of World Order*. London: Touchstone.

Ireland, P. (1994), *The Policy Challenge of Ethnic Diversity: Immigrant Policies in France and Switzerland*. Cambridge, Ma.: Harvard University Press.

Joppke, C., and E. Morawska. (2003), 'Integrating Immigrants in Liberal Nation-States,' in C. Joppke and E. Morawska (eds.), *Toward Assimilation and Citizenship: Immigrants in Liberal Nation-States*, ix, 243. Basingstoke: Palgrave Macmillan.

Juergensmeyer, M. (2003), *Global Religions: an Introduction*. New York, Oxford: Oxford University Press.

Kälin, W. (2000), *Grundrechte im Kulturkonflikt: Freiheit und Gleichheit in der Einwanderungsgesellschaft*. Zürich: NZZ-Verlag.

Kastoryano, R. (ed.) (2002), *Negotiating Identities: States and Immigrants in France and Germany*. Princeton, Oxford: Princeton University Press.

Kobayashi, A. (1993), 'Multiculturalism: Representing a Canadian Institution,' in J. Duncan and D. Ley (eds.), *Place/Culture/Representation*, pp. 205-31. London: Routledge.

Krause, K. (2004), 'Traveling Spirits – Transnational Healing in African Christian Churches in London.' *8th EASA Conference, Vienna, 2004*.

Kühlwein, W. (ed.) (1978), *Sprache und Kultur: Studien zur Diglossie, Gastarbeiterproblematik und kulturellen Integration*. Tübingen: Gunter Narr Verlag.

Kuper, A. (1999), *Culture: The Anthropologists' Account*. Cambridge: Harvard University Press.

Kymlicka, W. (1995), *Multicultural Citizenship: a Liberal Theory of Minority Rights*. Oxford: Clarendon Press.

Kymlicka, W. (2003), 'Immigration, Citizenship, Multiculturalism: Exploring the Links,' in S. Spencer (ed.), *The Politics of Migration: Managing Opportunity, Conflict and Change*, pp. 195-208. Oxford: Blackwell.

Lewis, P. (1997), 'The Bradford Council for Mosques and the Search for Muslim Unity,' in *Islam in Europe: the Politics of Religion and Community*. S. Vertovec and C. Peach (eds.), 103-128. Basingstoke: Macmillan.

Martiniello, M. (1997), *Sortir des ghettos culturels*. Paris: Presses de Sc. Po.

Martiniello, M. (1998), 'Accomodating Religious Pluralism in Britain: South Asian Religions,' in M. Martiniello (ed.), *Multicultural Policies and the State: a Comparison of Two European Societies*, 163-77. Utrecht: ERCOMER.

Martiniello, M. (ed.) (1998), *Multicultural Policies and the State: a Comparison of Two European Societies*. Utrecht: ERCOMER.

Martiniello, M. (2004), The Many Dimensions of Belgian Diversity. *Diversité Canadienne* 3: 43-46.

May, S. (1999), 'Critical Multiculturalism and Cultural Difference: Avoiding Essentialism,' in *Critical Multiculturalism: rethinking Multicultural and Antiracist Education.* S. May (ed.), 11-41. London: Falmer.

Mehlem, U., S. De Carlo, & C. Weth. (2004a), 'Understanding the Governance of Diversity in Europe.' *Unpublished paper prepared for the IMISCOE Cluster B6, 2004.*

Mehlem, U., & U. Maas. (2003), Schriftkulturelle Ressourcen und Barrieren bei marokkanischen Kindern in Deutschland. *Vol. I. IMIS. Materialien zur Migrationsforschung.* Osnabrück.

Mehlem, U., U. Maas, & C. Schroeder. (2004b), Mehrsprachigkeit und Mehrschriftigkeit bei Einwanderern in Deutschland,' in K. J. Bade, M. Bommes, and R. Münz (eds.), *Migrationsreport 2004), Fakten – Analysen – Perspektiven,* pp. 117-149. Frankfurt, New York: Campus.

Modood, T. (2003), 'Muslims and the Politics of Difference,' in S. Spencer (ed.), *The Politics of Migration: Managing Opportunity, Conflict and Change,* 100-115. Oxford: Blackwell.

Niekerk, M. van (2000), 'Creoles and Hindustanis. Patterns of Social Mobility in two Surinamese Immigrant Groups in the Netherlands,' in H. Vermeulen and J. Perlmann (eds.), *Immigrants, Schooling and Social Mobility: Does Culture Make a Difference?* 184-205. Basingstoke: Macmillan.

Parekh, B. C. (2000), *The Future of Multi-Ethnic Britain: Report of the Commission on the Future of Multi-Ethnic Britain.* London: Profile (Runnymede Trust).

Parekh, B. (2000), *Rethinking Multiculturalism: Cultural Diversity and Political Theory.* Basingstoke: Macmillan; Palgrave.

Penninx, R. (2000), 'Het Dramatische Misverstand,' in J. E. Overdijk-Francis and H. M. A. G. Smeets (eds.), *Bij Nader Inzien: Het integratiedebat op afstand bekeken,* 27-49. Bohn: Infoplus Minderheden, Stafeu and Van Loghum/Koninklijke Vermande, Houten/Lelystad.

Penninx, R., K. Kraal, M. Martiniello, & S. Vertovec. (2004a), *Citizenship in European Cities: Immigrants, Local Politics and Integration Policies.* Aldershot: Ashgate.

Penninx, R., K. Kraal, M. Martiniello, in *Citizenship in European Cities: Immigrants, Local Politics and Integration Policies.* R. Penninx, K. Kraal, M. Martiniello, and S. Vertovec (eds.), 70. Aldershot: Ashgate.

Pereira Bastos, S. (2001), *De Moçambique a Portugal: Reinterpretações identitárias do Hinduismo em diaspora (From Mozambique to Portugal: Identity Reinterpretations of Hinduism in Diaspora).* Lisbon, Orientália: Fundação Oriente.

Pfaff-Czarnecka, J.(ed.). (2004), *Death, Ri(gh)tes, and Institutions in Immigrant Switzerland. Rethinking Non-Discrimination and Minority Rights.* Turku: Institute for Human Rights, Abo Akademi University and Deutsches Institut für Menschenrechte.

Radtke, F. (1994), 'The Formation of Ethnic Minorities and the Transformation of Social into Ethnic Conflicts in a so-called Multicultural Society – the Case of Germany,' in J. Rex and B. Drury (eds.), *Ethnic Mobilisation in a Multi-Cultural Europe,* 30-7. Aldershot: Avebury.

Radtke, O., and M. Gomolla. (2002), *Institutionelle Diskriminierung: Die Herstellung ethnischer Differenz in der Schule.* Opladen: Leske und Budrich.

Rath, J., R. Penninx, K. Groenendijk & A. Meyer. (2001), *Western Europe and its Islam.* Leiden: Brill.

Reich, H. H. (2001), Sprache und Integration,' in K. Bade (ed.), *Integration und Illegalität in Deutschland,* 41-50. Osnabrück: Rat für Migration e. V.

Reich, H. H., & H.-J. Roth. (2002), *Spracherwerb zweisprachig aufwachsender Kinder und Jugendlicher. Ein Überblick über den Stand der nationalen und internationalen Forschung.* www.erzwiss.uni-hamburg.de/Insto2/indexo2.htm. Hamburg.

Riccio, B. (2001), Disaggregating the Transnational Community: Senegalese Migrants on the Coast of Emilia-Romagna. *Working Paper for the Transnational Communities Programme.* Oxford: University of Oxford.

Salentin, K. (2004), 'Ziehen sich Migranten in "ethnische Kolonien" zurück?,' in K. J. Bade, M. Bommes, and R. Münz (eds.), *Migrationsreport 2004. Fakten – Analysen – Perspektiven,* 97-116. Frankfurt, New York: Campus.

Sartori, G. (2002), *Pluralismo, Multiculturalismo e Estranei: Saggio sulla società Multietnica.* Milan: Rizzoli.

Scheffer, P. (2000), 'Het multiculturele drama,' in *NRC Handelsblad,* January 29.

Schiffauer, W. (2001), 'Ich bin etwas Besonderes. Wie ein junger Türke vom angepassten Gymnasiasten zum provozierenden Anhänger des fanatischen Islamisten Metin Kaplan wird,' in *Die Zeit,* 41 edition.

Schiffauer, W. (2004), 'Die Islamische Gemeinschaft Milli Görüs – ein Lehrstück zum verwickelten Zusammenhang von Migration, Religion und sozialer Integration,' in K. J. Bade, M. Bommes, and R. Münz (eds.), *Migrationsreport 2004. Fakten – Analysen – Perspektiven.* 66-96. Frankfurt, New York: Campus.

Schiffauer, W., G. Baumann, R. Kastoryano & S. Vertovec. (2004), *Civil Enculturation: Nation-State, Schools and Ethnic Difference in four European Countries.* New York, Oxford: Berghahn.

Shadid, W. A. R., & P. S. van Koningsveld. (1996), *Muslims in the Margin: Political Responses to the Presence of Islam in Western Europe.* Kampen: Kok Pharos.

Shadid, W. A. R. & P. S. van Koningsveld, (eds.) (2002), *Religious Freedom and the Neutrality of the State: the Position of Islam in the European Union.* Leuven: Peeters.

Silverman, M. (1992), *Deconstructing the National: Immigration, Racism and Citizenship in Modern France.* London: Routledge.

Soysal, Y.N. (1994), *The Limits of Citizenship: Migrants and Postnational Membership in Europe.* Chicago: University of Chicago Press.

Spencer, S. & A. di Mattia. (2004), *Introductory Programmes and Initiatives for New Migrants in Europe (unpublished paper).* Centre on Migration, Policy and Society (COMPAS) / Migration Policy Institute, Washington DC.

Statham, P. (2003), 'New Conflicts about Integration and Cultural Diversity in Britain: The Muslim Challenge to Race Relations,' in R. Cuperus, K. A. Duffek, and J. Kandel (eds.). *The Challenge of Diversity. European Social Democracy Facing Migration, Integration, and Multiculturalism.* Innsbruck, Vienna, München, Bozen: Studien Verlag.

Stasi, B. (2003), Commission de réflexion sur l'application du principe de laïcité dans la République, *Rapport au Président de la République.*

Stolcke, V. (1995), Talking Culture: New Boundaries, New Rhetorics of Exclusion in Europe. *Current Anthropology* 36: 1-24.

Sunier, T. (1999), 'Niederländisch-Islamische Staatsbürgerschaft? Ansichten über Islam, Bürgerschaft und Bürgerrechte unter Türkischen Jugendlichen in den Niederlanden,' in W. D. Bukow and M. Ottersbach (eds.), *Der Fundamentalismus-Verdacht: Plädoyer für eine Neuorientierung der Forschung im Umgang mit Allochtonen Jugendlichen,* 85-97. Opladen: Leske und Budrich.

Taylor, C. & A. Gutmann. (1992), *Multiculturalism and 'the Politics of Recognition': an Essay.* Princeton: Princeton University Press.

Todd, E. (1994), *Le destin des immigrés. Assimilation et ségrégation dans les démocraties occidentales.* Paris: Seuil.

Tosi, A. C. Demuth. (1985), *Multi-Cultural Education: Views from the Classroom,* Revised edition. London: British Broadcasting Corporation.

Verma, G. K. (ed.) (1989), *Education for All: a Landmark in Pluralism.* London: Falmer.

Verma, G. K. Social Cohesion and Tolerance.' *Second International Metropolis Conference,* Copenhagen, 1997.

Vertovec, S. (1998), 'Multi-multicutluralisms,' in *Multicultural Policies and the State,* 25-38. Utrecht: ERCOMER.

Vertovec, S. (1999), 'Introduction,' in Vertovec. S. (ed.), *Migration and Social Cohesion.* Cheltenham: Edward Elgar.

Vertovec, S. (ed.) (1999), *Migration and Social Cohesion.* Cheltenham: Edward Elgar.

Vertovec, S. (1999), Minority Associations, Networks and Public Policies: Re-assessing Vertovec, S. Relationships. *Journal of Ethnic and Migration Studies. [Offprint]:* 21-42.

Vertovec, S. (2001), 'Transnational Challenges to the "New" Multiculturalism.' *ASA Conference 2001, University of Sussex, 2001.*

Vertovec, S. forthcoming. 'Dimensions of Diaspora Among south Asian Religions,' in J. Hinnels and W. Menski (eds.), *From Generation to Generation: Religious Reconstruction in the South Asian Diaspora.* Basingstoke: Macmillan.

Vertovec, S. forthcoming. 'Religion and Diaspora,' in P. Antes, A. W. Geertz, and R. Warne (eds.), *New Approaches to the Study of Religion.* Berlin, New York: De Gruyter.

Vertovec, S. & C. Peach. (1997), *Islam in Europe: the Politics of Religion and Community.* Basingstoke: Macmillan.

Vertovec, S. & A. Rogers. (eds.) (1998), *Muslim European Youth: Reproducing Ethnicity, Religion, Culture.* Aldershot: Ashgate.

Werbner, P. (2002), *Imagined Diasporas among Manchester Muslims: the Public Performance of Pakistani Transnational Identity Politics.* Oxford: James Currey.

Westin, C. & E. Dingu-Kyrklund. (2000), *Integration Analysis Sweden.* CEIFO, Stockhom University.

Willett, C. (1998), *Theorizing Multiculturalism: A Guide to the Current Debate.* Oxford: Blackwell

Wilson, B. (1999), *La liberté de la langue des minorités dans l'enseignement: étude de droit international et de droit suisse.* Basel: Helbing & Lichtenhahn.

Wolf, R. & F. Heckmann. (2003), In Deutschland zu Hause – Politik, Geschichte und Alltagswissen für Zuwanderer und Einbürgerungswillige. *Evaluationsbericht zum Modellprojekt Integrationskurse an das Bayerische Staatsministerium für Arbeit und Sozialordnung, Familie und Frauen und das Bildungszentrum Nürnberg.* Bamberg: Europäisches Forum für Migrationsstudien.

Zachary, G. P. (2003), *The Diversity Advantage: Multicultural Identity in the New World Economy.* Boulder, Colorado: Westview.

Zolberg, A. & W. L. Long. (1999), Why Islam is like Spanish: Cultural Incorporation in Europe and the United States. *Politics and Society* 27:5-38.

8. Identity, Representation, Interethnic Relations and Discrimination

José Bastos, Aitor Ibarrola-Armendariz, João Sardinha,
Charles Westin and Gisela Will[1]

1. Introduction

Social identities are of crucial concern. Collective social identities stand out and are articulated when groups coming from different social, cultural, 'racial', national, ethnic, religious and linguistic backgrounds share societal space in public places and arenas, in residential areas or when people compete in schools and in the labour market. 'Race', ethnicity and nation are represented in these identities, stereotypes and collective/social representations. However, the concept of representation also pertains to issues of power and influence in political assemblies, that is, political representation of the interests of disadvantaged 'racial', ethnic and social groups. In this chapter we will cover a broad range of issues with a number of perspectives on interethnic relations in EU member states.

Dealing with relations between national, ethnic, 'racial', religious and cultural groups in concrete societies leads to differential outcome, depending on historical and demographic factors. In some countries this will primarily entail a focus on majority-minority relations (ethno-territorial, linguistic, religious, cultural minorities) in the nation-state. In other countries, countries of immigration, the focus will rather be on relations between native-born populations and migrants and their descendents (first and second generation) as well as between different migrant groups. In a third set of countries, probably most of the present 25 EU members states, interethnic relations will apply to ethno-cultural and ethno-territorial minority-majority relations as well as relations between groups of migrant origin and native populations. The term interethnic relations covers a broad range of encounters between people and groups of diverse origins that take place in European societies of immigration. Often the emphasis is on problematic dimensions or aspects of these relations – racism, social exclusion, discrimination, segregation, inequality and injustice. However, interethnic relations should also be understood to include processes of incorporation and acculturation often referred to as assimilation, integration and comparable terms, as well as various aspects of diversity management.

Although we will start from the broad field of study of identity, interethnic relations and discrimination, including minorities within societies that do not have a migration background (or a very ancient one), we will focus more specifically on the nexus with migration. Our central question is concerned with how migration and integration affect the social and geographical space of the receiving (multiethnic) society, across social class and gender.

A number of both interdisciplinary and intersectional theoretical and methodological approaches will be presented. A range of different empirical sources will be considered and hence also the use of various methods. Quantitative data from national surveys of group perceptions, attitudes, belief-systems, experiences of discrimination and injustice will provide empirical input, as well as in-depth interviews and case studies of specific groups and communities, studies that can be set up longitudinally as well as cross-sectionally.

It is of the utmost importance to focus on the institutional structures of racism and discrimination, and to uncover the concealed social structures that generate and perpetuate unequal opportunities. In order to analyse these structures we will need to be methodologically innovative.

In this chapter we have arranged the overview of the most important literature around three basic concepts in the field: *identity, interethnic relations* and *discrimination*. In treating these three core issues we followed a pattern of introducing the core themes, discussing concepts and definitions used in the literature, tracing their historical legacies and the major debates, outlining theoretical accomplishments and indicating methodological issues related to the themes. In two additional sections we have for each theme looked at their added value for the European context and new research questions. A bibliography for each of the three themes has been compiled. Within the space constraints of this chapter we only refer to the most important references. The full bibliography is available in the full state of the report at the IMISCOE website (www.imiscoe.org).

2. Identity

The issue of identity and ethnicity have become central issues since well-known social scientists have made us aware of the challenges posed by the emergence of a new type of human being (Fromm 1947, 1970; Riesman 1950; Marcuse 1964) and of a new type of society (Lasch 1991; Baudrillard 2003; Lyotard 1979; Foucault 1966, 1975; Giddens 1991; Jameson 1998, Castells 1997): 'our world, and our lives, are being shaped by the conflicting trends of globalization and identity' (Castells 1997: 1). That shift also results in a new kind of politics, the politics of identity (Calhoun 1996).

In the social sciences, this radical change, based upon the work of Marx and Freud (Zaretski 1996), resulted in a macro-level shift from the study of societies and of macro-political relations, to the micro-level of interpersonal relationships and of individual and group identity strategies (Camilleri 1990); in the preference for the study of socially-organised subjectivity (Barth 1969; Berger & Luckman 1966; Scheff 1996; Bastos 2000) over objectivising methods; in a move from the study of processes of acculturation and assimilation to the study of identity resistance and ethnic emancipation; in the abandonment of behavioural studies in favour of the study of mythologies, cultural productions and ideologies (Barthes 1957; Lévi-Strauss 1977; Jameson 1998; Hall 1988, 1997) and, finally, in the passage from the study of the exotic to that of the researcher's own group.

In anthropology, the move away from colonial and empire-building anthropology (Stocking 1982) resulted in a critique of structural functionalism and Lévi-Straussian structuralism, in the introduction of a multidimensional concept of identity (Erikson 1950), in the demystification of colonial ethnographies based on non-Western anthropologies, in the sub-alternisation of the concepts of culture (Barth 1969) and society (Ingold 1996) and, last but not least, in a theoretical-pragmatic focus upon the emotional dimension of intergroup identity processes (Scheff 1996), namely of interethnic relations in the context of plural states and of the pluralisation of nation-states, resulting from their 'reversed colonisation' (Ballard 2003) by uncontrollable migratory fluxes.

Central concepts and definitions

Identification, identity, identity strategies, ethnic identities, identity representations and politics of identity are the main concepts in the field. Identification in the psychological sense can be defined as the permanent process of transforming oneself to become as the Other (Freud 1923), and the accumulative result of this structuring process in biography and history. In this sense, identification is based upon love and is a form of ambivalent love, idealisation and respect of the Other. Identifications produce an enrichment of the self and the pluralisation of the cultural and psychological personality (Freud 1897). In political terms, the process of identity/identification is reversed; the state identifies subjects and groups, trying to objectify subjects and trying to impose them a fixed subaltern identity.

Identity in the sociological sense may be defined as a structural representation of self and of Others (as persons, groups or categories of
social beings), creating images of order, permanence, belonging, unity,
distinction and moral superiority. Identities are based on ontogenetic
bodily experiences, being in the case of collective identities reified and
transferred to images of societies symbolised as supra-individual bodies
(Durkheim 1912). In the same historical process, the image of significant Others, as parents, is also transferred in religion to transcendental
figures of families of Gods and Demons.

Identity strategies are defined as 'procedures worked out (at the conscious or at the unconscious level of elaboration) by a social actor (individual or collective) for the attainment of one, or more than one, (conscious or unconscious) objectives; these procedures are elaborated as a
function of the interactive situation, depending on diverse determina-
tions (socio-historical, cultural, psychological) of that situation' (Lipianski et al. 1990: 24). Strategies 'define a situation of tension that one
tries to resolve to obtain a gain (or an identity victory). [...] Tactically,
the actors react in function of the representation they have about what
is the problem in the situation, the gains and the objectives perceived,
but also in function of the state of the system in which they are implied and that pressures them permanently to act in one or other direction' (Kastersztein 1990: 30-31).

Ethnic identities belong to the process of organisation of the world
as ordered multiplicity and to the process of contestation of the hierarchies of the world system (Wallerstein, 2004). They create symmetries,
based in identity representations of groups, between state powers and
the image of distinct social subgroups with distinct biographies (languages, origins, bodies, group/ethnic religions, etc.) fighting for afflu-
ence and distinction (Bourdieu 1979). Although it is true that 'the discourse concerning ethnicity tends to concern itself with subnational
units, or minorities of some kind or another' (Chapman et al., 1989:
17), majorities and dominant peoples are no less ethnic than minorities
(Eriksen 1995).

Politics of identity are based on a critique of the ideological discourse
of Western democracy. Our ideologies of democracy presume boundaries and imply exclusions that we find very hard to justify internally to
the discourse of democracy. Social theory has been shaped by this re-
pression of certain aspects of the issue of identity (Calhoun 1996).

Historical legacies and debates

Against old clichés, Calhoun reminds us that 'tolerance is no invention
of the modern West'; democracy was founded on the idea of nation,
the 'production of a common discourse about collective matters of pub-

lic concern' and the conviction 'that individual identity was a product of self-construction, was open to free choice, and was not simply given by birth, or divine will'; but those ideological constructions were elitist and exclusionary: 'the individuals facing the market were prototypically male [white, Anglo-Saxon protestants], property-owning or labour-selling heads of households; they were free, though the law still recognised [black] slavery. [...] were prototypically property-owning male speakers of the dominant language of the nation. Thus individualism ironically repressed difference' (Calhoun 1996: 2-3) and produced 'race' distinctions and racial ideologies scientifically sustained by evolutionism and social Darwinism.

The debate between 'essentialists' (Geertz 1963), situationists (Mitchell 1956) and instrumentalists (A. Cohen 1974) can be reduced to a false problem when identity presentations (adaptive or tactical) are not confounded with self-representations, when synchrony is not opposed but articulated with biographical and historical diachrony and when identity motivations to insist in antagonistic acculturation (Devereux & Loebb 1943) are articulated with instrumental motivations and with emancipating politics of identity, in an integrative point of view. As Roosens insists, 'ethnic identity can take its drive and pattern from an interplay of oppositions with outsiders, but it mostly combines this source of differentiation with an internal source of identification. [...] Unlike boundaries, which make people different from each other and maintain ethnic division, origins, inversely, make people identical within the same group, creating and maintaining ethnicity from the inside' (Roosens 1996: 85).

Theory

Identification, the psychological foundation for the creation of we-ness, has been seen, since Rousseau, as the basis for people's collective action against the unjust power of aristocratic elites. For Freud, in the dialectics of generations, successive identifications are the cumulative result of the structural loss of successive illusions of participation in the being of the object(s), producing three forms of closeness of the self: character (the basis for personal identity representations), ideal formation (a substitutive transformation of primary identification) and investment in collective identities (a result of secondary identifications); this structural process re-enhances the dialectics of desire (and guilt), identity vulnerability (shame, resulting from triadic social comparison with rivals and with ideals) and narcissistic sublimation (pride and self-esteem). In linguistic terms, the process of identification substitutes the verb to have [the object(s)] with the verb to be (as ideal, but not the ideal). Against sublimation (secondary identification as the basis for

identity and participation), power and action are the contraries of this
process of emergency of a new generation: power as the idealised image of the omnipotent father, action as the result of ambivalence, rivalry and the impulse to symmetrisation, leading to the incorporation of
the power of the other that will be challenged in/by the next generation.

For Erikson, group identity is a style and an ethos resulting from the
pseudo-speciation of mankind (1968: 41) linked not only to divergent
socio-genesis – that is, to 'differences in geographic and historical perspectives (collective ego-space-time) and to differences in economic
goals and means (collective life plan)' (ibid.: 48), 'guided by common
images of good and evil' (ibid.: 44) and by 'ideological perspectives that
provide a convincing world image' (ibid.: 31), – but also to the use of
other groups as a screen of 'projection for the negative identities which
were the necessary, if most uncomfortable, counterpart of the positive
ones', and also as denigrated terms of comparison that fulfils 'the function of reaffirming for each pseudo-species its superiority over all
others.' (ibid.: 41) In this perspective, '[...] men's need for a psychosocial
identity is anchored in nothing less than his socio-genetic evolution',
that is, in the organization of the world in national and ethnic units,
with divergent group identities. Ego identity is simultaneously a form
of conscience and a sense: '[...] in its subjective aspects, is the awareness of the fact that there is a self-sameness and continuity to the ego's
synthetisizing methods, the style of one's own individuality, and that
this style coincides with the sameness and continuity of one's meaning
for significant others in the immediate community. [...] the mutual
complementation of group identity and ego identity, of ethos and ego,
puts a greater energy potential at the disposal of both ego synthesis
and social organization.' (ibid.: 50)

More recent formulations put emphasis on a certain degree of liberty
and a certain capacity of action of the individuals to choose their in-
and out-groups and put much less emphasis in the reality of group
identities; manipulating the processes of categorization and of comparison, persons integrated in groups can achieve positive identities, but
can also desert groups when they are stigmatised with negative identities (Tajfel 1981); manipulating a plurality of partial identities, situated
on different levels, individuals can face different arenas with different
presentations and can conceal their real (inner) identity by presenting
a series of virtual identities that meet (their ideas about) relevant social
consensus (Goffman 1963); facing social contradictions and manipulating their relations to different others, they can define their identity
strategies. Socio-historical groups are now seen as imagined communities (Anderson 1983) and group identities as presumed identities
(Weber 1922) or as tactic reifications and ideal constructions (Devereux

& Loebb 1985: 253-290) used for rhetorical social comparisons and controls. Even the notions of societies, groups and communities are contested as dubious concepts, suffering from reifications that essentialise the enormous diversities found 'within' (Baumann 1996).

In this context, ethnic identities emerge as the largest form of identification of individuals with a socio-historical group, within the organisation of the world system; and ethnic groups are seen as a form of social organisation. Group differentiation depends not on isolation or antagonism, but from processes of systematic dichotomisation of ethnic status, creating identity boundaries that persist despite a flow of personnel across them. In these terms, the sharing of a common culture is not the cause but the first consequence of persistent ethnic dichotomisation. 'To the extent that actors use ethnic identities to categorise themselves and others for purposes of interaction, they form ethnic groups in this organizational sense' (Barth 1998: 9-15).

Methodology and measurement

Under different designations, the description of patterns of culture, in the form of the psychology of the peoples and anthropological psychology, has a long philosophical and essayistic tradition in Europe, from Kant (1991/1798) to Fouillée (1902), and from Keyserling (1929) to Madariaga (1952). In the United States, this tradition was appropriated between the 1930s and 1960s by the Culture and Personality School and its derivates, based upon fieldwork, in the typological differentiation of patterns of culture and in the systematic study of patterns of child socialisation. Advancing in the direction of cross-cultural psychology, while avoiding the use of the concept of identity, McClelland (1961) compared the expression of different patterns in the official schoolbooks of a number of different countries, and Hofstede (1984, 1991) compared the answers to a questionnaire on work motivation carried out among the professional employees of the same multinational corporation in over fifty different countries.

In the Anglo-American and Anglo-Saxon tradition, from Katz and Braly (1935) to Tajfel (1981), the study of group identity was subsumed under the concept of stereotype, based on the use of adjective checklists. Peabody (1988), reviewing these studies, defined the bases for a critique of the concept of stereotype and its subsequent rejection, and proposed a new definition of group judgement, itself rejected since it did not withstand the critique. Like previous authors, Peabody was using simple identity questionnaires, administered to non-representative samples of a few dozen university students.

Taking his distance from Peabody, Bastos constructed a research instrument for the investigation of the system of identity social represen-

tations of members of socio-historical groups (the MIQ) and applied it
to representative samples of the Portuguese population (Bastos 2000,
2002) and of inhabitants of its nine metropolitan regions (Bastos
1995). The aim was a measurement of: (a) the degree to which self-
and hetero-representations were shared; (b) the relational economy between the definition of personal identity and the definition of identity
attributed by the respondents to their own national, regional, or ethnic
in-group; (c) the relational economy between the definition of regional
identities and national identity, and their relation with the quality of
life of each region and with the identities projected upon other European nationals; (d) the relational economy of personal identity, the
identities (national and regional) collectively attributed to the in-groups
and European out-groups (in the national context), or to regional out-
groups; (e) the relation of all these representations with complementary ideal identities; (f) the relational economy of all these representations with processes of angelisation and diabolisation of in- and out-
groups; and g) the economy of the articulation of these macro-repre-
sentations with category representations of gender and generation provided by the same informants, likely to introduce bio-cultural connotations ('familialist') to the area of political representations.

The same research instrument was applied by other researchers (E.
Correia 1993; S. Bastos 1995; Madeira 1999; Batoréu 2001; A. Correia
2001; Rodrigues 2002; Rodrigues & J. Bastos 2005) to study the system of identity social representations of exploratory samples of nationals of former Portuguese colonies (Cape-Verdeans from four islands of the archipelago) and of ethnic or ethno-religious communities
in Portugal (Gujarati Hindus, Sunni Muslims of Afro-Indian origin,
Cape-Verdeans, Angolans), in France (Cape-Verdeans and Portuguese)
and in Hungary (gypsies), as well as samples of university students in
Sardinia, Granada and Rabat (Pimentel 1993; Mourão 1997; Ribeiro
1996).

These studies enabled us to de-essentialise completely the concept of
identity representation, demonstrating that representations are strictly
personal, that the degree of superimposition and convergence of identity attributions both to the in- and the out-group are always partial;
and that, on the whole, the representations have a highly delirious
rhetorical economy (Marx 1844; Durkheim 1912; Freud 1974/1930), an
element that highlights the identity vulnerability underlying the process, as well as its defensive and compensatory function to the trau-
matic structure of the world system.

European added value

The political tradition that, in the USA, resulted in identity politics, is a European tradition based upon the detection of a relative compatibility and complementarity of the works of Marx and Freud (Reich 1929; Fromm 1947; Marcuse 1964; Foucault 1966; Zaretzki 1996; Godelier 1995). This theoretical complementary focuses upon the anthropological paradox that gives the world system its dramatic and problematic dimension – the fact that identification, cooperation and solidarity in the control of the natural world may be accompanied by exploitation, domination and extermination in intra- and intergroup relations, resulting in the most grievous form of suffering for the human species (Freud 1930).

The issue of the structural ambivalence of the human species cannot be reduced to any rationalist and technocratic project of diversity management, since no individual, group or elite may step outside and above this dramatic human ambivalence. Its two vectors give rise to two different types of social science, as incompatible and complementary as two images, gestaltically combined by the process of foreground-background inversion. These are, on the one hand, the mechanistic or organicistic and transcendental social sciences of the 19th century, which became structural-functionalist in the first half of the 20th, compatible with their most drastic revisionisms (symbolic interactionism and the most extreme formulations of social transcendental constructivism); on the other, critical and emancipatory social sciences, from a more Freudian current to a neo-Marxist one. In anthropology, structural ambivalence manifests itself in the way the school of cultural relativism devoted itself to a demonstration of the infinite variability of cultural behaviour, namely in respect of the double standard on intergroup relations, in the very same process in which, simultaneously, it was irreflexibly observed how its 'civilized' peoples were gradually exterminating dozens of 'primitive languages and peoples' (Lévi-Strauss 1984).

On the other hand, authors such as Barth (1969) are in the foreground of the subjectivist shift in the social sciences. They do so by equating the concept of ethnicity to that of identity, by making the concept of culture subaltern and by making the concept of identity the decisive concept in the permanence of interethnic and even in the processes of ethnic revitalisation.

New questions

Defined as stereotypes and denigrated as intellectual and moral errors, social representations of identity (Bastos 2000) in interethnic relations

have been until now under-studied in the artificial, un-historical context of experimental social psychology (Tajfel 1981) or even tabooed in
the context of social sciences. Once we demonstrate the fact that (a) individuals construct their self-representations on the establishment of a
positive comparison with the representation of their social in-groups
(national, ethnic, etc.) and (b) individuals construct the self-representations of their in-groups in contrast with their representation of out-
groups, chosen or imposed for comparison, (c) and link these self- and
group-representations to the economy of their vulnerable self-esteem,
the analysis of systems of identity representations requires further research in different social and political contexts. This should be connected to different aspects of group idealisation, historical conflict, racist confrontations or creation of more inclusive identities, as in the
case of the construction of a European identity, in the context of international competition, economic crisis and increased uncontrolled immigrations.

3. Interethnic relations

Despite the great currency it has acquired lately in anthropology, sociology, political science and several other fields, it is evident that in both
popular and academic discourse much confusion surrounds the concept of ethnicity. On the one hand, ethnicity and ethnic imagery are
sometimes used as synonyms (or should we say, euphemisms) for
'race'. This is true especially in countries like Germany or Israel, where
the latter term is loaded with some gruesome historical connotations.
On the other hand, a more accurate – but also more complex – conceptualization would shift the emphasis to ethnicity as a representation of
group consciousness and collective identification. Thus, ethnicity becomes one of the key factors in identity-formation processes as it is
said to include such features as: a common ancestry (or the myth of
it), memories of a shared past, aspects of a common culture (language,
religion, kinship, etc.), a connection with a homeland and a sense of
solidarity (or belonging).

The advantages of this conceptualization are that a) it embraces
many of the issues around which societies have organised and
struggled for centuries and b) it underlines the relational nature of the
term, as it entails a relation between human collectives within a certain
territory. As a result of the centrality that this relational character and
the conflicts of views/interests it often raises, the relevance of interethnic relations to migration studies seems beyond any question. Consequently, in spite of the elusive usages that the concept of ethnicity or
ethnic identity sometimes receives – as when it is considered just a fic-

tion or something imagined as a result of exogenous (material or ideo-logical) factors – it is evident that it plays a crucial role in the ever-changing relations of human groups within given social contexts.

In the broad and intricate field that the study of interethnic relations covers, the interests of the IMISCOE participants are primarily related to migration issues in the European context. All the participants share a preference for the situationist view of ethnicity as opposed to a pri-mordialist one, which would think of an *ethnie* as something static and monolithic. We agree, therefore, with Horowitz (1985: 4) when he ex-plained that 'shifting contexts make ethnicity now more, now less pro-minent.' This is true not only about the ebbing and flowing of ethnic issues at different historical junctures, but also with respect to particu-lar national/social contexts.

A second element shared by most of the participants is the socially constructed nature of ethnicity, which means that although some pri-mordial ties may be in place, groups and individuals are still able to cut and paste from various cultures and ethnic heritages.

One last point in common is that, in order to understand fully how interethnic relations condition the multiple affiliations that an immi-grant may adopt, it is essential to analyse the ways they intersect with other social categorizations such as gender, class, religion, etc. Most participants are, therefore, interested in context-specific empirical work that would unveil the kind of dynamics (and identities) that phenom-ena like ethnic differentiation, racialisation, post-colonial mobility, ra-cial amalgamation, transnationalism, stereotyping of the Other, under-representation and so on are bound to produce. The focuses of the ana-lyses are very specific and widely different (e.g. the crystallisation of in-tergroup relations in colonial times and its impact on contemporary so-cieties, colonial intercultural intimacy/sexuality, interactions between different types of ethnic identities (migratory and ethno-territorial), forms of exclusion and inclusion in receiving countries, etc.). There is in all of them, however, a clear attempt to explain some of the condi-tions (and obstacles) met by immigrant contingents in the light of the-ories and ideas that derive from studies of interethnic relations.

Some basic concepts

Since it is quite impossible to summarise in this limited space the abundance of concepts that discussions of interethnic relations have la-tely generated, we offer here just a number of key terms that keep sur-facing in much of the literature on the topic. It is important to clarify at the outset, though, that their definitions may change significantly depending on the (academic/national) tradition and the context in which they are being used.

To start with, it would be important to demarcate the specific place that ethnicity occupies among a number of related terms. As has been pointed out above, although sometimes used as synonymous with race, ethnicity does not carry the elements of insurmountable cultural and social (biological, in earlier days) differentiation that 'race-thinking' habitually does. Likewise, it is important to mark the difference between ethnic group and nation, which Benedict Anderson (1983: 6) defined as an imagined political community, which has moral claim over a certain territory. For some, ethnicity is precisely characterised by the dissociation between that collective culture and any particular territory. An expressivist view of ethnicity, however, may come close to our understanding of nation in that in both cases great emphasis is given to the feeling of communality and sense of sameness that underlies their ideological framework (see Yinger 1994).

Finally, even further apart from ethnicity is the concept of nation-state, which comes into existence when the inhabitants of a nation establish legal claims over a territory and become its citizens. As opposed to nations and ethnic groups, which are largely anthropological categories, a nation-state is a legal community.

There is another set of concepts, which also seem to threaten the specific place of ethnicity, this time, as it were, from below. Relations of kinship, neighbourhood, community, etc. may share a number of features with ethnic groups. However, what distinguishes these concepts from ethnic affiliations is that in the latter the roles played by members toward one another or toward the community as a whole are not specified. It would be inaccurate, though, to say that *ethnies* are without structures of social relations. Status and social differentiation do, of course, show up within ethnic groups, but the overarching sense of togetherness and communality often brings the members together in their struggles for higher purposes and overshadows any other considerations and intra-group distinctions.

So far we have referred to two major views or approaches to ethnicity, one primordialist (which thinks of ethnic heritage and culture as an inalterable essence that brings certain people together) and the other situationist (which believes that individuals will belong to a group depending on the kind of project they are engaged in). This second approach seems more useful and realistic in the sense that ethnic identity is primarily determined here by the constant frictions that emerge with other groups. Moreover, this view of ethnicity allows us to deal with such distinct issues as the adoption of alternating identities by migrant workers in receiving countries or the varying attachment (and claim) of an ethnic group to a certain territory. In both instances it is evident that ethnicity is being somehow instrumentalised in order to attain specific goals – be it a promotion or a raise in salary, or the formation of a new nation. What is clear to many specialists (see, for example, Hutchinson & Smith 1996) is that ethnic groups are becoming more and more like political parties that will use any of the cultural and social resources at hand to achieve the purposes defined by their leaders. In the opposite direction would go the expressivist or anti-globalist conception of ethnicity, which appeals to feelings of belonging to a particular community. In an anonymous world governed by global flows of capital, information, technology etc., most of us want to enjoy the warmth and affect of 'our' people. This is even truer about human contingents living in foreign environments or those other ethnic groups that, for historical reasons, have been dispossessed of important fragments (language, land, folklore etc.) of their identity.

It also seems important to refer to a handful of concepts that describe the processes undergone by ethnic identities when they come into contact with other – usually more powerful – groups in society. In this sense, we could speak of assimilative processes when the ethnic individual adopts the values and behaviour of the majority group, thus leaving behind her/his own cultural heritage. Less drastic than this wholehearted surrender to the dominant culture are processes of (segmented) acculturation (Portes & Rumbaut 2001), which means that there is a high level of identification with the majority but the individual also retains elements of his earlier identity.

The ideal situation is of course that of the 'fully-integrated' ethnic person who thinks and behaves just like the natives but still identifies with those who share her/his ethnic roots. On the opposite extreme would be those individuals who end up marginalised both in the dominant society and from their own group as they seem unable to achieve the levels of identification required by any of the two groups. No need to explain that conditions of social exclusion are frequently closely related to some of these processes (e.g. problems of mixed bloods in colonial settings). While it is a fact that the political and administrative machinery of states can contribute to the segregation of significant segments of their population, the newcomers' competence to complete some of these processes is also a determining factor.

Historical legacies and current debates

Although it would be interesting to trace the shifting meaning of the term ethnic from its very roots in the Greek *ethnós* (a people), it is definitely more productive to concentrate on those dimensions of the term that still have an impact on our way of thinking about ethnic relations. Thus, the connotations associated to the concept up to the 19th century do not seem very relevant today as hardly anybody would consider that being an ethnic means being pagan or a gentile. Beginning in the early

19th century, however, the concept underwent a radical transformation
as it began to be linked – especially in the Anglo-Saxon world – with
racial features. What we nowadays still call the 'objective attributes' of a
group of people (be they physical features, or more recently cultural)
were often the first aspect taken into account to identify and classify
them into different *ethnies*. Only a few decades after that modification,
ethnography, the discipline that describes the social life, customs, and
institution of human groups, made its appearance. During these early
years of the study of the ethnic, the term was frequently synonymous
(due to the influence of Romantic worldviews) with the folk/Volk,
which would encompass the particular styles of art, music, food, clothing, etc. characteristic of a people/region. In popular usages of the
term, this meaning has been generally retained and so it is not at all
unusual to hear today about ethnic festivals, cuisines, celebrations, etc.

From the mid-19th century, and running parallel somehow to the
ethnographic studies, the first anthropological investigations (sometimes called then ethnological) were beginning to be carried out. These
investigations were mostly interested in building theories that would
explain the evolution of particular cultures. However, the term ethnicity
was scarcely used in these studies as most theories conceived the various human communities in isolation and essentially different from
each other on account of biological differentiation. Highly influenced
by evolutionary theories, many of these models based their postulations
on processes of natural selection that resulted from the competitions
and conflicts between clans and tribes. Even in the early 20th century,
some Russian researchers were still defending that the *ethnie* was primarily a biosocial entity that could only be explained by looking into
the attachment of the people to a land and culture. Some of these
views worked their way into some of the primordialist theories that
were fairly current in the mid-20th century and which kept emphasising the affective components, primordial links and common culture as
the bases on which the identity of a people was built.

It is not until the late 1960s and early 1970s that, due to a great extent to processes of decolonization and the appearance of ethnic minority political activism, we observe a significant change in the approach
to ethnicity and ethnic groups. The Norwegian anthropologist Fredrik
Barth (1969) was very likely the key figure in causing a paradigm revo-
lution in the field. His main contribution was to argue that ethnic
identification was not something primordial and inalterable but, rather,
depended on the circumstances and purposes defined by a certain
group. This approach, which is still very much alive and kicking, found
its roots in functionalist sociology which tends to consider the strategic
use of cultural heritages for specific economic or political goals. One
major change observable in the works of Barth, Cohen (1969), Epstein

(1958) and other situationists is that much more attention is given to the political and socio-economic context, and that the interaction between different groups is crucial in the conformation of their identity.

Current debates (although they began already in the late 1980s with Horowitz [1985]) rotate very much around the issue of whether ethnic consciousness (and identity) are constructed, created, manipulated and utilized for political purposes. From the perspective of some situationists/instrumentalists, 'ethnic identities are created in the dynamics of elite competition within the boundaries determined by political and economic realities' (Brass 1991: 16). A further step in the volatilisation of the concept of ethnicity has resulted from what is referred to as the constructivist approach, which basically underlines the fluidity and contingency of ethnic identities as they always pertain to very specific social and historical conditions. This is not so radically different from what Barth was stating a number of decades ago but, as a result of the momentum gained by other areas of study (e.g. post-colonial, border studies, immigration, etc.), the concept of ethnicity has been newly relativized. The field works proposed by some of the IMISCOE members is symptomatic of this diversity as they cover studies of ethnic relations in transnational settings, between different types of ethnic groups, and even within the ethnic groups themselves.

Theories

Not to repeat ideas about the models/theories commented on above, we will refer here to a few theoretical approaches that have gained much centrality in the past two decades. Although neither primordialist (based on objective physical/cultural attributes) nor expressivist theories (based on a sense of belonging and common identity) have been completely put aside (see Berghe 1967), new phenomena like globalisation, liberal capitalism, technological innovations, and new transnational communities require a revision of the concept of ethnicity as a source of meaning and identity. Scholars like Castells (1997: 59), for instance, even argue that ethnicity (as it has been traditionally conceived) does no longer 'provide the basis for communal heavens in the network society [...] as a basis for reconstruction of meaning.' Yet a number of models, most of them constructivist and behaviourist – since they focus on several codes and group interactions that are characteristic in contemporary societies – have gained great currency among analysts in ethnic studies.

One of these is the 'interculturalist' model which is especially interested in displaced/immigrant groups needing to adjust to new environments. According to this theory (see Wimmer 2004; Marger & Obermiller 1987), the cultural baggage of the newcomer not only plays a key role as a shock absorber but it helps to establish difference as a value that the dominant group needs to learn to respect and appreciate. A second model would be that of ethnic resistance, which investigates the strategies used by minority groups to protect and promote their own identity and political agendas. This theory has maintained that ethnic individuals often come together to fight external competition and to find new ways of bettering their status and increasing their prestige in a given society (Shapiro & Kymlicka 1997). In a number of ways, the kind of strategies studied by this model are equally observable in immigrant groups and ethno-territorial minorities around Europe, which also have a long tradition in fighting for linguistic, environmental and cultural rights that were often denied to them in the past.

There is also what has been called an ecological model, which studies urban environments as a basis for ethnic group formation. The kind of communities formed in Britain by Pakistanis, in Germany by Turks, or in Spain by Moroccans could definitely be considered from this perspective, since they have often formed cities within cities in several of the big urban centres in these countries. Finally, a fourth theory much in vogue in recent years is that of hybridity. Whether the term used is amalgamation, miscegenation, race mixture, mestizaje, métissage, creolization, transculturation or cultural fusion, it is clear that the analysis of racial and cultural mixing has become one of the most enticing subfields in interethnic relations. As Robert Young (1995: 27) remarked, the study of race mixture is essential because 'it shows the connection between the racial categories of the past and contemporary cultural discourse.'

Methodology and measurement

As was mentioned earlier on, most IMISCOE members prefer to depart from empirical and quantitative studies. Given the specificity of the aspects to be assessed and the constructivist theoretical basis that they favour, it seems only natural that field work should come first and, from there, build towards qualitative (maybe even theoretically-oriented) analysis. Again, methodologies seem as diverse and multifarious as the research topics proposed, for while some of the projects may require longitudinal studies of specific groups of immigrants, others will rest on interviews with a variety of collectives – which could belong to both the immigrant contingents and the receiving society. In order to make methodologies more uniform, consensus should be reached to establish objects of study that are more easily comparable or contrasted. Such a course, however, is not an easy one, also in view of the fact that both research planning and funding are at variance.

Several of the participants have expressed their difficulties to measure such aspects of interethnic relations as sexual relationships across race lines, degree of inclusion and integration in educational systems, or correspondences between ethnic and social taxonomies in colonial times and today's discourses. Still, there are other areas where the data collected may be very revealing as to the levels of exclusion and discrimination suffered by ethnic contingents such as migrant workers and persons from previously colonial nations. Perhaps the area where the prospective findings of this sub-cluster would be most useful is that of the participation of ethnic minorities in institutions and social dynamics. Ideally, it should be possible to establish how those levels of participation compare in different regions around Europe and what the factors are preventing it in some countries.

European added value and future research

The topic of interethnic relations should be at the very top of the priorities on the EU agenda since it encompasses such urgent and problematic matters as social exclusion, segregation, disregard of basic human rights, under-representation, and unequal opportunities. These types of injustices are present, in one form or another, in most of the European countries and their causes and consequences need to be thoroughly investigated before steps can be taken to revise earlier policies and practices. The main aim of a majority of the analyses proposed here is to detect some of the obstacles (institutional barriers, racialised discourses and images, social prejudice, stereotypes, etc.) that are preventing large segments of the population from integrating fully into the receiving society because of their ethnic background. This task seems especially urgent when, despite the allegedly multicultural make-up of the societies in several European states, we still hear on a daily basis of blatant cases of discrimination and social abuse against immigrants. It is clear, then, that we are very far from the kind of post-ethnic world that David Hollinger (2000: 165-72) recently claimed for and which would be based on a pluralism and cosmopolitanism that would do away with ethno-racial markers and classifications of any kind.

A second, and perhaps more compelling, reason to promote the study of interethnic relations and the expansion of multicultural policies are the reactionary attitudes observed around Europe based on the perception of an Islamic threat, triggered by such events as the attacks in New York City, Madrid, London and the murder of Dutch filmmaker Theo van Gogh. If Muslims were already being categorised as the archetypal Other by some right-wing leaders, this kind of reaction does nothing but exacerbate the animosity against a group that has been repeatedly targeted as unassimilable (see Sartori 2001). To build an EU on principles of differentiation and marginalisation of the culturally Other would be one of our worst errors at this historical juncture.

4. Discrimination

To discriminate against someone means to treat this person differently than others on the basis of his or her belonging to some social group or category, be it gender, race, religion or ethnicity. The victim of discrimination is treated differently because he or she is seen to represent a social group that is held in low esteem. One cannot speak of discrimination when persons are treated on the basis of their personal individual characteristics or merits. Furthermore, those who engage in discriminatory behaviour act on the strength of seeing themselves as representing some group or category that is in its right to claim preferential treatment or priority.

Usually the party that discriminates will enjoy a superior position in relation to the party that suffers discrimination. This superior position may be founded in access to more resources, more power, larger numbers or real or assumed legitimacy. Discrimination implies a departure from the principle of equal treatment. It is really only in societies where equality is a basic value and objective, in political democracies, that discrimination is regarded as an essential societal problem. In other political systems discrimination is usually an inherent part of the system itself, as was the case in South Africa during Apartheid.

Differential treatment may be to the advantage of a particular group. We speak of positive (or affirmative) discrimination in those cases. Negative discrimination, on the other hand, that is to say, differential treatment that is to the disadvantage of some vulnerable group, reduces this group's opportunities and space for action, and is a social and political problem. The existence of discrimination in a society is a serious problem for those who are hit by it, but it also implies major costs to society because many people's capacities and potentials are not used to achieve the common good.

Discrimination hits individuals, and hence it may appear to be about individual relations and interactions. But the implications are broader: it is about group relations in society where individual actors are perceived as representatives of the groups they belong to. In theory, any group can be the target of discrimination or act as the discriminating party. However, we know from decades of research that groups with low access to power are more likely to be discriminated against, and groups in a position of power are more likely to be the ones that discriminate.

Central concept

Affirmative action stands for compensatory programmes that include measures of positive discrimination that aim to empower disadvantaged groups in education, in the labour market, in political representation and so on through the allocation of quotas. The terminology of negative and positive discrimination, however, may be confusing. What is experienced as positive treatment of one group by that group will be regarded as negative treatment of another group by that other group. This is a principal criticism of affirmative action.

Another distinction is between subjective experienced discrimination and objective discrimination determined by a third party. Subjective discrimination is about the victim's experience of having been subjected to negative differential treatment. Objective discrimination is established through independent, usually legal, criteria.

Racism is a wider concept than discrimination. It stands for a complex of ideas that defend and justify differential treatment of people who are categorised as special on certain grounds. It is about degrading treatment of people who are classified according to their phenotypal markers, culture or origin. In a racist society the ruling class or people legitimises differential treatment and it is maintained by means of the power instruments of society. Racial ideology permeates societal institutions and its political, economic and social structure. Even in societies that are not organised according to racial principles (as South Africa was), there may be parties and organisations that seek to justify racial division. While ideological racism obviously will include discrimination, it is not always the case that discriminatory actions are expressions of ideological racism.

One consequence of systematic discrimination in the housing market is segregation. Segregation is a serious problem because much of welfare service is distributed according to spatial criteria – education, health care, leisure time activities, social services, religious congregations etc. Although we may recognise that some instances of segregation may depend on a minority group's wish to live together, segregation is normally an outcome of market mechanisms that in complex ways may reinforce subtle forms of discrimination.

Many definitions point out that prejudice is to judge beforehand, usually negatively, of groups or individuals on the basis of traits attributed to the group. In the early literature on prejudice and discrimination it was often stated that discrimination was the action that corresponded to the prejudicial view. Or in other words, prejudice was the attitudinal component of discrimination. By influencing and moulding people's attitudes to becoming more benevolent one would be able to counteract discrimination. It was also believed that a major problem of prejudice was its character of erroneous or incomplete information about the group that was the object of prejudiced views.

The relation between prejudice and discrimination is not all that simple. Many people with prejudiced views about a certain group would not dream of discriminating against members of the group in actual practice. It is also perfectly conceivable that persons who do not hold prejudicial views against some particular group nevertheless might engage in discriminatory acts against members of that group. Central to prejudice according to the classic book by Gordon Allport (1954) is that it is not open to reason, it is emotional, not intellectual. It serves as a defence against ideas, values or thoughts that are felt to threaten the prejudiced person's own values, beliefs and lifestyle. This emotional side to prejudice distinguishes it from another concept, that it sometimes is confused with, the stereotype. A stereotype is usually understood as a simplified mental representation (collective and/or social representation) of some category of persons, institutions or events, and on the whole shared by many others in society. Stereotypes have traditionally been understood as conceptions that groups have of others (other groups). This refers to what has been termed heterostereotypes. Logically there must also exist autostereotypes, stereotypes of one's own group, better known as collective identities.

An important distinction needs to be made between individual discrimination and institutional (or possibly institutionalised) discrimination. In the former case the individual is the perpetrator, in the latter case an institution or organisation is responsible. Institutional discrimination may depend on specific rules and regulations within an organisation. These rules may intentionally or unintentionally have discriminatory consequences. In analyses of institutional discrimination it is of importance to penetrate the purposes and justification of these rules and how well they are anchored in the organisation. While psychological motives may be identified in cases of individual discrimination (sense of threat, insecurity, hostility, antipathy, identity processes) the motives of institutional discrimination usually pertain to interests in profit, economic rationality, bureaucratic efficiency and so on.

Farley (1988, 361) subsumes under the term individual discrimination (here racist and ethnic discrimination) 'any behaviour on the part of an individual which leads to unequal treatment on the basis of race or ethnicity'. This individual discrimination might occur because of prejudices and clichés. It has to be pointed out here, however, that there is not necessarily a causal connection between prejudices and discrimination. A person who is prejudiced against foreigners might, despite of that, politely serve a non-native client as his or her interest in making business is predominant. Or another person who doesn't have xenophobic attitudes is forced to behave in a discriminating way by group pressure (see e.g. Farley 1988: 40ff.; Heckmann 1992: 125ff.).

Institutional discrimination (here racist and ethnic discrimination) is defined by Farley (ibid.) as, 'Arrangements or practices in social institutions and their related organisations that tend to favour one racial or ethnic group (usually the majority group) over another'. Another important category in the area of discrimination is perceived discrimination, defined as any behaviour or practice on the part of an individual or organisation that is perceived as discrimination, independently of whether actual discrimination has occurred or not.

Intentional and unintentional discrimination is another distinction, although discrimination is usually thought of as an intentional act. What unintentional discrimination refers to are acts that the victim may experience as discriminatory although the perpetrator does not intend to discriminate. In an institutional context such situations may arise when rules or laws no longer correspond to changed conditions as a result of societal developments. The task is therefore to identify such situations and to alter the rules.

The concept of structural discrimination encompasses institutional discrimination but is broader in scope. It refers to structural processes of social categorisation, to differential power and power structures in society and to the very basic values upon which a society operates.

Historical legacies and debates

The consequences of discrimination may stretch from massive outcomes that affect an entire society to effects that only hit a few individual persons. The causes of discrimination need to be sought in a combination of cultural, political, economic, social and psychological factors. Some single isolated factor will rarely explain discrimination.

Discriminatory actions are usually difficult to observe and record as they take place. The perpetrator will usually not compromise himself in front of a researcher with a camera and tape recorder. Covert methods of observation have therefore been employed. A researcher may for instance pose as a job seeker belonging to some minority group, and record how he or she is treated by the employer. The German journalist Günter Wallraff used this method a number of times to expose the discriminatory treatment of Turkish labourers in Germany (Wallraff 1985).

The International Labour Office (the ILO) regards discrimination as a very serious problem in advanced industrial societies, and has therefore recommended governments to carry out research using covert methods to expose discriminators and name companies and organisations that commit discriminatory offences (Beijl 2000). The Council for Social Science Research in Sweden decided that it could not support this kind of research because it goes against basic research ethics. One important ethical principle is that persons who are interviewed in social science research should beforehand give their informed consent whether they agree to participate or not. In order to do so they should be fully informed about the objectives of the research. Those who defend covert methods maintain that discrimination is a very serious problem in society and that a minor departure from the ethical rules is a lesser harm.

The subjective experience of having been the victim of differential treatment may not necessarily meet the criteria of what is an independently established act of discrimination. But there is usually some correlation between groups that experience themselves as victims of discrimination and other legally or scientifically objective data about distributions of resources. People's subjective experience of discrimination can be surveyed by means of questionnaires and interviews and this material may provide important circumstantial evidence about discrimination and not in the least about contexts of discrimination.

The European Monitoring Centre on Racism and Xenophobia has sponsored research on racist attitudes in the member states (Eurobarometer 1997; Thalhammer et al. 2001). We find interesting country differences. In surveys from 1997 and 2000 the least racist views were found in Southern Europe and Ireland (all fairly new countries of immigration) while the most hardened racist views were expressed in countries of Central and Western Europe (France, Germany, Belgium and Austria). The UK, the Netherlands and the Nordic countries held an intermediate position. It needs to be borne in mind though that recently things have changed quite dramatically to the worse, both in the Netherlands and Denmark. We need to be cautious about drawing conclusions from this kind of comparative research.

Attitudinal research can provide important information about stereotypes, collective identities, belief systems and group evaluations, and this information does have a certain bearing on increasing our knowledge about the mechanisms of discrimination. The current debate today is however not about attitudes and stereotypes but about structural discrimination, which is an entirely different matter.

The famous Swedish sociologist Gunnar Myrdal wrote a groundbreaking book in the 1950s on structural discrimination. It was called *An American Dilemma*. Myrdal unravels the contradictions in American society that are at the very basis of structural discrimination, namely between the democratic creed, codified in the constitution, and racism with its roots in the slave system. One of the important challenges for Europe is to scrutinise the foundational values of our own societies,

and not in the least to have a close look at the national ideals and values underpinning these societies.

Theory

Research into discrimination has, on the one hand, been concerned
with the effects and consequences of discrimination, and, on the other
hand, with the causes of discrimination. Both approaches are important in the work to counteract discrimination. Theoretical work, however, has primarily focused on trying to determine social conditions,
factors and structures that give rise to discriminatory behaviour. Within
political economy there is a long tradition of theoretical modelling
based on the groundbreaking work of Gary Becker in *The economics of
discrimination* (1957). A survey of various theories of discriminations
was presented by Mats Lundahl and Eskil Wadensjö (1982). Both
authors have continued to publish in the field of discrimination. Theories of discrimination in political economy are to a large extent concerned with unequal treatment in the labour and housing markets.
Theories have highlighted problems of differential treatment that arise
in a dual labour market consisting of expensive organised labour and
another sector of cheap non-organised labour. The former category
usually consists of native, usually skilled labour, while the second category will often consist of imported, unskilled labour hired on a temporary basis. Various conflicts of interest on discriminatory consequences
tend to arise in this kind of system.

Sociologists such as Edna Bonacich (1972) and Michael Hechter
(1975) have proposed theories along similar lines. Bonacich developed
a theory of the split labour market, which specifically focused on racial
dimensions in the labour market, and Hechter developed a theory of
the cultural division of labour based on the recruitment of Irish labour
to English industry during the early stages of industrialisation in the
UK. Urban geographers and sociologists have developed theories about
how an originally middle-class residential area through the interplay of
market mechanisms, discrimination and neglect over a period of time
may change much of its population and become an impoverished segregated ghetto, while, on the other hand, a working-class suburb in
other circumstances may undergo a process of gentrification. Other sociological approaches relate discrimination to the differential distribution of power in society and are primarily concerned with social structures that enhance and maintain discriminatory treatment (Bhabha
1994; Gilroy 1987; Hall 1997).

Social psychology has contributed with various theories linking discrimination to ethnocentrism (LeVine & Campbell 1972), reference
groups and segregated networks. The most important work in this field

is represented by the studies originating from Henri Tajfel's social identity theory (Tajfel 1974, 1978) according to which out-group discrimination and in-group-favouritism serve to promote a positive social identity. John Turner (1978) carried on Tajfel's theoretical work into a social psychology of group interaction. Psychological work relating to discriminatory behaviour has focused on a number of different approaches ranging from learning theory, aggression and the authoritarian personality theory. The central focus of psychological work has mainly been on prejudicial attitudes rather than discriminatory behaviour. Two of the classic works are Adorno's study of the authoritarian personality (Adorno et al. 1950) and Allport's treatise of prejudice (Allport 1954).

A principle shortcoming of most of the theoretical work on discrimination and discriminatory behaviour has been the lack of interdisciplinary approaches. Power, market mechanisms, social structure, intergroup perceptions, categorization and identity processes are all involved one way or the other. Most explanations offered in the literature, however, tend to be monocausal. In order to develop multifactor models the conditions of social causality need to be analysed in depth.

Methodology and measurement

One difficulty in the area of discrimination are the varying definitions of the term discrimination. A second problem is that discrimination may manifest itself in many different forms. These problems become all the more visiblewhen it comes to the methodology of measurement.

The analysis of the situation of migrants in different areas of society such as the labour market, education system or housing market shows that great differences still exist between natives and migrants. However, it is methodologically very difficult to establish the extent to which the aforementioned disparities in the basic institutions of society among the various groups can be traced back to forms of discrimination or to other factors: differences in the opportunities to obtain education might be a result of different social backgrounds (e.g. level of education of the parents) and disadvantages in the labour market might be caused by different abilities and preconditions of human capital (educational and professional qualifications, language skills, etc.).

In principle, only the residual amount, that is, the disadvantage one faces after taking other factors (human capital) into account, displays the actual degree of discrimination (Alba et al. 1994: 210; van Suntum & Schlotböller 2002: 43). A quantitative study carried out by Granato and Kalter (2001) attempted to measure precisely this residual amount mentioned above. The authors studied the possible general discrimination of non-Germans whilst controlling human capital resources (that

is, by comparing the situation in the labour market of German employees with non-German employees who had the same abilities and preconditions of human capital). The following independent variables
were considered in the analyses: educational qualification, nationality,
generation, gender and age. In multivariable analyses, research was undertaken into whether the inequality between Germans and non-Germans remains, even whilst controlling further independent variables.
In the generation-related results of the analyses, it is apparent that if
qualifications are taken into account, the effects of nationality are dramatically reduced for the second generation. Roughly summarised, the
results of this study show that differing human capital resources play
the dominant role when an explanation is needed for the poorer positioning of second-generation migrants in the labour market.

In a similar vein, Alba et al. (1994) attempted to deduce discrimination indirectly from still existent ethnic differences as a remaining residual category after all the important explanatory factors/variables had
been checked. The following control variables were employed: length
of residence, generation status, socio-economic status of the parents,
the conditions in the place of residence, gender, the number of children in the household, cultural identities (operationalised by the existent language skills), orientation towards the society of origin (intention to return, remittances, identity as native or migrant, continuity in
the school career) and the ethnic composition of the place of residence.
Alba et al. determined that even after checking all these factors significant disadvantages remain, particularly for children of Turkish and Italian parents. Also here the question is whether this residual effect can
be attributed to discrimination, since one cannot be completely certain
if the decisive explanatory factors have been controlled.

This difficulty in measuring discrimination is also revealed in the
fact that there is no systematic registration based upon ethnicity and
hence no national statistics of cases of discrimination. Individual cases
are collected and documented only by various organisations which are
consulted by people subject to discrimination.

Disregarding the difficulty in measuring discrimination and the definition of discrimination, however, forms of subjectively perceived discrimination also play a decisive role in the feelings and behaviour of
migrants. In many studies, people of migrant backgrounds were asked
about personal experiences of discrimination in various areas in life.
Subjectively perceived discrimination influences the integration of migrants and their children. 'If the host society is perceived as "closed"
and prejudiced, this may lead to a reinforcement of ethnic ties with negative consequences for the cultural, social and identificational processes' (Heckmann et al. 2001: 63). Thus, the individual perception of

discrimination is also of importance, irrespective of the extent to which this subjective perception corresponds to the actual discrimination.

European added value

As the European Community expanded through the inclusion of new member states, diversity has increased, not in the least with regard to legal practices. Thus it became imperative to link member states and bring them closer to each other through the harmonisation of rules and regulations in a wide range of practices. Since economy, work and business were always regarded as being of central importance, the Community would sooner or later have to do something about racial discrimination because of its overall negative effects on the economy. However, before the Amsterdam Treaty, the basic legal instruments for policy to counteract racial and ethnic discrimination were not at the disposal of the Community. The will to combat racism was expressed in terms of resolutions and declarations, also obvious in article 13 of the Amsterdam Treaty.

These resolutions and declarations express the Community's intention to combat racism and racial discrimination, but concrete action depends on the goodwill of the political bodies of the member states. Resolutions and declarations do not automatically secure the power to take legal action against discrimination. These initiatives are rather concerned with dissemination of information, attitude formation and public opinion moulding. They clearly express the conviction that the concept of race is a misconception, and that racism is about wrong ideas and irrational values. Attitude change is an essential element of the struggle against racism. While this obviously is part of the truth, it neglects or at least does not consider the systemic, political and institutionalised aspects of racism and discrimination. Resolutions and declarations hardly affect the ways in which institutional structures operate.

New questions

Discrimination needs to be researched at various levels. We need to understand the social mechanisms that generate discriminatory behaviour. While individual prejudices and individual discriminatory and degrading treatment will hurt the targeted individual's feelings and violate his or her integrity, it is institutional and structural factors that maintain group and class differences in society with regard to resources and access to power. The welfare state along with legislation aims to change these differences, but has not been entirely successful. Legislation may be too weak. The burden of proof may be too high. An essential task is to strengthen anti-discriminatory legislation, to convict those who break the law and to empower those who are victims of discrimination. An important task for research is to identify social structures that maintain discrimination at various levels, to analyse the mechanisms of discrimination and to bring about change. This means analysing the structures of various societal institutions such as the police, the judiciary, the educational system, the labour market, social welfare systems and health care.

5. Conclusion

The task that was assigned to our research cluster is to bridge the gaps between four areas of social science research, all greatly significant to the central IMISCOE concerns of integration and social cohesion in countries of immigration. Intuitively it is obvious that identity issues, interethnic relations, representation and discrimination link up with one another. The questions that we have asked ourselves are: How do we formulate this theoretically? What building blocks do we select out of the multitude of theoretical approaches presented in the literature for each of these four research domains?

We started by trying to juggle with all four issues at once. Fairly soon it became obvious to us that this would not work. Subsequent work in our cluster may therefore be described as a process somewhat resembling phenomenological reduction. It involved the deconstruction of our intuitive understanding of the cluster's task. Hopefully this will be followed by a stage of reconstruction and re-establishment of the four conceptual domains into a new holistic understanding.

The first concept that we put aside was representation. Our justification was that issues of representation are included in identity discourse in terms of social (or collective) representations. However, it also enters the discrimination context as empowerment through political representation. Thus our state of the art report has three points – interethnic relations, identity and discrimination.

Ethnicity is the second concept to be put aside for a while. The following strategy was adopted. Ethnicity has been subsumed within the main identity concern. As a consequence of this step, the cluster reorganised its work into two streams. One stream has concentrated on putting together an edited volume on identity, which in turn is to serve as a platform for a research proposal on comparative identity research. The other stream has been working to develop a research proposal for a comparative study on discrimination research using a variety of approaches.

The principal task for the future then is to reconstruct the four concepts theoretically with emphasis on linkages, commonalities and med-
iations in a multidimensional, comprehensive understanding of this
special field of knowledge.

Note

1   All active members of the cluster contributed to the C7 state of the art report. The
    authors mentioned here worked on the condensed version given in this chapter.

Literature

Adorno, T. W., Frenkel-Brunswick, E., Levinson, D.J. & Sanford, R.N. (1950). The Authori-
    tarian Personality. New York: Harper & Row.
Alba, R., Handl, J. & Müller, W. (1994), Ethnische Ungleichheit im deutschen Bildungs-
    system (Ethnic dissimilarities in the German education system), Kölner Zeitschrift für
    Soziologie und Sozialpsychologie 2/1994: 209-237.
Allport, G. (1954), The Nature of Prejudice. Cambridge, Mass.: Addison-Wesley.
Anderson, B. (1983), Imagined Communities. Reflections on the Origin and Spread of Nation-
    alism. London: Verso.
Ballard, R. (2003), 'The South Asian Presence in Britain and its Transnational Connec-
    tions', in H. Singh, and Vertovec, S. (eds.) Culture and Economy in the Indian Dia-
    spora. London: Routledge.
Barth, F. (ed.) (1969), Ethnic Groups and Boundaries. The Social Organzation of Culture
    Difference. London: George Allen & Unwin. Also (1998): Prospect Heights, Ill: Wave-
    land Press, Inc.
Barthes, R. (1957), Mythologies. Paris: Seuil.
Bastos, J. (2000), Portugal Europeu. Estratégias Identitárias Inter-nacionais dos Portugueses.
    Oeiras: Celta.
Bastos, J. (2002), (ed.) Antropologia dos processos identitários, Ethnologia, Nova Série, nº 12-
    14, Lisbon, FCSH and Fim de Século.
Bastos, J. (ed.) (1992), Antropologia das estratégias identitárias, (número temático), Eth-
    nologia (ns), no. 12-14. Lisbon: Departamento de Antropologia da FCSH e Fim de Sé-
    culo.
Bastos, S. (1995), 'Do corpo ao cosmos: contributo para o estudo projectivo das represen-
    tações simbólico-identitárias dos hindus-gujeratis residentes em Lisboa', in Yanez Ca-
    sal, A., (ed.), Ser Português em Portugal. Lisbon: FCSH, 3º volume, mimeo.
Batoréu, F. (2003), Jovens muçulmanos. Estratégias identitárias, Lisboa: FCSH, tese de licen-
    ciatura em Antropologia, mimeo.
Baudrillard, J. (1970), La société de consommation: ses mythes, ses structures. Paris: Galli-
    mard.
Baumann, G (1996), Contesting Culture. Discours of identity in multi-ethnic London. Cam-
    bridge: Cambridge University Press.
Becker, G. (1957), The Economics of Discrimination. Chicago: The University of Chicago
    Press.
Beijl. R. Z. de (2000), Documenting discrimination against migrant workers in the labour
    market. Geneva: ILO.

Berger, P. L. & Luckman, T. (1966), *The Social Construction of Reality. A Treatise in the So-ciology of Knowledge*. Garden City, N.Y.: Doubleday.

Berghe, P. van den (1967), *Race and Racism: A Comparative Perspective*. New York: John Wiley & Sons.

Bhabha, H. (1994), *The Location of Culture*. London: Routledge.

Bonacich, E. (1972), 'A theory of ethnic antagonism: The split labour market'. *American Sociological Review*, vol. 37, Oct., 547-559.

Bourdieu, P. (1979), *La distinction. Critique sociale du jugement*. Paris: Les Éditions de Min-uit.

Brass, P. R. (1991), *Ethnicity and Nationalism*. London: Sage Publications.

Calhoun, C. (ed.) (1996), *Social Theory and the Politics of Identity* [1994]. Oxford: Blackwell Publishers.

Camilleri, C. (ed.) (1990), *Stratégies identitaires*. Paris: PUF.

Castells, M. (1997), *The Information Age: Economy, Society and Culture*, Vol. II – *The Power of Identity*. Malden, MA: Blackwell Publishing.

Chapman, M., McDonald, M. & Tonkin, E. (1989), 'Introduction', in E. Tonkin, McDo-nald, M. & Chapman, M. (eds.), *History and Ethnicity*, 1-21. London: Routledge.

Cohen, A. (1969), *Custom and Politics in Urban Africa*. London: Routledge & Kegan Paul.

Cohen, A. (1974), 'Introduction: The Lesson of Ethnicity', in A. Cohen (ed.), *Urban Ethni-city*. London: Tavistock

Correia, A. C. (2001), *Chamem-nos Roma: os Ciganos na Hungria*. Lisbon: FCSH, tese de licenciatura em Antropologia, mimeo.

Correia, E. P. (1993), *Identidade e confronto: contributo para o estudo das representações so-ciais identitárias dos Cabo-Verdianos*. Lisbon: FCSH, mimeo.

Devereux, G. & E. M. Loebb, (1985), 'Acculturation antagoniste', in G. Dévereux, *Ethno-psychanalyse complémentariste*, 253-290. Paris: Flammarion.

Durkheim, É. (1985), *Les forces élémentaires de la vie réligeuse* [1912]. Paris: PUF.

Epstein, A. L. (1958), *Politics in an Urban African Community*. Manchester: Manchester University Press.

Eriksen, T. H. (1993), *Ethnicity & Nationalism. Anthropological Perspectives*. London & East Haven, Con.: Pluto Press.

Erikson, E. H. (1950), *Childhood and Society*. New York: Norton.

Erikson, E. H. (1968), *Identity: Youth and Crisis*. New York & London: W. W. Norton & Comp.

Eurobarometer (1997), *Racism and Xenophobia in Europe*. Luxembourg: Eurobarometer Opinion Poll no. 47.1

Farley, J. E. (1988), *Majority-Minority Relations*. Englewood Cliffs, NJ: Prentice Hall.

Foucault, M. (1966), *Les Mots et les Choses*. Paris: Gallimard.

Fouillée, A. (1902), *Esquisse psychologiqye des peuples européens*. Paris: Félix Alcan.

Freud, S. (1897), 'Manuscrito L', anexo à carta a Fliess de 2 de Maio de 1897, in J. M. Masson, (ed.), *A correspondência completa de Sigmund Freud para Wilhelm Fliess, 1887-1904*. Rio de Janeiro: Imago Editora, LTDA, 1986, 242.

Freud, S. (1923), *Gesammelte Schriften*. Bd 6, Zur Technik; Zur Einführung des Narziss-mus; Jenseits des Lustprinzips; Massenpsychologie und Ich-Analyse; Das Ich und das Es. Vienna: Internationaler psychoanalytischer Verlag. Psychologie collective et analyse du Moï, in *Essais de Psychanalyse*. Paris: Payot, 1972, 83-175.

Freud, S. (1930), *Das Unbehagen in den Kultur*, Vienna: Internationaler psychoanalytischer Verlag. O Mal-estar na civilização, in *Obras Psicológicas Completas de Sigmund Freud*, vol. XXI, 1974, pp- 81-173, Rio de Janeiro: Imago.

Freud, S. (1974), Totem e tabu [1913], in *Obras Psicológicas Completas de Sigmund Freud*, vol. XIII, 17-191, Rio de Janeiro, Imago.

230   JOSÉ BASTOS ET AL.

Fromm, E. (1947), *Man for Himself: An Inquiry in the Psychology of Ethics.* New York: Holt, Rinehart & Winston Inc.

Fromm, E. (1970), *The Crisis of Psychoanalysis. Essays on Freud, Marx and Social Psychology.* New York: Holt, Rinehart & Winston Inc.

Geertz, C. (ed.), (1963), *Old Societies and New States.* New York: Free Press

Giddens, A. (1991), *Modernity and Self-Identity. Self and Society in the Late Modern Age.* Cambridge: Polity Press.

Gilroy, P. (1987), *There ain't no black in the Union Jack.* London: Routledge.

Godelier, M. (1996), *L'Énigme du Don.* Paris: Librairie Arthème Fayard.

Goffman, E. (1963), *Stigma. Notes on the Management of Spoiled Identity.* Englewood Cliffs, NJ: Prentice-Hall, Inc.

Granato, N. & Kalter, F. (2001), *Die Persistenz ethnischer Ungleichheit auf dem deutschen Arbeitsmarkt: Diskriminierung oder Unterinvestition in Humankapital?* www.social-science-gesis.de/ Mitarbeiter/ZUMA/Mitarbeiterpages/granato.htm accessed 07 03 2006.

Hall, S. (1988), *The Hard Road to Renewal: Thatcherism and the Crisis of the Left.* London: Verso.

Hall, S. (1997), 'Old and New Identities, Old and New Ethnicities', in A.D. King, (ed.). (1997), *Culture, Globalization and the World-System. Contemporary Conditions for the Representation of Identity,* 41-68. Minneapolis: The Minnesota University Press.

Hall, S. (ed.) (1997), *Representation. Cultural Representations and Signifying Practices.* London: Sage Publications.

Hechter, M. (1975), *Internal Colonialism: The Celtic fringe in British National Development, 1536-1966.* London: Routledge & Kegan Paul.

Heckmann, F. (1992), *Ethnische Minderheiten, Volk und Nation. Soziologie inter-ethnische Beziehungen* (Ethnic minorities, the people and the nation. Sociology of interethnic relationships) Stuttgart: Lucius & Lucius.

Heckmann, F., Lederer, H. & Worbs, S. (eds.) (2001), *Effectiveness of National Integration Strategies towards Second Generation Migrant Youth in a Comparative European Perspective. Final Report to the European Commission.* Bamberg: EFMS.

Hofstede, G. (1984), *Culture Consequences. International Differences in Work-Related Values.* London: Sage Publications.

Hofstede, G. (1991), *Cultures and Organizations. Software of the Mind.* London: McGraw-Hill Book Company.

Hollinger, D. (2000), *Post ethnic America: Beyond Multiculturalism.* New York: Basic Books.

Horowitz, D.L. (1985), *Ethnic Groups in Conflict.* Berkeley: University of California Press.

Hutchinson, J. & Smith, A.D. (eds.) (1994), *Nationalism.* Oxford: Oxford University Press.

Ingold, T. (1996), *Key Debates in Anthropology.* London & New York: Routledge.

Jameson, F. (1998), *The Cultural Turn. Selected Writings on the Postmodern, 1983-1998.* London & New York: Verso.

Kant, E. (1991), *Anthropologie du point de vue pragmatique (Anthropologie, 1798).* Paris: J. Vrin.

Kastersztein, J. (1990), 'Les stratégies identitaires des acteurs sociaux', in C. Camilleri (ed.), *Stratégies identitaires.* Paris: PUF, 27- 42.

Katz, D. & Braly, K. W. (1935), 'Racial Prejudice and Racial Stereotypes'. *Journal of Abnormal and Social Psychology,* 30, 175-193.

Keyserling, C. de (1929), *Europa, análisis spectral de un continente.* Madrid: Espasa-calpe.

Lasch, C. (1991), *The Culture of Narcissism. American Life in an Age of Diminishing Expectations [1979].* New York & London: W. W. Norton & Company.

LeVine, R.A. & Campbell, D.T. (1972), *Ethnocentrism: Theories of Conflict, Ethnic Attitudes and Group Conflict.* New York: John Wiley and Sons.

Lévi-Strauss, C. (1984), *Paroles données.* Paris: Plon.

Lipianski, M., I. Taboada-Leonetti & A. Vasquez (1990), 'Introduction à la problématique de l'identité', in C. Camilleri et allii, *Stratégies identitaires*. Paris: PUF, 7-26.

Lundahl, M. & Wadensjö, E. (1982), *Unequal Treatment. A Study in the Neo-Classical Theory of Discrimination*. Stockholm: Swedish Institute of Social Research.

Lyotard, J. F. (1979), *La condition postmoderne: rapport sur le savoir*. Paris: Minuit.

Madariaga (1952), *Portrait of Europe*. London: Hollis & Carter.

Madeira, C. (1999), 'Na luta pelo reconhecimento'. Cidadania, espaço e identidade numa comunidade luso-angolana. Lisbon. *FCSH, relatório de investigação do Projecto Portugal Plural*, vol. 4, mimeo.

Marcuse, H. (1964), *One-Dimensional Man. Studies in the Ideology of Advanced Industrial Society*. Boston: Beacon Press.

Marger, M. N. and P. J. Obermiller, (1987), 'Emergent Ethnicity Among Internal Migrants' in *Ethnic Groups*, vol. 7, 1-17.

Marx, K. (1975), 'Contribuição à crítica da filosofia do direito, de Hegel' [1844], *Escritos de juventude*. Lisbon: Edições 70, 1975.

McClelland, D. (1961), *The Achieving Society*, New York: D. van Nostrand Company, Inc.

Mitchell, C. (1956), *The Kalela Dance. Aspects of Social Relationships among Urban Africans in Northern Rhodesia*. Rhodes-Livingstone Institute / Manchester University Press.

Mourão, M. de Fátima (1997), *Contribuições para o estudo das representações sociais identitárias dos "andaluzes" face a referentes externos portugueses e marroquinos*. Lisbon: FCSH, tese de licenciatura em Antropologia Social e Cultural.

Myrdal, G. (1944), *An American Dilemma. The Negro Problem and Modern Democracy*. New York: Harper & Brothers.

Peabody, D. (1988), *National Chatacteristics [1985]*. Paris & Cambridge: Éditions de la Maison des Sciences de L' Homme & Cambridge university Press.

Pimentel, I. (1993), 'Na outra margem'. *Uma abordagem às representações sociais identitárias dos marroquinos*. Lisbon: FCSH, tese de licenciatura em Antropologia Social e Cultural, mimeo.

Portes, A. & R.G. Rumbaut, (2001), *Legacies. The Story of the Immigrant Second Generation*. Berkeley: University of California press.

Reich, W. (s.d.), *Materialismo dialéctico e Psicanálise* [1929]. Lisbon: Editorial Presença.

Ribeiro, D. C. (1996), I Sardi. Contribuição para o estudo dos processos identitários e das representações sociais identitárias na ilha da Sardenha. Lisbon: *FCSH, tese de licenciatura em Antropologia Social e Cultural*.

Riesman, D. (1950), *The Lonely Crowd*. New Haven: Yale University Press.

Rodrigues, E. (2003), Contribuição para o estudo dos processos identitários entre os imigrantes portugueses em França. Um estudo de caso entre luso-descendentes residentes no 7ème arrondissement parisiense. Lisbon: *FCSH, tese de licenciatura em Antropologia*, mimeo.

Rodrigues, E. & J. G. P. Bastos (2005), As estratégias identitárias dos cabo-verdeanos em França, Relatório do Projecto, *Portugal Multi-étnico*. Lisbon: CEMME, mimeo.

Roosens, E. (1996), 'The primordial nature of origins in migrant ethnicity', in H. Vermeulen and C. Govers (eds.), *The Anthropology of Ethnicity. Beyond 'Ethnic Groups and Boundaries'*. Amsterdam: Het Spinhuis, 81-104.

Sartori, G. (2001), *La sociedad multiétnica. Pluralismo, multiculturalismo y extranjería*. Madrid: Taurus.

Scheff, T. (1996), 'Emotions and Identity: A Theory of Ethnic Nationalism', in C. Calhoun, (ed.) *Social Theory and the Politics of Identity*. Cambridge. Mass: Blackwell Publishers.

Shapiro, I. & W. Kymlicka (eds.) (1997), *Ethnicity and Group Rights*. New York: New York University Press.

Stocking, G.W. (1982), *Race, Culture and Evolution. Essays in the History of Anthropology*. Chicago: University of Chicago Press.

Suntum, U. van & D. Schlotböller (2002), *Arbeitsmarktintegration von Zuwanderern –Einflussfaktoren, internationale Erfahrungen und Handlungsempfehlungen (Integration of immigrants on the labour market – factors of influence, international experience and advice for actions)*. Gütersloh: Verl. Bertelsmann Stiftung.

Tajfel, H. (1974), 'Social identity and intergroup behaviour', *Social Science Information*, 13, 2, 65-93.

Tajfel, H. (1981), *Human Groups and Social Categories. Studies in Social Psychology*. Cambridge: Cambridge University Press.

Tajfel, H. (ed.) (1978), *Differentiation between Social Groups*. London: Academic Press.

Thalhammer, E., Z. Vlasta & E. Enzenhofer (2001), *Attitudes towards Minority Groups in the European Union. A Special Analysis of the Eurobarometer 2000 Survey*. www.eumc. eu.int.

Turner, J. (1978), 'Social categorization and social discrimination in the minimal group paradigm', in H. Tajfel (ed.), *Differentiation between Social Groups: Studies in the social psychology of intergroup relations*. London: Academic Press.

Wallerstein, I. (2004), *World-systems Analysis: An Introduction*. Durham: Duke University Press.

Wallraff, G. (1985), *Ganz unten*. Köln: Kiepenheuer & Witsch.

Weber, M. (1922), 'What is an Ethnic Group?', in M. Weber, *Economics and Society* [1968], quoted in M. Guibernau & J. Rex (eds.) (1997), *The Ethniciy Reader. Nationalism, Multiculturalism and Migration*. Cambridge: Polity Press, 15-26.

Wimmer, A. (ed.) (2004), *Facing Ethnic Conflict. Toward a new Realism*. Lanham, MD.: Rowman & Littlefield Publishers.

Yinger, M. J. (1994), *Ethnicity Source of Strength? Source of Conflict?* Albany: University of New York Press.

Young, R. (1995), *Colonial Desire: Hybridity in Theory, Culture, and Race*. London: Routledge.

Zaretsky, E. (1996), 'Identity Theory, Identity Politics: Psychoanalysis, Marxism, Post-Structuralism,' in C. Calhoun (ed.), *Social Theory and the Politics of Identity*, 198-215. Cambridge, Mass: Blackwell Publishers.

9. Time, Generations and Gender in Migration and Settlement

Russell King, Mark Thomson, Tony Fielding and Tony Warnes

The key *problematique* of this chapter is to understand how migration and the integration of migrants unfold *through time, across generations and as gendered processes*. This is an extremely broad canvas on which to try to paint a picture of the temporal and socio-demographic dimensions of the processes of immigration and settlement in Europe.

Our first task is to stress the practical and theoretical importance of time in the study of migration. This is dealt with in section 1, where we deal in concepts and generalities. As a stimulus to think through the time factor in migration we briefly present two theoretical perspectives on 'time': the one of Hägerstrand and that of Cwerner. In section 2, we move to a more methodological analysis, and set out a series of possible strategies for comparatively studying the role of time in migration. Parts 3 and 4 review two specific epistemologies for studying migration through time: The *life-course approach* and *longitudinal studies* of international migrants. These four sections, then, represent our attempt to introduce, theorise and operationalise the critical dimension of time into the study of international migration and integration in Europe. The succeeding three parts of the chapter switch the focus away from time as a continuous and longitudinal variable, towards a range of cross-sectional and cross-cutting axes of analysis: gender, the family and generations. Each of these is time-dependent or incorporates the temporal factor in some fashion, but time as such is not the defining variable. Section 8 concludes by pointing up key findings and indicating some priorities for research.

1. Highlighting the role of time in the study of international migration

Conventionally conceptualised as a time-space phenomenon, the temporal dimension is often central in definitions of migration, for instance as a relocation to another place *for a significant period of time*, or as a *permanent or semi-permanent shift* of residence, either within or to another country. Moreover, there are often implicit thresholds of time and distance contained within definitions of migration, in order to differentiate migration from other, shorter-term and shorter-distance forms of mobility. Thus, migration may be defined as a semi-permanent, long-distance change of the place of residence; whereas a short-distance move is regarded as residential relocation, and short-term moves such as tourism or business trips are regarded as temporary mobility (Malmberg 1997: 23). But where, exactly, does migration 'begin'? In reality migration merges easily, but confusingly, with other forms of mobility. Take, for example, seasonal moves: the East European migrant construction worker who moves to a Western European country for a few months a year, or the 'residential tourists' or 'snowbirds' who escape the harsh weather of Northern Europe by wintering in southern Spain or the Canary Islands. Clearly, the temporal 'edges' of migration are very hard to define.

Now, when we move from definition to the *analysis* of migration, the distance factor tends to take over. Much theorising of migration, especially by geographers, sees distance as the explanatory or independent variable. For Boyle *et al.* (1998: 5-33), migration is a quintessentially *spatial event* to be mapped by the means of flow-arrows and choropleths of migration intensity. For Hammar *et al.* (1997) the concept of *migratory space* is used to bring together findings pertaining to the causes of migration and its relationship to development – the concept is not just physical space but also 'larger opportunity structures, social life and subjective images, values and meanings' that condition propensity for migration (Faist 1997: 247-8, 252). Thus, the measurement of distance can be straightforward mensuration in kilometres, or modified by actual or symbolic barriers such as mountain ranges, international frontiers or socio-cultural distance (language, religion, ethnicity etc.). For economists modelling migration flows or propensities, the distance variable may be both spatial and expressed as gradients of wages, real incomes, unemployment or perceptions or expectations of these. In all these studies, time tends to disappear behind the battery of distance, economic and social variables, and to be lost from the maps, graphs and regressions.

Two strands of work are noteworthy for their attempt to reclaim the central importance of time in the study of human migration: the classic work of the Swedish geographer Torsten Hägerstrand in the field of time geography; and the more recent initiative of the Brazilian sociologist Saulo Cwerner in exploring the multiple embeddedness of time in migration and of migration in time.

Torsten Hägerstrand's 'time geography'

Hägerstrand believed that the criteria for good social science 'are not to be found along the spatial cross-section but along the time-axis and in the particular sequence of events which makes up the life of each individual human being' (Hägerstrand 1975: 3). Key components of time geography are, firstly, the *time-path* of movement: in Pred's words (1977: 208), 'a weaving dance through time-space' from birth till death. Second, fixed points (home, workplace, community centre) are termed *stations*; it is here that individuals meet to form a group (an 'activity bundle') for a particular purpose, which might be related to a longer-term *project* such as creating a family, sustaining a livelihood, building a house, educating their children. Such projects might be *idealistic* (such as the notion of migrating to America to make one's fortune), but they are also *situational*; they are dependent on time and place and individuals' relations with each other and with the structures of authority; they become 'going concerns in the flow of real life' (Hägerstrand 1982: 324).

Next, Hägerstrand draws attention to three kinds of time-geographical constraints that condition people's abilities and opportunities to carry out various activities and projects, including migration (Malmberg 1997: 144). First, there are *capacity* or *capability* constraints, where the individual lacks the physical, financial and social means to realise certain acts; for migrants, distance and travel costs are obvious examples. Second, there are *coupling* constraints, whereby the individual cannot move abroad because of personal or family obligations or the impossibility of being engaged in two or more projects in different locations at the same time. Third, *steering* constraints are mechanisms created with the intention of facilitating, or blocking, access to migration – such as special incentive schemes for certain categories of migrants or immigration laws to prevent migration. These sets of constraints enabled Hägerstrand to focus not just on what people do and where they move, but also what they are *free* or *able* to do by way of actions and movement. By analogy, they also help the researcher to trace the barriers which prevent certain events – like migration – from occurring. As some recent key writings have shown, it is as important to explain non-migration as it is to explain why people do move (Fischer *et al.* 1997; Hammar and Tamas 1997); and a clear distinction needs to be made between *aspiration* and *ability* to migrate (Carling 2002).

From the point of view of comparative research on international migration and its evolution over time, a major limitation of the time geography of Hägerstrand and his disciples (e.g. Carlstein 1982; Carlstein *et al.* 1978) is its preoccupation with daily, weekly and seasonal rhythms of mobility, localised studies of individuals and very small samples. Little mention is made of long-distance emigration. On the one hand, it should not be too difficult to enlarge the scale of these stylised mappings from the farm or the village to embrace the reach of modern international migrations. A recent study of immigrant professionals in Denmark tries to do exactly that (see Liversage 2005). On the other hand, a move to larger scales of migration and to larger life-path datasets does present problems of representation. Multiple life lines would intersect, tangle and coalesce into a spaghetti-like vision where meaningful patterns in the data would probably be lost. Statistical generalisation and computer-generated colour-based diagrams may be two possible ways forward (Southall and White 1998).

Saulo Cwerner's 'times of migration'

We now turn to the recent work of Saulo Cwerner whose stimulating paper 'The Times of Migration' (2001) mirrors the title of his Lancaster PhD (1999). Cwerner notes (2001: 8) that the literature on the sociology of time almost completely overlooks migration. Instead, Cwerner draws inspiration from a little-known early foray into time, culture and migration by Elchardus *et al.* (1987) and from the more recent work of Lash and Urry into the transformation of time and the increasing mobility of people as fundamental aspects of the new social landscape of flows and signs (Lash and Urry 1994; Urry 2000).

In the most original part of his analysis, Cwerner (2001: 17-30) sets out an eight-fold conceptual framework for the 'times of migration'. The first three (strange, heteronomous and asynchronous times) are concerned with practical and symbolic levels of adjustment to the host society and so are more or less pressing issues from the moment of arrival. The second group (remembered, collage and liminal times) becomes more expressive as the immigrant experience develops. And the final pair (nomadic and diasporic times) are part of the long-term temporal outlook of the migrant experience.

- *Strange times.* Immigrants arrive with their own temporal baggage, some of which has to be jettisoned in order to conform to the socio-temporal organisation of life in the host society. A whole new semiotics of time has to be learnt: adjustment to the weather and seasons, to punctuality and the different pace of life, and so on.
- *Heteronomous times.* Migrants become subject to different laws and rules which create temporal alienation and are largely unavoidable, like the 'time rules' for the issue of visas and work permits.
- *Asynchronous times.* Immigrants engage a series of strategies to keep in touch with their country of origin via newspapers and magazines, videos, letters, telephone calls, satellite TV, email and the Internet. As these communicative media become more instant and accessible, migrants can to some extent overcome the time lags and 'resynchronise' with their homeland.
- *Remembered times.* Remembered times are activated and expressed both through a general feeling of nostalgia and via specific events

and material artefacts – photographs, memorabilia, national food, music and dances.
- *Collage times*. When moving abroad, immigrants have to contend with the fact that their own memories and narratives are challenged by alternative images of themselves and their homeland which circulate in the media of the host nation. Immigrants are faced with stereotypes and caricatures of themselves and their country of origin.
- *Liminal times*. For many migrants the nature of their migration is seen as temporary and transitional; they are in a constant state of indecision. This is partly because of the way they see their own migration project – as temporary yet open-ended – and partly because of the lack of certainty imposed by the host society's rules and regulations about immigration.
- *Diasporic times* represent the times of long-term settlement; they thrive when immigrant communities recreate, to some extent, the rhythms of social life of the homeland in the host society, reinstating a new kind of familiar time in place of the earlier uprootings of migration.
- *Nomadic times*. Between the liminal and the diasporic, migrants are seen as the bearers of new time conceptualisations and practices; as 'time pioneers' who are able to problematise and challenge dominant temporal constructs and devise new ways of thinking about and using time.

From Cwerner's path-breaking attempt to theorise the temporal aspects of international migration, three sets of points emerge. First, the focus on the temporal experience of migrants 'can illuminate the nature of migration itself, its twists and turns, meanings and ambivalence, and the way that [...] it dis-places and re-embeds people and communities around the world' (Cwerner 2001: 32). Second, there is the double challenge to the definition of the nation-state and to migration and citizenship policy. Transnational migrant practices blur traditional ethnonational allegiances and identities. Diasporic and nomadic times are crucial elements in new discourses that challenge the citizenship model of the nation-state, although there is a reflective backlash here in the way that newly-reinforced national identities are often articulated *against* the immigrant Other.

Policy-wise, immigration measures are often constructed on the basis of short-term issues which violate the time horizons of migrant life paths and livelihoods and which show little concern for migrants' marginal and vulnerable status. Thirdly, despite the tautologously temporal nature of time, Cwerner's analysis is essentially a kind of cross-sectional study of different dimensions of time which does not fully allow the life histories of migrants to emerge. This leads into the next three sections of this chapter, which are more methodological and deal with, in turn, a typology of methods for comparison, the life-course approach and longitudinal studies.

2. Comparative strategies for studying time in migration

Here we set out a range of more pragmatic methodologies for studying migration and migrants from a temporal perspective. Our emphasis is specifically on *comparative* studies, both across space and, more particularly, across and through time. Time can be considered either as a continuous variable (through life-history profiles of individual migrants or migrant groups) or as a discontinuous one (comparison of different time periods as cross-sections). Zelinsky's (1971) well-known *hypothesis of the mobility transition* effectively integrates within a historical timeframe the phases of 'modernisation' with demographic evolution and migratory types in a powerful (but essentially Western) spatio-temporal model that deserves to be updated into the 'new age' of migration (Castles and Miller 2003).

Nancy Green (1999), meanwhile, has proposed a useful typology for comparative migration studies and has advanced some powerful arguments (but also caveats) for the historical comparative method. The process of international migration embodies an explicit or implicit comparison between past and present, one place and another, two languages and two sets of cultural norms. Comparison goes beyond the specificity of national and ethnic case studies; it enables the researcher to understand what is specific and what is general in the phenomenon of migration – in other words what is structural, what is localised and what lies in the agency of the migrants themselves. Green points out (1999: 60) that the comparative method implies a triple choice: that of the subject (in our case, migration and integration), that of the unit (the migrant groups to be studied) and that of the level of analysis (the family, the city, the country, etc.). But expectations of what the comparative method can achieve should not be too high. While two cases are usually better than one, care must be taken in the choice of the cases to be compared.

Green goes on (1999: 67-71) to identify three common types of comparison in migration studies. The first is the *linear model*, which builds an implicit 'before and after' comparison into the history of the individual migrant's experience: his/her migration and life history (Demuth 2000). The second, the *convergent model* has been used frequently in studies of different immigrant groups in one place. Generally, a city or a country is the reference point and 'cultural origins' of groups are taken as key explanatory variables for the varying modes and rates of adaptation and incorporation over time (e.g. Niekerk 2004; Vermeulen and Penninx 2000). Thirdly, the *divergent model* locates the explanation of difference at the points of arrival by studying immigrant groups of the same origin in different places of settlement (e.g. Foner 1979; Gabaccia 2000). Compared to convergent studies, divergent studies are rare, perhaps because the premise of such a comparison works against the notion of group unity. However, the study of single ethno-national groups in different destinations is potentially important in order to evaluate the relative weight of migrant cultural factors vis-à-vis economic and other factors at the place of settlement.

The above three-fold classification can be extended. Some comparisons can be *parallel* rather than convergent or divergent; an example is the study of Manfrass (1991) which compares Turks in Germany with Algerians in France. Other studies combine convergent and divergent approaches, such as Zontini's (2002a, 2002b) 'double comparative' study of Moroccan and Filipino women in Bologna and Barcelona. And we should not overlook the possibility of building the host-society population into our comparative frameworks; or, where relevant, the home-society non-migrant population.

Lucassen (2004) rightly points out that, although the models in Green's typology are by nature historical, based on migrant processes expressed through time, they are, nevertheless, essentially *synchronic* because the analysis is restricted to one specific time period of a few decades of migration and settlement. *Diachronic* approaches compare migrants across explicit time periods and may, in turn, be combined with the linear, convergent and divergent models of Green. *Diachronic linear* studies are not very common; they compare different cohorts of the same migrant group in the same destination at different time periods. Such studies are usually implicit in general histories of the migration of certain groups with a long-term experience of migration (e.g. Jackson 1963). *Diachronic convergent* studies are more common: in this case two or more immigrant groups are compared across two periods of time in the same location – city, region, country (e.g. Lucassen and Penninx 1997; Lucassen 2004). Finally the *diachronic divergent* type looks at the cross-time comparison of a migrant group in different destinations (e.g. Fraser 1992).

The value of comparative historical research on migrant groups remains potentially powerful; it can reveal long-term lessons from the past about family structures, generational evolution, social networks, education, employment, residential mobility and housing, mixed marriages and other aspects of integration which may not yet be evident in recent immigrations.

3. International migration and the life-course

Life-course approaches in migration studies focus on the connections between age, place and mobility; between the changing life-course, patterns of international migration and consequent implications for migrants and the sending and receiving societies. Key topics in this sociological approach are the socially-constructed roles and positions of people at different ages, both within their families and in relation to society. It is these, rather than the individual's physical or mental states, that have been transformed by urbanisation, industrialisation and post-modernisation processes. The relevance to migration is immediately apparent: the life-course framework contextualises not only individual and group decisions about the timing of migrations but also their formative influences and outcomes.

It is common knowledge that certain age cohorts have higher propensities to migrate than others (Bogue 1968; Rogers and Castro 1981, 1986). Not surprisingly, the highest peak in the migration profile coincides with the transition from education to work; this is the point in the life-course at which individuals are likely to be, and need to be, most geographically mobile. Given that most migration research has been on working-age migrants – consistent with the previous emphasis on economically-driven labour migrations within and into Europe – we here pick three 'new mobilities' as examples of age-related migration: children, students and retired people. In reality, child, student and retirement migrations are deceptively simple categorisations and, as we shall shortly see, each breaks down into a number of subtypes.

Children as migrants

Study of child migrants cuts across academic disciplines, although the extant literature remains quite limited. We can identify two interrelated but distinct areas of research: the processes behind the actual migration of children and the difficulties child migrants experience upon arrival. Cutting across this division are five main subtypes: refugees and asylum seekers, victims of trafficking, migrant children with EU citizenship, migrant children of third-country nationals (TCNs) and inter-country adoptees.

Refugee- and asylum-seeking children migrate for a variety of reasons, often with family members and other adults, but occasionally by themselves. Children may flee with the family unit out of fear of ethnic or racial persecution, or because the family has been forcibly displaced from their home or out of severe poverty and deprivation. The circumstances causing flight, the ensuing journey to safety and experiences in the country of asylum all have an impact on migrant children's physical and emotional well-being. Their flight also exposes them to greater risks than adults, and they may have very little, if any, control over their final destination (see Ayotte 2000).

Due to their vulnerability, separated children are often victims of trafficking. Statistics on child trafficking are not readily available because of its hidden nature. It is recognised, nonetheless, as a growing phenomenon in Europe, especially where it takes place for sexual exploitation (Campani et al. 2002; IOM 2002; Kelly and Regan 2000; Ruxton 2000; Wolthius and Blaak 2001).

Children vulnerable to trafficking exhibit similar characteristics to child asylum seekers: flight from war-torn countries, from poverty or from lack of opportunity. More restrictive immigration controls in EU countries have also made children more vulnerable to trafficking and its expanding criminal networks (Salt and Stein 1997).

In contrast to the previous two types, children of EU migrant families do not experience migration with anything approaching the same degree of trauma and uncertainty. Children's social entitlements in the host state can however be contingent on the migrant worker-parent's continued residence in the same country, or, if the family status is not recognised under Community law, children may be excluded from the benefits of citizenship (Ackers and Stalford 2004).

The fourth type of child migrants are those without EU citizenship – children of third country nationals. Whilst EU citizens are guaranteed a right to family life (and, therefore, family reunification) under Community law, the right for TCNs living in EU member states to be joined by family members remains largely a matter for domestic law. This right has been undermined by recent legislative changes in EU member states which have tightened conditions for entry of family members (Kofman 2004). Once children of TCNs have moved into the host country, their entitlements, for example to education, are again derived from their relationship with the parent-worker.

The final type are inter-country adoptees. Inter-country adoption (ICA) is a global phenomenon: over 100 countries participate and more than 30,000 children are adopted each year (Selman 2002). The nature of ICA has changed from providing families for children to finding children for families (Triseliotis 1993: 419). This raises some fundamental questions about ICA. Is it in the 'best interests' of adopted children? Under which circumstances is it morally acceptable to remove children from poorer societies to provide families for childless people in richer nations? Does ICA exploit vulnerable people and countries and encourage a trade in children? What effects does it have on the identity of the children adopted? (Warren 1999).

International student migration

Students are one of the main under-researched elements of the contemporary European international migration scene (King 2002: 98-9). This lack of acknowledgement extends both to the simple enumeration and mapping of flows and distributions, and to the conceptualisation of student mobility as a specific form of migration (if, indeed, it can be considered as a 'pure' migration). Their mobility patterns are unlike those of previous generations, when opportunities to study and travel abroad were much more limited – both by the fact that far fewer people went on to tertiary education and by the slower speed and higher cost of European travel. Global, European and regional cities – from London, Paris and Brussels to Barcelona, Frankfurt and Milan – offer growing opportunities, through the ongoing internationalisation of business and economic life, to graduates to pursue both their careers and their lifestyle aspirations. The social geographies of these often hyper-mobile young people – where they live, their lifeworlds, identities, hopes for the future – are waiting to be systematically documented.

The most publicised form of student mobility within Europe is the Erasmus scheme which has been sponsoring intra-EU mobility by offering 'mobility grants' to more than 1 million students since its inception in 1987. Student migration flows also take place between European countries and the rest of the world. Population geographers have thus far missed a wonderful opportunity to create maps of student migration and to chart its growing global and European significance. The source data are there but the analyses have yet to be made.

Interesting possibilities also exist for explaining and modelling the patterns of origin–destination flows within and beyond Europe and their evolution through time. How does international student mobility fit into the scheme of things as regards theories of migration? To what extent do we need new theories of educated youth mobility, or can we rely on existing migration models? Some see the phenomenon as a subset of elite or high-skilled migration (Findlay 2002) – more precisely as a *potential* flow of qualified and professional workers – or as a product of globalisation, particularly the globalisation of higher education (Altbach and Teichler 2001). Another theoretical perspective sets student mobility within a more cultural frame, as part of a wider grouping of 'youth mobilities' and 'mobile identities' which also include independent travel, backpacking, working holidays etc. (Battisti and Portelli 1994; Clarke 2004). Cultural studies perspectives are also at the heart of some interesting work done on students' identities and integration patterns abroad. Are they the 'new strangers' (Murphy-Lejeune 2002) or do they successfully integrate?

Migration and retirement: the 'greying' of migration?

After the age of fifty, the likelihood of moving peaks among people in their early sixties and is positively related to income, social class and house ownership. Long-distance moves (including international migration) are most likely among married couples and those who have been most mobile earlier in life. These moves are particularly pronounced from large metropolitan areas and, not being balanced by counter-flows (unlike most other migration streams), have a significant redistributive effect on the location of the elderly population, as shown most clearly for Florida in the United States and the French and Italian Riviera coasts (Rogers 1989). Analysis of census data and surveys of retirement migrants have enabled the characteristics of the participants in these long-distance migrations to be described. Retirement moves are now prominent in international migrations by Northern Europeans, and displace many thousands a year to Mediterranean destinations (King *et al.* 2000).

Whilst student and recent-graduate migrants are likely to be found in the major urban centres and university cities of Europe, wealthy retirees are more likely to seek out pleasant rural and coastal landscapes, especially those in Southern Europe with a warm climate. However, the relationship between international migration and old age is much more complex than simply thinking of the British in the Dordogne or Germans in Majorca. The following four multiple interconnections between migration, ageing and retirement can be identified:

- the retirement migration of wealthy Northern Europeans to coastal and rural settlements in Southern Europe;
- the retirement-in-place of earlier waves of labour migrants, originating from Southern Europe, North Africa and other poor countries, in the cities and industrial areas of Northern Europe where they have spent most or all of their working lives;
- the return/retirement migration of these labour migrants back to their countries and villages of origin;
- the problems of survival and care suffered by older people in areas of emigration where they have been 'left behind' by the departure of most of the rest of the population, including their own family members.

Of these four, the first type, generally known as *international retirement migration*, has been thoroughly researched in recent years. Some studies adopt a comparative divergent approach, looking for instance at the British in various destinations (King et al. 2000); others take a convergent comparative approach – for instance Rodríguez et al. (1998) compare several North European groups in southern Spain. Yet others focus in-depth on a single group in one destination: the British in Fuengirola (O'Reilly 2000) or the Swiss on the Costa Blanca (Huber 2003).

The second type of retired migrants consists of the millions of labour migrants who, since the early 1950s, have moved within or into Europe and have subsequently 'aged in place' (Warnes et al. 2004: 311). These migrants mainly came from poor rural backgrounds, had little education, took on low-skilled and low-paid manual jobs and have endured a lifetime of disadvantage and deprivation, including poor housing and racial discrimination. They have now reached retirement age in massive numbers, and will continue to do so in the next few years (White 2006). Yet only now are these generations of older immigrants living in precarious conditions being 'discovered' (Bolzman et al. 2004; Fibbi et al. 1999; Gardner 2002).

The third type of retirement migration, the *return of retired labour migrants to their homelands*, has also been little studied. The 'return of retirement' was described by Cerase (1974) in his typology of return migration of Italians from the United States. Often, however, returning retirees have difficulty reintegrating after so long away. A solution for many retired labour migrants is to circulate between their place of origin and the immigrant host society, spending part of the year in each (Rodríguez and Egea 2006).

Finally, we must not overlook the *older people who remain in their home countries*, stripped of their families and support systems by mass emigration. Often the economies and welfare systems of their countries are too poor and disorganised to provide state pensions or proper health and social services. Such older people would normally expect their children and other close relatives to support them both materially and if they become frail or sick. When their children migrate to another country, especially one that is far away, they lose this emotional and practical support and become, in effect, 'orphaned elders' (King and Vullnetari 2006).

Life-course stages as a stimulus of migration

Put simply, contemporary highly-developed or post-modern societies display three life-course stages, characterised successively by childhood and socialisation, economic and family production, and retirement. These can be termed the first, second and third ages of the contemporary life-course. The sequence stimulates migration both directly and in subtle ways that play out over time. As individuals and households progress from one stage to the next, their 'optimum location requirements' change and the transitions stimulate many to migrate, as we have seen above.

More subtle connections between life-course stages and migration arise first because the calculation of where it is best to live is not simply for one day or the next month, but is to a greater or lesser extent a long-term prospective assessment. Migrants are of course concerned with their short-term earnings and standard of life, but they are also motivated by better prospects in the years to come for themselves and for their partners and dependants. However, it is also the case that some migrants fail in their goals – say to find a well-paid job or a high-quality residential setting for retirement – and therefore reverse their decision and return. Others realise (or knew all along) that migration entails losses as well as gains. Many distance themselves from close relatives and friends; go to countries in which they cannot speak the language or have little knowledge of the local job and housing markets or social and health services; and migrate to countries in which they are 'outsiders', with fewer rights and entitlements than the citizens, and in which they may be subject to discrimination, exploitation, exclusion and abuse.

Many migrations can be rated a success or failure within a few weeks or months. The life-course paradigm draws our attention, however, to the long-term consequences for the migrant, their dependants and descendants, and indeed the family members that they leave in the regions of origin.

Life-stages, human capital and the consequences for migration

The concept of human capital (the accumulation of material, educational and social resources) is useful in illuminating the long-term consequences of being an international migrant. Many components of comparative advantage at the two major life transitions, from the first to the second ages and from the second to the third, are the same. Assets and income condition the material standard of life at all life stages, but both a priori reasoning and observation suggest that other dimensions of human capital – such as social networks or health – have markedly different weights at the two major life-stage transitions.

Variations in the resources that a migrant has accumulated arise in several ways. Aspects of a person's migration and family histories influence the locations of and the relationships with their close and extended kin – and therefore the availability of both routine and 'crisis' informal social and instrumental support. Then, the migrant's personal history interacts with the national policy towards immigrants to determine their state welfare entitlements – pensions, income benefits, health and personal social services, and social or subsidised housing and long-term care.

As in the general population, a migrant's educational and occupational backgrounds correlate with their lifetime earnings and income and assets in old age. Socio-economic background strongly influences migrants' knowledge of the host country's welfare system and their ability to make use of the available services, especially through their language skills. These capacities are modified by information received from relatives and friends, and by whether the migrant can turn to a community association for advice. Access to and the utilisation of services will also be strongly influenced by the receptiveness of the country's housing, health and personal social services agencies and their staff to immigrants and ethnic minorities. In short, both for young economic migrants and for retirement and amenity-seeking older migrants, there are complex relationships between their migration history, current social position, national policies, and their access to social security, housing privileges and informal and formal care (Warnes and Ford 1995).

The life-course interacts with international migrations and particularly their long-term outcomes in a yet more intricate way. On a global scale wide differentials in levels of well-being and economic opportunities associate with the forms and durations of the life-course. International migrants relocating from the least developed to the most developed world regions not only move (by definition) between countries and levels of economic development, but also into socio-demographic and welfare environments that are quite different from those that they leave. The long-term consequences for their social position and welfare are profound.

Over the last century and more, the nature of the life-course and the disposition of its stages have been radically transformed. This has several implications for international migrants, particularly those who move between 'level of development' zones. Most economic migrants from poorly to highly developed countries enter a 'life-course stage context' that differs greatly from that in which they have been socialised or gained early work experience. Their socialisation and skills acquisition put them in a weak position in competitive labour markets. They are particularly ill-prepared to finance their retirement.

The decision to move hundreds or thousands of kilometres for work has substantial impacts on the daily lives and the medium- and long-term prospects of not only the migrants but also their families and others. From the perspective of the migrants, and in relation to the long-term consequences of international migration on both origin and destination countries or regions, the 'decision to migrate' needs to be conceived as a *diachronic* process which has both a 'formation' period and outcomes that play out over time, and which involves several decisions with consequences for many people.

Multiple affiliations and residences

Radical improvements in international transport and travel in recent decades, combined with the spread of high incomes and wealth, have recently introduced another complication in the relationship between the life-course and migration, and not only for the most affluent. There is growing evidence from Northern European countries, specifically the Netherlands, Belgium, Norway, Sweden and Switzerland, that long-term international migrants who reach retirement are choosing to maintain links and residences in both their adopted and their origin countries (and some in third countries too).

Second-home ownership and the growth of peripatetic residential patterns introduce further complexity into mobility patterns over the life-course. Seasonal migration is increasing among the young retired population in North America. Little hard information on the same phenomenon exists in Europe, but there is no doubt that increasing numbers of retired people are spending many weeks or months in Mediterranean resorts (Gustafson 2001, 2002; Myklebost 1989). No clear distinction exists between a long winter-break holiday and a seasonal migration between multiple homes.

The relationship between household change and residence is also growing more complicated for younger adults. Rising age-participation rates in tertiary education and vocational training are spreading the transitional or adolescent life-course stage of alternating residence patterns, associated in England and Wales with university students. Private households of unrelated young-adult individuals in rented, leased or mortgaged properties are becoming more common in Britain and North America and in other European countries too. Pre-marriage and post-divorce sexual unions lead frequently to cohabitation in single households, themselves difficult to monitor using standard sources. Over the past few years, the custom has grown of stable partners keeping two properties; often one is near a city centre and occupied during the working week, while the other is extra-metropolitan and retreated to at weekends. Other configurations, with shared properties in remoter rural areas or abroad, have also multiplied.

These new social forms represent subtle transformations of the life-course within the second age, particularly with respect to social reproduction and family roles. They prompt the suggestion that the coincidence between a 'minimal household unit', nuclear family group or other co-resident group and a single dwelling unit is breaking down. Contemporary lifestyles increasingly involve peripatetic residential patterns at two or more addresses, and increasingly too cross-nationally. These will be exceptionally difficult to measure using conventional sources.

4. Longitudinal studies of international migrants

Despite a widely-held view that longitudinal data offer the best basis for an understanding of migration processes, there are surprisingly few studies of immigration and integration in the countries of the EU that fully depend upon this form of data. There are many reasons for this; among the most important is the paucity of data. Longitudinal datasets are very expensive to generate (if based on censuses) and are very limited in the range of material they contain (if based on population registers).

Are we to interpret this absence to mean that there is little of value to be expected from a longitudinal approach? Not at all. But it does mean that we are encouraged to emphasise more the *potential* for such studies than their already-established contribution. Existing contributions can be grouped under six headings:

- *Qualitative studies: the oral history approach.* Many believe that one of the best ways to develop an understanding of the longitudinal profile of a migrant's life is through oral history (Thomson 1999).
- *Other qualitative studies.* Related to the above, but not dependent on interviews, relying instead on historical data from family archives and genealogical society records, are the longitudinal studies of migration histories. Thus far, most such studies have been on internal migration (e.g. Pooley and Turnball 1998), but it is to be expected that this genre of research in the future will encompass international migration flows as well as internal ones.
- *Quantitative studies and methods of analysis.* There is a shortage of migration research using longitudinal datasets. The paucity of datasets beyond the British Census's Longitudinal Study (a 1 per cent sample linked across the four censuses since 1971, analysed by Fielding 1995, amongst others) is partly to blame, but there are other approaches such as the 'triple biography' favoured by Courgeau and Lelievre (1989) that, surprisingly, have not been taken up.[1] This gap between the rich potential for quantitative studies using longitudinal data and the sad reality of current research can probably be explained by the methodological chasm between the *qualitative mentalities* of most migration researchers and the significant demands for *quantitative skills* arising from the more statistical approaches.
- *Empirical research on immigrants using panel studies.* The richest datasets for longitudinal research are panel studies. This is where a group of people are contracted to provide information on their lives as they unfold over time through repeated rounds of surveys. Very labour-intensive, and therefore expensive, panel studies need time to accumulate value and tend to contain rather limited samples of the

population (Eckbert 1996). This can have the result of ruling out any detailed work on subsamples of ethnic minorities.

- *Empirical research on emigrants using panel studies.* There is, on the other hand, a growing literature on *emigrants* using panel studies (e. g. Klinthall 2003; Schmidt 1997). Constant and Massey (2003) used the German Socio-Economic Panel to investigate return migration of Turks; they found that the propensity to return, over the 14-year study period, was linked to low-status employment and the sending of remittances.
- *Event history analysis.* This technique relates continuous biographical and profile data to discrete events occurring at particular points in time (and space), thereby investigating the relationship between continuous-time and discrete-time variables. The aim is to uncover causal relationships and to map out a system of causal relations in social processes (Blossfeld and Rohwer 2002: vii). Boyle *et al.* (1998: 50) acknowledge its potential for enabling hypotheses, explanations and inferences to be linked to research questions on migration behaviour and outcomes.

5. Gender

The topic of gender is all-encompassing in research into migration and integration; yet the theoretical aspects of gender-selective migration have only been addressed since the early 1980s. It is now widely appreciated that incorporating gender into research on the migration process is fundamental to a full understanding of the 'migrant experience' as well as for a complete grasp of the consequences of immigration and integration policies. But this realisation has not yet been put into practice; some migration research remains gender-blind. Gender cannot, of course, simply be reduced to a discussion about women. Gender is a *relational* social category implicated in a range of social relations linked to the process of migration (Anthias 2000: 24).

Women (and wider questions of gender relations) were often completely invisible in early migration research, as they were in other areas of social science. The gender-blind male dominance of migration research up to the 1980s leads to a fatal analytical flaw. This is that *descriptions, analyses and explanations for the migration of 'people', by aggregating the very different characteristics, motivations, agencies and relations of men and women, end up by failing to accurately portray the migration behaviour of either sex.* This silence was broken in the early-mid-1980s by a number of landmark statements on the role of migrating women which challenged the status quo in migration research, key among which was Annie Phizacklea's edited book *One Way Ticket* (1983).

Among other questions raised were those concerning the domestic/ public model of women's status in relation to different spheres of activity. These first-wave studies of migrant women, however, only went so far. The complexity of gender relations through the migration process was not yet fully explored, nor was male migration analysed from a gender perspective.

In the 'second wave' of literature on migration and gender, emerging since the late 1990s, a more *flexible conceptualisation* of migrant women and of gender relations in migration processes more generally was formulated, proposing a more transformatory interpretation of female migration by viewing structures as both constraining *and* enabling (Phizacklea 1998: 26; see also Goss and Lindquist 1995). A second key element was the *feminisation* of international migration. Feminisation of migration flows means that women play an increasingly significant role, both quantitatively and as social actors, in most types of migration. The real point about the feminisation thesis is recognising the increased agency and independence of women in migration flows and systems. Reappraisals of some earlier migration streams revealed that women had always been migrating as independent individuals and as pioneers, sometimes on their own, sometimes alongside, or separated from, their male counterparts (Gray 1996; Phizacklea 2003a: 26-7). But the later decades of the twentieth century also witnessed the emergence of single-sex migration streams. All-female migrations are linked to the perpetuation or reappearance of live-in domestic work as an employment sector for migrant women in a wide range of European and other countries (within Europe, especially Italy, Spain and Greece) and to the increasing willingness of European governments to allow the entry of migrant women working as live-in domestics and as careers for the elderly.[2]

A third perspective of recent research on gender and migration comes from the new literature on *transnational migration*. In their critique of the transnational approach, which they criticise for not 'bringing gender in' enough, Pessar and Mahler propose a theoretical framework focused on 'gendered geographies of power' to facilitate 'a more nuanced transnational examination of how gender articulates with migration' (2003: 815). Pessar and Mahler do go on to acknowledge (2003: 819-823) that much new work on transnational migration *does* foreground gender – for instance in studies of refugees and state policies, on women's role in remittances, on women and transnational families, on gendered discourses of work and responsibility and on return attitudes and behaviours. But much of this work is North American; only very recently is comparable European research emerging. This new European work covers a diversity of gender-migration-transnationalism interactions, including Islam, employment and other eco-

nomic roles, family and care duties, transnational mothering etc. (see
e.g. Andall 2000; Salih 2003; Zontini 2004). This leads us to perhaps
the key question regarding migration and gender: what do past and
contemporary (female) migrations reveal about the changing nature of
patriarchal relations of migration?

Throughout many accounts on gender and migration one can find a
range of perspectives. Some lay emphasis on migration as a potentially
liberating and transformatory experience, through which women are
able to regain a measure of control over their lives and destinies. Other
analyses are more negative: gender is seen as another layer of the multiple oppression of migrant women – structurally discriminated against
as migrants, as women (both by the host society and within their own
ethnic group), as members of the labouring underclass, as racially stigmatised and, finally, as accepting these oppressive structures.

By and large recent research has tended to document migrant women's success in escaping old patriarchal structures. At least for some
groups, women's wage-earning gives them some independence within
the household sphere, leading to a more flexible division of labour in
the home, and less sex-segregation in social and public spaces (Brettell
2000: 110). The new sense of control gained by women through migration, however, raises a different set of questions about return migration. Like all aspects of the migration process, the dynamics of return
are highly gendered. Often it is observed that, despite a general yearn-
ing for home which is commonly shared by both sexes, women are
more reluctant to go back since it would mean giving up new-won free-
doms and returning to a situation in which female employment opportunities are lacking and conservative social conditions constrain women's social relations.

6. The family

To write about the role of the family in migration and integration is
also, almost inescapably, to write about gender and the life-course;
hence, in the relevant previous sections we have already given some
hints about family and household dynamics in migration.[3] In this section we first propose a typology of family migration pathways. We then
examine the role of the family/household approach, both from the
standpoint of emigration from the home country and from the perspective of arrival and integration in the destination country. Finally, we
engage in a more theoretical and critical discussion of the family/
household approach, especially as regards its ethnocentric and normative nature.

Types of family migration

Where they exist, European case studies of international family migration have tended to assume traditional paradigms of family organisation – the nuclear family above all – and have not fully explored or even acknowledged the variety of family and household types which derive from diverse home-country settings or are evolving amongst European populations or developing within specific transnational migration contexts.

Several different family-migration trajectories can be identified. The following typology builds on that suggested by Kofman (2004: 244-7):

- *Whole-family migration* – where the entire family (typically a nuclear family of husband, wife and young children) is the unit of migration, moving all together at the same time.
- *Migrations of family reunion* – where the 'primary migrant' from an already-existing family, having lived abroad for a certain period of time, brings over his or her remaining family members, usually spouse and children, and perhaps also parents.
- *Family formation* by migrants in the host society – where two single migrants form a partnership/marriage in the destination country and create a new family there.
- *Marriage migration* – where a single migrant (or member of the 'second generation') takes a spouse from the home country or from another country of the migrant community's diaspora and brings him/ her to the country of immigration, where the new family is formed.
- *Split-family migration* – the case where, typically, only one member of the family migrates, leaving the rest behind.

The above are the main 'ideal types'; many further variations exist. Taking a time-based perspective, families can be created, split and then re-unified through different stages of the migration cycle. The life-history approach sees a complex interweaving of family stages with migration events: family formation or dissolution may set the scene for or trigger migration; and migration in turn may provide opportunities for, or in other cases constrain, particular family formations. Personal and intra-family relationships and dynamics can also play a significant role – such as separation, divorce or a woman migrating to flee an abusive husband.

Home- and host-country perspectives

Increasingly, the family is seen as the most appropriate unit of analysis in the examination of emigration behaviour, especially as regards the decision making process and the causes and consequences of migration (Boyd 1989; Hugo 1999: 54-5). On the one hand, the migration decision is often made within the context of the needs and constraints of the whole family. On the other hand, many of the impacts of the migration of one or more family members are acutely felt by the family members 'left behind'. These effects are both positive and negative. On the positive side, remittances improve living conditions and enable investments to be made; and women may be empowered by the absence of husbands, fathers and brothers. On the negative side, the absence of family members is keenly felt by the non-migrants and the local economy may decline due to the absence of labour.

From the perspective of the country of immigration, family migration and family reunion are processes which generally favour long-term settlement and integration. The family provides a crucial setting for immigrants' integration, through its multiple links to various institutions and activity spheres within the host society – work, education, the health service, the neighbourhood, etc. Ever since the closure of mass labour recruitment schemes in the 1970s, family reunion has been the main immigration gateway into the European Union. Nowadays, more than three-quarters of the EU's (legal) annual inflow of immigrants is accounted for by spouses, children and other family members.

Another host-country perspective to be noted is the demographic one. Europe's 'second demographic transition' sees a number of distinctive developments within European populations that can affect the context of family migration (Kaa 1987, 1999). Unprecedentedly low fertility regimes, demographic ageing and international migration provide new contexts for how families and households organise themselves within, and beyond, Europe. Family-based 'replacement migration' now looms large in current debates over European population development (United Nations 2000). Such immigration contributes significantly to what little demographic growth exists in European countries in recent years, both due to the crude aggregate numbers of new (net) immigrants and, more particularly, to their younger age structures and higher fertilities. Of course, it has to be recognised that family-based immigration cannot be the *sole* solution to Europe's declining and ageing population.

Theorising and deconstructing the family in European migration

Having mapped out these preliminary typologies on family/household migration, it is important now to consider, from a more theoretical and critical point of view, the genealogy of the family approach to migration. During the 1980s, theorisation and explanation of migration began to shift from an individual-scale focus to intermediary institutions such as families, households and social networks. One important conceptual thread emerged out of the discipline of economics where the *new economics of migration* moved beyond the modelling of migration behaviour predicated on individuals' rational choice to a focus on the family as the effective decision making unit (Stark 1984, 1991). Under the 'new economics', families and households act collectively not only to maximise expected income but also to minimise risks and to hedge against 'market failures' such as crop damage or unemployment. Stark and his colleagues were then roundly criticised for failing to acknowledge tensions and conflicts within the household and for making the assumption that the household, like the individual of neoclassical economics, was a 'rational' decision making unit. For, as Phizacklea (2003b: 85) memorably wrote, opening the 'black box' of the family often reveals a 'can of worms', and 'families and households are not the cosy, rational decision making units that some accounts would have us believe'. Writers such as Hondagneu-Sotelo (1994), Phizacklea (2003b) and others argue for an analytical shift which recognises that households and families are deeply implicated in gendered and cross-generational ideologies and practices. The household, in other words, has its own internal political economy in which access to power and resources is structured along generational and gender lines.[4] Moreover, the household is itself positioned within wider structures and relations such as social class, social networks and other migration-relevant institutions.

The deconstruction of the terms 'household' and 'family' in migration research is taken one stage further by Gunilla Bjerén (1997: 233-8) who stresses their inherent ethnocentrism and questions their cross-cultural validity. The pre-eminent assumption of the nuclear family (husband, wife, two or three children, living together in their own home) reifies a model which is both culturally specific (especially to Europe and North America) and now increasingly outdated in areas where it was held to be the 'norm'.

7. Generations of migrants

This section discusses patterns of social mobility and integration of the children of immigrants, the second generation. Many of the European second generation are finishing their education, and trying to transfer their acquired knowledge and skills to the workplace. Some find this transition from school to work particularly challenging, and experience the insecurities inherent in low-paid, temporary work or unemployment. Others may take advantage of so-called 'ethnic niches' in the economy, although more ambitious aspirations amongst the second generation mean that many are reluctant to assume the 'immigrant' jobs their parents held. A third group are surpassing their 'white' peers both in education and in the workplace.

Academic interest in the second generation has brought a development in the comparative dimension of research on integration processes. Not only are researchers able to contrast patterns of integration of distinct ethnic groups, but they can also highlight the relative socio-economic performance of different generations of immigrants from the same ethnic background. Are the children of immigrants, for example, performing better in education and the labour market than their parents did? Are they achieving a higher occupational status or is the incidence of unemployment greater amongst the second generation compared to the first?

Theories of second-generation integration

We can formulate two sets of determinants that shape the integration processes of the second generation: external factors, such as levels of discrimination and the degree of social and residential segregation; and factors intrinsic to ethnic groups, including the ability to access social support networks, level of education and skills and the amount of financial resources available. Intrinsic cultural values, though they risk attributing behavioural differences to 'culture' alone (Vermeulen 2000: 3), offer further insights into why certain ethnic groups attain higher levels of social mobility than others, despite similar socio-economic backgrounds. An apt example is the value that immigrant parents attach to their children's education. In other words, structural and socio-cultural factors are seen to interact to produce a 'complex process of assimilation in the second generation' (Zhou 1997: 1000). Ethnic communities possess social networks that provide moral and material resources to uphold immigrant values and traditions through private education, whilst some second-generation immigrants are able to benefit from 'ethnic niches' created in the labour market by the established immigrant community.

As the children of immigrants in Europe follow the transition from the school to the workplace, academics researching ethnic groups in Europe have used Portes and Zhou's (1993) US-based theory of 'segmented assimilation' to describe the integration and mobility patterns of the second generation. The theory of 'segmented assimilation' has been criticised on a number of counts (Crul and Vermeulen 2003).[5] It pays little attention to the notion that ethnic groups might actually inhibit social mobility of their members, in particular the female second generation. Neither does the theory pay sufficient attention to internal differences within ethnic groups that might account for different pat-

terns of social mobility and integration. Also, differences between national receiving contexts – obviously more relevant in Europe than in
the US – do not feature as explanatory factors.

The European second generation

Recent studies on immigrant integration in Europe (e.g. Andall 2002;
Bolzman et al. 2003; Crul and Vermeulen 2003; Modood et al. 1997;
Niekerk 2004; Tribalat 1995) testify to a growing interest in the second
generation. European cross-national studies, however, have yet to
emerge on the position of the second generation, although research is
in progress.[6] There are some important points to bear in mind when
undertaking this type of cross-national comparative research:
- In comparing the 'same' ethnic group in different countries, internal
  differences within the emigrant community should be acknowledged, such as socio-economic background, first-generation education, migration 'push' factors, religion and ethnicity.
- Datasets are to be used with caution, often being incomplete and
  not sufficiently disaggregated. National differences in recording statistics on ethnic groups also make cross-national studies problematic.
- Structural changes over time to the economy, as well as in levels of
  racial and ethnic tolerance, influence the extent to which the second
  generation from different waves of migration are able to integrate
  into mainstream society.
- The definition of the second generation is not without ambiguity,
  especially when statistics do not distinguish between native- and foreign-born children of immigrants (Portes 1994). Many researchers
  define the second generation as native-born children or those who
  arrived before primary school (e.g. Andall 2002; Crul and Vermeulen 2003). The term 1.5 generation (or 'in-between' generation)
  broadly refers to children who migrated after starting their school
  careers.[7] An unambiguous definition of the third generation – the
  grandchildren of immigrants – is even more elusive.

The remainder of our discussion addresses the integration processes of
the European second generation in two specific areas: education and
the labour market.

Education
Several indicators point to the educational performance of the second
generation: school attendance rates, highest level of qualification, drop-
out rates and the numbers repeating school years (Crul and Vermeulen

2003). Poorer levels of education and higher drop-out rates are influenced by:

- Social and economic exclusion – The confluence of low socioeconomic position of parents, residence in disadvantaged areas and poor educational results is well charted. Many immigrant families in Europe are of working-class origin. Statistics indicate that foreign pupils concentrate in schools with disproportionate numbers of children with 'educational difficulties'.
- 'Discrimination' in education – Whilst knowledge of the native language does not guarantee success at school, some European countries rely on children's skills in the native language to place them in higher or lower educational streams. Teachers' expectations for pupils, influenced by children's racial or ethnic characteristics, highlight a more direct form of discrimination.
- Ethnic cohesion and values – Respect for parents' aspirations and expectations can foster a sense of social cohesion within family and community networks that influences, negatively or positively, school performance.
- Supportive role of family members – Older siblings can play a pivotal role in the education of younger brothers or sisters. Where parents have inadequate skills in the official language of the country of settlement, older siblings can provide early exposure to the language, help with homework, liaise with teachers and give general encouragement.

Educational attainment in the European second generation varies within and across different ethnic groups. We have outlined above some possible reasons for this variety, but fuller explanations lie in the dynamic interplay between structure, culture and agency. Cultural factors may offer useful explanations, most plausibly when ethnic groups have similar socio-economic profiles. Culture, though, should not be reified, but explained by reference to the social pressures on individuals to conform to the values of the wider ethnic community. Structural factors add another dimension to further explain divergent trends within the 'same' ethnic group, for instance where the children of pioneer migrants live and are educated in less disadvantaged areas.

Upward mobility as gauged by educational attainment is a general trend from one generation to the next, and indeed from the 1.5 generation to the second (Crul and Vermeulen 2003; Simon 2003). Given that many of the European labour migrants – the parents of the second generation – had limited opportunities at school, this should not be too surprising. Two concerns remain, however: firstly, that this upward trend conceals those children who drop out and/or fail to gain sufficient qualifications; and, secondly, that a number of the second genera-

tion are experiencing difficulties in the transition from school to the labour market.

Labour market

Several indicators help determine how well second-generation immigrants are performing in the labour market: unemployment levels, differences between level of qualifications and job status, earnings, employment status (permanent or temporary) and the presence of ethnic
minorities in more senior positions. We can also compare their position to that of their parents, and to the 1.5 generation, to measure the
degree of mobility between generations.

There are somewhat worrying trends in the employment status of
the European second generation. Possible explanations are:

- Economic opportunities and expectations – The second generation
  may not be able, or (understandably) willing, to perform the same
  'immigrant' jobs their parents held. With appropriate educational
  skills increasingly in strong demand, the second generation suffers
  due to the high numbers who either drop out of school unqualified
  or gain few qualifications. The resulting transition to the labour
  market, especially for the least qualified, is at best problematic and
  at worst may foretell a scenario of 'second-generation decline' (Gans
  1992).
- Ethnic cohesion – High levels of social capital in ethnic communities can facilitate a smooth transition to the workplace for the European second generation. However, the 'closed' or introverted nature
  of this ethnic social capital may prevent the second generation from
  accessing the same opportunities for social mobility, particularly via
  higher education, as in more open, individualised communities
  (Crul and Vermeulen 2003: 983).
- Discrimination in the workplace – Many academics highlight racial
  and ethnic discrimination as a factor in limiting the second generation to their 'own, marginal economic circuits' (Crul and Doomernik
  2003: 1057) and as a reason for their high unemployment rates (Simon 2003; see also Fibbi et al. 2003). Two other forms of discrimination need to be noted: religious and sexual. Muslims are particularly affected by religious discrimination in the labour market; potential employers look unfavourably on women wearing the 'hijab',
  or on the observation of religious rituals such as prayers (Ahmad et
  al. 2003: 32-3). Sexual discrimination adds another layer to the multiple oppression of migrant women, who may suffer discrimination
  within their own ethnic groups as well as from the host society.

8. Conclusion and prospects for research

The first sections of this chapter have the theoretical ambition of 'bringing time into' the conceptualisation of migration. Disciplinarily situated in geography, our account reaches out to establish dialogue with history. It also develops methodological issues connected to time-related research designs. The second half of the chapter makes an effort to embrace the empirical literature on various topics – gender, family, age and generation – mapping this research along broad theoretical lines. Here we go beyond discipline barriers to take on board and integrate sociological, anthropological and historical studies. This approach allows us to trace possible future lines of development.

The clear implication is that migration must not be thought of as a single relocation decision by an individual at a moment in time. Such a conception neglects important aspects of the formative and decision making processes and, crucially, pays no attention to the outcomes and consequences of the migration in both the short and long terms. Secondly, migrations need to be understood in their household, family and temporal contexts. Thirdly, as the length of retirement has grown to a significant period for most people, the migrant's economic calculations are increasingly influenced by his/her prospects and opportunities not only in the second age but also in the third age. Fourthly, we need a deeper ethnography of migration decision making, with studies that consider the influence and interest of the closest relatives of the migrant cross-sectionally and in the future. Finally, migration policies will increasingly need to be informed not only by the labour-market and economic growth implications for the host country, but also by considerations of the extent to which the social welfare and quality of life of the migrants when they reach the third age are protected and raised to the national norms.

Like much social research, migration research is only beginning to redress the imbalance that is the legacy of the male domination of the profession. But the gender ignorance of many (male) migration scholars sets up a counter-tendency in some cases to remorselessly stress the gender (female) dimension. This, in turn, tends to squeeze out other key demographic categories such as children and old people, or to override other social categories such as class or ethnicity, or to simply ignore the male dimension altogether. Moreover, the study of *male migration* from a gendered perspective also gets overlooked. The ideal research design should firstly aim at a more nuanced analysis encompassing the intersections ('intersexions', cf. Bottomley *et al.* 1991) of gender with race/ethnicity, class, nation, family structures etc. (Brah 1996; Yuval-Davis and Anthias 1989). Secondly it should recognise that gender is at base a *relational concept* – the one gender being construed in relation to the other. Hence the migration of women can only be fully understood in relation to the migration and social power of men; and vice versa. In other words, 'the migration of men as well as of women is predicated on the time-space strategies of persons of the other sex' (Bjerén 1997: 226, emphasis in original). Even this powerful statement presents the danger of an essentialised binary, since in reality the migration of men/women is simultaneously affected by the activities and strategies of persons of the same sex too.

Migration is one of the powerful influences destabilising the notions of household and family, even when these latter terms are used in an unrefined, unproblematised sense. But international migration also brings together different aetiologies of family and household. Quite apart from the need to be able to identify the cultural significance of home-country conceptualisations of family and household in the context of immigration to another country, a further challenge is to recognise when it is the *act and circumstances of migration itself* which produce variants in the practice and meaning of family and household. Indeed such practices may be 'forced' on migrants by the immigration control policies and legal/citizenship regimes of the receiving countries.

The status of the second generation in the labour market offers few definitive answers to the question of their integration. Social mobility, as in education, is discernible between the first and second generations: most children of immigrants enter more qualified and skilled occupations than their parents. Higher levels of education and vocational training explain this. The position of the second generation varies widely across Europe, however, which is partly the result of differences in national educational systems and the existence or absence of training schemes. Certainly generic policies in the national context have a considerable impact, for good or for bad, on second-generation integration (Crul and Vermeulen 2003: 982-4). Where policies fail the second generation, indicated by high levels of unemployment and poor educational attainment, there is a serious risk of underclass formation in parts of ethnic groups, and polarisation within the 'same' communities.

Integration, though, is also about the degree to which the second-generation feel they belong and can participate in society (outside the school and the labour market). Where discrimination occurs within institutions, it can profoundly affect the life chances of the second generation. Discrimination, though, leaves the classroom or workplace with its perpetrators. Integration should therefore be addressed in a more holistic way to include, among others, questions of citizenship and identity.

Notes

1   The triple biography consists of three separate histories: family and friendship relationships; education, training and work records; and the unfolding location and migratory paths. One then explores the relationship *between* these three histories to discover which is connected to, or determines, which, at what times and in what contexts.

2   The employment of migrant women to relieve Western European women of the necessity to do certain household tasks contains not a little feminist irony and suggests the importance of placing the issue of the presence of migrant women in such feminised work niches into a wider gender analysis. As Phizacklea (1998: 33-4) points out, 'women from poor countries [...] allow women in more affluent countries to escape the drudgery of housework in conditions which sometimes approximate to a contemporary form of state-facilitated slavery. The increasing incidence of paid domestic work highlights the hollowness of the supposedly new "spousal egalitarianism". The hiring of a full-time domestic worker means that patriarchal household and work structures can go unquestioned, women pursuing a career *and* a family need not "rock the boat" and any guilt over exploitation is assuaged by the knowledge that a less fortunate woman is being provided with work. Thus racialized and class privileges are preserved as well as patriarchal structures and privileges'. See also Bridget Anderson's definitive volume *Doing the Dirty Work* (2000), based on fieldwork in Athens, Barcelona, Bologna, Paris and Berlin, which stresses, in addition, the *racialisation* of domestic labour in Europe.

3   We use the terms family and household somewhat interchangeably. Nevertheless there is an analytical distinction: *family* involves an aggregation of individuals based on close kinship ties (although the extensiveness of these ties can vary from one culture to another); *household* comprises a collection of individuals, not necessarily related, living in the same dwelling. Hence households are defined by co-residence; families can be divided by migration or separation. In fact, migration is a major factor which disturbs the normally close correspondence between family and the household.

4   Portes (1997: 816) cautioned against taking the 'can of worms' argument too far. He acknowledged that men, women and children within a household may struggle and clash over conflicting migration-related goals. But he also argued that an exclusive focus on these internal differences runs the risk of ignoring the fact that households *do* pool resources to organise their migration decisions and *can* act as units despite internal contradictions.

5   Portes and Zhou (1993) outlined two alternative 'modes of incorporation' to the classical, linear process whereby the second generation achieves social and economic mobility into 'white, middle-class America': 'downward assimilation' into the 'native underclass' resulting in permanent poverty and marginalisation; or socio-economic advancement but with the second generation upholding the traditions and values of the immigrant ethnic community.

6   Notably the TIES ('The Integration of the European Second Generation') project coordinated by Maurice Crul at the Institute of Migration and Ethnic Studies, University of Amsterdam. This project compares three immigrant communities – Turks, Moroccans and the ex-Yugoslav second generation – across seven destination countries (Austria, Belgium, France, Germany, the Netherlands, Spain and Switzerland). Currently (mid-2006) the project is entering its fieldwork phase.

7   Simon (2003), however, defines the 1.5 generation as children born abroad but who emigrated before the age of 10. These terms also do not appear to account for children of mixed parentage; e.g. with one foreign- and one native-born parent.

Literature

Ackers, L. and Stalford, H. (2004), *A Community for Children? Children, Citizenship and Internal Migration in the EU*. Aldershot: Ashgate.

Ahmad, F., Modood, T. and Lissenburgh, S. (2003), *South Asian Women and Employment in Britain: The Interaction of Gender and Ethnicity*. London: Policy Studies Institute.

Altbach, P. G. and Teichler, U. (2001), 'Internationalisation and exchanges in a globalised university', *Journal of Studies in International Education*, 5: 5-25.

Andall, J. (2000), *Gender, Migration and Domestic Service. The Politics of Black Women in Italy*. Aldershot: Ashgate.

Andall, J. (2002), 'Second-generation attitude? African-Italians in Milan', *Journal of Ethnic and Migration Studies*, 28: 389-407.

Anderson, B. (2000), *Doing the Dirty Work. The Global Politics of Domestic Labour*. London: Zed Books.

Anthias, F. (2000), 'Metaphors of home: gendering new migrations in Southern Europe', in Anthias, F. and Lazaridis, G. (eds.) *Gender and Migration in Southern Europe*. Oxford: Berg, 15-47.

Ayotte, W. (2000), *Separated Children Coming to Western Europe: Why They Travel and How They Arrive*. Plymouth: Save the Children UK.

Battisti, F. and Portelli, A. (1994), 'The apple and the olive tree: exiles, sojourners, and tourists in the university', in Benmayor, R. and Skotnes, A. (eds.) *Migration and Identity*. Oxford: Oxford University Press, 25-51.

Bjerén, G. (1997), 'Gender and reproduction', in Hammar, T. et al. (eds.) *International Migration, Immobility and Development*. Oxford: Berg, 219-46.

Blossfeld, H. P. and Rohwer, G. (2002), *Techniques of Event History Modeling: New Approaches to Causal Analysis*. Mahwah NJ: Lawrence Erlbaum.

Bogue, D. (1968), *Principles of Demography*. New York: Wiley.

Bolzman, C., Fibbi, R. and Vial, M. (2003), *Secondas – Secondos: le Processus d'Intégration des Jeunes Issus de la Migration Espagnole et Italienne en Suisse*. Zurich: Seismo.

Bolzman, C. Poncioni-Derigo, R., Vial, M. and Fibbi, R. (2004), 'Older labour migrants' well-being in Europe: the case of Switzerland', *Ageing and Society*, 24: 411-29.

Bottomley, G., de Lepervanche, M. and Martin, J. (eds.) (1991), *Intersexions: Gender/Class/Culture/Ethnicity*. Sydney: Allen and Unwin.

Boyd, M. (1989), 'Family and personal networks in international migration: recent developments and new agendas', *International Migration Review*, 23: 638-70.

Boyle, P., Halfacree, K. and Robinson, V. (1998), *Exploring Contemporary Migration*. London: Longman.

Brah, A. (1996), *Cartographies of Diaspora: Contesting Identities, Gender, Racism, Ethnicity*. London: Routledge.

Brettell, C. B. (2000), 'Theorizing migration in anthropology: the social construction of networks, identities, communities and globalscapes', in Brettell, C. B. and Hollifield, J. F. (eds.) *Migration Theory: Talking Across Disciplines*. New York and London: Routledge, 97-135.

Campani, G., Lapov, Z. and Carchedi, F. (2002), *Le Esperienze Ignorate: giovani migranti tra accoglienza, indifferenza, ostilità*. Milan: Franco Angeli.

Carling, J. (2002), 'Migration in the age of involuntary immobility: theoretical reflections and Cape Verdean experiences', *Journal of Ethnic and Migration Studies*, 28: 5-42.

Carlstein, T. (1982), *Time Resources, Society and Ecology: On the Capacity for Human Interaction in Space and Time*. London: George Allen & Unwin.

Carlstein, T., Parkes, D. and Thrift, N., eds. (1978), *Timing Space and Spacing Time*. London: Edward Arnold, 3 vols.

Castles, S. and Miller, M. J. (2003), *The Age of Migration*. London: Macmillan (3rd edition).

Cerase, F. P. (1974), 'Migration and social change: expectations and reality. A case study of return migration from the United States to Southern Italy', *International Migration Review*, 8: 245-62.

Clarke, N. (2004), 'Free independent travellers? British working holiday makers in Australia', *Transactions of the Institute of British Geographers*, 29: 499-509.

Constant, A. and Massey, D.S. (2003), 'Self-selection, earnings and out-migration: a longitudinal study of immigrants to Germany', *Journal of Population Economics*, 16: 631-53.

Courgeau, D. and Lelievre, E. (1989), *Analyse Démographique des Biographies*. Paris: Institut National d'Etudes Démographiques.

Crul, M. and Doomernik, J. (2003), 'The Turkish and Moroccan second generation in the Netherlands: divergent trends between and polarization within the two groups', *International Migration Review*, 37: 1039-64.

Crul, M. and Vermeulen, H. (2003), 'The second generation in Europe', *International Migration Review*, 37: 965-86.

Cwerner, S. B. (1999), *The Times of Migration. A Study of the Temporalities of the Immigrant Experience*. University of Lancaster: PhD Thesis in Sociology.

Cwerner, S. B. (2001), 'The Times of Migration', *Journal of Ethnic and Migration Studies*, 27: 7-36.

Demuth, A. (2002), 'Some conceptual thoughts on migration research', in Agozino, B. (ed.) *Theoretical and Methodological Issues in Migration Research. Interdisciplinary, Intergenerational and International Perspectives*. Aldershot: Ashgate, 21-57.

Ekbert, J. (1996), 'Labour market careers among young Finnish immigrants in Sweden', *Quarterly Review*, 34: 371-84.

Elchardus, M., Glorieux, I. and Scheys, M. (1987), 'Temps, culture et coexistence', *Studi Emigrazione*, 86: 138-54.

Faist, T. (1997), 'From common questions to common concepts', in Hammar, T. et al. (eds.) *International Migration, Immobility and Development*. Oxford: Berg, 247-76.

Fibbi, R., Kaya, B. and Piguet, E. (2003), *Le Passeport ou le Diplôme? Etude des Discriminations à l'Embauche des Personnes d'Origine Etrangère sur le Marché du Travail Suisse*. Neuchâtel: Forum Suisse pour l'étude des Migrations et de la Population.

Fibbi, R., Bolzman, C. and Vial, M. (1999), 'Italiennes et Espagnoles en Suisse à l'approche de l'âge de la retraite', *Revue Européenne des Migrations Internationales*, 15: 69-93.

Fielding, A. J. (1995), 'Migration and social change: a longitudinal study of the social mobility of immigrants in England and Wales', *European Journal of Population*, 11: 107-21.

Findlay, A. M. (2002), 'From Brain Exchange to Brain Gain: Policy Implications for the UK of Recent Trends in Skilled Migration from Developing Countries'. Geneva: *ILO International Migration Paper 43*.

Fischer, P. A., Martin, R. and Straubhaar, T. (1997), 'Should I stay or should I go?' in Hammar, T. et al. (eds.) *International Migration, Immobility and Development*. Oxford: Berg, 49-90.

Foner, N. (1979), 'West Indians in New York City and London: a comparative analysis', *International Migration Review*, 13: 284-97.

Fraser, A. (1992), *The Gypsies*. Oxford: Blackwell.

Gabaccia, D. (2000), *Italy's Many Diasporas*. London: UCL Press.

Gans, H. (1992), 'Second-generation decline: scenarios for the economic and ethnic futures of the post-1965 American immigrants', *Ethnic and Racial Studies*, 15: 173-92.

Gardner, K. (2002), *Age, Narrative and Migration: The Life Course and Life Histories of Bengali Elders in London*. Oxford: Berg.

Goss, J. and Lindquist, B. (1995), 'Conceptualising international migration: a structuration perspective', *International Migration Review*, 29: 317-51.

Gray, B. (1996), 'The home of our mothers and our birthright for ages? Nation, diaspora and Irish women', in Maynard, M. and Purvis, J. (eds.) *New Frontiers in Women's Studies*. London: Taylor and Francis, 164-87.

Green, N. L. (1999), 'The comparative method and poststructural structuralism: new perspectives for migration studies', in Lucassen, J. and Lucassen, L. (eds.) *Migration, Migration History, History: Old Paradigms and New Perspectives*. Bern: Peter Lang, 57-72.

Gustafson, P. (2001), 'Retirement migration and transnational lifestyles', *Ageing and Society*, 21: 371-94.

Gustafson, P. (2002), 'Tourism and seasonal retirement migration', *Annals of Tourism Research*, 29: 899-918.

Hägerstrand, T. (1975), 'Space, time and human conditions', in Karlqvist, A., Lundqvist, L. and Snickars, F. (eds.) *Dynamic Allocation of Urban Space*. Farnborough: Saxon House, 3-12.

Hägerstrand, T. (1982), 'Diorama, path and project', *Tijdschrift voor Economische en Sociale Geografie*, 73: 323-39.

Hammar, T. and Tamas, K. (1997), 'Why do people go or stay?' in Hammar, T. et al. (eds.) (1997) *International Migration, Immobility and Development*. Oxford: Berg, 49-90.

Hammar, T., Brochmann, G., Tamas, K. and Faist, T., (eds.) (1997), *International Migration, Immobility and Development*. Oxford: Berg.

Hondagneu-Sotelo, P. (1994), *Gendered Transitions: Mexican Experiences of Migration*. Berkeley: University of California Press.

Huber, A. (2003), *Sog des Südens. Altersmigration von der Schweiz nach Spanien am Beispiel Costa Blanca*. Zürich: Seismo.

Hugo, G. (1999), 'Key issues in international migration today', in: *Migration at the Threshold of the Third Millennium*. Vatican: Pontifical Council for the Pastoral Care of Migrants and Itinerant People, 31-63.

IOM (2002), *Trafficking in Unaccompanied Minors in the European Union*. Paris: IOM.

Jackson, J. A. (1963), *The Irish in Britain*. London: Routledge and Kegan Paul.

Kaa, D. van der (1987), 'Europe's second demographic transition', *Population Bulletin*, 42: 1-57.

Kaa, D. van der (1999), 'Without maps and compass? Towards a new European transition project', *European Journal of Population*, 15: 309-16.

Kelly, L., and Regan, L. (2000), *Rhetorics and Realities: Sexual Exploitation of Children in Europe*. London: Child and Woman Abuse Studies Unit.

King, R. (2002), 'Towards a new map of European migration', *International Journal of Population Geography*, 8: 89-106.

King, R. and Vullnetari, J. (2006), 'Orphan pensioners and migrating grandparents: the impact of mass migration on older people in rural Albania', *Ageing and Society*, 26: in press.

King, R., Warnes, A. M. and Williams, A. M. (2000), *Sunset Lives: British Retirement Migration to the Mediterranean*. Oxford: Berg.

Klinthall, M. (2003), *Return Migration from Sweden 1968-96: A Longitudinal Analysis*. Stockholm: Almqvist and Wiksell.

Kofman, E. (2004), 'Family-related migration: a critical review of European studies', *Journal of Ethnic and Migration Studies*, 30: 243-62.

Lash, S. and Urry, J. (1994), *Economies of Signs and Space*. London: Sage.

Liversage, A. (2005), *Finding a Path. Labour Market Life Stories of Immigrant Professionals*. Copenhagen: Copenhagen Business School PhD Series 34/2005.

Lucassen, L. (2004), 'Why historical comparisons matter. The integration of Poles and Turks in Germany (1870-2004)'. Paper presented at the conference *Integration of Immigrants from Turkey in Austria, Germany and Holland*, Istanbul, 27-28 February 2004.

Lucassen, L. and Penninx, R. (1997), *Newcomers: Immigrants and their Descendants in the Netherlands*. Amsterdam: Het Spinhuis.

Malmberg, G. (1997), 'Time and space in international migration', in Hammar, T. et al. (eds.) *International Migration, Immobility and Development*. Oxford: Berg, 21-48.

Manfrass, K. (1991), *Türken in der Bundersrepublik: Nordafrikaner in Frankreich. Ausländerproblematik im deutsch-französichen Vergleich*. Bonn: Bouvier.

Modood, T., Berthoud, R., Lakey, J., Nazroo, J., Virdee, S. and Beishon, S. (1997), *Ethnic Minorities in Britain: Diversity and Disadvantage. The Fourth National Survey of Ethnic Minorities*. London: Policy Studies Institute.

Murphy-Lejeune, E. (2002), *Student Mobility and Narrative in Europe: The New Strangers*. London: Routledge.

Myklebost, H. (1989), Migration of elderly Norwegians, *Norsk Geografisk Tidsskrift*, 43: 191-213.

Niekerk, M. van (2004), 'Afro-Caribbeans and Indo-Caribbeans in the Netherlands: pre-migration legacies and social mobility', *International Migration Review*, 38: 158-84.

O'Reilly, K. (2000), *The British on the Costa del Sol: Transnational Identities and Local Communities*. London: Routledge.

Pessar, P. and Mahler, S. (2003), 'Transnational migration: bringing gender' in, *International Migration Review*, 37: 812-46.

Phizacklea, A. (ed.) (1983), *One Way Ticket. Migration and Female Labour*. London: Routledge and Kegan Paul.

Phizacklea, A. (1998), 'Migration and globalisation: a feminist perspective', in Koser, K. and Lutz, H. (eds.) *The New Migration in Europe*. London: Macmillan, 21-38.

Phizacklea, A. (2003a), 'Gendered actors in migration', in Andall, J. (ed.) *Gender and Ethnicity in Contemporary Europe*. Oxford: Berg, 23-37.

Phizacklea, A. (2003b), 'Transnationalism, gender and global workers', in Morokvasic, M. et al. (eds.) *Crossing Borders and Shifting Boundaries*. Opladen: Leske + Budrich, 79-100.

Pooley, C. and Turnbull, J. (1998), *Migration and Mobility in Britain since the 18th Century*. London: UCL Press.

Portes, A. (1994), 'Introduction: immigration and its aftermath', *International Migration Review*, 28: 632-9.

Portes, A. (1997), 'Immigration theory for a new century: some problems and opportunities', *International Migration Review*, 31: 799-825.

Portes, A. and Zhou, M. (1993), 'The new second generation: segmented assimilation and its variants among post-1965 immigrant youth', *Annals of the American Academy of Political and Social Science*, 530: 74-98.

Pred, A. (1977), 'The choreography of existence: comments on Hägerstrand's time-geography and its usefulness', *Economic Geography*, 53: 207-21.

Rodríguez, V. and Egea, C. (2006), 'Return and the social environment of Andalusian emigrants in Europe', *Journal of Ethnic and Migration Studies*, 32: in press.

Rodríguez, V., Fernández-Mayoralas, G. and Rojo, F. (1998), 'European retirees on the Costa del Sol: a cross-national comparison', *International Journal of Population Geography*, 4: 183-200.

Rogers, A. (1989), 'The elderly mobility transition: growth, concentration and tempo'. *Research on Aging*, 11: 3-32.

Rogers, A. and Castro, L. J. (1981), 'Age patterns of migration: cause-specific profiles', in Rogers, A. (ed.) *Advances in Multiregional Demography*. Research Report RR-81-6, Laxenburg, Austria: International Institute for Applied Systems Analysis, 125-59.

Rogers, A. and Castro, L. J. (1986), 'Migration', in A. Rogers and F. Willekens (eds.), *Migration and Settlement*, Dordrecht: Reidel, 157-209.

Ruxton, S. (2000), *Separated Children in Europe: A Programme for Action*. International Save the Children Alliance and UNHCR.

Salih, R. (2003), *Gender in Transnationalism: Home, Longing and Belonging among Moroccan Migrant Women*. London: Routledge.

Salt, J. and Stein, J. (1997), 'Migration as a business: the case of trafficking', *International Migration*, 35: 467-94.

Schmidt, C. M. (1997), 'Immigrant performance in Germany', *Quarterly Review of Economics and Finance*, 37: 379-97.

Selman, P. (2002), 'Intercountry adoption in the new millennium: "The quiet migration" revisited', *Population Research and Policy Review*, 21: 205-25.

Simon, P. (2003), 'France and the unknown second generation: preliminary results on social mobility', *International Migration Review*, 37: 1091-1119.

Southall, H. and White, B. (1998), 'Mapping the life course: visualising migrations, transitions and trajectories', in Unwin, D. and Fisher, P. (eds.) *Case Studies of Visualisation in the Social Sciences*. Joint Information Systems Committee/ESRC Technical Report 43, 97-116.

Stark, O. (1984), 'Migration decision making: a review article', *Journal of Development Economics*, 14: 251-9.

Stark, O. (1991), *The Migration of Labour*. Oxford: Blackwell.

Thomson, A. (1999), 'Moving stories: oral history and migration studies', *Oral History*, 27: 24-37.

Tribalat, M. (1995), *Faire France. Une enquête sur les immigrés et leurs enfants*. Paris: La Découverte.

Triseliotis, J. (1993), 'Inter-country adoption: in whose best interest?', in Humphrey, M. and Humphrey, H. (eds.) *Inter-country Adoption: Practical Experiences*. London: Routledge, 119-37.

United Nations (2000), 'Replacement Migration: Is it a Solution to Declining and Ageing Populations?' New York, UN Population Division, *Working Paper 160*.

Urry, J. (2000), *Sociology beyond Society: Mobilities for the Twenty-First Century*. London: Routledge.

Vermeulen, H. (2000), 'Introduction: The role of culture in explanations of social mobility', in Vermeulen, H. and Perlmann, J. (eds.) *Immigrants, Schooling and Social Mobility: Does Culture Make a Difference?* Basingstoke: Macmillan, 1-21.

Vermeulen, H. and Penninx, R. (eds.) (2000), *Immigrant Integration: the Dutch Case*. Amsterdam: Het Spinhuis.

Warnes, A. M., Friedrich, K., Kellaher, L. and Torres, S. (2004), 'The diversity and welfare of older migrants in Europe', *Ageing and Society*, 24: 307-26.

Warnes, A.M. and Ford, R. (1995), 'Migration and family care', in Allen, I. and Perkins, E. (eds.) *The Future of Family Care*. London: Her Majesty's Stationery Office, 65-92.

Warren, C. (1999), 'Inter-country Adoption: A Social Work Perspective'. Norwich: *Social Work Monographs, No. 171*.

White, P. (2006), 'Migrant populations approaching old age: prospects in Europe', *Journal of Ethnic and Migration Studies*, 32: in press.

Wolthius, A., and Blaak, M. (2001), *Trafficking in Children for Sexual Purposes from Eastern Europe to Western Europe*. Amsterdam: ECPAT International.

Yuval-Davis, N. and Anthias, F. (eds.) (1989), *Women-Nation-State*. London: Macmillan.

Zelinsky, W. (1971), 'The hypothesis of the mobility transition', *Geographical Review*, 61: 219-49.

Zhou, M. (1997), 'Segmented assimilation: issues, controversies, and recent research on the new second generation', *International Migration Review*, 31: 975-1008.

Zontini, E. (2002a), 'Towards a comparative study of female migrants in Southern Europe: Filipino and Moroccan women in Bologna and Barcelona', *Studi Emigrazione*, 145: 107-35.

Zontini, E. (2002b), *Family Formation and Gendered Migrations in Bologna and Barcelona*. University of Sussex, DPhil thesis in Contemporary European Studies.

Zontini, E. (2004), 'Immigrant women in Barcelona: coping with the consequences of transnational lives', *Journal of Ethnic and Migration Studies*, 30: 1113-44.

10. The Multilevel Governance of Migration

Giovanna Zincone and Tiziana Caponio[1]

1. The making of migration policy: Exploration of the field

The study of the processes of policy making for immigration and immigrant incorporation should be considered as a 'young' research field; most of the research in this area consists of 'grey literature' (i.e. PhD dissertations and research reports).

Policy-making seems to represent a sort of fourth-generation research topic. *First generation* studies were essentially concerned with the demographic composition and evolution of migration flows into and immigrant stocks within European countries. *Second generation* research has focused primarily on immigrants' economic integration and their social behaviour. The *third generation* has dealt mainly with integration policies and political participation. Lastly, the *fourth generation* has tackled the problem of understanding how immigrant and immigration policies are decided upon and carried out. More recently, a new generation is starting to carry out research on the issue of the multilevel governance of immigrants and immigration.

In order to better understand multilevel governance we investigate decision making processes by adopting an analytical perspective that focuses on the following dimensions: 1) the various levels of government at which decisions are made (i.e. the central State, Regions/Länder/Cantons/federated states; provinces and more frequently – as we shall see below – municipal administrations) and the relations between these different levels of government[2], either more top-down or more bottom-up oriented; and 2) not just formal decision making processes but also semi-formal and informal ones (i.e. bottom-up pressures arising from civil society)[3]. Examples of such semi- and informal processes are the roles played by trade unions, NGOs, immigrant associations, social movements, experts and media. A bottom-up orientation includes two types of perspectives: a) inputs from lower levels to upper levels, and b) inputs from civil society to the public arena. This kind of analysis began in the late 1980s, spurred by changes in public decision making mechanisms – processes of power fragmentation and devolution to both lower levels of governments and civil society organisations (Pierre 2000; Scharpf 1993). This perspective looks to both changing patterns of public-private (and civil society) relations and to the redefinition of traditional hierarchical governing structures (Pierre 2000).

In the domain of immigration and immigrant incorporation, multi-level governance still represents a poorly investigated research object. This topic has developed unevenly in Europe both in time and in the themes that have become the focus of researchers' interest. The main factors accounting for such differences often seem to mirror aspects of the national policy making structure or machinery.

Genesis and development

The genesis of research on the making of migration policies varies considerably across European countries. In this section we present some hypotheses on the factors that may account for such differences.

The first factor that hypothetically matters is the timing of migration flows and immigrants' settlement. This accounts particularly in the case of Poland (Mazur-Rafal 2005) and Ireland (Mac Einri 2004), where immigration represents a very recent phenomenon, starting in the late 1990s, and migration studies are still essentially of a first and second generation type.[4] In other words, the timing of the immigration appears to have some impact on the maturity of migration studies. In general, these appear to be more developed and established in the countries with a longer history of immigration (i.e. France, Great Britain, Germany, Switzerland, Austria, Belgium and Sweden). Here, third-generation studies have achieved a high degree of maturity, as pointed out by classical comparative studies on citizenship rights models (Brubaker 1992; Hammar 1985 and 1990; Ireland 1992; Schnapper 1992; Soysal 1994; Wihtol de Wenden 1988).

However, we do not find a well-established *fourth*-generation literature in any of the countries mentioned above and this kind of study already represents quite a relevant research field in most of the 'new' immigration countries, such as Italy (Zincone & Caponio 2004), Spain (Morén-Alegret 2004) and Greece (Apostolatou 2004). The timing of migration flows and immigrant settlement seems sufficient to explain the case of Ireland, but other explanations are necessary in order to account for most of the other countries.

A second factor that may help to explain the varying degree of development of migration studies among different European countries might be the maturity of policy-oriented studies in political science. The policy analysis literature emerged in political science in the United States in the early 1970s as an attempt to study more closely how political systems functioned in practice, not only in theory (Howlett & Ramesh 1995; Nelson 1996; Parsons 1995). In Europe, the development of such an approach has been uneven (Nelson 1996; Parsons 1995; Peters 1995; Regonini 2001). In the Anglo-Saxon and Nordic countries, established traditions of interest intermediation and negotiation appear to have favoured the political scientist's concern for research on policy making processes. As for immigration, this seems to be the case in the Netherlands, where the first studies on immigration and integration policy making were carried out by a group of public administration and political science scholars of the University of Amsterdam (Hoppe 1987), and in Great Britain, where the first studies on the making of race relation policies were carried out in the early 1990s (see Hatton 2004).

A similar explanation seems to apply to the case of Austria (see Kraler 2004). Studies on the making of Austrian migration policies began to appear already in the mid-1980s (Matuschek 1985; Wimmer 1986; Bauböck & Wimmer 1988) in the context of political science research on labour relations and neo-corporatist arrangements. Interest in this line of research diminished shortly thereafter (in the second half of the 1990s) when social partnership entered a phase of deep crisis. However, such a hypothesis does not completely account for the cases of Germany and Sweden – two traditionally neo-corporatist countries where interest in the making of migratory policies is more recent and not primarily focused on labour relations.[5]

In most of continental Europe other academic traditions have prevailed, mirrored in the study of policy making processes (Regonini 2001). In the case of France, for instance, historical narratives have always been preferred by political scientists to model-building (Guiraudon 2004b). In Southern Mediterranean countries the policy approach is a late arrival to political science. However, the consolidation of policy analysis coincided with the consolidation of migration studies, thus favouring the relatively quick emergence of a *fourth* generation type of literature. This seems to be the case in Italy, where the policy approach started to gain momentum only in the early 1990s (Regonini 2001: 46), and was adopted by political scientists soon thereafter in order to investigate immigration-related issues as well.[6]

Another factor that may explain the emergence of the immigration literature with a policy making orientation appears to be related to academics' and experts' participation into the making of migration policy. This happened in Belgium (Lafleur 2004), France (Guiraudon 2004b), Greece (Apostolatou 2004), Italy (Zincone & Caponio 2004), the Netherlands (Penninx et al. 2005), Spain (Morén-Alegret 2004), Sweden (Widgren & Hammar 2004, Tamas 2004), Switzerland (Gerber & Cattacin 2004), and lastly Poland (Mazur-Rafal 2005), Hungary (Nyíri et al. 2001) and the Czech Republic. These same academics who had direct experience in migration policy making appear to have promoted the undertaking of studies on the decision making processes, often relying upon their direct experience as a source of data.[7]

Finally, the genesis of the literature on European level policy making processes can be related with the timing of the country's entry into the EU. In the case of Austria, researchers' attention toward European institutions in the area of migration policy started in 1995, after the country's accession to the EU (Juen et al. 1996, Perchinig 1996). In general, the EU level has gained more and more relevance after the Treaty of Amsterdam (1997) and the incorporation of immigration policy into the first pillar. This increase in significance is demonstrated by the growth of research in this field over the last five years (Geddes 2000, Guiraudon 2000, 2003 and 2004a, Monar 2001, Stetter 2000, Uçarer 2001, Di Gregorio 2004, Lahav 2004). This increase in interest has taken place even though the Treaty of Amsterdam represents only a tentative and partial step towards the communitarisation of immigration and immigrant policies. Migration flows, nationality laws, and voting rights policies have not been included in the Amsterdam first pillar, nor in the EU Convention.

As for the new EU countries such as Poland, Hungary and the Czech Republic, accession to the EU has undoubtedly influenced research on migratory policy, which in the late 1990s turned more and more to the analysis of the impact of the *acquis communautaire* on national legislations (see: Kaczmarczyk & Okólski 2002 on Poland; Boldizsár 1997, Aszalós 2001 on Hungary; Tychtl 2001 on the Czech Republic). Particularly in the case of Poland, research is attempting to figure out its future role as an EU border country.

Thematic specialisation

As mentioned above, the study of the making of migration policy has developed unevenly in Europe not only in terms of emergence but also in terms of the themes of research and problem definition. To account for differences and similarities, we can hypothesise that at least three families of factors are significant: 1) the pressure of 'problems'; 2) differences and similarities in the decision making structure in the form of state (more or less decentralized) and in the policy styles and institutional legacy in traditional minorities conflict resolution; 3) differences in the governance structure, such as the specific role played by informal and semi-formal actors and the level of governance institutionalisation, especially in the cases of neo-corporatist arrangements or representative bodies aimed at including religious minorities.

Pressure of 'problems'. Asylum policy, for instance, has received a great deal of researchers' attention in the United Kingdom (Hatton 2004), owing to the increase in the number of asylum seekers registered in this country during the 1990s. This is also the case in new EU member countries such as the Czech Republic, where the relatively high number of asylum seekers produced analyses on asylum policies (see: Pořízek 2004; Janů & Rozumek 2004), and Hungary (Béla 1997). In the case of Greece, most of the studies are concerned with regularisation measures (Apostolatou 2004). This feature can be explained by the particular evolution of migration flows towards this country, which only began in 1991 after the collapse of the Albanian communist regime and consisted almost exclusively of illegal entries. On the contrary, in the case of France, local integration policies are progressively coming under greater scrutiny, given the pressures on public schools exerted by people who are second-generation migrants (Morel 2002) and deteriorating suburbs, the so-called *banlieues* (Moore 2004). Another example is provided by the increasing attention of researchers towards public opinion, moods and attitudes on immigration. It appears that in many countries – such as Italy (Zincone & Di Gregorio 2002), Austria (Plasser & Ulram 1991 and 1992, Kuscheij & Pilgram 2002) and Switzerland (Gerber 2003) – the emergence of these attitudes have followed the electoral success of right-wing parties that hold anti-immigrant positions.

The general structure of the decision making. Differences can be detected in at least two aspects. First of all, the existing studies seem to emphasise the national or local level of governments according to the structure of the state. This is particularly evident in the case of Greece, where existing studies on decision making focus almost exclusively on the national level[8] (Apostolatou 2004), as well as in Poland (Mazur-Rafal 2005), the Czech Republic and Hungary. Studies on federalist and/or decentralised countries, on the other hand, tend to pay attention mainly to local levels – either federated states, regions or municipalities – as pointed out by the cases of Germany (Bosswick 2004), Austria (Kraler 2004), Spain (Morén-Allegret 2004) and Italy (Zincone & Caponio 2004).

The second factor that may be related to the general decision making structure is represented by national policy styles and policy legacy. Here we mean the consolidated institutional patterns of mediating conflicts with internal linguistic and religious minorities as well as with an emerging working class. In the Netherlands (Aluffi & Zincone 2004, Soysal 2004), for example, the incorporation of immigrant organisations into the pillar system, originally developed in order to accommodate the country's religious diversity, might explain the particular interest of Dutch researchers in the relations among immigrant associations, Muslim minorities and the institutional opportunity structure (Koopmans 2004, Fennema & Tillie 2004, Vermeulen 2002). Accordingly, in Austria the crucial relevance of labour relations and neo-corporatist arrangements accounts for the particular emphasis of policy making studies on the role of unions in the immigration policy field (Härpfer et al. 1992, Gächter 2000). However, in the case of France, researchers' attention has always been centred on the state Republican ideology of incorporation[9] (Guiraudon 2004b), possibly explaining why the role of minorities and social actors in decision making processes has been under-investigated.

In order to account for differences in the study of the making of immigration and immigrant policy, *the governance structure* should also be considered. The weight and relevance of informal actors varies considerably across countries, a feature of the governance model which appears to be mirrored somewhat by policy making analyses. In the case of Italy (Zincone & Caponio 2004), Germany (Bosswick 2004) and Spain (Morén-Alegret 2004) the traditional role played by third sector organisations in the provision of social services may explain the particular interest of researchers in these countries for NGO participation in migration policy making.

In the following section, we focus more directly on how the multilevel governance of immigration has been investigated so far by looking at the main studies carried out at the different levels of policy making. The third section of this essay is devoted to the description of the main theoretical models and methodological approaches that can be found in this nascent literature, detailing the specific research techniques that are employed within it.

2. The study of the multilevel governance of migration: Territorial levels and analytical perspectives

The majority of the studies on the making of immigration and immigrant policies usually focus on actors' horizontal relations in decision making processes at a specific territorial level (i.e. at a national, local or European one). However, there are also a number of studies that analyse the relations among actors at different levels. This is what we called the multilevel governance of migration policies: the *new* generation type of research in migration studies.

The analyses of multilevel governance relations have been approached from two main perspectives: top-down and bottom-up. The top-down perspective looks at policy making as a process going from higher level institutions and/or from formal policy making arenas (parliament, government, bureaucracy etc.) to lower level (peripheral) and informal social actors. The bottom-up approach is concerned with two types of processes. One type is a process going from lower levels of government to the higher ones (from local administration to the central/regional government or from nation-states to EU institutions). The second type is the process that goes from informal actors in civil society to public formal arenas (the representative and executive institutions that act as formal policymakers at the various territorial levels). Below we shall first describe studies on migration policy making that were carried out at the different territorial levels, eventually identifying those that are also concerned with the analysis of multilevel governance relations.

Given that the existing body of literature on policy making in the immigrant and immigration field is not particularly well developed, it seems reasonable to include research that did not investigate this subject directly, but nevertheless contains information that can be helpful in our study. The following section describes these indirect migration policy making studies.

Studies indirectly addressing policy making.

Three clusters of research that indirectly investigate policy making processes can be identified: explanatory policy output studies, research on the political discourse on immigration, and studies on immigrants' mobilisation and political participation.

The *first cluster (explanatory policy output studies)* consists of a set of analyses seeking to identify the main factors that explain either national or local policy outputs. Studies on *national immigrant and immigration policy*, for instance, have often highlighted external constraints, such as international agreements and EU requirements (Borrás 1995, Juen et al. 1996, Soininen 2002), or path dependency – the legacy of past policy intervention on a specific issue[10] (Bleich 2003). On the other hand, media and public opinion pressures from below have also been acknowledged, especially by British scholars in order to explain the introduction of restrictive asylum policies in the UK (Boswell 2003; Cwerner 2004; Dell'Olio 2004; Rudolph 2003).

Studies on *local policy outputs* should be considered as 'late arrivals'. Some of the more relevant ones have been carried out in the context of the UNESCO Most Metropolis Project[11], with the purpose of surveying the structure of local immigration and the policies undertaken by local governments. Drawing on these materials, Alexander (2003 and 2004) undertakes a comparative cross-city and cross-country study on 17 cities, with the purpose of explaining differences in local policy-outputs. The author explains differences in terms of local government attitudes, taking into consideration just formal decision making institutions.[12] However, the more in-depth analysis of 'policy trajectories' in Rome, Amsterdam, Birmingham and Tel Aviv enables us to understand that local government cannot be assumed to be monolithic – a unitary actor

with a consistent will. A variety of actors are involved in concretely defining immigrant policies, and some of them belong to civil society organisations. In many cases, some kind of bottom-up process (i.e. from
civil society to the public arena) can be recognised.

The *second cluster – policy framing and political discourse* – includes a
number of studies that were carried out essentially at the national level
in order to find out how political parties define the immigration issue
in their electoral manifestos and/or political programmes.[13] These studies focus on political parties that participate in formal decision making arenas (i.e. in parliament or in government) or are willing to enter
these arenas as in the case of electoral campaigns. The bulk of these
studies do not explore the relationship between parties' programmes
and propaganda, on the one hand, and political strategies, on the other.
An exception to this tendency is Zuser's study (1996) that points out
how the anti-immigrant political discourse in Austria was not an invention of Haider's Freedom Party (FPÖ), but rather a successful attempt
by the Minister of the Interior of the previous Austrian People Party
and Socialist Party government to exploit negative public opinion in order to strengthen his role in the migration policy making arena.

The *third cluster – immigrants' political participation* – is concerned
with explaining degrees and patterns of immigrants' mobilisation and
participation. Studies have also been carried out in this context in order
to assess the influence of immigrant organisations on both national
and local policy outputs.[14] This body of research focuses on a classical
informal actor, and thus looks more closely to bottom-up influences
and pressures. According to this literature, the opening of the 'institutional opportunity structure' through policies aimed at providing financial and organisational resources for immigrant associations is likely to
have a positive impact on foreigners' civic participation and on their associations[15] (Horta 2003; Soysal 2004; Fennema & Tillie 2004; Vermeulen 2002). These studies have not yet told us if highly-structured
immigrant associations are likely to play a more significant role in the
policy making process than less structured ones. By contrast, such a
question is the central concern of the research described below that directly investigates the role of immigrants in decision making processes.

The making of national migratory policies and laws

The national level is certainly the most thoroughly investigated. These
studies usually focus on policy-processes taking place in national formal arenas, such as the parliament or government. However, a small
number of studies adopt both a top-down perspective (implementation
analysis and outcome evaluation) and a bottom-up perspective (influ-

ences and pressures from civil society, informal actors and from lower administrative levels to the national one).

Many studies focus on the formal relations among high-level actors. They aim to reconstruct processes of law-making in order to investigate political parties' negotiation and coalitions on the migration issue. This is the case with the analysis carried out in Italy by Zucchini (1999) on the centre-left 1998 law, and by Colombo and Sciortino (2003) on centre-right reformation in 2002. Central bureaucracies and parliaments have also been investigated by looking primarily at high-level policy making processes. This is the case with Baldwin-Edwards and Fakiolas (1998), who show how the bureaucracies of national ministries in Greece have a clear preference for traditional structures and values. Viet (1998), however, points out a more innovative attitude in the case of France. There the bureaucracy appears to be more oriented toward renewing established institutional structures and practices in order to cope with new events and changes in the pressure made by immigrants.

Other studies are more concerned with governmental action than with parliamentary negotiation, and pay more attention to both civil society actors and local levels. Alink (2002), for example, analyses how national decision makers in the Netherlands dealt with two immigration crises – the arrival in 1985 of hundreds of Tamil asylum seekers and the case of a Turkish family threatened with repatriation after eight years of illegal residence. As pointed out by the analysis, in both cases policymakers showed a clear preference for regular policy (i.e. for the routines and the established belief system characterising that policy sector) vis-à-vis initiating reforms. However, other actors mobilised in reaction to such a conservative attitude in order to influence the outcome. Third-sector organisations and pro-immigrants activists, in particular, succeeded (at least partially) in pressuring for a redefinition of the issue. The positive solution of the Tamil crisis demonstrates the effectiveness of this pressure. Dreef (2004) takes a similar approach in her analysis of the political and administrative developments that occurred in relation to the Amsterdam garment workshops during the period from 1980-1997. She contrasts the attitudes of national decision-makers towards illegal work with the tradition of toleration that has characterised the Amsterdam administration towards such kinds of informal economic activity. However, the study shows how local government officials were not able to form a 'counter-coalition' and reach a compromise. National level decisions prevailed as a result.

Similarly, Pérez-Díaz, Álvarez-Miranda and Gonzáles-Enríquez (2001) analyse the reform of the Spanish Foreign residents Law (LO 4/2000), as well as its counter-reform (LO 8/2000) which occurred in 2000 after the Popular Party obtained absolute majority in the legislative elections. The study reconstructs the heated public debates and protests that followed the counter-reform, pointing out how this apparent policy U-turn of the Spanish government represented a move *away from* the discourse of domestic policy actors and *towards* the moods of EU policymakers.

Since the mid-1980s, an increasing number of studies have focused on experts' influence on the national policy making processes within parliamentary and governmental institutions. The research/policy making nexus has been investigated in-depth in France (Tissot 2002, Feldblum 1999), the Netherlands (Penninx 1984, 1985, 1988, 1992, 1998 and 2005), Sweden (Hammar 2004) and Belgium, where a report on this matter has been funded by the Belgian Federal Science Policy Office (Adam et al. 2004). Here again a distinction can be made between the French and Swedish studies that focus essentially on top level decision making, and the Dutch and Belgian studies that analyse more directly the influence of experts in the overall policy process.[16]

In the case of Sweden, Hammar (2004) points out that the participation of experts in policy making processes is the expression of an agreement between opposed political parties to treat migration policy in a technical, pragmatic way. French studies, on the other hand, analyse primarily the processes of policy framing and definition. Tissot (2002), for example, reconstructs the genesis of French *politique de la ville* (urban renewal policy), showing how this was strongly influenced by the views and theories of urban sociologists and social scientists in general. Feldblum (1999) on the other hand, reconstructs the 1980s debate on citizenship, pointing out how an epistemic community (i.e. the Marceau Long Commission) was able to build an extended consensus on nationality reforms and integration politics, even though reforms were not concretely brought about.

As mentioned above, studies in the Netherlands and Belgium represent an attempt to assess experts' influence in the different phases of the policy making process – from problem recognition to implementation. Penninx's (1984, 1985, 1988, 1992 and 1998) efforts have been primarily directed towards investigating the role played by researchers in Dutch policy making on immigration since the end of the 1970s, when political consensus started to emerge regarding the need to develop a consistent immigrant policy. Similarly, the Belgian study (Adam et al. 2004) is oriented towards assessing the influence of experts and research on the main phases of the policy-process (i.e. agenda setting, policy formulation and implementation) as well as examining possible ways of improving reciprocal knowledge utilisation between policymakers, academia and stakeholders.[17]

Studies on Italy by Zincone (1998) and Zincone and Di Gregorio (2002) acknowledge the crucial role played by expert committees and top-level civil servants in the long process that led to 1998 law. However, Zincone's (1998) analysis also considers bottom-up decision making processes that originate in the peripheries (i.e. when street-level bureaucrats come under pressure from civil society to adopt *contra legem* practices – especially where inclusion of undocumented immigrants in health services and children's education were concerned – which were gradually incorporated into formal public measures to the point of becoming laws). Civil society actors are particularly effective in Italy, because they constitute a strong advocacy coalition (Zincone & Di Gregorio 2002) that has proven itself to be able to take part in each phase of the policy making process. Composed primarily of Catholic third-sector organisations but including left-wing unions, lay associations and parts of the magistracy as well, such an advocacy coalition can count on a constant window of opportunity because Catholic parties are present in both left-wing and right-wing political coalitions.[18]

Bottom-up analyses aimed at reconstructing the policy networks in which mobilisation by lower-level actors results in participation in the immigration policy making arena, have also been carried out in other countries. In Greece, for example, Kiprianos et al. (2003) focus on the positions of political parties, labour unions and NGOs during the public debate on the first and second regularization bills in order to account for their influence. In Spain, Aragón Bombín (1996) analyses the first decade of foreigners legislation and acknowledges the influence of some trade unions, NGOs and immigrant associations.[19]

NGOs have been carefully investigated not only in the case of Italy (Zincone 1998; Zincone & Di Gregorio 2002), but also in Germany. An example is the study carried out by Bosswick and Bronnenmeyer (2001), who have described the ability of German voluntary organisations to interact with the government levels (from community/local to the central state) that are most resource-rich and influential in the immigration policy field. Pressures arising from social movements appear to be far more relevant in Spain and Switzerland than in Germany – particularly from the anti-racist movement, which has been successful in putting the integration issue on the political agenda and in building new cognitive frameworks (for Spain see Donaldson et al. 1998; for Switzerland see Gerber 2003).

The local level: Implementation processes and policy networks

Local authorities and institutions play a dual role in the governance of immigrants' policies. On the one hand, they are responsible for the implementation of national legislation, which is an adaptive process that implies more than simply executive activities. On the other hand, they are called upon to answer to the demands of their local societies and to initiate new policies in order to cope with these demands. This second role has been focused on only recently.[20]

The research that is directly addressing the study of local policy making reflects this dual role and can be classified into two main categories: classical implementation studies and studies that analyse local policy making as a process starting from below (i.e. from local policy networks and/or organisations in civil society that are mobilised on a specific issue).

Implementation studies are generally aimed at analysing how national laws and policies are carried out at the local level and whether or not and to what extent the stated goals are achieved. The more traditional version of these studies is represented by the pioneering analysis carried out by Selznik (1949) and the later implementation study of Pressman and Wildavsky (1973). In both cases, the purpose was to identify distortions and *implementation deficits* that might undermine the achievement of stated policy goals. In the policy analysis literature these have usually been classified as top-down studies, since the analysis moves from higher-level policy programmes and/or norms to assess if and to what extent lower levels conform to them.

This classical implementation framework has been adopted mainly – if not exclusively, as we shall see below – for the investigation of immigration policies such as procedures of regularisation and the renewal of permits. This is the case with Skordas (2000), who analyses the complications that arose during the implementation of the first regularisation programme in Greece, and with Zucchini's (1998) research on the 1995 regularisation in Italy.[21] A main finding of these studies is that administrative discretion is one of the main sources of failure in policy implementation. Fasano and Zucchini (2001), for example, point out how police headquarters (*questura*) in Italy[22] implemented the permanent stay permits (*carta di soggiorno*) that were introduced by law nr. 40/1998 in an extremely discretionary way, asking often for documents which were not explicitly mentioned by the law. The study carried out by Jawhari (2000) on the implementation of the Residence Act in Austria emphasises the power of the lowest administrative level (the implementing agency) which had an interest in preventing a system breakdown, and therefore in rejecting a large number of cases for more or less arbitrary reasons.

Local civil servants' behaviour has also been explained by looking at administrative cultures. This is the approach adopted by a number of studies carried out in France (Spire 2003), Germany (Cyrus & Vogel 2003), Greece (Psimmenos & Kassimati 2003), Italy (Triandafyllidou 2003) and the United Kingdom (Düvell & Jordan 2003). These last four[23] were aimed at determining if street-level bureaucrats' behaviour and policy frames were influenced by the late-1990s EU-level institutions' more positive view of the economic advantages of immigration. What emerges is a substantial continuity of established administrative practices, directed essentially at controlling and restricting immigrants' presence.

A small number of implementation studies have also focused on national and/or regional social integration programmes by lower tiers of government, usually municipalities. Damay (2002), for example, investigates the 'Integration-cohabitation Programme' promoted by Brussels' Region in 1990, and Pelàez, Donaldson, Gonzáles and Montardit (2002) analyse the implementation of the so-called Icària Programme (early 1990s) in Osona, Catalunia. Both programmes were launched with the purpose of empowering local governance; empirical evidence, however, points out how implementation processes engendered dynamics that led to the failure of these promoted- and sponsored-from-above policy networks.

Policy-making processes at the local level are not necessarily activated by higher-level government policy programmes. They may be looked at from a bottom-up perspective, as processes starting from below. They may be initiated within horizontal networks or by specific civil society actors and organisations that are mobilised on a particular issue.

A number of studies carried out in Italy[24] (Zucchini 1997; CeSPI 2000; Caponio 2002, 2003 and 2004; Campomori 2005), and in Germany (Bosswick & Will 2002) point out that the differences among local policy networks are particularly important for understanding differences in immigrant incorporation policies at the local level. Analyses of local policy making processes such as those carried out by Caponio (2004) for the cases of Milan, Bologna and Naples, and by Campomori (2005) for the three medium-sized cities of Vicenza, Prato and Caserta, emphasise how policy networks reflect established models of public/third sector relations.[25] The 'policy engine' appears to be more centred on local government in the cases of Bologna and Prato, but the role of third sector organisations appears to be crucial in promoting new initiatives in Milan and Vicenza.[26]

A similar approach characterises the study carried out by Bosswick and Bronnenmeyer (2001). They investigate multilevel governance relations between NGOs and the various levels of government in Germany (see earlier partof this section) and also carry out two in-depth studies of Nürnberg and Mönchengladbach. These case studies analyse city council horizontal policy networks by evaluating the local integration of services, the cooperation among the various actors (especially as far as NGOs are concerned) and the eventual coordinating or integrating role played by the city council.[27]

Studies carried out in France look at local policy networks as means of policy innovation and change: cultural difference, which is officially denied by the national republican model of immigrant incorporation, is concretely accommodated through local policy networks within which immigrant associations and cultural mediators play a crucial role (Moore 2004; Gaxie et al. 1999; Morel 2002; Wihtol de Wenden & Leveau 2001). Allasino et al. (2000) explain policy change as driven by policy entrepreneurs in their analysis of an urban crisis in a disadvantaged district of the city of Turin with a high density of foreign residents. In this specific case, the vice-major (S. Salvario) succeeded in initiating a new policy network that involved all of the concerned actors (i.e. the residents' committees, the two mosques, immigrants' representatives, the district church, the Jewish community, etc.) and in launching innovative projects.

Along with the policy networks that were mentioned above, local level studies have also attempted to assess the influence of specific categories of informal actors (i.e. immigrant associations and NGOs) in decision making processes. Research findings suggest that the influence of immigrant associations is quite variable. In a comparative research study on immigrant policies in Barcelona and Lisbon, Morén-Alegret (2002) finds that although both cities have introduced local advisory councils, the immigrant organisations that are taking part in these councils are usually co-opted actors who are funded by local administrations. By contrast, Marques (2004) points out that immigrant organisations can influence local policy making processes under two conditions: 1) if they have the right to vote in administrative elections (local franchise) and 2) if they are organisationally strong. On the one hand, voting rights give immigrant associations significant contractual power because the party in office will attempt to secure the votes of the minority population through favourable policies. On the other hand, the organisational structure is important in order to redistribute policy benefits to ethnic constituencies. A sort of 'virtuous patronage cycle' seems to be at work.

Case studies on the role of NGOs in local policy making have been carried out in the Spanish regions of Madrid (Araujo 2004), Andalusia (Dietz 2000) and Catalunia (Casey 1996 and 1998). In the last study, the role of NGOs in the elaboration of the first Catalan government plan on immigration in 1993 is analysed, while the first two analyses are more concerned with the role of NGOs in managing local level immigrant policies.

We can draw some preliminary conclusions from this very brief review of local policy making studies. One is that implementation – which is far from being just an automatic enforcement of national or regional laws and programmes – appears to be a stage in which policy goals are redefined. Another is that administrative discretion and the dynamic relations among actors might be regarded either as policy making pathologies or as positive adaptations to changing local contexts.

Additionally, bottom-up approaches show us that policy networks at the local level can involve autonomous policy action as well, and frequently promote innovation (as in the cases of France and Italy). The role and influence of immigrant associations vary considerably in the cases summarised above, but these conclusions are based on a limited sample; apart from classical studies on immigrant participation at the local level (see first part of this section), studies adopting a policy making orientation perspective are still uncommon.

The European level

In this section we limit our survey primarily to Europeanisation processes, thereby temporarily neglecting important analyses concerning the more general study of the supra-national dimension of policy making.[28] The choice of focusing on the European level is due not only to high salience, but also because it fits better into a multilevel governance perspective: it is a level which is more clearly and consistently connected with the national level and, to a certain extent, the local one. It can be more easily approached in terms of top-down and bottom-up perspectives and studied with the common instruments of the policy analysis. However, this does not mean that these instruments have been widely applied. If studies on the making of immigration and immigrant incorporation policies are 'latecomers', then studies on the Europeanisation of this policy sector are even more recent arrivals.

Two main research threads can be distinguished in the literature on the European level: 1) studies analysing processes of European integration and policy communitarisation, which are concerned with the progressive shift of policy competencies from the member states to the EU and 2) studies centred on processes of Europeanisation that deal with the impact of European norms and policies on the national ones.

In the first set of studies – those on the European integration of the migration policy field three research clusters can be identified: a) the identification of factors that explain member states' transfer of powers and functions to the EU; b) the analysis of the attempts undertaken by national governments and/or coalitions of governments to influence specific pieces of EU legislation; and c) studies aimed at assessing the role of civil society in EU policy making. These threads of literature appear to be consistent with the bottom-up perspective on multilevel governance (see above). However, the last two are still in an embryonic stage, as we shall see below.

The first group of bottom-up studies consists of a series of analytical accounts of the events that have led to the contemporary partial communitarisation of immigration and asylum policies. The communitarisation is not complete because crucial issues such as migration flows, citizenship and voting rights are still not communitarised. The aim of this group of studies is to explain why member states first agreed to cooperate and surrender at least part of their sovereignty in favour of Community institutions.

Various hypotheses and interpretations have been advanced. Guiraudon (2000 and 2002), for example, maintains that until the year 2000, the process of European integration on these issues was fundamentally driven by national European governments that have an interest in finding decision making arenas that are sheltered from the public eye and not subject to strong political control. This process, called 'venue-shopping', enables member state governments to introduce restrictive policies without having to face awkward situations of opposition. According to Guiraudon, this hypothesis is confirmed by the slow – and often more symbolic than practical – aperture to Community institutions other than the national government-representing Council.[29] Similarly, Channac (2002) points out that since the 1970s-80s, national governments have attempted to develop new supra-national arenas and decision making processes that are quite different from both the classical international organisations (more institutionalised, visible and independent from nation-states) and traditional intergovernmental cooperation, which is aimed at preserving niches of state sovereignty in new multilateral and supra-national orders. Uçarer (2001) stresses the active entrepreneurial role played by the European Commission, which was able to take advantage of a few initial 'windows of opportunity' in a context in which a specific Directorate-General on Justice and Home Affairs did not exist (until 1999) and funding from the Community budget was not available (until 1996).

According to other interpretations (Monar 2001, Stetter 2000) the main factor pushing national governments to adopt more 'communitarised' forms of decision making in the area of immigration is the poor performance of the decision making system itself. This system includes the strong procedural constraint of the unanimous vote, which has made it particularly difficult to reach decisions on highly conflictual but nonetheless relevant matters such as immigration and asylum policy.[30] The importance of 'problem' pressure (i.e. the evolution of immigration and asylum in Europe) has also been stressed by Monar (2001). The pressure exercised on governments by international criminal organisations and activities is listed as one of the 'drivers' of international cooperation. Leading ideas, namely the ideal and project of an 'area of freedom, security and justice', are another factor again singled out by Monar (2001). Once this project had been announced on a large scale and legitimised by public speeches, it became a 'steady factor of change'.

The second research thread is more concerned with analysing how individual governments or coalitions of governments have concretely influenced specific EU decisions. There are very few studies on this topic, and yet they yield interesting analyses on European-level policy making processes. Geddes (2000 and 2003), for example, points out that a strong influence is exerted on EU migratory policy by the traditional European countries of immigration (i.e. Germany, France and Great Britain). Being a traditional country of immigration gives these states greater legitimacy during Community negotiations and provides a larger and more authoritative legislative background and set of policy instruments, thereby making it possible for them to steer – if not determine – Community political strategies. Di Gregorio (2004) explains the minimal influence of Italy in EU policy making as a consequence of a lack of a coherent 'spoils strategy' that is demonstrated by the fact that the country has appointed only a few high-level functionaries and temporary experts.

Contrary to the literature on the national and local levels that was examined above, informal actors at the European level have been poorly investigated up to this point. Furthermore, the findings of EU-level studies are contradictory. According to Lahav (2004), the most conspicuous informal actors have been mostly promoted, co-opted and controlled by the national governments. On the contrary, in two recent pieces of research, Guiraudon (2003, 2004a) points out that, at a certain point in the evolution of immigration and asylum policies in the European Union, a sort of coalition that favoured integration policies coalesced that included not only the EU Commission but also pro-migrant NGOs. This alliance began to oppose the EU Council's restrictive orientation. However, Favell and Geddes (1999) say that the role played by the pro-migrant lobbies has been limited and was not the result of mass mobilisation, but of an elite pressure group that included the epistemic community of researchers. Civil society and public opinion are rarely taken into account in this second group of studies.[31]

Analyses of the processes of Europeanisation, which are concerned with the application of European norms at a national level, adopt essentially a top-down perspective. Studies adopting this perspective are less numerous than the one previously mentioned. Two comparative works (Geddes 2003; Bigo & Guild 2003) and five case studies (Martiniello & Rea 1997; Vink 2002; Di Gregorio 2004; Guiraudon 2004a; Calvès 2002) seem to have initiated this research path. The Belgian (Martiniello & Rea 1997), Dutch (Vink 2002) and (especially) the Italian case[32] (Di Gregorio 2004) demonstrate that, at least in these countries, migration policies are highly conditioned by European developments. In the French case, Calvès (2002) shows that even though parliamentarians were able to circumvent the most problematic issues in the transposition of the 2000 EU 'race directive', the impact of the EU on migration policy-frames was still effective in a subtle way. Evidence of this effectiveness are the soft norms and managerial concepts that have pervaded French race relations policy since that time (i.e. mainstreaming, monitoring). What emerges from these works is that the communitarisation of immigration policies has produced considerable impacts on the national political systems, even in periods when Community decisions were non-binding and cooperation in the Council was only of the intergovernmental type.[33]

In sum, our review indicates that the literature on the EU level is clearly dominated by works that fall within the field of theories of European integration, while there is still little research that could be truly defined as studies of the process of Europeanisation.[34] In the first group of studies, the great majority of existing work is still aimed at identifying the main factors that account for states' cooperation and integration. Research that analyses bottom-up influences arising from specific governments and/or civil society actors, thereby looking more in-depth at multilevel governance relations, are still in a nascent phase. Completely absent are attempts to ask the question whether there is an ongoing spontaneous process of convergence among EU member states that is driven by diffusion, and to see which factors could possibly promote or discourage this process.

3. Approaches in the study of the multilevel governance of migration: theories, methods and research techniques

The large majority of the studies surveyed above do not refer to explicit theoretical frameworks and perspectives. Concerning methodology, case studies prevail and there is a clear preference for qualitative research techniques. These features are very much in accordance with the more general orientation that characterises policy studies literature.[35] Here we shall come back to some of the studies mentioned above in order to highlight the main – even if often implicit – theoretical approaches underlying this nascent literature.

First of all, *system analysis* appears to underlie studies on national policy making that distinguish between different decision making and implementation phases, each one having a specific function and involving different actors. The policy-cycle approach is adopted explicitly in Adam et al.'s (2004) study on the research/policy nexus in Belgium. This work has the purpose of assessing the function and impact of experts in each phase of the policy making process. Also, Zincone and Di Gregorio (2002) adopt a system analysis framework and combine it with the advocacy coalition framework[36] in order to better account for the different actors taking part in each phase of the decision making process. A number of studies carried out by Penninx (1984, 1985, 1988, 1992 and 1998) are based on the policy-cycle metaphor but adopt a more long-term perspective, looking at the evolution of experts' participation in the Dutch policy making process over a period of 30 years. System analysis is present in all of the theses that consider 'problems' pressure and the negative feedback of previous decisions in explaining both policy changes and possible convergences between progressive and conservative parties or party coalitions (Zincone & Di Gregorio 2002).

A considerable number of studies adopt some kind of cultural explanation of policy making processes. Two different meanings of culture seem to emerge: 1) the *strong version* that considers cultures to be coherent systems of norms and beliefs that strongly influence individual actors; and 2) the *soft version* that looks at the policy frames that guide actions and learning processes. An example of the first type is represented by research on the administrative cultures of street-level bureaucrats (Cyrus & Vogel 2003; Psemmenos & Kassimati 2003; Triandafyllidou 2003; Düvell & Jordan 2003) that was aimed at revealing how market-oriented policy principles and relatively open borders might find resistance in already consolidated belief systems that are traditionally concerned with law and order, immigration control and restriction. On the other hand, a soft culturalist approach appears to underlie studies that explain public policy making as processes aimed first at building policy-frames – problem definitions that, once agreed upon by the concerned actors, are assumed to influence the identification of possible policy instruments. By contrast, a discrepancy between change in the conceptualisation of the issue and relative continuity in policies has been observed in Italy (Zincone 2006).

A soft cognitive approach centred on policy learning also lies behind studies of local policy networks as drivers of policy change in France. In order to accommodate cultural difference, these networks have included immigrant associations and cultural mediators, thereby opening up the traditional republican approach to innovative experimentation (Morel 2002; Gaxie et al. 1999; Moore 2004).

Neo-institutionalist perspectives, on the other hand, put a particular emphasis on path dependence and policy legacy. This seems to be the case with the studies that show how, especially at a local level, immigration and/or immigrant incorporation policies are shaped more by established actors' relations and local institutional arrangements than they are by general strategies that are embedded in programmes or laws decided by higher levels of government (Zucchini 1998; Fasano & Zucchini 2001; Damay 2002) or political majorities (Caponio 2004). The role of path dependence and policy legacy has been underlined in the making of nationality laws (Brubaker 1999; Zincone 2005).

Finally, quite a number of studies adopt a rational action paradigm such as rational choice, public choice, or game theory. In the case of Germany, for example, NGOs are often regarded as strategic actors who are able to identify and put pressure on the more fruitful levels of government in terms of resources and influence in the immigration policy field (Bosswick & Bronnenmeyer 2001). According to Crowley (1999: 23), xenophobic right is too strong to be ignored by any government, but too weak to govern. This theory leads to the assumption that a conservative party can incorporate xenophobic attitudes, but it cannot be excessive if it wants to maintain a good coalition potential. In addition to parties and conservative coalitions, progressive coalitions can also take decisions that restrict immigrants' inflows or their rights because of the influence of anti-immigrant public opinion and the fear of losing elections (Hansen 2000). The illusion of recovering approval leads centre-left coalitions to take measures when elections are approaching, while right-wing leaders can increase their chances to lead conservative coalitions directly by voicing pro-immigrant attitudes – thereby positioning themselves at the centre. Both the centre-left and the centre-right use rhetoric inspired by law and order, whereas – at the same time – they approve mass regularisations in order to balance the need of satisfying the electors' anti-immigrant attitudes with the need of responding to pressures from the alignment by pro-immigrant advocacy coalitions and entrepreneurs (Zincone 2006). According to Freeman's point of view (1995), which follows a classic thesis by Edelman (1964), governments are inclined to keep the borders not totally closed and to promote immigrants' rights because the advantages of policies in favour of immigrants are selective (pro-immigrant groups and entrepreneurs), while costs are diffusive – they fall on all of the citizens.

Bureaucracies have been regarded as interest-oriented actors, exploiting margins of discretion in order to avoid the risks of system breakdown and work overload (Jawhari 2000).

Some of the approaches mentioned above come in other guises, such as in analyses of European policy making where at least three theoretical perspectives can be singled out: *intergovernmental, neofunctionalist* and *governance*.[37] *Intergovernmentalism* can be linked to rational choice and game theory, since the focus is on the utilitarian strategies of national governments, and is highlighted in the studies carried out by Guiraudon (2000) and Channac (2002). *Functionalism* can be linked to systemic/functionalist analysis (answers to 'problem' pressures and to negative feedback of the previous decision making cycle) and to neo-institutional analysis (path dependence, the importance of accommodating new models of governance and new institutions to the old ones). The analyses of Monar (2001) and Stetter (2000) mentioned above can be located in this cluster.

The multilevel governance perspective is focused on the relations among actors. Examples are provided by the few existing studies that are aimed at identifying bottom-up influences arising from a) national governments or coalitions of governments (Geddes 2000 & 2003; Di Gregorio 2004) and b) civil society actors (Lahav 2004; Guiraudon 2003 & 2004).

This brief review suggests that the use of the main conceptual tools of policy analysis such as policy cycles, policy network, policy entrepreneur, path dependency, etc., is gaining more and more ground in this nascent literature. What appears to be still lacking is a more aware and direct relation with mainstream policy-analysis research, which would situate the study of the making of migration policy in clearer theoretical frameworks.

Some steps forward could be taken eventually in the direction of a more systematic use of comparative research. Even though comparison (both diachronic and synchronic) is gaining ground, synchronic comparison usually deals with cross-city comparison within a specific country, and only rarely with cross-country comparison (especially as far as the literature on local policy making is concerned). The combined cross-country and cross-city comparison is far less common. This is a promising exercise, which appears to be useful for determining to what extent local decision making processes are conditioned by the specific national legal system and which kinds of similarities and dissimilarities can be detected *ceteris paribus*.

Finally, regarding research tools, a clear prevalence of qualitative techniques emerges from the analysis of the literature. Common examples of these techniques are in-depth semi-structured interviews with key actors and/or observers and the analysis of documents (especially of parliamentary proceedings and other official documents). Studies on street-level bureaucracy have also relied on participant observation in order to get a better understanding of civil servants' practices and attitudes towards immigration. However, there are other research tools that might contribute to and enrich the reconstruction of policy processes. Opinion polls and newspaper and media analysis, which are quite well established in immigration studies, could be reoriented to find out the actual capacity of the media to influence the decision making process.[38]

4. Conclusive remarks

The study of the multilevel governance of migration has already produced interesting findings and raised research questions that deserve
to be further developed and investigated. In this review we have em-
phasised the innovative perspective of the studies that have dealt with
this governance, since they proved capable of revealing the informal actors and procedures that lie behind formal decisions and decisions makers. However, a one-sided governance analysis may also lead to disregard of two important elements of policy making processes: formal
competence and rules that deeply influence actors' relations and policy
making processes (what we define as the *decision making structure*) on
the one hand; and changes and consequent challenges coming from
the environment, such as international crises, political challenges and
economic and demographic constraints.

A future research agenda on the multilevel governance of migratory
policies has to take seriously into consideration these possible risks. In
order to overcome them, we suggest three strategies:

1. A shift back towards taking into account features and possible
   changes in the *formal distribution of competencies among different institutions*. Special attention should be paid to the building of ad hoc
   departments, offices and commissions directly dealing with immigration issues at different levels of governments. Even more relevant for the making of immigration and immigrants' policies could
   be redistributions of competencies and power among bodies between different levels of governance.
2. A *further step towards systems analysis*, which might prove useful to
   detect possible external factors influencing policy making processes.
3. *Interdisciplinary collaboration* of lawyers, economists, demographers
   and international relations scholars; this will lead to more attention
   to external constraints such as rules and laws on the one hand, and
   market demands, international events and terrorism threats on the
   other.

Such emphasis on formal policy making structures and external pressures does not imply, however, an abandonment of the governance approach. On the contrary, a future agenda should entail a *reinforcement
of the bottom-up perspective* by focusing more on the relations between
formal and informal actors. *At the EU level*, the role of both *specific
member states' governments* and *civil society* actors needs to be further
analysed. Furthermore the role of *civil servants* should be a priority in
research on EU policy making processes. As for *the civil society actors
who are mobilised on the immigration issue, immigrant associations* –
whose role is still uncertain – and *social movements* in general, should

be more carefully investigated. Social movements have been studied only incidentally in Spain (Morén-Alegret 2004) and Switzerland (Gerber & Cattacin 2004).

Finally, another under-researched area is the *analysis of the relations between different levels of government*. With some exceptions (see the cases of Italy and Germany), the interplay between different levels of government in decision making processes on immigrant and immigration is still poorly investigated. This is the case, even though this domain appears to be crucial in order to better understand the governance of migration policy.

As for methodology, in view of the present prevalence of national case studies in research, an important step forward lies in systematic cross-national comparisons. In doing so, two points should be stressed.

1. Both *diachronic and synchronic comparisons* would doubtless help in reinforcing the empirical dimension of this body of literature, thereby enabling better-grounded analyses and possibly generating a truly cross-national debate on the making of migration policy. Diachronic comparison is particularly useful to shed light on continuities and ruptures in policy making processes. On the other hand, synchronic cross-country and cross-city comparisons have proven to be useful in acquiring a better understanding of how European national and local societies deal with the immigration issue.

2. *Greater attention to different variables influencing public policies* (such as population, immigrant presence, per capita income, etc.) is likely to enrich considerably this emerging research field when comparing towns of different size.

Finally, on a more prescriptive plan, the research review points out the problematic nature of the so-called research-policy nexus (Penninx et al. 2004; La Fleur 2004). Martiniello (2004), for instance, has underlined that policymakers often select researchers and studies according to their own political priorities, and that the risk of being used as a legitimising instrument is difficult to avoid. Policy evaluation (especially of policy making processes) may be useful in improving policy implementation and – as far as the field of immigration is concerned – in escaping from ideological impasses and promoting more pragmatically-oriented policy interventions. Therefore, *policy evaluation* can represent an important *fifth generation* development for immigration and immigrants studies. Such a new generation of studies may help policy to learn and revise itself, provided that it is scientifically strong enough to resist immediate political needs and demands. In doing so, the IMISCOE network might offer a concrete platform for improving dialogue between researchers and policymakers at large, by involving not only

politicians but also public officers and private sector workers and organisations who are involved in the formulation and implementation of
concrete policies and practices.

Notes

1   This chapter is based on an extended version compiled by Zincone et al. (2004), and
     presented to the first Annual IMISCOE conference held in Coimbra, 34 December
     2004. It relies upon the contributions of researchers from all over Europe, both
     affiliated and not affiliated to IMISCOE institutions, who have been asked to deliver
     Country Reports on the state of the art of this literature in their countries. Country
     Reports have been delivered on: Austria (Kraler 2004), Belgium (Lafleur 2004),
     France (Guiraudon 2004b), Germany (Bosswick 2004), Greece (Apostolatou 2004),
     Ireland (Mac Einri 2004), Italy (Zincone & Caponio 2004), the Netherlands
     (Penninx et al. 2005), Portugal (Oliveira, Malheiros and Fonseca 2004), Spain
     (Morén-Alegret 2004), Switzerland (Gerber & Cattacin 2004) and the United
     Kingdom (Hatton 2004). We received helpful suggestions on Scandinavia from
     Elena Dingu-Kyrklund, on Poland from Monica Mazar-Rafal, on Hungary from
     Endre Sik, and on the Czech Republic from Marek Canek. We are grateful also to
     Catherine Wihtol de Wenden and to Ellie Vasta.
2   See the so-called *intergovernmental relations* school, concerned with changing patterns
     of previously hierarchical relations (Hollingsworth et al. 1994, Kooiman 1993,
     Scharpf 1993 and 1997).
3   See the *interest intermediation school*, that focuses essentially on horizontal relations
     between public on the one hand, and private and third sector organisations on the
     other (Rhodes 1996 and 1997, Marsh 1998).
4   The timing also plays a role in the Czech Republic, though the generations of
     research identified above cannot be totally applied. It has been noted that imported
     concepts (such as multiculturalism) have sometimes preceded the developing of
     migration flows (see Baršová 2005). The same seems to hold true for Hungary,
     where research on immigration has steadily developed in the late 1990s, moving
     from *first generation* to more policy oriented studies (see for instance: Fullerton et al.
     1997).
5   For the German case, see Bosswick (2004). In the case of Sweden, research on policy
     making has essentially developed in the context of increasing disillusionment
     towards national integration policies which are formally aimed at achieving equality,
     freedom of choice and partnership (Westin & Dingu-Kyrklund 2003).
6   Zincone & Caponio (2004) have pointed out that the first studies explicitly
     investigating Italian policy making date back to 1998 (see also: Zincone 1998,
     Zucchini 1999).
7   This is not the case in the United Kingdom, where a lack of reflexive observation has
     been pointed out (Hatton 2004) despite the significant participation by researchers
     as actors in British policy making and implementation.
8   The only exception is the study carried out by Psimmenos & Kassimati (2003) on the
     implementation of the first regularisation law in Athens (see section 2.2). However,
     this study adopts a clear top-down approach, looking at how street-level bureaucrats
     conform to – or depart from – national directives.
9   For an appreciation of the republican assimilationist model as compared with the
     English pluralist and the German ethnic ones, see Schnapper 1992.

10 Bleich (2003), for instance, has undertaken a comparative investigation on race politics in France and the United Kingdom, and has pointed out how the British race relations system and French antiracist legislation stem from different sources (the US model in the former and the negative legacy of Vichy and the Nazi era in the latter).

11 See: www.unesco.org/most/p97. A similar cross-city/cross-country comparison is the one carried out by Ethnobarometer (2003).

12 Attitudes are reconstructed only through the observation of policy outputs, not through an analysis of policy making processes.

13 See, for example, Hagelund (2003) on the Norwegian Progress Party, De Witte & Klandermans (2000) on extreme right-wing parties in Flanders and the Netherlands, Celeya (1997) on the 1996 electoral speeches of the Socialist and Popular parties in Spain, Oliveira (2000) on Portuguese governmental elite discourse on 'cultural affinity' and Fermin (1999) on the changing viewpoints on multi-ethnic society and minorities' policy of Dutch political parties between 1977 and 1995.

14 These appear to be particularly developed at a local level, where a wide array of participation instruments has been put forward by European cities during the 1980s and 1990s (Vertovec 1999). For a cross-local and cross-national analysis, see Koopmans' (2004) broad study of the involvement of migrants and ethnic minorities in public debates and mobilisation in Germany, the United Kingdom and the Netherlands.

15 However, Boussetta (2000) contends that immigrants' political participation can be understood by looking at institutional channels alone and emphasises the internal differentiation and divides within ethnic communities at both the level of strategy and identity in his study of Muslim representation in Belgium cities.

16 As for new EU member countries, the role of researchers in the migratory policy making has been recently addressed in the Czech Republic (Uherek 2004). In Hungary academics appear to be deeply involved in the debate on the reform national legislation (Nyíri, Tóth & Fullerton 2001), but analytical accounts on their role are lacking.

17 However, Martiniello (2004) contends that, given the highly contentious and politically sensitive nature of migration-related issues, elected politicians holding executive offices are often particularly careful to select the research projects that may be directly useful in terms of policy making.

18 Catholic NGOs have also proven to be crucial in the decision making processes that led to the centre-right Bossi-Fini law. According to Zincone (2002), they succeeded in putting pressure on small Catholic parties in order to soften up the more radical anti-immigrant programs of the Northern League.

19 As for an account on the role of associations on integration and citizenship policies in France, see: Wihtol de Wenden & Leveau 2001.

20 Ireland is an exception (Mac Einri 2004). It has a highly centralised public administration, and, contrary to other European countries, no process of local/regional empowerment has been undertaken. This relative lack of power and resources seems to explain the lack of local immigration and integration policies.

21 This study focuses on two different cities (Turin and Brescia) and highlights two different ways of solving the ambiguities of national regulations. In Turin, the *Questura* (Police Headquarters) organised regular meetings with the municipal Immigration Office, unions and third-sector organisations in order to agree upon a common understanding of regularisation procedures. In the case of Brescia, the process was far more fragmented because there was no established collaboration between the *Questura* and the other actors who were interested in immigrant rights.

22 The study was carried out in three medium-sized cities in the Lombardy Region (Brescia, Sesto S. Giovanni (near Milan) and Busto Arsizio near Varese).

23 These have been published in a special issue of the *Journal of Ethnic and Migration Studies* that was edited by Jordan, Stråth & Triandafyllidou (2003).

24 See also the Cluster C9 Country Report on Italy (Zincone & Caponio 2004).

25 However, according to Caponio (2002 and 2004), elected politicians also play a role, at least at the beginning of their mandate when they need to consolidate consensus around the definition of the immigration issue that was promoted during the electoral campaign. On the contrary, Campomori (2005) places greater emphasis on *policy frames*, which reflect on the one hand, administrative structures and routines (the organizational dimension), and consolidated models of public-private interaction and influence relations (political dimension) on the other.

26 In the cases of Naples and Caserta, third-sector organisations are usually the only ones that are mobilised on the issue, with only a minor involvement on the part of the local administration. In Naples, this situation has started to change, at least partly, since 1995 (Caponio 2004).

27 See also Bosswick & Will (2002), where the authors explain differences in the integration measures implemented in eleven Hessian cities by looking at various factors, such as local administrations' organisational aspects; the economic, demographic and ethnic situation; and the actors mobilised in the local immigration policy field.

28 As mentioned in the introduction, studies on supranational and transnational policy making are very few, and often are more concerned with policy outputs than with policy processes. In other words, while there are studies that attempt to assess the impact of international laws on national migratory policies (see for instance: Soysal 1994 and Joppke 1999), they do not usually analyse the mechanisms through which such an impact is produced.

29 Another work by Guiraudon (2002) confirms that this system is dominated by the governments of the member states and above all by the structures of the home affairs ministries.

30 According to Monar (2001), consciousness of such procedural constraints first emerged in the so-called 'laboratories' (i.e. the Council of Ministers of the European Union, the Trevi Group and the Schengen system) – decision making arenas in which, in his opinion, the foundations were laid for what later become the community *acquis* in Justice and Home Affairs.

31 When it does happen, two contrasting theses emerge – one being top-down and the other bottom-up oriented. According to the first of these (McLaren 2001) national elites are able to mould and redirect the perceptions and attitudes of their political communities of reference on immigration and asylum. By contrast, Lahav (2004) maintains that political influence goes in the opposite direction: it is pubic opinion that strongly conditions government choices and that this explains the clear prevalence of restrictive policies that are driven by mass identity orientations and defensive attitudes. However, a similar analysis of public opinion carried out by Kessler and Freeman (2003) provides different evidence and shows a tendency towards an openness to foreigners throughout Europe, more or less.

32 The greatest impact on Italy is also confirmed by the research conducted by Geddes (2003) in which one can see that the countries of Southern and Eastern Europe have been the ones most influenced by community orientations.

33 EU influence has been carefully investigated in new member countries, since accession to the Union implied the adoption and implementation of the *acquis com- munautaire* as a whole without derogations. Case studies have been carried out in Po- land (Iglicka et al. 2003), Hungary (Béla 1997, Boldizsár 1997) and the Czech Repub-

lic (Drbohlav 2001, 2003 and 2004, Barša 2004). For more detailed analyses including also the cases of Estonia and Slovenia see: Nyíri et al. 2001.

34   This confirms a trend that is common to all of the policy sectors that are already communitarised in some way. The theoretical corpus on European integration has a solid tradition (starting from the 1950s-'60s), while that on Europeanisation has seen significant growth only recently. This asymmetry is linked primarily to the history and evolution of the Union's political system and its relationship with its member states. It is thus understandable that the first thread of studies to develop has been the one that aims to explain the processes that have led (and lead) member states to progressively transfer (or not to transfer) parts of their sovereignty in migration and asylum matters to the EU. It is only later that the thread that seeks to comprehend the impact of community decisions and policies on the member states has developed.

35   However, recourse to quantitative tools is not excluded in the policy-analysis literature. Wildavsky (1979), for example, speaks of the 'art and craft of policy analysis' to stress that different research techniques might prove to be useful in serving the researcher's needs.

36   See Sabatier & Jenkins-Smith (1993) for more on this concept.

37   It might be useful to recall briefly the fundamental hypotheses that form the basis of these approaches. Neo-functionalism (Holland 1993, Schmitter 1996) hinges on the two concepts of incrementalism and the spill-over effect. It postulates that, thanks to the political action of the European Commission (often allied with national and supra-national interests and pressure groups), European integration is a process that develops gradually but in an irreversible manner. This is the case because each time that a transfer of sovereignty from the national to the community level occurs in a specific sector, it brings new needs that induce further transfers upwards (the spill-over effect). Intergovernmentalism (Milward 1992, Moravcsik 1991 and 1993) upholds instead the thesis that European integration has occurred and occurs only because it is considered to be advantageous by the nation states. This means that 'the community system has been accepted so far by national governments only in that it has enabled them to strengthen rather than weaken their control over home affairs' (Moravcsik 1993: 507). The multilevel governance approach has developed as an alternative to the two cited above, and was elaborated only in the late 1990s (Marks et al. 1996, Hix 1998). The objective of this approach is to avoid considering European integration as necessarily a zero-sum game in which the winner (whether it is the EU or the member states) takes all. On the contrary, the EU is depicted as a 'non-hierarchical, regulatory and deliberative model of governance' (Hix 1998).

38   An interesting way of looking to the newspapers is demonstrated by Statham & Guiraudon (2004) in their attempt to assess the relevance of the European versus the national public arenas on the immigration issue by analysing the relevance assigned to the two venues by national newspapers.

Literature

Adam, I., P. Balancier, M. Brans, E. Florence, D. Jacobs, M. Martiniello, A. Rea, M. Swyngedouw & T. Van der Straeten (2004), *Recherches et Politiques Publiques: le cas de l'immigration en Belgique*. Gent: Academia Press.

Alexander, M. (2003), 'Local policies toward migrants as an expression of Host-Stranger relations: a proposed typology', *Journal of Ethnic and Migration Studies*, 29 (3): 411-430.

Alexander, M. (2004), 'Comparing local policies toward migrants: an analytical framework, a typology and preliminary survey results', in R. Penninx, K. Kraal, M. Martiniello & S. Vertovec, *Citizenship in European Cities. Immigrants, Local Politics and Integration Policies*. Ashgate: Aldershot.

Alink, F. (2002), 'Coping with crises in Dutch immigration policy: the impact of crisis management on the outcome of crisis', paper presented at the *ECPR Joint Sessions*, Turin 22-27th April 2002.

Allasino, E., L. Bobbio & S. Neri (2000), 'Crisi urbane: che cosa succede dopo? Le politiche per la gestione della conflittualità legata all'immigrazione', *Polis*, 13 (3).

Aluffi, R. & G. Zincone (2004), *The Legal Treatment of Islamic Minorities in Europe*. Leuven: Peeters.

Apostolatou, A. R. (2004), *Immigrant and immigration policy making. The case of Greece*, IMISCOE Working Paper/ Country Report. http://www.imiscoe.org/working papers.

Aragón Bombín, R. (1996), 'Diez años de política de inmigración', *Migraciones*, 0: 45-59.

Araujo, S. (2004), *Gobernando a distancia: el papel de las ONG en la gestión de la integración de inmigrantes*, paper presented at the *IV Congreso sobre Inmigración en España*. Girona: Catalan public universities.

Aszalós, Z. (2001), *Hungary*, in P. Nyíri, J. Tóth & M. Fullerton (eds.), *Diasporas and Politics*, 181-205. Budapest: Institute for Political Science of the Hungarian Academy of Sciences.

Baldwin-Edwards, M. & R. Fakiolas (1998), 'Greece: The Contours of a Fragmented Policy Response', in M. Baldwin-Edwards & J. Arango (eds.), *Immigrants and the Informal Economy in Southern Europe*, 186-204. London: Class.

Barša, P. (2004), *Managing Immigration and Integration in Europe and in the Czech Republic*, www.policy.hu/barsa/Final_Research_Paper_html.html

Baršová, A. (2005), 'Integrace přistěhovalců v Evropě: od občanské integrace k multikulturalismu', paper presented at the *conference Current disputes over multiculturalism*, 24 January 2005. http://aa.ecn.cz/img_upload/9e9f2072be82f3d69e3265f41fe9f28e/ABarsova_Integrace_pristehovalcu_v_Evrope.pdf.

Bauböck, R. & H. Wimmer (1988), 'Social Partnership and "Foreigners Policy"', *European Journal of Political Research*, 16: 659-681.

Béla, J. (1997), 'The Management and Regulation of Refugee Affairs in Hungary in View of Accession to the European Union', in M. Fullerton, E. Sik & J. Tóth (eds.), *From Improvisation toward Awareness? Contemporary Migration Politics in Hungary*, Budapest: Institute for Political Science of the Hungarian Academy of Sciences.

Bigo, D. & E. Guild (2003), 'La mise à l'écart des étrangers. Les effets du Visa Schengen', *Culture et conflits*, double special issue, 49-59.

Bleich, E. (2003), *Race Politics in Britain and France: Ideas and Policymaking since the 1960s*. Cambridge: Cambridge University Press.

Boldizsár, N. (1997), 'The Acquis of the European Union Concerning Refugees and the Law in the Associated States', in M. Fullerton, E. Sik & J. Tóth (eds.), *From Improvisation toward Awareness? Contemporary Migration Politics in Hungary*, Budapest: Institute for Political Science of the Hungarian Academy of Sciences.

Borrás, A. (ed.) (1995), *Diez años de la Ley de Extranjería: Balance y Perspectivas*. Barcelona: Fundación Paulino Torras Doménech.

Bosswick, W. (2004), 'Immigrant and immigration policy making. The case of Germany', country report presented at the *first IMISCOE Annual Conference*, Coimbra, 3-4 December 2004.

Bosswick, W. & V. Bronnenmeyer (2001), *Integrationsmaßnahmen der Wohlfahrtsverbände. Gutachten für die Unabhängige Kommission 'Zuwanderun'*. Berlin: Bundesministerium des Inneren.

Bosswick, W. & G. Will (2002), *Integrationsangebote in ausgewählten hessischen Kommunen und ihre institutionelle Umsetzung*. Wiesbaden: Hessisches Sozialministerium.

Boswell, C. (2003), 'Burden-Sharing in the European Union: Lessons from the German and UK Experience', *Journal of Refugee Studies*, 16 (3): 316-335.

Boussetta, H. (2000), 'Institutional theories of immigrant ethnic mobilisation: relevance and limitations', *Journal of Ethnic and Migration Studies*, 26 (2).

Brubaker, R. (1992), *Citizenship and Nationhood in France and Germany*. Cambridge, MA: Havard University Press.

Calvès, G. (2002), '"Il n'y a pas de race ici"'. Le modèle français à l'épreuve de l'intégration européenne', *Critique internationale*, 17.

Campomori, F. (2005), 'Integrare l'immigrato? Politiche di accoglienza a Vicenza, Prato e Caserta', in T. Caponio & A. Colombo (eds.), *Stranieri in Italia. Migrazioni globali, integrazioni locali*, 235-266. Bologna: Il Mulino.

Caponio, T. (2002), 'Policy networks e immigrazione. Il caso delle politiche sociali a Milano e a Napoli', in A. Colombo & G. Sciortino (eds.), *Assimilati ed esclusi. Stranieri in Italia*, 253-282. Bologna: Il Mulino.

Caponio, T. (2003), 'Politiche locali per gli immigrati e innovazione istituzionale. Il caso dell'Isi del Comune di Bologna', *Polis*, 17 (2): 257-282.

Caponio, T. (2004), 'Immigrazione, politica e politiche. I casi di Milano, Bologna e Napoli', *Rivista Italiana di Politiche Pubbliche*, 1: 23-55.

Casey, J. (1996), 'El papel de las organizaciones no gubernamentales en la elaboración de políticas públicas. El caso de la integración de inmigrantes extranjeros en Cataluña', *Dossiers Barcelona Associacions*, 20, Ajuntament de Barcelona.

Casey J. (1998), *Non-Government Organizations (NGOs) as Policy Actors: The Case of Immigration Policies in Spain*, PhD Thesis, Departament de Ciencia Política i de Pret Públic, Universitat Autònoma de Barcelona.

Celaya, C.N. (1997), 'La política en la frontera: inmigración y partidos políticos en España durante 1996', *Migraciones*, 2: 27-57.

CeSPI (2000), 'Migrazioni e politiche locali: l'esperienza italiana nel quadro europeo', in Agenzia Romana per la preparazione del Giubileo (ed.), *Migrazioni. Scenari per il XXI secolo*, dossier di ricerca, Roma, 2.

Channac, F. (2002), 'The evolution of international decision making processes concerning migrations. A comparison between formal and informal multilateral fora', paper presented at the workshop 'Immigration policies: between centre and periphery, national states and the EU'at the *ECPR Joint Sessions*, Turin, 22-27 April 2002.

Colombo, A. & G. Sciortino (2003), 'La legge Bossi-Fini: estremismi gridati, moderazioni implicite e frutti avvelenati', in J. Blondel & P. Segatti (eds.), *Politica in Italia. I fatti dell'anno e le interpretazioni*, 195-215. Bologna: Il Mulino.

Crowley, J. (1999), 'The Politics of Belonging: Some Theoretical Considerations', in A. Geddens & A. Favell, *The Politics of Belonging: Migrants and Minorities in Contemporary Europe*, 15-41. Aldershot: Ashgate.

Cyrus, N. & D. Vögel (2003), 'Work-permit decisions in the German labour administration: an exploration of the implementation process', *Journal of Ethnic and Migration Studies*, 29 (2): 225-255.

Cwerner, S. B. (2004), 'Faster, Faster and Faster: the Time Politics of Asylum in the UK', in *Time & Society*, 13 (1): 71-88.

Damay, L. (2002), 'The integration-cohabitation programme of the government of the Brussels's Region: mutations of public action and constructions of norms', paper presented at the workshop 'Immigration policies: between centre and periphery, national states and the EU' at the *ECPR Joint Sessions*, Turin, 22-27 April 2002.

Dell'Olio, F. (2004), 'Immigration and Immigrant Policy in Italy and the UK: Is Housing Policy a Barrier to a Common Approach Towards Immigration in the EU', *Journal of Ethnic and Migration Studies*, 30 (1): 107-128.

De Witte, H. & B. Klandermans (2000), 'Political racism in Flanders and the Netherlands: explaining differences in the electoral success of extreme right-wing parties',
Journal of Ethnic and Migration Studies, 26 (4): 699-717.

Dietz, G. (2000), *El desafío de la interculturalidad: el voluntariado y las organizaciones no gubernamentales ante el reto de la inmigración*. Barcelona: Fundación 'La Caixa', Granada:
Laboratorio de Estudios Interculturales.

Di Gregorio, L. (2004), *La politica migratoria italiana nel quadro europeo. Quale e quanta
europeizzazione?*, PhD Thesis in Political Science, University of Florence.

Donaldson M., A. Montardit, L. Pelàez & J. Monteserín (2002), '¿Hasta dónde llegan las
fronteras? Inmigración, leyes de extranjería y movimientos sociales', in P. Ibarra, S.
Martí & R. Gomà (eds.), *Creadores de democracia radical. Movimientos sociales y redes de
políticas públicas*. Barcelona: Icaria.

Drbohlav, D. (2001), 'The Czech Republic', in C. Wallace & D. Stola (eds.), *Patterns of Migration in Central Europe*, 203-226. Houndmills, Basingstoke: Palgrave Publishers.

Drbohlav, D. (2003), 'Czech Republic', in J. Niessen, Y. Schibel & R. Magoni (eds.), *EU
and US Approaches to the Management of Immigration*. Brussels/Prague: Migration
Policy Group. http://www.migpolgroup.com/uploadstore/Czech%20Republic.pdf.

Drbohlav, D. (2004), *Volume II – The Czech Republic. The Times They Are A-Changing*, in:
Migration Trends in Selected EU Applicant Countries. Vienna, International Organiza-
tion for Migration. http://www.iom.int//DOCUMENTS/PUBLICATION/EN/IO-
M_II_CZ.pdf.

Dreef, M. (2004), *Politiek, migranten en informele economie. Politieke en bestuurlijke ontwik-
kelingen ten aanzien van de Amsterdamse confectieateliers, 1980-1997*, PhD Thesis, Amsterdam, IMES.

Düvell, F. & B. Jordan (2003), 'Immigration Control and the Management of Economic
Migration in the United Kingdom: Organisational Culture, Implementation, Enforcement and Identity Processes in Public Services' *Journal of Ethnic and Migration Studies*, 29(2): 299-336.

Edelman, M. (1964), *The Symbolic Uses of Politics*. Chicago: University of Illinois Press.

Ethnobarometer (2003), *The Ethnobarometer Report. Migrants Integration in European Cities*. Rome: Ethnobarometer.

Fasano, L. & F. Zucchini (2001), 'L'implementazione locale del testo unico sull'immigrazione', in Fondazione Cariplo-ISMU (ed.), *Sesto rapporto sulle migrazioni 2000*, 39-50.
Milano: Franco Angeli.

Favell, A. & A. Geddes (1999), 'European Integration and the Nation-State: Institutiona-
lising Transnational Political Action', *EUI Working papers*, 32.

Feldblum, M. (1999), *Reconstructing Citizenship. The Politics of Nationality Reform and Immigration in Contemporary France*. Albany (NY): Suny Press.

Fennema, M. & J. Tillie (2004), 'Do immigrant policies matter? Ethnic civic communities
and immigrant policies in Amsterdam, Liège and Zurich', in R. Penninx, K. Kraal,
M. Martiniello & S. Vertovec, *Citizenship in European Cities. Immigrants, Local Politics
and Integration Policies*. Aldershot: Ashgate.

Fermin, A. (1997), *Nederlandse politieke partijen over minderhedenbeleid 1977-1995*, PhD
Thesis, Rijksuniversiteit Utrecht. Amsterdam: Thesis Publishers.

Freeman, G. (1995), 'Modes of Immigration Politics in Liberal Democratic States', *International Migration Review*, 29 (4): 881-913.

Fullerton, M., E. Sik & J. Tóth (eds.) (1997), *From Improvisation toward Awareness? Contemporary Migration Politics in Hungary*. Budapest: Institute for Political Science of
the Hungarian Academy of Sciences.

Gächter, A. (2000), 'Austria: Protecting Indigenous Workers from Immigrants', in R.
Penninx & J. Roosblad (eds.), *Trade Unions, Immigration, and Immigrants in Europe*,

1960-1993. A Comparative Study of the Attitudes and Actions of Trade Unions in Seven West European Countries, 65-89. New York/Oxford: Berghahn Books.

Gaxie, D., P. Laborier, M. De Lassalle, I. Obradovic & A. Taiclet (1999), 'Les politiques municipales d'integration des populations d'origine étrangere', *Migrations Études*, 86.

Geddes, A. (2000), *Immigration and European Integration*, Manchester: Manchester University Press.

Geddes, A. (2003), *The Politics of Migration and Immigration in Europe*. London: Sage.

Gerber, B. (2003), *Die antirassistische Bewegung in der Schweiz: Organisationen, Netzwerke und Aktionen Reihe 'Sozialer Zusammenhalt und kultureller Pluralismus*. Zürich: Seismo Verlag.

Gerber, B. & S. Cattacin (2004), *Immigrant and immigration policy making. The case of Switzerland*, Country report prepared for the first IMISCOE Annual Conference, Coimbra, 3-4 December 2004.

Guiraudon, V. (2000), 'European integration and migration policy: vertical policy making as venue shopping', *Journal of Common Market Studies*, 38 (2): 249-269.

Guiraudon, V. (2002), 'Logiques et pratiques de l'Etat délégateur: les compagnies de transport dans le contrôle migratoire à distance', *Cultures et Conflits*, 45, 51-79.

Guiraudon, V. (2003), 'The Constitution of a European Immigration Policy Domain: A Political Sociology Approach', *Journal of European Public Policy*, 10 (2): 263-282.

Guiraudon, V. (2004a), 'Construire une politique européenne de lutte contre les discriminations: l'histoire de la directive "race"', *Sociétés contemporaines*, 53, 11-32.

Guiraudon, V. (2004b),' Immigrant and immigration policy making. The case of France', country report prepared for the *first IMISCOE Annual Conference*, Coimbra, 3-4 December 2004.

Hagelund, A. (2003), 'A matter of decency? The Progress Party in Norwegian immigration politics', *Journal of Ethnic and Migration Studies*, 29 (1): 47-65.

Hammar, T. (1985), *European Immigration Policy. A Comparative Study*. Cambridge: Cambridge University Press.

Hammar, T. (1990), *Democracy and the Nation State*. Aldershot: Avebury.

Hammar, T. (2004), 'Research and Politics in Swedish Immigration Management 1965-1984', in *Towards a Multilateral Migration Regime. Special anniversary Edition dedicated to Jonas Widgren*. Vienna: ICMPD.

Hansen, R. (2000), *Immigration and Citizenship in Post-War Britain*. Oxford: Oxford University Press

Härpfer, C., M. Wammerl, R. Bauböck & C. Palt (1992), *Ausländerbeschäftigung und Arbeitsmarktverwaltung*, unpublished Project Report. Vienna: Institute for Conflict Studies.

Hatton, J. (2004), 'The state of the art of research on migration policy making and implementation in the UK', country report prepared for *the first IMISCOE Annual Conference*, Coimbra, 3-4 December 2004.

Hix, S. (1998), 'The Study of the European Union II: The 'New Governance' Agenda and its Rivals', *Journal of European public Policy*, 5(1): 38-65.

Holland, M. (1993), *European Community Integration*. London, Pinter.

Hollingsworth J. R., P. C. Schmitter & W. Streek (eds.) (1994), *Governing Capitalist Economies*. Oxford: Oxford University Press.

Hoppe, R. (1987), *Etniciteit, Politiek en Beleid in Nederland*. Amsterdam: University of Amsterdam Press.

Horta, A. P. B. (2003), *Struggling for Recognition: Immigration Policies and Migrants' Political Participation in Post-colonial Portugal*. Lisbon: Universidade Aberta.

Howlett, M. & M. Ramesh (1995), *Studying public policy: Policy cycles and policy subsystems*. Toronto/New York: Oxford University Press.

Iglicka K., P. Kaźmierkiewicz & M. Mazur-Rafał (2003), 'Poland', in J. Niessen & Y. Schibel, *EU and US approaches to the management of immigration. Comparative perspectives.* Brussels: Migration Policy Group.

Ireland, P. R. (1994), *The policy challenge of ethnic diversity: immigrant politics in France and Switzerland.* Cambridge, Mass.: Harvard University Press.

Janů, I & M. Rozumek (2004), *Azylové právo ES. Pohled a role nevládních organizací*, Organization for Aid to Refugees. http://aa.ecn.cz/img_upload/c16177daf2c782a8ab9b9 d2c6a914ec7/Azylov__pr_vo_EU.pdf.

Jawhari, R. (2000), *Wegen Überfremdung abgelehnt.* Vienna: Braumüller.

Joppke, C. (1999), *Immigration and the Nation-State.* Oxford: Oxford University Press.

Jordan, B., B. Stråth & A. Triandafyllidou (2003), 'Comparing cultures of discretion', *Journal of Ethnic and Migration Studies*, 29 (2): 373-395.

Juen, G., B. Perchinig & P. Volf (1996), 'Migrationspolitik – Zur Europäisierung eines Gastarbeitermodells', in E. Talos & G. Falkner (eds.), *EU-Mitglied Österreich. Gegenwart und Perspektiven: Eine Zwischenbilanz*, 201-222. Vienna: Manz.

Kaczmarczyk, P. & M. Okólski (2002), 'From net emigration to net immigration. Socioeconomic aspects of international population movements in Poland', in R. Rotte and P. Stein (eds.), *Migration Policy and the Economy: International Experiences*, 319-348. Munich: Hanns Seidel Stiftung.

Kessler A. & G. Freeman (2003), 'Beyond Fortress Europe? Public Opinion on Immigration and Asylum in the EU', paper presented at the *Annual meeting of the The American Political Science Association*, 27 August 2003.

Kiprianos P., S. Balias & V. Passas (2003), 'Greek Policy towards Immigration and Immigrants', *Social Policy and Administration*, 37 (2): 148-164.

Kooiman, J. (ed.) (1993), *Modern Governance.* Newbury Park: Sage.

Koopmans, R. (2004), 'Migrant Mobilisation and Political Opportunities: Variation Among German Cities and a Comparison with the United Kingdom and the Netherlands', *Journal of Ethnic and Migration Studies*, 30(3): 449-470.

Kraler, A. (2004), 'Immigrant and immigration policy making. The case of Austria', country report prepared for the *first IMISCOE Annual Conference*, Coimbra, 3-4 December 2004.

Kuscheij, H. & A. Pilgram (2002), 'Fremdenfeindlichkeit im Diskurs um "Organisierte Kriminalität"', in K. Liebhart, E. Menasse & H. Steinert (eds.), *Fremdbilder, Feindbilder, Zerrbilder. Zur Wahrnehmung und diskursiven Konstruktion des Fremden*, 39-56. Volume 5 of the Series The Investigation, Explanation and Countering of Xenophobia and Racism. Klagenfurt/Celovec: Drava.

La Fleur, J. M. (2004), 'Immigrant and immigration policy making. The case of Belgium', country report presented at the *first IMISCOE Annual Conference*, Coimbra, 3-4 December 2004.

Lahav, G. (2004), *Immigration and Politics in the New Europe.* Cambridge: Cambridge University Press.

Mac Einri, P. (2004), 'Country profile: Ireland', country report presented for the *first IMISCOE Annual Conference*, Coimbra, 3-4 December 2004.

Marks, G., F. Scharpf, P. Schmitter & W. Streeck (eds.) (1996), *Governance in the European Union.* London: Sage.

Marques, M. M. (2004), 'The dynamics of immigrant participation in local civil society', paper presented at the *Metropolis International Conference*, Geneva, 29 September 2004.

Marsh, D. (1998), *Comparing Policy Networks.* Philadelphia: Open University Press.

Martiniello, M. & A. Rea (1997), 'Construction européenne et politique d'immigration', in M. Coenen & R. Levin (eds.), *La Belgique et ses immigrés – Les politiques manquées.* Bruxelles: de Boeck-Université.

Martiniello, M. (2004), 'Le champ des études migratoires et ethniques en Belgique', in I. Adam et. al. (2004), *Recherches et Politiques Publiques: le cas de l'immigration en Belgique*. Gent: Academia Press.

Matuschek, H. (1985), 'Ausländerpolitik in Österreich. 1962-1985. Der Kampf um und gegen die ausländische Arbeitskraft', *Journal für Sozialforschung*, 25 (2): 159-198.

Mazur-Rafal, M. (2005), 'Country profile: Poland', country report presented at the *IMISCOE C9 workshop*, Turin, 18-19 March 2005.

McLaren, L. (2001), 'Immigration and the new politics of inclusion and exclusion in the European Union: The effect of elites and the EU on individual-level opinions regarding European and non-European immigrants', *European Journal of Political Research*, 39: 81-108.

Milward, A.S. (1992), *The European Rescue of the Nation-state*. Berkeley: University of California Press.

Monar, J. (2001), 'The Dynamics of Justice and Home Affairs: Laboratories, Driving Factors and Costs', *Journal of Common Market Studies*, 39 (4): 747-764.

Moore, D. (2004), 'Migrants as mediators in a comparative perspective', in R. Penninx, K. Kraal, M. Martiniello & S. Vertovec, *Citizenship in European Cities. Immigrants, Local Politics and Integration Policies*. Aldershot: Ashgate.

Moravcsik, A. (1991), 'Negotiating the Single European Act', in S. Hoffmann & R. O. Keohane (eds.), *The New European Community. Decisionmaking and Institutional Change*, 41-84. Boulder/San Francisco/Oxford: Westview Press.

Moravcsik, A. (1993), 'Preferences and Power in the European Community: A Liberal Governmentalist Approach', *Journal of Common Market Studies*, 31 (4): 473-524.

Morel, S. (2002), *Ecole territoires et identités. Les politiques publiques françaises à l'épreuve de l'ethnicité*. Paris: L'Harmattan.

Morén-Alegret, R. (2002), 'Gobierno local e inmigración extranjera. Aproximación a los casos de Barcelona y Lisboa durante los años 90', *Migraciones*, 11: 25-81.

Morén-Alegret, R. (2004), *Immigrant and immigration policy making. The case of Spain*, IMISCOE Working paper/Country Report, Amsterdam: IMISCOE. http://www.imiscoe.org/working papers

Nelson, B. J. (1996), 'Public policy and Administration: an Overview', in R. Goodin & H. D. Klingemann (eds.), *A new Handbook of Political Science*, 559-594. Oxford: Oxford University Press.

Nyíri P., J. Tóth & M. Fullerton (eds.) (2001), *Diasporas and Politics*. Budapest: Institute for Political Science of the Hungarian Academy of Sciences.

Oliveira, N. (2000), 'Discursos políticos sobre minorias imigrantes: a construção de uma "questão",' *Working Paper Series*, n. 16. Lisbon: SociNova.

Oliveira, C., J. Malheiros and L. Fonseca (2004), 'Portuguese immigration policy: the state of the art', country report presented at the *first IMISCOE Annual Conference*, Coimbra, 3-4 December 2004.

Parsons, W. (1995), *Public Policy: an Introduction to the Theory and Practice of Policy Analysis*. Cheltenham: Elgar.

Pelàez, Ll., M. Donaldson, R. González & A. Montardit (2002), 'Las redes de apoyo a la inmigración y las políticas locales: El caso del programa Icària', in I. Blanco & R. Gomà (eds.), *Gobiernos Locales y Redes Participativas*, 255-276. Barcelona: Ariel.

Penninx, R. (1984), 'Research and policy with regard to ethnic minorities in the Netherlands. A historical outline and the state of affairs', *International Migration*, 22 (4): 345-366.

Penninx, R. (1985), 'Onderzoek met betrekking tot minderheden in Nederland', in A. Martens & F. Moulaert (eds.), *Buitenlandse minderheden in Vlaanderen-België. Wetenschappelijke inzichten en overheidsbeleid*, 233-254. Antwerpen/Amsterdam: De Nederlandse Boekhandel.

Penninx, R. (1988), *Minderheidsvorming en emancipatie. Balans van kennisverwerving ten aanzien van immigranten en woonwagenbewoners 1967-1987*. Alphen aan den Rijn: Samsom.

Penninx, R. (1992), *Wie betaalt en wie bepaalt? Onderzoeksbeleid van de overheid m.b.t. minderheden en de invloed van onderzoek op beleid*. Den Haag: Ministerie van Binnenlandse Zaken.

Penninx, R. (1998), 'Over machtsverhoudingen tussen politiek, beleid en onderzoek. De casus van minderhedenstudies en -beleid', *Sociale Interventie*, 7 (4): 175-181.

Penninx, R., B. Garces Mascareñas & P. Scholten, (2004), *Policy-making related to immigration and integration. A review of the literature of the Dutch case*. IMISCOE Working Paper/Country Report, Amsterdam: IMISCOE http://www.IMISCOE.org/workingpapers/index.html

Penninx, R. (2005), 'Bridges between research and policy? The case of post-war immigration and integration policies in the Netherlands', *UNESCO/International Journal on Multicultural Societies*, 7, (1): 33-48.

Perchinig, B. (1996), 'Migration und Migrationspolitik in Österreich 1995', *RIMET-Bericht Österreich für die Europäische Kommission*. Vienna: GD V, mimeo.

Pérez-Díaz, V., B. Álvarez Miranda & C. González-Enríquez (2001), *Espanya davant la immigració*. Barcelona: Fundació 'La Caixa'.

Peters, G. (1995), *The Politics of Bureaucracy*. New York: Longman.

Pierre, J. (ed.) (2000), *Debating governance: Authority, Steering and Democracy*. Oxford: Oxford University Press.

Plasser, F. & P. Ulram (1991), 'Die Ausländer kommen! Empirische Notizen zur Karriere eines Themas und der Bewußtseinslage "im Herzen Europas"', in G. Ofner, A. Khol & A. Stirnemann (eds.), *Österreichisches Jahrbuch für Politik 1990*. Vienna/Munich.

Plasser, F. & P. Ulram (1992), 'Ausländerfeindlichkeit als Wahlmotiv? Analyse der Wiener Gemeinderatswahl 1991', in A. Khol, G. Ofner & A. Stirnemann (eds.), *Österreichisches Jahrbuch für Politik 1991*. Vienna: Munich.

Pořízek, P. (2004), *Komplexní analýza azylového systému v ČR včetně navržení legislativních a praktických opatření k jeho zefektivnění*. Brno: SOZE http://soze.hyperlink.cz/Komplexní%20analýza%20azylového%20systému%20v%20ČR.pdf.

Pressman, J. & A. Wildavsky (1973), *Implementation*. Berkeley: University of California Press.

Psimmenos, I. & K. Kassimati (2003), 'Immigration control pathways: organisational culture and work values of Greek welfare officers', *Journal of Ethnic and Migration Studies*, 29 (2): 337-371.

Regonini, G. (2001), *Capire le politiche pubbliche*. Bologna: Il Mulino.

Rhodes, R. A. W. (1990), 'Policy Networks. A British Perspective', *Journal of Theoretical Politics*, 2 (3): 293-317.

Rhodes, R. A. W. (1996), 'The New Governance. Governing without Government', *Political Studies*, 44: 652-667.

Rhodes, R. A. W. (1997), *Understanding Governance: Policy Networks, Reflexivity and Accountability*. Buckingham: Open University Press.

Rudolph, C. (2003), 'Security and the Political Economy of International Migration', *American Political Science Review*, 97 (4): 603-620.

Sabatier, P. A. & H. C. Jenkins-Smith (1993), *Policy Change and Learning. An Advocacy Coalition Approach*. Boulder: Westview Press.

Scharpf, F. W. (ed.) (1993), *Games in Hierarchies and Networks. Analytical and Empirical Approaches to the Study of Governance Institutions*. Frankfurt: Campus.

Scharpf, F. W. (1997), *Games Real Actors Play: Actor-Centered Institutionalism in Policy Research*. Oxford: Westview Press.

Schmitter, P.C. (1996), 'Examining the Present Euro-Polity with the Help of Past Theories', in G. Marks, F. Scharpf, P. Schmitter & W. Streeck (eds.), *Governance in the European Union*, 1-14. London: Sage.

Schnapper, D. (1992), *L'Europe des immigrés*. Paris: Burin.

Selznick, P. (1949), *TVA and the grass roots; a study in the sociology of formal organization.* Berkeley: University of California Press.

Skordas, A. (2000), 'The regularisation of illegal immigrants in Greece', in P. de Bruycker (ed.), *Regularisations of illegal immigrants in the European Union*, 343-387. Bruxelles: Bruylant.

Soininen, M. (2002), 'Exploring EU ethnic diversity and anti-discrimination policy – a Swedish perspective', paper presented at the workshop *'Immigration policies: between centre and periphery, national states and the EU'* at the ECPR Joint Sessions, Turin, 22-27 April, 2002.

Soysal, N.Y. (1994), *Limits of Citizenship. Migrant and Postnational Membership in Europe.* Chicago: University of Chicago.

Soysal, N.Y. (2004), 'Postnational Citizenship. Reconfiguring the Familiar Terrain', paper presented at the International *Conference: Tranforming Citizenship? Transnational Membership, Participation and Governance*, Campbell Institute of Public Affairs, Syracuse University, April 2004.

Spire, A. (2003), *Sociologie historique des pratiques administratives à l'égard des étrangers en France*, PhD Thesis in sociology, Université de Nantes.

Statham, P. & V. Guiraudon (2004), 'Different Paths of 'Europenization'? Evidence from the Public Debates over Europe in Britain and France', paper presented at the International *Conference: One EU-Many publics?*, Stirling, 5-6 February 2004.

Stetter, S. (2000), 'Regulating migration: authority delegation in justice and home affairs', *Journal of European Public Policy*, 7 (1): 80-103.

Tamas, K. (2004), 'International Migration Control: Swedish Migration Policy from 1985 to 2004', in *Towards A Multilateral Migration Regime*, 35-64. Vienna: ICMPD.

Tissot, S. (2002), *Réformer les quartiers. Enquête sociologique sur une catégorie de l'action publique*, PhD Thesis in Sociology, EHESS.

Triandafyllidou, A. (2003), 'Immigration policy implementation in Italy: organisational culture, identity processes and labour market control', *Journal of Ethnic and Migration Studies*, 29 (2): 257-297.

Tychtl, P. (2001), 'Czech Republic', in P. Nyíri, J. Tóth & M. Fullerton (eds.), *Diasporas and Politics*, Budapest: Institute for Political Science of the Hungarian Academy of Sciences.

Uçarer, E. M. (2001), 'From the Sidelines to Center Stage: Sidekick No More?' The European Commission in Justice and Home Affairs, *European Integration online Papers (EIoP)*, 5 (5).

Uherek, Z. (2004), 'Use of social science research on migration policy in the Czech Republic', *International Social Science Journal*, 56 (179): 101-113

Vermeulen, F. (2002), 'Immigration policy and ethnic organisations in Amsterdam, 1960-1990. A local historical approach', paper presented at the workshop *'Immigration policies: between centre and periphery, national states and the EU'* at the ECPR Joint Sessions, Turin, 22-27 April 2002.

Vertovec, S. (1999), 'Minority associations, networks and public policies: re-assessing relationships', *Journal of Ethnic and Migration Studies*, 25 (1): 21-42.

Viet, V. (1998), *La France immigrée. Construction d'une politique. 1914-1997.* Paris: Fayard.

Vink, M. P. (2002), 'Negative and Positive Integration in European Immigration Policies', *European Integration online Papers* (EIoP), 6 (13).

Westin, C. & E. Dingu-Kyrklund (2003), 'Immigration and Integration of Immigrants and their Descendants: The Swedish Approach', in F. Heckmann & D. Schnapper (eds.), *The Integration of Immigrants in European Societies. National Differences and Trends of Convergence*. Stuttgart: Lucius & Lucius.

Widgren, J. & T. Hammar (2004), 'Research and Politics in Swedish Immigration Management 1965-1984', in *Towards A Multilateral Migration Regime*, 11-34. Vienna: ICMPD.

Wihtol de Wenden, C. (1988), *Les immigrées et la politique. 150 ans d'évolution*. Paris: Press de Sciences Po.

Wihtol de Wenden, C. & R. Leveau (2001), *La bourgeoisie. Les trois ages de la vie associative issue de l'immigration*. Paris: CNRS Editions.

Wildavsky, A. (1979), *Speaking Truth to Power*. Boston: Little Brown and Company.

Wimmer, H. (1986), 'Zur Ausländerbeschäftigungspolitik in Österreich', in H. Wimmer (ed.), *Ausländische Arbeitskräfte in Österreich*, 5-32. Frankfurt am Main, New York: Campus.

Zincone, G. (1998), 'Illegality, Enligthenment and Ambiguity: A Hot Italian Recepy', *South European Society & Politics* 3 (3): 43-81.

Zincone, G. (2002), 'Immigrazione', in F. Tuccari (ed.), *Il governo Berlusconi. Le parole, i fatti, i rischi*. Roma-Bari: Laterza.

Zincone, G. (2005), 'Historical Developments', in M. Arena, B. Nascimbene & G. Zincone (eds.), *Legal and Political Overview: Italy*, NATAC research project on 'The acquisition of nationality in EU member states: rules, practices and quantitative developments'. Catholic University Nijmegen, Centre for Migration Law, forthcoming.

Zincone, G. (2006), 'The Making of Immigration and Immigrants Policies', *Journal of Ethnic and Immigration Studies*, forthcoming.

Zincone, G. & T. Caponio (2004), *Immigrant and immigration policy making. The case of Italy*, IMISCOE Working Paper/Country Report, Amsterdam, IMISCOE. http://www. IMISCOE.ORG/workingpapers/index.html.

Zincone G., T. Caponio & L. Di Gregorio (2004), *The multilevel governance of migration. State of the art*, IMISCOE Working Paper/State of the art Report, Amsterdam: IMISCOE. http://www.imiscoe.org/working papers.

Zincone, G. & L. Di Gregorio (2002), 'Il processo delle politiche di immigrazione in Italia: uno schema interpretativo eclettico', *Stato e Mercato*, 66 (3): 37-59.

Zucchini, F. (1997), 'Le politiche pubbliche locali per l'immigrazione', in Fondazione Cariplo-Ismu (ed.), *Secondo rapporto sulle migrazioni 1996*, 75-86. Milano: Franco Angeli.

Zucchini, F. (1998), 'L'implementazione della politica pubblica per l'immigrazione: i casi di Torino e Brescia', in Fondazione Cariplo-ISMU (ed.), *Terzo rapporto sulle migrazioni 1997*, 173-189. Milano: Franco Angeli.

Zucchini, F. (1999), 'La genesi in Parlamento della legge sull'immigrazione', in Fondazione Cariplo-ISMU (ed.), *Quarto rapporto sulle migrazioni 1998*, 61-72. Milano: Franco Angeli.

Zuser, P. (1996), 'Die Konstruktion der Ausländerfrage in Österreich. Eine Analyse des Öffentlichen Diskurses 1990', in *Reihe Politikwissenschaft*, 35, Vienna, Institut für Höhere Studien/ Institute for Advanced Studies. http://www.ihs.ac.at/publications/pol/pw_35.pdf.

11. Conclusions and Directions for Research

Rinus Penninx

1. Understanding the new dynamics of migration and settlement

The foregoing chapters have illustrated abundantly that international migration and integration of immigrants have become hot topics in Europe. First of all, the fact of immigration into Europe and its tendency to grow is undeniable, although the timing and size of different immigration patterns vary. There are solid indications that immigration will persist and most likely increase in the coming decades. On the demand side such indications can be found in the demographic developments in Europe with its decline of natural growth and greying population, and in labour market developments that indicate a demand in an increasing number of sectors that cannot be met by local supplies. On the supply side, people motivated by political, social or economic reasons (or all three) to leave for an expected better life elsewhere presently outnumber the demand. This migration pressure from outside[1] will increase rather than decrease, helped by communication media and transport facilities that cover an ever wider audience and clientele in a globalising world.

However, it is not only the sheer number of people crossing borders that have brought the topics to the top of the agenda of public and political discourse and policy making. The phenomenon of migration itself has changed in a globalising world, as have the states and societies that 'send' and 'receive' immigrants and their reactions to migration. These changes have given rise to new dynamics that are not yet fully understood, let alone that adequate policy responses for the 'management' of these migration processes and the consequences for sending and receiving societies are within reach. International migration and integration have become contested topics and the public and political discussion is frequently phrased in analytical concepts and terminology of the past. The content of such discussions is often dominated by normative undertones, even to the extent that empirical evidence is disregarded. In the European case it is particularly the mismatch between the traditional norm of not being immigrant societies and the facts of a continuously increasing proportion of the resident population being of immigrant origin that creates ambivalences in perceptions and policies. Therefore there is an urgent need for research to feed the public and political discourse on migration and settlement with both analytical insights and concomitant empirical data.[2]

The state of the art of research as presented in the foregoing chapters contains a double message. On the one hand, there is a growing amount of research available that is not adequately disseminated and thus under-used.[3] On the other hand, there are significant gaps in empirical data and, more importantly, there is also the general recognition that research still fails to produce comprehensive insights on present migration processes and their consequences for migrants and their communities, and for countries of origin and destination. Researchers need to develop new perspectives and comprehensive analytical approaches that enable us to understand better the dynamics of migration and settlement in Europe in the present and future era. In the following sections, I will briefly elaborate on the question how research efforts should be improved to produce better knowledge, for science itself and as a sound and solid basis for public and political discourse and policy making. In section 2, the concrete question is how research in this field should best be organised as a precondition for good research results. In section 3, possible new definitions of the field, units to be studied, new perspectives and questions to be asked will be discussed. In the final section, I will give some examples of research lines and projects that are being developed presently within IMISCOE. Most of these ideas spring from the work reported in the chapters of this book, but they also cut across their boundaries.

2. Challenges for the organisation of research

As we have seen in the foregoing chapters the development of research in Europe has not kept pace with developments in the field it studies. The most common qualification of the weakness of European research on migration and integration issues is that it is fragmented. Three forms of fragmentation are regularly brought up: lack of comparative research, lack of cooperation between disciplines and lack of integration of the different levels at which phenomena are studied.[4] Such weaknesses of the present European research call for specific efforts in the organisation and methodology of research for the future. I will briefly dwell on each of these causes of fragmentation and indicate how these could possibly be remedied.

Systematic comparison as a strategic tool

Throughout the chapters that have taken stock of research there seems to be a consensus both on the lack of comparative research and on the expectation that systematic comparison will bring our knowledge base a big step forward. But what does this mean in practice? The challenges here lay on different levels that all have relevance in the design of a comparative research framework. The first and most practical level is that of basic administrative data that are often used by researchers. In chapter 2, it was reported that cross-national comparability of seemingly simple data such as those on migration is profoundly problematic. The problem is that administrative data (of any kind) are collected within a specified institutional context for specific purposes, using definitions that reflect their particular tasks, assumptions and preoccupations. The problem for scientists (apart from the validity and reliability of the data within the system in which they are collected) in using such data for comparative purposes is essentially twofold: do they measure the same phenomenon?[5] And are they complete or representative? Critical assessment of comparability is thus a fundamental requirement here, possibly leading to practical proposals for change.

The second level is that of the design of comparisons. Chapter 9 has indicated that the kind of comparison we choose to make directly relates to the specific questions that we would like to answer. A research design that compares different immigrant populations within one national or local context will draw attention, by the choice of the design, to factors *within these immigrant populations* that explain the differential outcomes, while a design that compares the same ethnic group within different national or local contexts will focus on factors *within these contexts* that explain differences in outcomes. The same holds for comparisons in which time is additionally and explicitly brought into the design. There remains significant work to be done to develop a tool of rigid comparison and combine the different forms of design in such a way that they are complementary. That should preferably be done in an internationally coordinated research programme.

The third level is that of concepts and terminology. The fact that the same terms are used in different national or local contexts – for example integration policy or multicultural policies – may create the illusion that the same phenomena are dealt with. Empirical research, however, has shown that not only the ideas and assumptions behind such policies are different, but that the practice and measures of such policies vary considerably in different places and situations.[6] Another complication is that academic concepts may, in public and political discourse, get a normative connotation that makes it difficult for scholars to use such concepts particularly in communication with a broader audience.

Chapter 6 has described this phenomenon for the concepts of assimilation and integration and chapter 7 for the concept of multiculturalism. We therefore need to design analytical frameworks in which such abstract concepts and notions are operationalised in such a way that empirical data can be collected in the same way in different contexts.[7]

Working on systematically comparative research is thus scientifically a significant challenge, and a costly one in practice, but it will bring research a fundamental step further. At the same time it will provide a sound basis for policymakers who are looking increasingly across borders to see how other countries are dealing with the dilemma's they are confronted with.[8]

Multidisciplinarity/Interdisciplinarity

Critiques on the involvement of various disciplines in the study of migration and settlement in the preceding chapters essentially refer to two aspects. The first is the observation that in the past the research field has been dominated by a limited number of disciplines, often anthropology, sociology, social geography, economics and law, while other disciplines came in relatively late such as political sciences and history.

The second is that disciplines often develop their research and perspectives in relative isolation – this point is made strongly for economists in chapter 5 for example, but it can also be applied to other disciplines like history and law – and that comprehensive multidisciplinary research is rare, let alone interdisciplinary research projects.[9]

The challenge for future research is thus to transcend the old division of disciplines in research on international migration and settlement of migrants. Such cooperation across disciplines can be done most fruitfully when participants in such endeavours work from the strength of their own discipline. This means that researchers should not be isolated or isolate themselves from their discipline (to form another isolated thematic field of research on migration and settlement), but act as active links between their discipline and the thematic field: stimulating research on the thematic theme within the discipline and bringing the special expertise from the discipline to the thematic field. In practice this should be done at two levels. The first is to create multidisciplinary organisational structures which bring disciplines together and stimulate exchange and cooperation.[10] The second, deeper, level is to conceive and implement interdisciplinary projects and programmes in which such cooperation is built in *ex ante* into the central questions and design, the collection of material and is integrated into the analysis and reporting.[11]

Integrating levels of analysis

Yet another form of fragmentation relates to levels of units of analysis and the lack of integration of these levels. This may express itself in the form where (mostly qualitative) research on the micro-level of small groups does not seem to have any relation with (mostly quantitative) research on the aggregate level of groups or categories.[12] This is a classical kind of fragmentation that is not unique to the field of migration and integration, but this observation does not make the challenge to overcome it any easier.

The fragmentation may also take a more space-based form, particularly when the unit of analysis refers to the different levels at which societies are politically organised and policy efforts are involved: the borough, the city, the region, the national state and supra-national or international agents. While the nation-state has been an important level from the beginning and has dominated in research, there is a growing body of research on the local level on the one hand, and on the international and supra-national level on the other. The relations between these levels and the complex way in which they influence each other, however, are yet to be explored.

This form of fragmentation has a special dimension in the European context. Since the early start of Europeanisation in the form of the European Economic Community up to the present European Union an ever more significant supra-national level has developed. In its early phase – starting back as far as the 1950s – mobility within the European Economic Community and later the European Union has been a topic of complicated interaction between national governments and the European Commission (Goedings 2005), while discussions focusing on immigration from outside the EU have grown in importance since the 1980s, and integration policies since 2003.[13] There is a growing awareness among researchers that there is a need to overcome this fragmentation, and at the same time an expectation that this will greatly enhance our understanding of policies and policy making in the field.[14]

3. New perspectives on immigration and integration research in Europe

Apart from improvements in the organisation of research by involving relevant disciplines, using comparison as a strategic tool and designing research that comprises more levels and the interaction between them, the state of the art of the preceding chapters suggested time and again that there are also significant challenges in terms of the development of new theoretical and analytical perspectives. The term 'perspective' here means looking at the field from a different angle and thus asking different questions, taking other units of analysis as a starting point and collecting new kinds of empirical material. These suggestions can be brought together under three headings.

Rethinking the relation between migration and settlement

International migration and integration (or its alternative terms such as assimilation, incorporation or settlement) have established themselves as more or less independent fields of research and theory (see chapters 2 and 3 for migration and chapters 4-7 for integration). This is also partly reflected in the way the IMISCOE network has initially structured its research clusters. The first – international migration – is then defined as the spatial movement, voluntary or forced, of persons across political borders as a process, together with its causes and consequences. The second pertains to the process of settlement and integration of immigrants and their descendants in the society of destination and the consequences this has for these societies.[15] Most of the existing body of theories in these fields is being developed on the basis of experience in traditional Anglo-Saxon immigration countries and by researchers from these countries.

Though it is useful to start from that knowledge and build on it, at the same time, it transpires from the foregoing chapters that there are at least two kinds of problems, stemming from such definitions and focus and the implied division between migration and integration research. The first kind of questions arise when we see migration and integration as self-contained and independent fields of research, thus decoupling migration from settlement. As noted in the introduction and subsequent chapters, international migration in recent decades has changed in character: the migration process has become more complex, more fluid and less permanent. The implicitly assumed once-off movement and the time sequence of migration followed by a settlement process is increasingly blurred.

The second set of issues refers to a specificity of the European context: having defined itself as a set of non-immigration countries has had far-reaching consequences both for international migration and integration separately, but also for the nexus between the two fields. There is a new tendency in policy thinking that sets integration requirements as criteria for the selection and admission of immigrants (see, for example, Carrera 2006).

There is thus a need to reformulate the research field as one complex field rather than two separate ones and introduce new perspectives and questions that focus on this more complicated interconnectedness.

Focusing on the migrants themselves, one of these new perspectives is that of transnationalism. This notion basically challenges the above-mentioned assumptions of once-off movements, followed by gradual settlement, by asking pertinent questions about the nature and continuity of the ties of migrants with several places and communities and thus their simultaneous 'integration' in them. Focusing on both sending and receiving societies a number of new questions also arise (or are put in a different light) that interconnect migration and integration. For example: how are migration and development issues influenced by new migration patterns, by the formation of transnational communities and by integration policies in destination countries? How do arguments related to integration (and concrete policy measures in that field) influence admission and immigration policies and practices and the patterns of continued immigration and return?[16]

Shifting the focus from migrants to society[17]

There is another observation on the state of the art of migration and integration research that hints at the need to introduce new perspectives: the fact that nearly all research focuses primarily on migration, immigrants and their integration, while the societal systems into which the phenomenon of migration and the immigrants themselves are to be integrated is taken for granted.[18] It is interesting to observe that when the effects of migration on societal structures are studied, it is mainly from a sending-country perspective, as illustrated in chapter 3. Migration and development are apparently a topic that is relevant and applicable for countries that send migrants rather than for countries that receive them. The effects of migration on social structures in sending countries have been studied under headings such as brain drain, effects on families and households, on peasant economies, local markets, etc. More recently, the developmental potential of migration and migrant communities for the regions of origin found much attention. To put it ironically, migration research has looked more at the societal effects of the 'absence of migrants' in sending countries than at the societal effects of the 'presence of migrants' in receiving ones.

But if we really want to make sense of the difficult terms integration and social cohesion[19] – beyond the political attractiveness of their semantics on the global, European and nation-state level – we must include in our analysis the effects of migration on the societal structures in Europe as well. Europe and its nation-states have become – in an uneven process – a world region of international migration. If migration is linked to major social dynamics, as is claimed by migration researchers and increasingly accepted as common sense knowledge, then it needs to be demonstrated to what extent migration has effected the core structures of European immigrant-receiving societies themselves. How has international migration become part of the evolutionary development of these societies beyond political or other kinds of intentions? From such a perspective the social dynamics of integration and social cohesion are both necessarily embedded in the structural changes that are an outcome also of the unintended and differentiated effects of international migration itself on the various realms of society.

This general perspective leads to a focus on such issues as the short-term and long-term effects of migration and the presence of immigrants on the various societal realms such as politics, the economy, law, science, education, health, religion, mass media, arts, sports and the family. It allows us to study migration as a form of social mobility, institutionalised in modern society (based on its differentiation structure). In asking such questions for each of the mentioned domains, several social levels should be taken into account, such as the institutional level, that of organisations, networks and their interactions.

Such new lines of research can be illustrated by taking the examples of the effects of migration on the *health care system* and *educational system*. In the health care realms there is more to be studied than just the integration of newcomers into the existing provisions of health care. Migration affects not only the composition of patients, but also concepts of illness and disease, modes of communication and cultural expectations and the organisation of care and composition of staff. Since the health care system is – among others – strongly based on processes of social interaction, questions arise as to how its various organisations cope with the cultural and ethnic diversity of their new clients. Comparable questions can be asked for other institutional fields, like the educational system, where probably even more than in the case of the health system questions of causes and consequences of societal change and migration have two directions: on the one hand, what are the effects of structural changes of the (higher) education system on migration flows (e.g. students, teachers, scientists etc.), and on the one other, what are the effects of the presence of migrants and their children on the educational system?

Perspectives 'from outside'

The foregoing observations on new perspectives refer to imbalances within the thematic field of international migration, integration and social cohesion and suggest ways to address them. But this thematic area is not to be regarded as an isolated one. Taking a different angle may yield unexpected insights. The preceding chapters have shown several times that new issues and questions arise when their particular fields are seen in a broader perspective, of which I mention here only two examples.

The first involves looking at international migration as just one of the forms that spatial mobility may take. Systematic comparison with other forms of mobility that do not imply crossing national borders, such as internal migration, or that have a shorter time horizon, such as cross-border commuting, tourism and business travel, may bring the special characteristics and underlying mechanisms of international migration to the fore.

The mobility perspective can also be applied to the social mobility of individuals and groups within a given societal system asking for the empirical study of how international migrants fit in and compare to other groups and categories.

Another broader perspective is the one that nowadays goes under the term of globalisation. From such a perspective, important questions arise as to how physical migration of people across borders relates to the 'travel' of money, of goods, of ideas and cultural and religious meanings and practices across these same borders, some of which are physical but other much less so, or not at all. And what do such relations mean for how we should look at the process of settlement.

4. Examples for the way forward

Applying the foregoing suggestions for organisational changes in research and taking into account the ideas for new perspectives opens in theory nearly endless possibilities for promising future research. Making strategic choices is the only option in practice. This is exactly the strategy that IMISCOE is implementing. During the first two years three special projects have been started to prepare new strategic research lines that combine – in various forms – the suggestions for improvement listed above. These three new research lines – still in a nascent phase at the time of this publication – will be described here briefly as examples for a possible way forward.

The first one – given the acronym EUROLINKS – aims to study Europe as an established and continuously changing migration system. It creates a common framework for understanding migration to Europe in terms of both various interconnections between geographical areas and complicated cause and effect explanations of migration. The central question is: How does a migration system as it has developed within the present EU and between the EU and adjacent areas – the Mediterranean rim and Central and Eastern Europe – interact with increasing social and economic interdependencies between these areas? The basic idea is to conceptualise migration as partly caused and evoked by broader economic, political, social and cultural developments and partly contributing to these developments itself.

The primary research question will be addressed in a programme of coordinated research projects that will focus on different migration subsystems within or to Europe. The evolution of such subsystems will be studied in terms of both their historical context and their present and possible future forms, with a particular focus on the interconnections between economic, political and cultural linkages and migration processes. The basic units of analysis will be migration systems at the country-to-country level chosen strategically to untangle the various contextual and substantive factors (like specific characteristics of migrants themselves, the institutional architecture, policy variations etc.) and therefore include a) countries that have the same sending area (e.g. Turkey-to-Germany or Turkey-to-Netherlands); b) country-to-country sub-systems that have the same target area (e.g. the Turkey-to-Germany or Poland-to-Germany systems); c) destination countries inside and outside the EU (e.g. Germany versus Switzerland); and d) comparisons of systems that have their roots in colonial or ex-colonial ties.[20] In addition, EUROLINKS will have to cover various (political, economic, socio-cultural) aspects of the interconnections between migration systems and larger systems.

The second research line – given the acronym INTPOL – focuses on the systematic comparative analysis of integration processes and related policies. Institutional arrangements and policies are important factors that may influence or steer integration processes. Even though local arrangements and policies are embedded in national systems, and even though national systems are increasingly embedded in supra-national systems like that of the EU, such institutional arrangements and policies may have differential mechanisms and implications at all these levels.

This leads to the central overarching research question: To what extent do different national and local institutional arrangements and policies result in differential outcomes of integration processes (the divergence hypothesis), and to what extent do comparable practical problems of integration lead to convergence in these processes and policies (the convergence hypothesis)? Specific questions such as how supra-national policies like EU policies influence processes of integration and related policies, or whether the approaches from one setting can be applied and/or converted to other settings can be formulated to supplement this general research question.

INTPOL starts from the assumption that the analysis of processes of integration and related policies is to be done empirically, comparatively and comprehensively and should take into account different relevant dimensions (political, economic, social and cultural). INTPOL will study the two sets of actors involved in this field: individuals, organisations and institutions of the immigrants themselves as well as actors at corresponding levels of the receiving society. It is the interaction between these two sets of actors that determines directions of processes of integration and ultimate outcomes.

Within such a general framework, specific and complementary case studies will be selected and implemented. In view of the large domain covered, it is envisaged to make strategic choices in which certain domains like education and health will have priority and certain comparisons are preferred, like those between cities or local policies.

The third research line – given the acronym SOCO – focuses on the political and social dynamics of migration and integration as phenomena of European societies. Often seen as a threat, migration is easily associated in Europe with defensive attitudes, xenophobia and racism on the individual level, and with political mobilisation against migrants and ethnic minorities on the group level. In its turn, such mobilisation may lead to counter-mobilisation like anti-racism movements and mobilisation of immigrants themselves.

These three forms of social movements stemming from migration and the interactions between movements, are taken as specific focus. In order to understand the dynamics involved in such processes and interactions, these processes will not only be studied in their national context and cross-nationally, but also in their historical dimension.

The central question of this research line is then: *How does migration affect political mobilisation in its potential threefold manifestation: anti-immigrant mobilisation, anti-racist mobilisation (or the solidarity movements) and political mobilisation of immigrants themselves? How do these different mobilisations interact?*

These three projects are examples of how the IMISCOE Network of Excellence approaches the issues of international comparison, interdisciplinarity and multilevel analysis in the fields of international migration and integration in the European context. This State of the Art, delivered by all research teams, sets out the challenge to contribute to a better understanding of migration and settlement in the coming years primarily as a development of science, and by the choice of the strategic topics at the same time as a service to better inform public and political discussions and policy making.

Notes

1 Migration pressure is conceived here simply as the number of people that would be willing to immigrate if they would be allowed to do so.

2   A collection of recent analyses of European policies and choices for the future was given the apt subtitle: 'A New Deal or a Continuing Dialogue of the Deaf?' (Papademetriou 2006).

3   On this point the IMISCOE Network of Excellence has set itself the task to disseminate research results not only as scientific publications through the IMISCOE book series and working papers, but also to a wider audience and to policymakers through special tools such as research briefs, policy briefs and policy workshops (see www.imiscoe.org).

4   One particular way of describing that fragmentation has been to point to relatively isolated national traditions of research. Such traditions have often developed in a context in which the funding of research is significantly influenced by policy interests. It implies a strong focus on the national case that may lead not only to a lack of cross-national comparison, but also to specific foci of research. In general more attention is given to migrants as the object of study (the dependent variable of the design) than the receiving society (the independent one). The crucial questions to be researched also reflect perspectives of receiving countries rather than those of sending countries. Some observers have coined the term 'methodological nationalism' for this phenomenon (Ali-Ali and Koser 2002, Wimmer and Glick-Schiller 2003). Recent publications such as Bommes (2006), Lavenex (2005) and Vasta and Vaddamalay (2006) substantiate (the limitations of) such national traditions in empirical comparison of countries.

5   This problem returns in another form as policy systems increasingly start to organise 'self observation' through monitoring systems and evaluations. Indicators of such observations, however, are deduced from the policy system itself.

6   See, for examples, Vermeulen (1997) and Vermeulen and Slijper (2003)

7   Within IMISCOE various initiatives have already been taken. On a still relatively abstract level the INTPOL-study by Heckmann and Bosswick (2006) has delivered an analytical framework for the comparative study of integration processes of immigrants. Within the TIES-project a systematic framework for the comparison of the position of the second generation of 4 immigrant groups in 8 countries and 15 cities has been developed during a 2-year period of preparation, including a standardised and piloted questionnaire (see www.imiscoe.org/ties).

8   The key word in such international exchanges has become 'to learn from best practices elsewhere'. However, there is a problem here too of comparability: since any practice – bad, good or best – is rooted in a much broader local and national institutional setting, the crucial question is whether a good practice is transferable from one institutional setting to another. It is the knowledge about the mechanisms of a good practice and the conditions under which it works that make it transferable, rather than the specific form it has taken at a certain moment and place. It is particularly on this point that research and policy can cooperate on a concrete level to the advantage of both. The recently started 'European Programme on the Role of Local Authorities in the Integration of Migrants', funded by the European Foundation is based on this principle: Some 30 European cities work together with 5 IMISCOE institutes comparing local practices in the field on the basis of analytical grids.

9   For practical purposes, I prefer to use 'multi-disciplinary' as a quality of research institutes, teams and programmes indicating that researchers of several disciplines are involved. I use interdisciplinary specifically as an adjective of research projects, indicating that the central questions and the design of the project is conceived as an integrated and complementary work across disciplines beforehand, which expresses itself in the coordinated collection of material, integrated analysis and reporting.

10 The IMISCOE Network of Excellence is an example of such an organisational structure at the European level. The extent of multidisciplinarity of its institutional members varies considerably, which makes the Network all the more important for its members.

11 For an interesting new contribution to this topic see: Bommes and Morawska (2005).

12 Admittedly in migration studies this cleavage has been discussed since the late 1980s and interesting new studies have introduced 'meso-level' mechanisms, particularly in the form of networks of different kinds, to bridge the gap. In integration studies, however, there is much less of an effort to bridge between the micro- and macro/aggregate level.

13 For a concise overview, see Van Selm and Tsolakis (2004).

14 One of the research clusters of IMISCOE has expressed this by renaming the specific topic of research 'The multilevel governance of migration and integration'.

15 See original IMISCOE proposal, Annex I: p. 9.

16 One specific research initiative is taken by a group of IMISCOE researchers that looks at the side-effects of naturalisation laws in the EU (such as preferential categories of persons who can show their descent from a (former) national citizen to acquire citizenship, and thus get rights of immigration) and regularisations or amnesties as phenomena where immigration and integration arguments and policies are strongly interconnected.

17 This section is heavily based on an internal discussion note written by Michael Bommes for the Board of Programme Leaders of IMISCOE, A Research Note on IMISCOE, document BPL-9-11/BD-8-11 of the meeting of 7 April 2006.

18 Although in the new rhetoric of integration policy the normative statement that integration is a two-sided process of change of migrants and the receiving society is accepted nowadays (see for example the Communication of the European Commission on Integration (European Commission 2003) and the Common Basic Principles for integration policies approved by the Conference of Integration ministers in Groningen (European Commission 2004), we see the same strong focus on immigrants in practice.

19 The concept of social cohesion has been broadly discussed in the introduction and several of the other chapters where it has also been explained that this is a theoretically diffuse and politically loaded term.

20 For the IMISCOE Network of Excellence this design offers the additional advantage of bringing research partners from Central and Eastern Europe and the Mediterranean Basin systematically into the work of the Network.

Literature

Ali-Ali, N. S. and K. Koser (2002), *New approaches to migration? Transnational communities and the transformation of home.* New York/London: Routledge.

Amato, G. d' and S. Baglioni (2006), *IMISCOE Network Feasibility Study. Social cohesion and immigration: actors, beliefs and dynamics of a contested space.* Forthcoming: – www.imiscoe.org.

Bommes, M. (2006), 'Migration and Migration Research in Germany', in: Ellie Vasta /Vasoodeven Vaddamalay (eds.): *International Migration and The Social Sciences: Confronting national Experiences in Australia, France and Germany.* Houndmills, Basingstoke: Palgrave Macmillan: 143-221

Bommes, M. and E. Morawska (eds.) (2005), *International Migration Research: Constructions, Omissions and the Promises of Interdisciplinarity.* Aldershot: Ashgate.

Carrera, S. (ed.) 2006, *The nexus between immigration, integration and citizenship in the EU*. CHALLENGE Collective Conference Paper, April 2006: www.ceps.be.

Entzinger, H., J. Schoorl and A. Fermin (2006), *EUROLINKS. IMISCOE Network Feasibility Study*. Forthcoming: www.imiscoe.org.

European Commission (2003), *Communication on Immigration, Integration and Employment*. 3 June 2003.

European Commission (2004), *Common Basic Principles for Integration*, adopted by the JHA Council on November 19, 2004.

Goedings, S.A.W. (2005), *Labor Migration in an Integrating Europe. National Migration Policies and the Free Movement of Workers, 1950-1968*. The Hague: Sdu.

Heckmann, F. and W. Bosswick (2006) *Integration and integration policies. IMISCOE Network Feasibility Study*. Forthcoming: www.imiscoe.org.

Lavenex, S. (2005), 'National Frames in Migration Research: The Tacit Political Agenda', in: M. Bommes & E. Morawska (eds.) (2005): *International Migration Research: Constructions, Omissions and the Promises of Interdisciplinarity*, Aldershot: Ashgate: 243-264.

Papademetriou, D.G. (Ed.), (2006), *Europe and its immigrants in the 21st century. A new deal or a continuing dialogue of the deaf?* Washington/Lisbon: Migration Policy Institute/ LUSO-American Foundation.

Selm, J. and E. Tsolakis (2004), 'EU Enlargement and the limits of freedom', *Migration Policy Information Source*, October 2004, see: www.migrationinformation.org/Feature/display.cfm?ID=224.

Vasta, E. and V. Vaddamalay (eds.) (2006), *International migration and the social sciences: confronting national experiences in Australia, France and Germany*. Houndmills, Basingstoke: Palgrave Macmillan.

Vermeulen, H. (ed.) (1977), *Immigrant policy for a multicultural society. A comparative study of integration, language and religious policy in five Western European countries*. Brussels/ Amsterdam: MPG/IMES.

Vermeulen, H. and B. Slijper (2003), *Multiculturalisme in Canada, Australië en de Verenigde Staten. Ideologie en Beleid, 1950-2000*. Amsterdam: Aksant.

Wimmer, A. and N. Glick-Schiller (2003), 'Methodological Nationalism, the Social Sciences, and the Study of Migration. An Essay in Historical Epistemology', *International Migration Review* 37 (3): 576-610.